MAUPASSANT

A LION IN THE PATH

Francis Steegmuller

The Universal Library

GROSSET & DUNLAP

NEW YORK

To Laurence Steegmuller

CONTENTS

PART THREE: THE END

PART ONE

MAUPASSANT
AND
FLAUBERT

CHAPTER 1

RUNAWAY COLT

THERE WERE TWO Norman weddings, a few months apart; and of the four people married, three are important to the story. In Rouen, on the ninth of November, 1846, a brief time after her brother Alfred had married a Mademoiselle Louise de Maupassant, Laure Le Poittevin married Gustave de Maupassant, her new sister-in-law's brother.

Laure's bridegroom was the son of a well-to-do Rouennais who was the local director of the national tobacco monopoly and a gentleman farmer, with a large property on the outskirts of the city. In his prosperity her father-in-law had revived the noble-sounding *de* in his name, which had fallen into disuse after the Revolution, and was even displaying—some say without complete respect for correct usage—a coat of arms bearing a marquis's coronet. His son had been brought up to be a gentleman of leisure and to use the coronet on his stationery; the young man was good-looking, a dandy, an amateur painter; a paternal allowance took care of expenses.

Laure's own family, the Le Poittevins, also bourgeois and with a coat of arms to be used if desired, were at least equally well off. Her father owned cotton mills in Rouen and had married the daughter of a wealthy

Fécamp shipowner, and Laure brought with her as dowry sufficient capital to provide an income somewhat larger than that which her husband received from his father. She also possessed a cultivation that was greater than her husband's. Much of her youth had been spent in the company of her dearly loved brother Alfred, who had been a student of literature and philosophy; and from him and from his intimate and adorer, a slightly younger Rouennais named Gustave Flaubert, she had acquired a familiarity with classical and modern letters and a knowledge of English that allowed her to read Shakespeare in the original. She was handsome in a strong-featured, almost masculine way, and she was known to be self-willed and independent in judgment. In an age of ruffles and furbelows she affected soft felt hats and sensationally short walking skirts that showed her ankles; early in her life she had ceased to observe all but the outermost forms of her religion; and her clothes, her cigarette-smoking, horseback-riding and Shakespeare-reading gave her a reputation for mild eccentricity in her provincial milieu. But though she was generally thought odd, everyone agreed that Laure was intelligent and "interesting"—words that no one ever seems to have applied to her husband.

The Maupassants (both of them were twenty-five) made a wedding trip to Italy, just as the Alfred Le Poittevins had done a few months before; and on their return to France they lived much as they wished, spending winters in Paris and the rest of the year in their native Normandy—partly in a villa at Etretat, a charming fishing village near Le Havre which was beginning to have a certain vogue as a summer resort, particularly with artists and with the English, and where several houses and parcels of land included in Laure's dowry

were located. In 1848 Laure, as well as the rest of her
brother Alfred's family and friends, was grief-stricken
by his untimely death at the age of thirty-two. Then,
sometime in 1850, she and her husband rented, near the
village of Tourville-sur-Arques, five miles inland from
Dieppe, the imposing Chateau de Miromesnil, an isolated, red-brick and white-stone Norman mansion
complete with corner towers and a sixteenth-century
chapel; and here, on the fifth of August, was born their
first son, Henri-René-Albert-Guy de Maupassant.

So, at least, say the local records, and so Laure herself
always maintained. "My mother," she later declared,
"told of what was happening, arrived at the chateau by
its avenue of beeches, which resembled the vault of a
cathedral, and at the far end of which was being celebrated the mystery of the birth of the new day. The
thought came to her that this child born at dawn would
enjoy a glorious destiny, like that of the sun mounting
toward the lofty splendors of the sky." There is indeed
a splendid beech avenue at Miromesnil, and it is possible
that the sun was rising at one end of it as Guy came into
the world; but like her words, Laure had a touch of the
grandiose and the spendthrift about her, and the renting
of the Chateau de Miromesnil seems to have been one of
her more extravagant gestures. Gossips in Fécamp,
where Laure's mother lived, have claimed that although
Laure had leased the big place for the express purpose of
bearing her child in its aristocratic setting (the name of a
chateau looking so well on a birth announcement), Guy
upset her plans by arriving early and uttering his first
cries in the more bourgeois surroundings of his grandmother's house, in a town justly celebrated for its pervasive odor of herring and cod. Mother and child (so
the gossips claim, and bring forth documents to "prove"

it) were quickly transferred to the chateau, and the birth was registered as having occurred there.

Wherever he was born, the boy received a vigorous welcome. "The roundness of my head," he said later, "is due to the old doctor who brought me into the world. He at once put me between his knees and gave my head a powerful massage, ending with the gesture of the potter who gives his vessel a good round shape with a twirl of his thumb. Then he said to my mother, 'See, I've given him a head as round as an apple. This will assure his having an active brain, and almost certainly a first-rate intelligence.' "

From the very beginning, Laure's maternity was marked by a jealousy that persisted to the end of her days. In her extreme old age, after Guy's death, her indignation was aroused by an article in a Paris newspaper, which declared: "Maupassant's *frère de lait* [that is, the son of Maupassant's wet-nurse] has just been appointed caretaker of Solferino park in Rouen. The writer's bust is in this park. It has been stated that there is a striking resemblance between the caretaker and his *frère de lait*." What angered the aged Laure was not the slur on her husband, the implication that he was not only Guy's father but the father of the wet-nurse's child as well—to that, at least, she made no reply—but rather the statement that Guy had had a wet-nurse. She had someone write a correction to the newspaper. "*I* was my son Guy's wet-nurse," she had herself quoted as saying, "and I will allow no one else to usurp the title. I cannot conceive how a woman could think she had a right to it simply on the ground of having nursed my child for four or five days at the most. Shortly after Guy's birth, when I was living with my mother at Fécamp, I suffered some slight indisposition, and a woman named Cavalier, the daughter of a neighboring farmer, was briefly called on. That was the extent of her services. In less than a week my dear baby was back at my breast, and he was weaned only at the age of twenty months."

Some time after Guy's birth the Maupassants left Miromesnil. The date is not certain—it was apparently their habit to move about from place to place in Normandy; but one of the reasons is said to have been that the loud and incessant cawing of crows in the beeches grated on Laure's nerves—the first existing mention of those sensitive and interesting fibres. Six years after Guy's birth, shortly before the appearance of his only brother Hervé (the name given each boy had a smart sound in itself and allowed full value to the sonorous family name), they rented another chateau, the Chateau Blanc, at Grainville-Ymauville near Etretat, less pretentious than Miromesnil, but apparently sufficiently suitable in Laure's eyes as a birth setting. Here they stayed another undetermined length of time.

The Chateau Blanc was the first home of which Guy retained a conscious memory, and he used both it and Miromesnil (separately, or in combination, and almost always with invented details) as settings for several of his stories. It was in just such a mansion as the Chateau Blanc that he placed his story *Clochette,* about

an old seamstress who came once a week, every Tuesday, to mend the linen. My parents were then living in one of those country dwellings called chateaux, but which are really just ancient, steep-roofed houses with four or five attached tenant-farms. I adored Mother Clochette. As soon as I was out of bed in the morning I would clamber up to the linen-room in the attic, where I would find her sewing, her feet on a little charcoal foot-warmer. She always made me take this and sit on it, lest I catch cold in the big frigid room. As she mended the linen with her

long, crooked, nimble fingers, she told me stories, stories
of village happenings; the story of a cow that had got out
of the stable and been found, one morning, standing in
front of Prosper Malet's mill, watching the wooden
paddles turn; or the story of an egg discovered in the
church tower, making everyone wonder how a hen had
ever got up there to lay it; or the story of Jean-Jean
Pilas's dog, who had traveled quite alone ten leagues
from the village and brought back his master's trousers
that had been stolen while drying outside the door after a
shower. She told me these naïve adventures in such a way
that they took on in my mind the proportions of unforgettable dramas, grandiose and mysterious poems;
and the ingenious stories invented by poets, which my
mother told me in the evening, had none of the flavor,
the appeal, the strength, of the peasant-woman's tales.

And apparently the Chateau Blanc was the scene of
another childhood memory, this one of fascination and
cruelty, that never left him:

I remember that even as a child I loved cats rather
strangely, often wanting to strangle them with my little
hands. One day, at the bottom of the garden near the
edge of the wood, I suddenly noticed something gray
rolling in the tall grass. I went to look; it was a cat,
caught in a snare, choking, half dead. It was writhing,
tearing at the earth with its claws; it kept leaping into
the air and falling back as though lifeless, and then beginning again; and its hoarse rapid breathing was like the
sound of a pump, a terrible sound that I can still hear.
I could have taken a spade and cut the snare, I could
have gone to find a servant or tell my father. But no,
I didn't move; and, my heart pounding, I watched with
a tremulous cruel joy until it died—it was a cat! If it
had been a dog I should rather have cut the copper wire
with my teeth than let it suffer a second longer. And
when the cat was dead, really dead, but still warm, I
went up to it and touched it, and pulled its tail. . . .

During these years at the Chateau Blanc, and in Paris where they still sometimes spent part of a winter, the Maupassants' marriage began to disintegrate; and the small Guy, who did indeed possess—whether or not because of the doctor's massage—an active brain and a first-rate intelligence, had occasion to do some rather precocious seeing and understanding.

"I was first in composition," he wrote his mother when he was nine, studying in a Paris lycée, "and as a reward Madame de X took me to the circus with Papa. It seems she was also rewarding Papa for something, but I don't know what."

And another day, when Guy and Hervé were invited to a children's party by Madame Z, and Hervé was sick and Laure said she would have to stay at home with him, and Monsieur de Maupassant eagerly offered to take Guy himself, Guy was slow in getting ready:

M. de Maupassant: Hurry up, or we shan't go at all.
Guy: You can't worry me that way, Papa. I know you want to go even more than I do.
M. de Maupassant: Come along! Tie your shoelaces!
Guy: *You* tie them.
M. de Maupassant: [Speechless.]
Guy: I said, '*You* tie them.' I won't go unless you do.
M. de Maupassant: [Speechless. Ties Guy's shoe-laces.]

Laure herself, many years later, told those anecdotes about Guy and his father with a complacency concerning her own role that was always part of her character. Her husband had rather quickly begun to stray, by now her son sensed the situation and was impertinent to him, and in the impertinence she took a pleasure which she never forgot. Perhaps there were also other, more violent things that Guy saw and understood. A story called

Garçon, un bock! (*Waiter, a Beer!*) tells of another boy in a chateau:

You remember the chateau where I lived as a child, where you used to visit me during vacation? You remember the great gray house in the middle of the park, and the long avenues of oaks stretching to the four points of the compass? You remember my father and mother, both so ceremonious and solemn and severe? I adored my mother, I was in awe of my father, and I respected them both, being accustomed to seeing the rest of the world respect them. To everyone in that part of the country they were Monsieur le comte and Madame la comtesse; and our neighbors in other chateaux, the Tannemars, the Ravelets, the Brennevilles, treated them with the highest esteem.

I was thirteen—gay, pleased with everything about me the way one is at that age, full of the joy of being alive. Then one day toward the end of September, just before I was to go back to school, I was playing wolf in the shrubbery of the park. As I was running among the branches and the leaves I caught sight of Papa and Mama walking in one of the avenues. I remember it as though it were yesterday. It was a gusty day, the whole row of trees was swaying and sighing, uttering little cries, those muffled, deep-drawn cries of a forest in the wind. Yellow leaves were flying about like birds, swirling, swooping, rushing up the entire length of the avenue like scurrying little animals. It was almost dusk, already dark in the woods. The whipping of the branches in the wind excited me; I was running all over the place, howling, pretending to be a wolf. As soon as I saw my parents I began to go toward them, moving stealthily, keeping myself hidden behind branches, meaning to surprise them as though I were a prowler. But when I was a few steps from them I stopped in terror, for I heard my father shouting.

"Your mother's a fool. Besides, it's not your mother's concern. It's yours. I tell you I need the money, and I want you to sign."

Mama defied him. "I will not. That money is Jean's. I am going to keep it for him. I have no desire to see you throw it away on the housemaids and your other women, the way you threw away your own money."

Papa was trembling with rage, and he turned and seized Mama by the neck and began to hit her in the face. Mama's hat fell off and her hair was shaken loose and tumbled down. She tried to shield herself, but couldn't. And Papa, as though he had gone mad, hit and hit and hit. She fell to the ground, hiding her face in her arms. Then he twisted her onto her back, and pulled her hands away from her face, and began to hit her again. For me it seemed that the end of the world had come, that the eternal laws had changed.

Everything was different for me after that day. I had caught a glimpse of the other side of things, the bad side, and I haven't seen the good side since. . . .

That situation is recurrent in Maupassant's fiction, appearing in late works as well as early; in the last-published of all his novels he speaks of someone sitting "stupefied, like a man who discovers that his mother or father has been guilty of a questionable action." Whatever he may have seen or heard in his childhood that so deeply impressed him, Laure decided when he was about eleven that fifteen years of marriage to his father was not an experience she wished to prolong. Divorce did not at that time exist in France, and in all but the most exceptional cases respectable families deemed married misery preferable to the notoriety of legal separation. But Laure was exasperated and strong-minded, and was not deterred by legalities or family pressure. Avoiding the more formal machinery of the courts, she induced her husband (apparently without too much difficulty) to agree in a magistrate's office that they should henceforth live separately, that she should retain control of her dowry, and that he should contribute an annual sum toward the support of Guy and Hervé, who would remain with her.

Thereafter, although Monsieur de Maupassant communicated with his wife and sons and sometimes visited them (on such occasions he was always seated at table at Laure's right hand as a guest, Guy sitting opposite her as host), he was banished from family intimacy. Later he was to complain that "Guy was always under his mother's influence, not a very affectionate son as far as I was concerned." And indeed Guy's partisanship was complete and permanent. "Poor woman!" he wrote of his mother in later years, at a moment when she was passing through further trials; "How she has been crushed, beaten, martyrized without mercy since her marriage!"

You speak of Etretat and the people gossiping so maliciously on its pretty beach [an old lady writes to a young one in Maupassant's story *Correspondance*]. That place is finished as far as I am concerned, but I once had a good time there. There were only a few of us then, some of us *gens du monde*—from the real *monde*, that is, not the *demi-monde!*—and the rest artists; and we all enjoyed each other's company. There was no scandal-mongering in those days. There was no insipid casino, full of people putting on airs, whispering about everybody else, dancing badly and being bored to tears: we made our own fun. Somebody's husband, I forget whose, conceived the idea of impromptu dances at a near-by farm, and we used to go there often, a whole group of us, someone at the head of the line playing a hurdy-gurdy, two of the men carrying lanterns, and the rest of us following behind, laughing and talking our heads off. We'd wake the farmer and his household, and they'd make us onion soup, and there'd be dancing under the apple trees. All the animals would wake up and wonder what was going on: we could hear the roosters crowing

and the horses stamping in the stables. On our cheeks,
flushed from dancing, we would feel the cool country
breeze, carrying the smell of grass and newly cut harvests. How far away it all is! Thirty years . . .

Such a charming summer resort was the fishing village
near Le Havre in the days before the Franco-Prussian
War, when Jacques Offenbach, composer of operettas,
was its summer king. By the time Maupassant wrote his
story it had become a bit more crowded, a bit
noisier. But it has always remained a pleasant little place,
and though a favorite no longer, and scarred like most
Norman coastal towns by the events of 1939–44, its
beach is still as Maupassant described it in *Adieu:*

Nothing so nice as this beach in the morning at
swimming time. It is small, and curved like a horseshoe,
and lies between two high white cliffs each pierced with a
strange open arch. One of the cliffs, enormous, flings a
giant buttress out into the sea; at the opposite end of the
beach crouches the other cliff, lower and rounder. The
crowd of women gathers on the narrow strip of shingle,
turning it into a garden of bright dresses planted there in
the frame of high rocks. The sun shines on the cliffs, on
the multi-colored parasols, on the blue-green sea; the
whole scene is gay and charming.

Almost down to the beach stretches the green
Norman countryside, with its richly cultivated fields and
the apple orchards that provide cider and Calvados and
fill the air in spring with the tints and the scent of their
blossoms. A few hundred yards from the sea, standing
among birches, willows, hawthorn and holly, was Les
Verguies, the villa, in which Laure now chose to live with
her sons, a pleasant white house surrounded by gardens.
The name meant Little Orchards, and had formerly been
given to that corner of the countryside, about which there
was a legend. In ancient times the lady of a near-by

manor, a noble and virtuous golden-haired Norman
beauty, was about to be seized by the leader of a boat-
load of pirates, who had caught sight of her as with her
ladies she was washing linen at a spring on the beach—
a spring still called *la fontaine d'Olive.* Her ladies fled,
and she, in her terror, vowed that if she were to escape
she would build a church. She did escape, and the church
foundations were laid near by. But the place she had
chosen was haunted by a devil, *"le diable des Verguies,"*
and three times the workmen, returning to their task in
the morning, found that he had moved the stones during
the night to another spot. That God, all-powerful, should
thrice allow the devil to have his way was interpreted to
mean that He, too, preferred the other location for His
church, and that is where it was built and where its
successor still stands, a few steps from Laure's villa.

The curé of the church taught Guy grammar,
arithmetic and Latin; and in the house, filled with old
family furniture, Rouen faïence and an agreeable air of
clutter and untidiness that Laure, always careless of
housekeeping, did little to banish, she herself tutored
him in other studies, assigning him lessons which he did
in the evening in his upstairs room; and she read him in
French the plays of Shakespeare which in her youth she
had read in English—his favorites seem to have been
Macbeth and *A Midsummer Night's Dream* with its
country echoes. And Laure went out with him into the
country, and she told him stories; all her life she was a
woman of great physical endurance when in command of
her nerves, and all her life she was a good storyteller.
"Often in the evening when my master was away,"
Maupassant's valet wrote years later, "Madame de
Maupassant used to tell me and her maid Marie of the
fantastic things she had seen in Corsica. Sometimes she

put so much impetuousness into her way of recounting
these strange, often mysterious adventures, that I used
to feel shivers running up and down my spine."

Chiefly, at Etretat, the boy who had already been
first in composition in his Paris school lived out of doors;
his life, in Laure's words, was that of a "runaway colt."
"Awakened by these country smells, a thousand memories of childhood came to my mind," he wrote of a walk
in the woods when he was older. "Now and then I sat
down on a bank to look closely at the innumerable flowers
whose names I had long known. I recognized them all,
as if they were the very ones I had seen years before."
He tramped and loafed in woods and fields, and especially he explored the beach at all tides; once he and
Laure were caught by rising water and together scram-
bled up one of the cliffs to safety and home. Laure
allowed him to make little voyages out into the Channel
with local pilots, and to go out in the local fishing boats
after herring and turbot; the children of these sailing
folk and of the peasants were his playmates, and he
learned to speak as they did, in the *patois* of that part of
Normandy. One day a lady of the Etretat gentry seemed
displeased that Guy should have brought with him on a
picnic outing a boy who was the son of a fisherman, and
she said with some hauteur: "Charles will carry the
basket." Guy replied: "Oh, we'll take turns. I'll carry it
first." He too was a member of the gentry, and that fact
was recognized on both sides; but from these early days
dates his lifelong enjoyment of the company and friendship of people different from himself in birth and education. Also among his friends were cousins who lived
near by; and especially during the summer, when Etretat
was lively, Les Verguies was full of young people or-
ganizing charades and picnics. He was an attractive and

popular boy, with his sturdy physique, his round head, and the large dark eyes that, according to Laure, came to him from a Creole ancestress; and always he was to look back on his early years in Etretat as the most delightful of his life. For him the name evoked a place of enchantment, a kind of paradise.

When he was about thirteen, the scene changed. It was time for him to begin acquiring more of an education than the curé and his mother could provide.

There was an excellent lycée in Le Havre, twenty miles from Etretat, but Laure did not send him there: she chose a small seminary at Yvetot near Rouen, where, outside the regular theological courses, young men were accepted for purely classical studies. Apparently Laure was in some ways like her father, Monsieur Le Poittevin, the mill-owner, who, after being a free-thinker all his life, was quite willing to conform to the custom of his society and admit a priest to his death-chamber; she was without religious beliefs, but she lived according to her social position in paying lip-service to the Church. She had never concealed her free-thinking from her sons, but she had seen to it that they learned their catechism and made their first communion like any other nominally Catholic children; and now she sent Guy to a religious school as she might have sent a daughter to a fashionable convent; it was attended by sons of the provincial aristocracy and gentry, and her boy would be sure to find there other boys of the class into which he had been born, boys who would presumably become his friends.

It was an unhappy choice; not yet, apparently, was Laure entirely aware of some of the characteristics which her son had already acquired. Guy's opinion of his fellow

seminarians is expressed in the almost unvarying tone of
scorn found in those of his stories which deal with chance
meetings in later life between former schoolmates; and as
to the place itself, with its high walls, black-robed priestly
teachers and rigid discipline ("Severe as Sparta, elegant
as Athens" was the seminary's motto, and at all seasons
rising time was five in the morning), it was a revolting
prison for one who had hitherto been a "runaway colt,"
and who at no time in his life, even as a very small child—
so he later said—was able to see anything but absurdity
in religious rites. He describes it in *Une Surprise* * as

a large, dreary building, full of curés, whose pupils were
almost without exception destined for the priesthood.
I can never think of the place even now without a
shudder. It smelled of prayers the way a fish-market
smells of fish. Oh! That dreary school, with its eternal
religious ceremonies, its freezing Mass every morning,
its periods of meditation, its gospel-recitations, and the
reading from pious books during meals! Oh! Those dreary
days passed within those cloistering walls! . . . We
lived there in narrow, contemplative, unnatural piety—
and also in a truly meritorious state of filth, for I well
remember that the boys were made to wash their feet
but three times a year, the night before each vacation.
As for baths, they were as unknown as the name of
Victor Hugo. Our masters apparently held them in the
greatest contempt.

At first Guy was miserably homesick, convincingly
pretended illness and was sent back to his mother; but in
Etretat he recovered too promptly and was returned.
Resigned to remaining, he did his work well—the school
reports speak highly of his progress and his conduct and
say that he was liked by everyone—but his one surviving
letter to his mother, although it speaks of his studies and
especially a copy of Racine that he hoped to win as a

* See: Four Hitherto Unreprinted Maupassant Stories, page 368.

prize, shows that other things continued uppermost in his mind:

You'll say I'm talking about it a long time ahead, but if it's all the same to you, instead of the dance you promised me for the beginning of the summer vacation I wonder if you wouldn't just invite a few friends for dinner, or even better—I mean if it's really the same to you—just give me half the money you'd spend on the dance, because that way I'll be able to buy myself a boat sooner. That's the only thing I've been able to think about since being back here—I don't mean just since Easter, but ever since coming back after last summer vacation. I don't want the kind of boat people in Etretat sell to summer people from Paris—they're no good; I'll go to one of the customs men I know and he'll sell me a fishing boat with a good round bottom, like the ones in the church [placed there by fishermen as votive offerings].

A year or so before Guy wrote from the seminary about his longing for a boat of his own, Laure had been in correspondence, for almost the first time since her brother's death, with his and her old friend Gustave Flaubert, who had, during the years that had gone by, become a literary celebrity. The publication and prosecution of *Madame Bovary* in 1857 had brought him notoriety and eminence; and now in 1862 he had sent her a copy of his newly published second novel, *Salammbô*. Laure thanked him, and her thanks brought a warm reply:

Your good letter touched me deeply, my dear Laure; it stirred old feelings, old feelings that are always young. It brought back to me, like a breath of fresh air, all the sweet perfume of my youth, in which our poor Alfred had so large a place. That memory never leaves me. Not a single day passes—I can almost say not a single hour—without my thinking of him. I am now acquainted

with what are commonly called "the most intelligent
men of the day," and I compare them with him and find
them mediocre. Not one of them has ever dazzled me the
way he used to. What excursions into the empyrean he
used to take me on, and how I loved him! I think I have
never loved anyone, man or woman, as much. When he
married I suffered the most painful jealousy: for me it
was a rupture, an uprooting. For me he died twice, and
I carry his memory with me constantly, like an amulet,
like something private and intimate. How often, in the
weariness of my work, or during an entr'acte in some
theatre in Paris, or alone beside the fire at Croisset on a
long winter evening, I turn to him—and see him, and
hear him! With delight and melancholy mingled I think
back on the interminable talks we used to have, talks
made up of everything from farce to metaphysics; I
think back on our reading, on our dreams and our high
aspirations! If I am worth anything today, it is certainly
because of those things. I have retained a great respect
for that part of my past: we were not commonplace, and
I have done my best not to become so.

I see all of you in your house in the Grande Rue,
strolling in the sunshine on the terrace beside the aviary.
I arrive, you call out a welcome. . . . How I should
love to talk about all that with you, dear Laure! We
have gone a long time without seeing one another. But
I have followed your life from a distance, and have sensed
and inwardly shared some of your sufferings. I have
"understood" you—to use the word in its old-fashioned,
romantic sense.

Since you mention *Salammbô*, you will be glad to hear
that my little Carthaginian is making her way in the
world. My publisher announces the second edition for
Friday. I wrote the book for a very limited number of
readers, and it turns out that the public is eating it up.
Blest be the god of the book trade! I was very glad to
know that it pleased you, for you know how I value your
intelligence, my dear Laure. You and I are not only
friends from childhood, but almost classmates: do you

remember our reading the *Feuilles d'automne* together at Fécamp, in the little upstairs room?

Please give my excuses to your mother and sister for not sending them copies, but I had very few to dispose of and a long list of people to send them to. Besides, I knew your mother was with you at Etretat and I counted on you to read to her. Kiss your boys for me, and to you, dear Laure, with two long handshakes, go best remembrances from your old friend.

In that letter, emotional as it is, the author of *Salammbô* did not exaggerate the memories he shared with Laure. Flaubert's parents and the older Le Poittevins had been friends, the two families of children had been brought up together in Rouen, and as adolescents Flaubert and Alfred Le Poittevin (each the godson of the other's father) had been inseparable. Alfred, five years the older, was a curious boy, sickly and sensual, melancholy and exalted, and at once romantic and skeptical; and for him Flaubert conceived a hero-worship as romantic as any part of his friend's temperament. In the Le Poittevin house with Alfred, sometimes with Laure as a third, Flaubert spent what were probably the happiest hours of his life, reading the philosophers and poets and discussing all possible worlds. Alfred produced a few writings, of a turgid, fashionably romantic character, and it was under his influence that Flaubert wrote his own early, romantic manuscripts—to Alfred were dedicated such frenzied effusions as *Agonies* and *Mémoires d'un Fou.*

But Alfred, despite all his qualities, lacked will, and to please his father he agreed to follow a legal career— an abhorrent prospect. His three years at law school in Paris separated the friends. And then the separation was prolonged, for when Alfred's law course ended Flaubert's began: like his friend, although more resentfully, he too

had bowed to paternal wishes concerning the choice of a
career. But soon Flaubert suffered a breakdown and
abandoned his legal studies; and when he returned home,
eager to renew the friendship, he found Alfred withdrawn
into a morbid, painful state of lonely and cynical unhappiness, a kind of melancholia. After Alfred's marriage
the two friends met but seldom. And then Alfred called
Flaubert to his deathbed. Flaubert watched beside him
for two days and nights, gave him the last kiss, wrapped
him in his shroud, saw the coffin nailed down and walked
behind it to the grave. He spent days in mourning, re-
living the hours he and Alfred had passed together, experiencing mystical and marvelous "intimations and in-
tuitions," as he wrote a friend: "A host of things have
been coming back to me, with choirs of music and clouds
of perfume." The happiness in the friendship had been
short-lived, but of an intensity that Flaubert fed on for
the rest of his life; and as intense as the happiness had
been the loneliness and jealousy and grief.

  Had Alfred Le Poittevin not died so young, Flaubert's
first novel might well have been a different kind of book
from *Madame Bovary*. For throughout Alfred's life Flaubert's writing had continued to be almost exclusively
romantic, and shortly after the funeral he began a long,
dramatic extravaganza, *La Tentation de Saint Antoine*,
which, when its final version was published many years
later, was dedicated to Alfred. But when the first version
of the *Tentation* was finished, the young poet Louis
Bouilhet, whom even before Alfred's death Flaubert had
begun to cherish as a friend, said it was a wretched rant-
ing failure, and persuaded the distressed author to tread,
rather unwillingly, more realistic paths. *Madame Bovary*,
the original and beautiful novel that was the result of
this experiment, made Flaubert's reputation; but its com-

position had meant four and a half years of immersion in uncongenial, bourgeois subject matter. The new novel, *Salammbô*, with its intense exoticism—the critic Sainte-Beuve complained of its "bizarre sensuality" and the author's "bloody imagination"—was in a sense a return to the old romantic material.

So that Flaubert's letter to Alfred's sister on the occasion of *Salammbô* is a mirror in which are reflected with a particular brilliance his thoughts of his old friend—memories, as he said, that had never left him at any time, but which must have been blooming with more than ordinary fragrance and profusion about the flamboyant Carthaginian story.

The letter to Laure, with its greeting to her sons (neither of whom Flaubert had as yet ever seen), was written from Paris, where for a number of years he had lived a few months each winter and spring with a man-servant, seeing his friends and enjoying a change from the loneliness and hard work which were his life during most of the rest of the year at his mother's house in Croisset, on the banks of the Seine near Rouen. Three years later, early in 1866, he was similarly in Paris for his winter and spring sojourn, this time beginning work on another novel, *L'Education Sentimentale;* and from his apartment he wrote to Laure again, for old Madame Le Poittevin, mother of Laure and of Alfred, had just died.

How can I express my bewilderment and my grief? I heard the terrible news only last night; I am still crushed. I love you too dearly to offer consolation and say banal things that make suffering even worse than it is. Weep, my poor friend, weep as much as you can. She whom you have lost merits all tears, for never was anyone more intelligent, good, devoted, charming. Such Easter vacations as I used to spend with you all at Fécamp! Such exquisite memories! Such conversations with Alfred and you! Nothing I have known since has begun to equal any of it. . . . What will happen to you now? How lonely you will be! How I pity you! Adieu, my poor Laure. Try to be brave for your boys' sake.

Laure's reply, written a week later, read in part:

If anything can ease a deep grief, it is to know that it is really understood, and your letter, my dear friend, has brought me the only consolation that has touched my heart. You have evoked the early memories we share, and as I write I can see that house on the Grande Rue, full of loved ones, now most of them gone. My poor old father, so worthy and good; my brother, so intelligent, so distinguished, so exceptional; and then my mother, my dear wonderful mother, departed last of all, to rejoin the others. How sad life is! And what bitterness time sows as it flies!

The terrible trial through which I have just passed found me stronger than you would have believed possible —stronger than I should have believed myself. I was able to stay to the end beside the remains of our dear departed—I sat through two nights looking at her face, which in the supreme calm of death took on something of its expression of former days. My poor sister hurried here when I summoned her, and threw herself sobbing in my arms; but when I suggested that she come with me to our mother's bedside her strength left her and I saw that she was in such a state that I begged her to return to her home, to her husband and children. She left, but the anguish of being away at such a time was even more impossible for her to bear, and the next day she found the courage to come and share my dreary vigil. I feel relieved by telling you these things, for I know your old and deep friendship. With me fate has been particularly harsh, and it is scarcely surprising that I should cling ardently to the past, so full of sweet memories; but that you, dear Gustave, living in the very whirlpool of artistic

life, in a celebrity that to others remains but a dazzling
dream—that *you* should have preserved, like me, such
a devotion to things gone by! You speak of them with
such feeling that it is easy to see that for you too the
past is the happiest time. . . .

Now I must turn my eyes toward the future. I have
two boys, whom I love with all my heart and soul, and
who will perhaps give me a few more happy days. The
younger is so far only a sturdy little peasant, but the
older is a young man, already serious-minded. The poor
boy has seen and understood many things, and he is almost too mature for his fifteen years. He will remind you
of his uncle Alfred, whom he resembles in many ways,
and I am sure that you will love him. I have just been
obliged to remove him from the seminary at Yvetot,
where they refused to give me the dispensation which
would allow him to eat meat on abstinence days as his
doctor ordered; surely a singular manner of interpreting
the religion of Christ! Guy is not seriously ill, but his
nerves are not strong and he needs a diet that will build
him up, and besides, he was not at all happy in the school.
The austerity of that cloistered life did not suit his impressionable, sensitive nature, and the poor boy felt
stifled behind those high walls that kept out all sound
of the outer world. . . .

"The terrible trial through which *I* have just passed
found *me* stronger than you would have believed possible. . . . My poor sister found the courage to come
and share *my* dreary vigil. . . . I have two boys who
will perhaps give *me* a few more happy days. . . . They
refused to give *me* the dispensation which would allow
him to eat meat. . . ." The author of *Madame Bovary*
had so analyzed his heroine that critics had accused him
of "using his pen as though it were a scalpel," of "dis-
secting" her; but living at the time he did, and living as
he did, in lifelong devotion and proximity to his own
mother, even Flaubert was probably not as aware as we

of the drives that are to be sensed in those words of
Laure's.

Her withdrawal of Guy from the seminary because of
the refused dispensation was not permanent. She seems
to have kept him at home the rest of that school year
and all of the next, giving him once again the freedom of
Etretat; and in October, 1867, before returning him to
the seminary, she sent him to Croisset to call on Flaubert
—or rather, since all courtesies were observed, on Flaubert's mother. Old Madame Flaubert, crusty, stiff, seldom pleased, has recorded in the only one of her letters
ever to be published the impression that Guy made:

Chère Madame [she wrote Laure] I cannot begin to
tell you how much pleasure your son's visit gave me. He
is a charming boy, and you must be proud of him. He
looks a little like you, and like our poor Alfred. He has
such a gay, humorous expression that it is impossible
not to feel drawn to him, and the friend who was with
him says that he is gifted in every way. Your old friend
Gustave is delighted with him, and asks me to congratulate you on having such a child. But why did you not
come with him? You would have given us such pleasure.

Back at the seminary, Guy found the place as dreary
as ever.

I don't know whether you know that barrack [he
wrote from Etretat during his spring vacation to his
cousin Louis Le Poittevin (Alfred's son)], that gloomy
monastery, home of curés, hypocrisy, boredom, etc. etc.,
out of which rises such an odor of priests' robes that it
permeates the whole town of Yvetot and permeates one's
self, too, even during the first days of vacation. To get
rid of it I have just read a book by J. J. Rousseau. I
didn't know the *Nouvelle Héloïse*, and it has served me at
the same time as a disinfectant and as pious reading for
Holy Week! I am alone here at Etretat and don't enjoy

having no one to walk with. Why don't you come to see us? I'd show you valleys and woods unknown to profane outsiders, and springs that come gushing out of our great rocks; and there amid the beauties of nature you could write some pretty poetry. I know that you don't need all those things to do good work, but I assure you that the sight of them would inspire you to finer efforts than ever, and at least I'd have some company on my walks.

Louis, a few years older than Guy, replied:

You say in your letter that a sort of fatality keeps us apart. Well, you know what it is, that fatality. Think, and you'll recognize it as clearly as I do: on your side you'll find the cloister and on mine the law school. Those are the only two obstacles to our reunion; without them we could see each other more often, climb the cliffs of Etretat or walk in the woods at La Neuville, talk, laugh, sing—and write poetry together, delicious pastime and matchless remedy against the boredom and mental fatigue caused by the law. You, too, I am sure, will suffer from the matter-of-factness and dryness of that science when you finish your literary studies and begin to work at the Code. It will take more than one day for your spirit, so passionately given to letters, to resign itself to such work. Very often, during months on end, I have felt my own spirit ready to revolt, and I really don't know how I have managed to continue a course of study so out of key with my character. For poetry seeks illusions, and nowhere are you less likely to find them than in law reports.

The letters of both embryo lawyers are written in such charming and free-flowing French that even if one didn't know the outcome one would suspect that neither the seventeen-year-old nor his cousin would ever practise at the bar. Indeed, on both sides of Guy's ancestry there was a greater degree of artistic and generally non-commercial imagination, or at least a greater tolerance of it,

than is commonly found in mercantile families. His Maupassant grandfather, the director of the tobacco ware-
house, had made no objection when his son and daughter
became amateur painters, transformed a barn on his
property into a studio and surrounded themselves with
a group of artist friends. A portrait of Guy's father in the
Rouen museum shows him with a sketchbook in his hand,
and we have seen how the grandfather had revived the
family *de* and did not insist on his son's following him
into business, but gave him an allowance to do with as
he pleased. On the Le Poittevin side there is said to have
been at the time of Louis XIV an ancestress named
Madame Bérigny who wrote verse and corresponded
with *beaux esprits*. Nor was Guy's Le Poittevin grandfather, the free-thinking mill-owner, without his fanciful
side. According to a family story that Laure liked to tell,
there was not far from Cherbourg a manor with a
haunted chamber. The ghost took the form of a black
sheep, seen by everyone who slept in the room. Laure's
father slept there one night and the sheep appeared and
spoke: "As long as you and your descendants own this
domain, good fortune will be with you." Monsieur Le
Poittevin bought the property. Such a capacity for fantasy did not prevent him from insisting that his imaginative son Alfred study and practise law; but late, too late,
toward the end of poor Alfred's life, he relented, and he
had, at least, never opposed Alfred's immersing himself,
and Laure with him, in the classics and in the romantic
literature of the day.

Thus, unlike many other young people who have become artists, Guy, son of an amateur painter and of a
lover of literature and friend of Flaubert, never had to
combat a home atmosphere hostile to the arts. Indeed
Laure claimed in after years that she had always thought

he would be a writer, that she had reached that con-
clusion by "deduction" from his resemblance to her dead
brother and his love of reading; and she declared that in
Etretat she had trained him to observe—to observe, especially, the changing face of nature—in deliberate preparation for his future profession. Whether or not Laure
consciously thought of her son at this time as a future
writer, Guy was certainly at seventeen and for several
years to come being schooled for a lawyer's career; and
on the surface, at least, her only activities in connection
with his writing seem to have been the reading and
preservation of the homesick verses that he sent her from
his Yvetot "barrack."

He was abruptly expelled from the seminary for improper behavior toward the end of his next-to-the-last
year, shortly after the exchange of letters with his cousin
Louis. According to Laure the improper behavior consisted of a burlesque, before hilarious schoolmates, of a
recent lecture by one of the holy fathers describing the
torments of hell, and the writing of a poem—a lament on
the occasion of a pretty cousin's marriage—that the
religious thought indecent. The seminary janitor delivered the boy to his mother's door one spring day with
the stoutly expressed opinion that "Monsieur Guy is a
good fellow just the same," and Laure rewarded him
with a glass of cider for his good judgment; then she
scolded Guy and then she held out her arms. His own
feelings can be imagined. Back once again in Etretat,
with its charming bay and its beach and the curving,
sheltering arms of its cliffs! Back until fall: Laure had
decided to send him, for his last year before the baccalaureate, to the lycée in Rouen. Once again free to tramp
and swim, sail and row; to picnic on the beach in the
moonlight; to watch Corot, Courbet and other artists

painting Etretat landscapes and seascapes; to play jokes
on summer visitors—to tell them that the battered fishing boats they saw transformed into cabins atop the
three-hundred-foot cliffs had been flung there by gigantic
waves during storms, to dress up in women's clothes and
shock an English old-maid tourist with outrageous un-
ladylike language; free to play in charades and parlor
theatricals at Les Verguies. It is easy to share his glee.

The expulsion resulted, of course, in Laure's becoming
just that much more pervasive in Guy's life—if any increase in her pervasiveness was by this time possible. She
had nursed him long and jealously; she told him, evenings
at the chateau, stories from the poets which may have
lacked the tang of the country stories told by old Clochette, but which he, nonetheless, remembered all his life;
she won his allegiance in her conflict with his father, and
after the separation made him a delightful home at Les
Verguies, with its legend and its charming rooms and
gardens; she gave him extraordinary freedom for a
French boy of his class and time, letting him roam the
countryside with peasants and even go to sea on the
treacherous Channel and have his own boat; she heard
his lessons and showed him the marvels of poetry. She
waited unusually long before sending him to school, and
she treasured his verses and was waiting for him at
vacation time, and now, after expulsion, she welcomed
him home again.

It is a familiar spectacle—the absorption of a sensitive boy by a charming, cultivated mother not quite intelligent or self-disciplined enough to know or to stop
what she is doing. Of the two most usual, alternative
consequences of such a relationship—physical indifference to women, or promiscuity—Guy from his teens did
not display the former. Once again it is Laure, speaking

in her old age, who tells the story. "His childhood was absolutely chaste. It was not until he was sixteen that he had his first liaison, with the lovely E . . . ; and their love was followed by a friendly affection which lasted a long time. He sought only high-class liaisons, and, like his brother, always respected his mother's house." These words of Laure's concerning Guy as a youth seem to indicate that according to prevailing standards he was a "good boy": more precisely, apparently, they mean that he seduced none of the peasant girls with whom he played, and that neither he nor Hervé went to bed with their mother's maids or brought their mistresses home. But that he should begin to have "liaisons" at sixteen—what could be more natural? For Laure, though as dominant a mother as it is possible to imagine, was also a Frenchwoman of her time; she was complacent in her *spiritual* conquest. In later years Guy, who had long since become physically utterly promiscuous, was in the habit of speaking unfavorably of womankind in general; and whenever he did so, Laure tells us, she was accustomed to demand: "And what about me?" "Oh, you!" Guy would answer—and Laure tells us that his answer never failed to "amuse" her—"You aren't like the rest of them."

In a poem called *Ex Voto*, an English poet has commemorated his escape from drowning in characteristic verses that begin:

> *When thy salt lips wellnigh*
> *Sucked in my mouth's last sigh,*
> *Grudged I so much to die*
> *This death as others?*

The adventure so memorialized took place off Etretat
during those summer months of 1868 following Guy's
expulsion from the seminary; and he has left his own
fantastic record of it and of events immediately following
it:

I was very young, and spending the summer on the
beach at Etretat.

One morning about ten o'clock I heard sailors crying
that a swimmer was going down off one of the cliffs:
ignorant of the terrible current that swept through the
open archway in the rock, he had been carried away.
They were setting out after him, and I decided to go
with them; but before we reached him he was picked
up by a fishing boat.

That same evening I learned that the rash swimmer
was an English poet, Algernon Charles Swinburne, recently arrived in Etretat as the guest of another Englishman, with whom I sometimes talked on the beach, a Mr.
Powell. This person, owner of a little cottage that he had
baptized Chaumière Dolmance [Dolmance Cottage: Dolmance being the name of the hero of the Marquis de
Sade's *La Philosophie dans le Boudoir*], was a source of
astonishment to the village because of his mode of life,
which was extremely solitary and seemed strange indeed
to local tradespeople and sailors unfamiliar with English
crotchets and eccentricities. Mr. Powell learned that I
had tried, though too late, to help his friend, and I received an invitation to lunch for the following day.

I found the two men waiting for me in a pretty,
shady garden behind a low, flint-walled, thatch-roofed
Norman house. They were both short, Mr. Powell stout,
Mr. Swinburne thin—thin and at first glance astonishing,
a kind of fantastic apparition. He made me think of
Edgar Allan Poe: there was long hair coming down over
an immensely high forehead, a face that gradually van-
ished into a tiny chin with a meager tuft of beard, a faint
bit of mustache hovering over fine, thin lips. This head,

which was enlivened by light-colored, inquisitive, staring eyes, was joined by an apparently endless length of neck to a body seemingly shoulderless—for Mr. Swinburne's chest gave the impression of being scarcely broader than his forehead. The entire body of this almost supernatural being was constantly agitated by a nervous twitch. He was very cordial, very hospitable; and the extraordinary charm of his intelligence captivated me at once.

Throughout lunch we talked of art, literature and humanity; and for me the opinions of the two friends illuminated the subjects of our conversation with a disturbing, macabre kind of light, for they had ways of seeing and understanding things that made them seem a pair of mad visionaries, drunk on poetry that was depraved and magical. Some of the tables in the house were covered with human bones, among them a skinned hand, the hand of a parricide, they said, with blood and dried muscles still coating the white bones. They showed me fantastic drawings and photographs, a whole collection of incredible curios. Around us, all the time, roamed a tame monkey, making faces at us, comical to a degree, constantly up to tricks—less a mere monkey, really, than a dumb friend of its masters and a sly enemy of all strangers.

The monkey was hanged, I heard later, by one of the Englishman's young men-servants, who had conceived a hatred for it. The corpse was buried in the middle of the lawn before the front door, and over it was placed an enormous block of granite which bore the simple inscription "Nip" and was equipped, like tombstones in oriental cemeteries, with a hollowed-out drinking place for birds.

A few days later I was again invited to lunch by the eccentric Englishman, this time to eat monkey meat, which had been especially ordered from a dealer in exotic animals in Le Havre. The mere smell of the roast as I entered the house filled me with dismay and convulsed my stomach, and the frightful taste of the animal left me with no desire ever again to try such a meal. . . .

That October Flaubert wrote from Croisset to his niece that Laure de Maupassant had dined with him and his mother—doubtless on the occasion of her visit to Rouen to place Guy in the lycée.

"But I have seen this town before!" Maupassant exclaimed years later, in a travel piece written in North Africa. "I had this bright vision long ago, when I was very young, in the lycée, learning about the Crusades in Burette's *Histoire de France*. I know this place so well! It is full of Saracens behind that crenellated rampart. That wall! It was so very clearly drawn in the picture-book, I remember, so regular and definite that one would have said it was cut out of cardboard." And a little Italian town that he visited during later travels and found full of magic made him write: "I at once fell to dreaming foolishly, the way one dreams at the memory of old fairy tales, the way I used to dream at night in the lycée, before going to sleep in the freezing dormitory, thinking about the novel I had been reading that day, keeping it well hidden under the lid of my desk."

Despite the freezing dormitory and the forbidden novels, the "odor of priests' robes," at least, was missing from the lycée; and in the city outside there were men to be visited with pleasure and profit, literary men who not only respected but encouraged one's poetry, men eminent but kind, whose acquaintance was a rare privilege for a *lycéen*. One of these was the friend whom Flaubert had clung to during the alienation from Alfred and following Alfred's death:

I was eighteen at the time, and in the last year of the lycée at Rouen. I had read nothing by Louis Bouilhet, though he was Flaubert's dearest friend. One day, when we were returning to the college after a walk, the master

in charge of our outing—a master who always made us
work, but who was one of the few we respected—made a
sudden motion of his hand as though to stop us; and
then he bowed, very respectfully and humbly, as doubtless one used to bow to a prince, to a large gentleman
coming toward us with his head thrown back and his
stomach thrown out, and who had long flowing mus-
taches and wore a pince-nez and the red ribbon of the
Legion of Honor. When he had passed, our master said
"That was Louis Bouilhet," and immediately began to
recite lines from *Melaenis*, charming, sonorous, amorous
lines caressing to the ear and to the mind like all good
poetry. That same evening I bought *Festons et Astragales*,
and for a month I was drunk on that stirring, subtle
poetry.

Still very young, I didn't dare ask Flaubert, whom at
that time I approached only with timid respect, to
introduce me to Bouilhet. I determined to go alone. He
lived in the outskirts of Rouen, in the rue Bihorel, one of
those interminable provincial streets that lead from city
to country. I pulled a wire beside a little door in a high
wall, and heard a bell tinkle in the distance. No one came
for a long time, and I was just about to go when I heard
footsteps. The door opened, and before me stood the
large gentleman whom my master had greeted so respectfully. He stared at me in surprise, waiting for me to say
something. But during the few seconds it had taken him
to turn the key I had completely forgotten the graceful,
flattering speech that I had spent the past three days
preparing. I simply murmured my name. He had long
known my family, so he gave me his hand and I went in.

That was but the first of many visits: for the next six
months Guy saw Bouilhet "every week, either at his
house or at Flaubert's":

One day I walked out the rue Bihorel to show my
poems to my illustrious and severe friend. When I
entered the poet's study I saw through a cloud of smoke
two large men sitting in armchairs smoking and talking:

Flaubert was there with Bouilhet. I let my poems remain
in my pocket, and I sat quietly in a chair in a corner,
listening. About four o'clock Flaubert rose to go. "Walk
me to the end of the street," he said. "I'll go on foot as
far as the boat." At the boulevard, where the Foire
Saint-Romain was in progress, Bouilhet suggested that
we take a walk among the booths, and the two big men,
taller than anyone else in sight, enjoyed themselves like
a couple of children, strolling slowly through the fair side
by side, exchanging remarks about the people they saw.
They played a game of guessing the characters of passers-
by from their faces, and mimicking them as they conceived them in imaginary husband-and-wife dialogues.
Bouilhet took the men's parts and Flaubert the women's,
and they made great use of Norman turns of phrase,
the drawling Norman accent, and the continually
astonished expression that Normans wear.

To Bouilhet, a minor and all but forgotten poet whom
it is still possible to read with pleasure, Maupassant
always felt a considerable debt. He wrote later that:

Bouilhet told me over and over again that a hundred
lines of poetry, maybe less, can make the reputation of an
artist if they are flawless and contain the essence of a
man's talent and originality even if he be of second rank.
This made me understand that continued work and
complete mastery of one's *métier* make it possible, on
some day of particular clairvoyance, of particular force
and drive, to bring to flower, if one is lucky enough to
find a subject in harmony with all the tendencies of one's
mind, a piece of work that is short, unique, and as nearly
perfect as lies in one's power.

The correction of Maupassant's poetry and the encouragement that he persevere were among the last
activities of Louis Bouilhet. He died on July 18, 1869,
nine days before Maupassant received his baccalaureate.
The grateful young *bachelier ès lettres* wrote the best
memorial he could, a poem of several dozen lines:

Il est mort, lui, mon maître; il est mort, et pourquoi?
Lui si bon, lui si grand, si bienveillant pour moi . . .

He began his law studies in Paris that Fall, but they
were soon interrupted by the Franco-Prussian war. He
quickly enlisted and found himself a private in the field.
His regiment, paralyzed by bad equipment, spent an
exasperating winter of inactivity in a snow-covered
Norman forest, the forest of Les Andelys; and there, one
day, "like a phantom," suddenly appeared Josephe, his
mother's maid, who had tended him as infant and small
boy, now bringing him, through the Prussian lines, clean
clothes, a ham, a leg of lamb, wine and other delicacies.
Josephe, "a woman with masculine features, a real
Normande," joined in the general feast; and when it came
time for her to leave she replied with "the look of a
lioness" to the commanding officer's repeated urgings
that she watch out for the enemy.

Eventually Guy's unit had to flee, and he wrote his
mother from somewhere in the stricken country:

I asked the driver of the Havre coach to see you and
give you news of me, but fearing he may not have done
so, I send you this line. I escaped with our retreating
army and was almost taken prisoner. I went from the
front to the rear to carry an order from the quartermaster
to the general—did over thirty-five miles on foot. After
walking and running the whole previous night delivering
orders, I slept on the stone floor of an icy cellar; if it
hadn't been for my good pair of legs I would have been
captured. I am very well. Adieu. Fuller details tomorrow.

And later, from Paris:

I'll write you a few more lines today because within
two days communications will be cut between Paris and

the rest of France. The Prussians are advancing upon us
by forced marches. As for the result of the war, there
is no longer any doubt—the Prussians are lost. They
realize it perfectly, and their only hope is to take Paris
by surprise, but we are ready for them. My father is at
his wits' end—he wants me absolutely to get into the
quartermaster's office here in Paris, and he keeps giving
me the most comical suggestions as to how to avoid
accidents. If I listened to him, I'd be asking for the post
of caretaker of the sewers, to keep myself out of the way
of bombs. Médrinal has written asking me to lend him
my Lefaucheux; I'm going to answer him that I have
promised it to cousin Germer. It will be a long time before
I let myself be put back in the quartermaster corps!
Médrinal can take the other rifle.

High-spirited lines! Pathetic, too, considering how
differently everything mentioned in them turned out.
Médrinal—whoever he was—and Guy's cousin Germer
may have borrowed the hunting rifles at Les Verguies
and gone out after Prussians as "irregulars" as so many
Frenchmen were doing amid the defeat of the armies;
but if they did, frustration awaited them. For after the
fall of Metz in October the war was practically over, and
the Prussians overran France as far as the Loire. Paris,
in Guy's opinion ready to receive the enemy, capitulated
after the famous siege of five months on January 29,
1871, the day after the signing of the armistice; and on
May 23 the new government signed the humiliating
treaty of Frankfort. And by that time Guy himself,
despite his fiery words, had capitulated to the urgings of
his father—who on this occasion makes one of his very
rare appearances in the paternal role: he had taken
and passed an examination for the quartermaster corps
and had been sent to the Rouen quartermaster office.
Rouen was evacuated by the Prussians on July 22, and

Guy was demobilized—his place taken by a paid sub-
stitute—before the end of the year.

And no sooner was the war over and military service
at an end, no sooner was Guy at home in Etretat, resting
before resuming law school, than another crisis arose.

The business affairs of the Maupassant grandfather,
the tobacco-director and gentleman-farmer, suddenly
collapsed; most of the unearned income so long enjoyed
by his son just as suddenly disappeared; and at the age of
fifty the elegant Monsieur de Maupassant, who had never
worked a day in his life, took a position in the office of a
Paris stockbroker. "By means of many privations," he
said in his old age, "I managed over a period of twenty-
five years to rebuild a small capital for myself"; and
among the privations he was obliged to institute was a
large part of the allowance which he had been sending
Laure for the support of his sons. The household at Les
Verguies was thrown into confusion. Several years of
law study awaited Guy, Hervé at fifteen needed much
more schooling; and for such projects Laure's ill-
budgeted income was insufficient.

An echo of part of the perplexity at Etretat, and the
first hint of who was to be its eventual resolver, are found
in a letter which Laure wrote that January, 1872. In the
Parisian newspaper *Le Temps* for January 26 had
appeared a blistering letter from Flaubert, excoriating
the members of the municipal council of Rouen for the
stupidity and pettiness of their recent refusal to allow
the erection of a statue to Louis Bouilhet in one of the
city parks; and a few days later Laure wrote Flaubert:

Guy is still here with me, and together we read your
letter, so eloquent, so indignant, so mocking. You gave us

some good moments here in our solitude, where distractions are rare, especially distractions of that quality.
My son wanted to write you, but I insisted on my pre-
rogative, and send you all his compliments along with
mine. We have fallen into the habit of talking of our
friends in the evening beside the fire, and your name
comes up constantly, as is only fitting. Guy has told me
of the last visit he paid you in Paris, and has shared with
me all the impressions he felt in hearing you read poor
Bouilhet's last poems. He assures me that you consulted
him occasionally; he felt proud, grown-up; I thank you
for what you are doing for my boy, for what you are to
him. . . . He will perhaps have difficulty finding his
right road.

Monsieur de Maupassant, just as he had obtained
Guy's transfer to the quartermaster corps during the war,
now found him a temporary road—a road then much
traveled by young men in need of regular salaries and a
certain amount of leisure for the cultivation of their
talents if they had any: a place in one of the ministries,
where at that time employment was secured not by
competitive examination as at present, but by recom-
mendation and connections. Belonging as he did to the
gentry of Normandy, one of France's chief maritime
provinces, Monsieur de Maupassant was acquainted with
navy officials, and shortly before Laure wrote her letter
to Flaubert he had had Guy apply for a position in the
Naval Ministry. The answer had been unfavorable; no
place was vacant. But later in the winter Monsieur de
Maupassant wrote himself to the naval minister, mentioning his important friends and enclosing another
application in his son's hand:

Monsieur le Ministre—I have the honor to request a
favor of Your Excellency which would be of the greatest
value to me: a position in the ministry. This would be all

the more precious in that it would permit me to continue
my legal studies which were interrupted by the war—a
project which would in no way hinder me from fulfilling
my duties with zeal and exactitude.

This time, although there was still no opening, a
friendly admiral made it possible for Guy to start work
in the ministry immediately without pay, so that he
would be on hand to be given the first position available.
Fairly soon, in October, he was named special assistant.
The following February, 1873, he was put on the payroll
at 1650 francs a year. During 1872 his father had given
him 1600 francs; now he reduced his allowance to 600
francs; and the total of 2250 francs which formed Guy's
income was just barely enough, however its modern
equivalent in francs or dollars might be calculated, for a
young man to live on carefully in Paris.

The runaway colt who had reveled in the freedom of
Etretat, the youth whose impressionable, sensitive nature
had rebelled at the restrictions of Yvetot, was now one
among thousands of government clerks. From Les
Verguies, with its orchards and gardens, with the sea at
the end of the road, he moved to the city: to a dark,
ground-floor room, with a solitary window opening on a
dark court, in the rue Moncey, a nondescript street in
lower Montmartre.

During his first days at the ministry, before his salary
had begun, while he was attending law classes and living
on what his parents could give him, a violent scene
occurred between father and son. While Guy was paying
a call on his father in Paris, Monsieur de Maupassant
reproached him for living extravagantly; and the bitterness of the boy who was beginning a life he hated in
advance burst all bounds. The poorest workingman in
Paris, Guy cried, was more of a father to his family than

Monsieur de Maupassant had ever been; and he rushed out of the house, locked himself in his own room and refused to see his father when he came to appease. He wrote a passionate account of the scene to his mother, enclosing an account of his meager spendings. Auspices were scarcely favorable for the career that his father had chosen.

CHAPTER 2

IDLER AND DISCIPLE

FOR GUSTAVE FLAUBERT, the years just before, during, and just after the Franco-Prussian war had been bitter ones.

His lonely existence in Croisset had always made him particularly prize his friends, and now his friends began to die, one after the other. Bouilhet's death in 1869, the beginning of the cycle, was shattering: "I have just buried a part of myself, an old friend whose loss is irreparable," he wrote; and to George Sand he said "In losing my poor Bouilhet I have lost my midwife, a friend who saw into my thoughts more clearly than I." A few months later came the death of Sainte-Beuve: "Still another gone! The little band diminishes! With whom to talk of literature now?" In February, 1870, died Jules Duplan, "a splendid fellow who loved me like a dog"; and in June it was the turn of Jules de Goncourt. "Except for you and Turgenev," Flaubert wrote George Sand, "I don't know a single mortal to whom I can pour out the things that are closest to my heart, and you both live so far away!"

Then, during the war, shut up at Croisset with his old mother and a family of refugee relations from one of the fighting zones, expecting from day to day the arrival of the Prussians as France lost one battle after another,

unable to work, Flaubert thought he would go mad. "I
assure you, Carolo," he wrote his niece who had fled to
England, "I cannot stand it! I am *dying of grief!*" For
a time he managed to throw off his despair, volunteering
for nursing duty at the Rouen hospital of which his
father had once been head, and becoming a lieutenant in
the Croisset company of the national guard. But the
disorganization was so discouraging that he resigned;
and then came the Prussian occupation of Normandy,
the house at Croisset was requisitioned, and Flaubert,
living with his mother and two billeted Prussian soldiers
in Rouen lodgings, had to do errands for the officers in
the Croisset house, providing them with hay and straw
for their horses. "What ruin!" he cried. "What sadness!
What misery!" The occupation was a humiliation and a
horror: "France is so low, so dishonored, so debased, that
I wish she would disappear completely." As for the
Prussians: "These officers who wear white gloves when
they smash your mirrors, who know Sanscrit and fling
themselves at your champagne, who steal your watch
and then send you their card, this war for money, these
people at once civilized and savage—they fill me with
more horror than cannibals. And everyone is going to
imitate them." The prospect of what the world would be
like after the war filled him with disgust: "The society
which is going to grow up out of our ruins will be military
and republican—that is, antipathetic to all my instincts.
'*Toute gentillesse*,' as Montaigne would have said, '*y sera
impossible*.' " And he likened the state of his country
to his own: "No one can recover from such a calamity.
Such blows ruin your intelligence irremediably. The
disasters which have befallen me during the past year and
a half (the loss of my dearest friends) have weakened my
whole being, and my resistance is less than I thought.

Like my poor country, I am humbled in my pride."

Back in Croisset after the armistice, he forgot what he could in work, determining to finish now a final version of the *Tentation de Saint Antoine*, and devoting himself also to Bouilhet's memory, getting a posthumous play produced at the Odéon and writing an introduction for an edition of the posthumous poems. His days were lonelier and sadder than ever: "The worst thing about the invasion for me is that it added ten years to the age of my poor dear old mother," he wrote George Sand. Both at Croisset and even in Paris, where he had to go for research and theater business, he was filled with an unending loneliness and sense of loss. "My evenings are very solitary and very sad," he wrote his niece from the city. "I keep thinking of how differently I used to spend them when poor Duplan was with me. I sit beside my window and look out at the Parc Monceau, which is charming, and then I go to bed very early." To Turgenev he wrote: "The idea that I shall see as much as I like of you this winter fills me with delight, like the prospect of an oasis. If you knew my solitude you would realize the exactness of the comparison. Whom to talk with now? Who, in our lamentable country, still concerns himself with literature?" And when his niece told him that she had a plan for a novel, he was delighted: "I insist that you show it to the Old Man! Do you realize how charmed I am to have you for a disciple? I, who have no literary friends left?"

And then, once again, came losses. "*Ma chère Laure,*" he wrote in April, 1872, "*My mother is dead.* She died yesterday morning. We shall bury her tomorrow. I am exhausted from fatigue and sorrow. *Je t'embrasse tendrement.*" And in October died Théophile Gautier, whom in his youth he had adored as a deity of the

Romantics and whom he had loved for years. "The death of old Théo is crushing to me," he wrote Turgenev. "For the past three years all my friends have been dying, one after the other, without interruption. I now know only one man in the world to talk with—you."

So many friends lost!

And yet, almost immediately after that last cry of loneliness following Gautier's disappearance, comes word that Flaubert was, at the age of fifty-one, *acquiring* a friend. "The next book that I will publish will carry on its fly-leaf the name of your brother," he wrote to Laure de Maupassant, just about the time Guy received his temporary appointment in the ministry. "For in my mind the *Tentation de Saint Antoine* has always been dedicated 'To Alfred Le Poittevin.' I talked with him about it six months before his death, and now I have finally finished this work which has occupied me, off and on, for twenty-five years! Your son is right to love me, for I feel a real friendship for him. He is witty, well-read, charming, and then he is your son, the nephew of my poor Alfred."

Since Guy's first visit to Croisset six years before on his way to the seminary, his own maturing and Flaubert's losses, to say nothing of Laure's letters, had, as it turned out, been preparing the younger man and the older for each other; and now the friendship blossomed rapidly.

I hear you spoken of so often [Laure wrote Flaubert from Etretat the following February, 1873], that I am impelled to write you and to thank you with all my heart and soul. Guy is so happy to see you every Sunday, to be allowed to stay for hours, to be treated with such flattering familiarity, that all his letters tell and re-tell the same thing. The dear boy writes me about what he does every day, about our friends whom he meets in Paris, about his distractions; and then invariably the chapter ends: "but the house I like best, the place where I enjoy going more than anywhere else, is Monsieur Flaubert's." I assure you that I do not find his words monotonous! On the contrary, I cannot tell you my joy in knowing that my son is so welcomed by the best of my old friends. For don't I count for something in your graciousness to him? The nephew resembles the uncle, you told me in Rouen; and I see, not without a mother's pride, that more intimate investigation has not entirely destroyed the illusion.

If you want to please me, take a few minutes and tell me, yourself, some of your news. And talk to me about my son; tell me whether he has read you some of his poems, and whether you think they show anything beyond mere facility. You know what confidence I have in you; I will believe what you believe, I will follow your advice. If you say yes, we shall encourage the boy in the path that he prefers; but if you say no, we shall have him learn wig-making or some such trade. So speak frankly to your old friend.

You have got ahead of me, my dear Laure [Flaubert replied]. For the last month I have been wanting to write you, to send you a declaration of affection regarding your son. I cannot tell you how charming I find him, how intelligent, good-natured, sensible and witty—in short, to use a stylish word, *sympathique.* Despite the difference in our ages, I consider him a friend, and then he so reminds me of poor Alfred. Sometimes I am really startled by the likeness, especially when he bends his head as he has a way of doing when he reads poetry.

We must encourage him in this taste for poetry that he has. It is a noble passion, a love of letters can be a consolation in times of misfortune, and he may even have some talent—who knows? So far he has not produced enough to make it possible for me to cast his poetic horoscope, and anyway, where is the man who can decide another's future?

I think our young friend something of an idler, not

too fond of work. I should like to see him undertake
something long and exacting, execrable though it might
turn out to be. What he has shown me is certainly as
good as anything published by the parnassians. With
time he will acquire an originality, an individual manner
of seeing and feeling (which is everything). As to the
result, as to his possible "success," what difference does
it make? The principal thing in this world is to keep
one's soul aloft, high above the bourgeois and democratic
sloughs. The worship of art gives one pride: no one can
have enough of it. Such is my morality.

Although Flaubert continued, in the years immediately following, to spend lonely and depressed months at
Croisset, busy at his ill-fated play *Le Candidat* and his
novel *Bouvard et Pécuchet*, with only his servant Emile
and his greyhound Julio for company, there is evident
in his letters, particularly between the "declaration of
affection" to Laure and the death of George Sand in
1876, a lessening of the lamentations of friendlessness
that had so long filled them. Along with Turgenev,
whom he had come to care for increasingly since
Bouilhet's death, Flaubert had found someone else—
someone who was to be the "disciple" that his niece, a
fashionable young woman who dabbled in painting, could
never have been for all his pathetic delight at the thought
that she might be, and who also could be a friend, despite
a thirty-year difference in age. "Madame Sand is now,
with Turgenev, my only literary friend," he wrote
shortly before sending off to Laure the "declaration of
affection." "Those two are worth a crowd of others, it is
true, but something nearer the heart would not be un-
welcome." It was that vacant place near the heart that
Maupassant came to fill.*

* Flaubert's inscriptions in the copies of two of his works which he gave
Maupassant in 1874 reveal the dual nature of the relationship. In *Le Candidat*
he wrote "To Guy de Maupassant. May this, young man, be a lesson to you!!!"

By October Laure was writing to Flaubert: "You are being so good to my son, so perfect with him, that I do not know how to thank you. The young man belongs to you heart and soul, and I am like him, all yours now and always."

Maupassant put it simply many years later: "Flaubert, whom I saw from time to time, conceived an affection for me."

"From time to time" meant Sundays at Flaubert's apartment if he was in Paris, and otherwise an occasional Saturday or Sunday at Croisset, where Guy turned up either alone or in the company of his cousin Louis Le Poittevin, who had become not a lawyer but a painter. By all accounts, Louis was a charming young fellow, like his cousin Guy; but even so, and despite the fact that he was Alfred's own son—indeed, perhaps in part because of that fact, because of the memories it brought of Alfred's marriage, when for Flaubert he had first "died"— Flaubert at no time expressed particular interest in him. Alfred's son remained an acquaintance; Alfred's nephew became the special friend.

I was a government clerk without a sou. I had a thousand modest and unrealizable desires; my existence was gilded with a thousand expectations. How simple and good and hard it was to live as I lived then, between my office in Paris and the river at Argenteuil! My one, great, absorbing passion for ten years was the Seine. That lovely, calm, ever-changing, stinking river, full of glamor and filth! I loved it so, I think, because it gave me a sense of life. Those walks along the flowering banks, my friends the frogs dreaming on the water-lily pads,

---

And in *La Tentation de St. Antoine*: "Guy de Maupassant, whom I love as a son." The absurd rumor for a time current in France, that Maupassant *was* Flaubert's son, has been disposed of by René Dumesnil in his *Guy de Maupassant*.

the white water-lilies themselves so dainty and fragile among the tall fine grass that suddenly brought to mind a Japanese print when out from behind a willow a king-fisher fled before me like a blue flame! How I loved it all, with an instinctive visual love that infused my entire body with a deep, natural joy!

As others remember tender nights, I remember sunrises in morning mists—floating, shifting vapors that suddenly turned ravishingly rose as the first day darted over the meadows; and I remember moonlight silvering the moving, flowing river with a gleam that was the flowering of all one's dreams.

And all those things I saw either on or beside a stream of foul water that carried seaward all the refuse of Paris.

And then the fun! There was a company of five of us, today all serious men. Then we were all poor, and we had founded, in a frightful café at Argenteuil, an indescribable colony consisting of a single room with several beds, where I passed what were certainly the maddest nights of my life. We cared for nothing but fun and rowing: for all but one of us the oar was a cult. I remember adventures so singular, farces so improbable, invented by those five good-for-nothings, that no one today could believe them. No one lives like that any more, even on the Seine!

The five of us owned a single boat, bought with great difficulty, and in which we laughed as we shall never laugh again. It was a broad skiff, a little heavy, but solid, spacious and comfortable. I will just sketch my companions. There was a short one, very sly, nick-named Petit Bleu [Red Ink; Dago Red]; a tall one, with a wild air and gray eyes and black hair, known as Tomahawk; another, witty and lazy, called La Toque [Skullcap]—the only one who never touched an oar, his excuse being that he would capsize the boat; still another, slender, elegant, well-groomed, whom we called N'a-qu'un-œil [One-Eye] after a then recent novel by Cladel and because he wore a monocle; and finally myself, christened by the others Joseph Prunier. We lived in per-

fect harmony, with but one regret: that we had no girl to
be our coxswain. A woman is indispensable in a boat. Indispensable because she keeps head and heart alert, because she enlivens, amuses, distracts, gives spice, and
looks decorative with her red parasol gliding past the
green riverbanks. But no ordinary coxswain would do for
us, who were so unlike everyone else. We needed someone
unique, fantastic, ready for anything—someone almost
unfindable. We had tried a number without success,
girls who understood nothing of the duties of a coxswain,
silly boating girls interested only in wine, not water. We
would keep them a single Sunday and let them go,
disgusted. Then, one Saturday night, N'a-qu'un-œil
brought us a little creature! . . .

Such is the beginning of *Mouche*, one of Maupassant's
last stories, an outrageous little tale of rowing life on the
Seine that was a favorite with French readers from the
moment of its publication and that was commented on in
a Paris newspaper, shortly after Maupassant's death by
a respectable gentleman named Robert Pinchon, municipal librarian of Rouen:

Even though Mouche's adventure has been greatly
exaggerated by the author to fit the requirements of his
story [Monsieur Pinchon declared], still it gives an idea
of the gaiety of the river life of which he speaks. I have
become a "serious man," but I always enjoy remembering those happy times, when in that gay company I was
known by the nickname of La Toque.

Now *Mouche*, which was printed in the *Echo de Paris*
without question when Maupassant wrote it, is a story
that no editor in America or England would dream of
printing in his periodical even today; and it makes us
smile that the head of a provincial library should openly
and proudly avow himself one of those who participated
in Mouche's "adventure," even though explaining that

Maupassant had "greatly exaggerated" it. It is difficult
to imagine the chief librarian in a large American or
English city delightedly putting forth his claim in print,
and over his own signature, to such participation,
considering what it consisted of.

There is nothing today, in France or elsewhere, quite
like the free-and-easy week-end river life of those days on
the Seine below Paris during the months of good weather.
"Every Sunday we all went somewhere in the near-by
countryside to roll on the grass or soak in the water.
Asnières, Argenteuil, Chatou, Bougival, Maisons, Poissy,
each had its habitués and its fanatics, and there was
passionate discussion of the merits and advantages of all
these places, so famous and delightful for the employees
of Paris," Maupassant wrote in *Le Père Mongilet* (*Old
Mongilet*). Renoir's famous canvas, *Le Déjeuner des
Canotiers*, painted at the restaurant Fournaise at Chatou,
is a scene from this happy existence, and, in *Yvette*,
Maupassant describes the floating cabaret La Grenouillère (The Froggery), moored beside an island in the
Seine and familiar to us from paintings by Renoir and
Monet:

An immense roofed barge, moored to the bank, was
laden with a mass of men and women eating and drinking
at tables, or standing about shouting, singing, dancing,
capering to the sound of a throbbing, tinny old piano.
A number of large, red-lipped, red-headed, foul-mouthed
girls were walking about undulating their busts and their
buttocks and eyeing everyone in invitation. Others were
dancing madly with half-naked young men in rowing
clothes and jockey caps. The whole place smelled of
sweat and face powder, of perfume and armpits. The
drinkers at their tables were downing liquors of all
colors—white, red, yellow and green; and they were
shouting and yelling for no reason except their own

violent need to make a noise, a purely animal necessity
to fill their own ears and heads with uproar. Every other
moment a swimmer jumped off the roof into the water,
splashing the nearest drinkers and making them scream
like savages.

It was an atmosphere of raucous cameraderie, of
rough-and-tumble farce, of swarms of prostitutes and
near-prostitutes and working men and girls out for a
good time, of rowing and sailing parties dotting the river
and converging at the cafés along the bank and at the
floating cabaret. It hadn't taken long for the young
swimmer and oarsman of Etretat, the water-lover now
living in a dark room in Paris, to discover the Seine.
"I row and swim, swim and row," he wrote his mother.
"The river rats and the frogs are so accustomed to see me
go by at any hour of the night with my light in the bow of
my boat that they come out to wish me good night."

Unlike most of the riverside habitués, Guy did not
restrict himself to week-ends:

My entire happiness at this time of my life lay in
rowing [he says in *Le Colporteur—The Peddler*]. I had a
room in a café at Argenteuil, and evenings I used to take
the bureaucrats' train—a long slow train that dropped
off at one suburban station after another men who were
paunchy and heavy because they seldom took exercise,
and whose trousers sagged because of the hours they
spent sitting at their desks. This train, which I always
imagined still smelled of the office, with its papers and
its files, took me to Argenteuil. My skiff was waiting, all
ready to dart over the water, and with long strokes I
rowed myself to dinner at Bezons or Chatou or Epinay
or Saint-Ouen. Then I rowed back, put away the boat,
and, when there was a moon, set off for Paris on foot.

There are other, slightly incoherent echoes of the life
in a letter he wrote during one of his first summers in
Paris to his friend Petit-Bleu:

Here is the news I promised you of our colony of
Aspergopolis. I sleep there about twice a week and fence
with Boullaud from five to seven in the morning. Not
much else new. Sunday we had a visit from Paul, coming
from Chatou with Berthe. As a climax, a friend of Paul's
who had brought them felt sick and couldn't row them
back, so I had to embark at ten P.M. to take the two
traveling turtledoves to their nest: I accomplished the
dangerous journey without accident. So many things
have happened since I began this letter! First of all, we
have been at Bezons with Mimi and Nini. . . .

And there are more echoes in another letter, which he
wrote in a French feebly approximating that of Rabelais:

Epistle from Master Joseph Prunier, boatman in the
waters of Bezons and neighboring parts to the very
esteemed Petit-Bleu:
After a goodly number of apéritifs, we began our feast
by consuming 2,591 bottles of wine of Argenteuil, 678
bottles of good wine of Bordeaux, 746 bottles of Pom-
mard, and 27,941 hogsheads of Ay. Thereupon we
commenced to feel of good cheer. But ill accustomed to
our Pantagruelian repasts, that old f— La Toque commenced to roll his eyes in such an odd and grievous
manner, followed by his belly rolling even more griev-
ously, that he at last fell to the floor and henceforth
stirred no more. At this we mopped him and washed him
and rubbed him, hoisted him and carried him and un-
dressed him and laid him out, completely besoused;
thereupon we recited at his bedside the prayers and
orisons of loafers, tipplers, wine-bibbers and the like,
with the effect that he slept, snored, made exceeding
wind all night long and awakened stiff and aching and
cold: head, neck, back, chest, arms, and everything.
And the morrow we did begin again. Now the day
whereon God the Father rested after creating both
heaven and earth, we arrived at Bezons. And that day
Prunier did many things, feats of navigation most
astonishing, marvelous and superlative, such as to row

from Bezons as far as Argenteuil a sailing ship so frightfully large that he thought he had left the skin of his
hands upon the oars. (Two beautiful whores were in said
sailing ship.) *Signed:* Joseph Prunier, Captain of the
Etretat.

From the first days of spring Maupassant's blood
boiled in his veins like sap [Petit-Bleu reminisced in
later years]. He thirsted for fresh air and country and
found it impossible to stay in Paris. We had rented a
room together in a dive at Argenteuil run by one Bétry
Simbosel at the sign of the "Petit-Matelot," and it
became a veritable dormitory the nights our friends
joined us. One fine day Maupassant and his friends
abandoned Argenteuil and the band split up. Those who
had more of a taste for frolicsome company went down
the Seine as far as Chatou and made their headquarters
at the Restaurant Fournaise, near La Grenouillère.
Joseph Prunier and Petit-Bleu stopped at Bezons, in the
inn kept by Poulin, next to the bridge. Naturally that
didn't hinder the two crews from joining forces on occasion, but Joseph Prunier needed quiet for his work. In
the autumn the two friends shot larks in the meadows
near by. When he talked about his hunting or his prowess
as walker or oarsman, this Norman Joseph Prunier, a
true Gascon of the North, always inflated the number
of his victims or kilometers, and his companion Petit-
Bleu, on whom some of his glory was reflected, took pains
not to contradict him. They were greeted as "the boys
from Bezons" when they appeared, like two wild
Indians, in Chatou, a more civilized community. There
were so many adventures that delighted Prunier in that
Bezons inn! One morning it was the innkeeper himself,
found hanged in his attic—the whole village came in to
get pieces of the rope [as good-luck souvenirs]. One night
it was our next-door neighbor, suddenly seized with the
pangs of childbirth and uttering piercing screams; the
midwife was late in arriving, and it was the never-shy
Prunier, aided by Petit-Bleu, who delivered the poor

creature as best he could. One night a husband of the vicinity came lamenting to Prunier that his wife had not come home. He was afraid she might have thrown herself into the river. The two friends, who knew very well that it wasn't in the river that she should be looked for, nevertheless pretended to drag the Seine to pacify the inconsolable husband, and brought him, at dawn, as the best they could provide in the way of a corpse, a dead dog fished up by Prunier near the dam. One day when a pretty Parisienne came to see them, Prunier thought it would be fun, in order to spare her the long walk from the station to the village, to fetch her in a handcart. The two oarsmen harnessed themselves to the shafts and it was in this equipage that the lady made her entry into Bezons. Maupassant enjoyed all the characters he met: the bourgeois and their better halves spending Sunday in the country, the bargemen, the peasants, the tramps, the washerwomen, the barber, the village pharmacist. He chatted and gossiped with them all, and not one of their comic traits escaped him.*

The meaning of Flaubert's phrase, "something of an idler," becomes abundantly clear. Maupassant was handsome, strong and vigorous—"a good-looking, well-built young fellow" is Zola's description of him at the time, and others mention his broad shoulders, powerful biceps, ruddy complexion and general outdoor look, and tell of how a wrestler, seeing him in his rowing clothes, took him for a member of his own profession. A good part of his life was always to be given over to the various kinds of exercise and dissipation that Flaubert, the cloistered artist, lumped together under the term "idling"; and in these penurious years of his twenties he did his idling on or beside the Seine. His work at the ministry was good —his chief's words of praise are still on file, and he was

* Pierre Borel et Léon Fontaine, "Maupassant avant la gloire," *Revue de France,* 5:385–410 (1927).

promoted more than once—but his thoughts were usually elsewhere; and one of his surviving letters of these days, a letter written to his cousin Louis in Rouen, filled with details and sketches of a boat that he wanted, is reminiscent of the homesick letter he had written Laure on the same subject from the seminary.

But despite the idling, a new occupation now began. "Read, in Turgenev's last book, *Histoires étranges*, the story called *l'Abandonnée*—it's a rare masterpiece," Flaubert wrote him the summer of the Rabelaisian drinking bout. And in a letter of lamentation to Laure, written in the midst of post-vacation blues after two glorious, all-too-short weeks in Etretat ("I've been up to scandalous things!" he had scribbled happily to Petit-Bleu in mid-vacation on one of those recent innovations, a postcard), Guy says "To try to cheer myself up a little I have just written something in the style of Daudet's *Contes du Lundi*. I'm sending it to you. Naturally it doesn't pretend to be anything—I wrote it in a few minutes. But send it back to me, please; maybe I can make something of it." A year later he writes her: "Try to find me sub- jects for stories—I could work on them a little during the day at the ministry."

As a boy and as a lycéen Guy had written poetry, and it was his poetry that Louis Bouilhet had seen and encouraged and that Flaubert had pronounced "as good as anything by the Parnassians." Now, at twenty-three, although he was to continue writing poetry for a number of years, he began to write stories.

Many a prose writer has begun as a poet: the shift seems to be a stage in certain kinds of literary maturing. Often, somewhere in the background of such a change, the presence of an immediate agent can be detected; and Laure, in her old age, said that in her son's case the agent was Flaubert. "If Bouilhet had lived," she said, "he would have made my son a poet. It was Flaubert who turned him to story writing." Perhaps Laure was right. "Don't worry," Flaubert wrote her during one of Guy's first winters in Paris. "I will do everything I can do for Guy because of you, because of Alfred, and because of Guy himself. He is a charming boy, and I love him dearly." Certainly Flaubert's "everything I can do" included above all else guidance in the writing of prose.

Flaubert was always faithful to the memory of Louis Bouilhet, just as to the memory of Alfred Le Poittevin, and the fact that Bouilhet had pronounced Guy a poet and encouraged him in verse-writing was no doubt sufficient reason for Flaubert to do the same—as indeed he continued to do for the rest of his life, even while training him in the writing of prose. But Flaubert—who had been so influenced by Bouilhet in his abandonment of romantic writing in favor of the realism of *Madame Bovary*— had become much more a part of the main literary current of the age than Bouilhet, who, despite his influence on Flaubert, remained somewhat provincial. Flaubert recognized that the greater use of realistic, or everyday, subject matter in literature made appropriate and inevitable an increase of prose narrative at the expense of verse, and he can scarcely have failed to appreciate the essentially narrative, flowing character of most of the poems that Maupassant showed him. Furthermore, the short story was becoming at this time increasingly popular, and newspapers were buying ever greater numbers of short tales, or *contes*, and printing them on their front pages. Alphonse Daudet, whose *Contes du Lundi* Maupassant had told Laure he was imitating, had so published numerous short tales in the 1860's and collected them under the celebrated title *Lettres de Mon Moulin* in 1866;

Zola had published a collection of short tales under the title *Contes à Ninon;* and such remembered and unremembered writers as Paul Arène, Ludovic Halévy, Gyp, Richard O'Monroy, François Coppée, Théodore de Banville, Armand Silvestre and Catulle Mendès were earning considerable money from their short stories, which appeared regularly in newspapers. "There has arisen," wrote the critic Jules Lemaître, "a whole Pléiade of short-story writers."

Flaubert's knowledge of all this, plus his memory of the penury in which Bouilhet had lived and his recognition of Maupassant's financial need, may have been among his reasons if he did, as Laure says he did, encourage the young poet to try the other medium. In any case, he was soon referring to him as his "disciple," his "pupil."

As to Maupassant's idleness, Flaubert made no attempt, during these early years, to suppress or combat it. "Since your Saturdays are sacred to rowing, and since I was in Paris only one day, last Saturday, on my way back from Switzerland, I wasn't able to see you," he wrote him matter-of-factly one summer; and he indicates his knowledge of a more urban type of idleness in a note to his niece: "My 'pupil,' Guy de Maupassant, is a friend of somebody connected with the Vaudeville theater"—a fact that is confirmed in a note from Guy to Petit-Bleu indicating that he possesses a source of free tickets to that playhouse.

Some of the forms that Guy's idleness took gave Flaubert considerable pleasure. "Lascivious author, obscene young man," he wrote early in 1875, "do not come to lunch here Sunday (I will tell you the reason), but if you don't go rowing drop in about two. It will be my last Sunday in Paris, and Turgenev has finally

promised to translate aloud Goethe's *Satyros*." The
salutation "Lascivious author" refers to a literary pastime of a different kind from a reading of the *Satyros*—to
the recent, highly diverting performance, before a select
audience of men only, of a farce written by Guy and
La Toque and called *A la feuille de rose, Maison Turque.*
The title, adapted from the name of a brothel in Flaubert's *Education Sentimentale,* was the name of the establishment in which the action took place; and the authors
and their friends in various costumes played the roles
of an innocent young married couple spending a night
in what turns out not to be a hotel, and also the roles
of the establishment's staff and clientele. "The solemn
occasion is set for Monday, the nineteenth of the present
month," Guy wrote a friend in advance of the performance. "Only men over twenty years of age and women
previously deflowered will be admitted." Characteristi-
cally, Laure was not kept in ignorance of the scabrous
event: "A few friends and I are going to put on a completely lewd play in Leloir's studio," her son wrote joyfully. "Flaubert and Turgenev will be in the audience.
I don't have to tell you we wrote it ourselves."

There was one casualty during those first years in
Paris: the project which Maupassant had told the minister a position at the ministry would enable him to carry
through. Unlike his uncle Alfred, unlike his cousin Louis,
but like Flaubert, he abandoned the study of law before
reaching the end of his course.

"My Little Father," Flaubert wrote his disciple in
November, 1875, in one of his first letters after installing
himself in a new Paris apartment, "it is agreed, is it not,
that you will lunch with me every Sunday this winter?
Till Sunday, then."

It was those Sunday lunches during the winter of 1875–76, when Flaubert was in Paris uninterruptedly from November until March, that marked the earliest intensification of Maupassant's literary training. He described it later:

Flaubert, whom I saw from time to time, conceived an affection for me, and I dared show him a few things that I had tried. He was kind enough to read them, and said: "I cannot tell whether you will have any talent. What you have brought me shows a certain intelligence, but don't forget what Buffon says: 'Talent is a long patience.' So—work." I worked, and returned to see him often, for it was clear that he liked me, and he took to calling me, laughingly, his disciple. For seven years I wrote poetry, short stories, longer stories, even a detestable play—none of which survive. The master read everything; then, the following Sunday, as we lunched, he criticized, gradually inculcating into me, bit by bit, two or three principles that sum up his long and patient teaching. "If you have originality," he used to say, "the essential is to release it; if you haven't, you must acquire it."

"Talent is a long patience . . ." It is a matter of considering long and attentively what you want to express, so that you may discover an aspect of it that has never before been noticed or reported. There is a part of everything that remains unexplored, for we have fallen into the habit of remembering, whenever we use our eyes, what people before us have thought of the thing we are looking at. Even the slightest thing contains a little that is unknown. We must find it. To describe a blazing fire or a tree in a plain, we must remain before that fire or that tree until they no longer resemble for us any other tree or any other fire.

That is the way to become original.

After repeating over and over again this truth, that there are not in the entire world two grains of sand, two flies, two hands or two noses that are absolutely the same, he made me describe, in a few sentences, a being or an object in such a way as to particularize it clearly, to distinguish it from all the other beings or all the other objects of the same race or kind.

"When you pass a grocer sitting in his doorway," he used to tell me, "or a concierge smoking his pipe, or a cab-stand, show me that grocer and that concierge, the way they are sitting or standing, their entire physical appearance, making it by the skillfulness of your portrayal embody all their moral nature as well, so that I cannot confuse them with any other grocer or any other concierge; and make me see, by means of a single word, wherein one cab-horse does *not* resemble the fifty others ahead of it or behind it."

Whatever you want to say, there is only one word that will express it, one verb to make it move, one adjective to qualify it. You must seek that word, that verb, and that adjective, and never be satisfied with approximations, never resort to tricks, even clever ones, or to verbal pirouettes, to escape the difficulty.

Every act, good or bad, is of importance for the writer only as a subject to be written about. No idea of good or evil can be attributed to it. It is good or bad solely as a literary document.

[Flaubert] did not think of "*styles*," as of a series of particular moulds, each bearing the mark of some writer and into which that writer casts his ideas; he believed in *style*—that is, a unique, absolute manner of expressing a thing in all its color and intensity.

Those are only a few of the many passages, scattered here and there through Maupassant's works, in which he does his best to tell us of Flaubert's literary principles (and his own: at no time does he make a distinction between them). But even allowing for the fact that at Sunday lunch Flaubert doubtless made his pronouncements with something of a teacher's emphasis and simplification, Maupassant's expositions of them are always somewhat crude and naïve, like a series of awkward, rather scrambling jumps from one high spot to another in what must have been Flaubert's discourse. Unlike Maupassant, Flaubert never published a treatise on his literary principles: indeed it was one of his principles not to do so, but to embody them in the one place where he thought they belonged—his fiction; but his correspondence is rich in comment on writers and writing, and it is there, rather than in Maupassant's inadequate attempts at exposition, that one can learn most profitably what Flaubert believed and sense what his talk must have been like.

You are young [Flaubert wrote during these same years to another young literary man who had sought his advice]. Work for a long time in solitude, and without hope of recompense, without any idea of publishing. Do as I did: I was thirty-seven when *Madame Bovary* appeared. You are lost if you think of making any profit from your work. You must think only of Art in itself, and of perfecting it for yourself in your own way. All the rest follows from that. And do not think that the life of a literary man like myself is "strewn with flowers": you are in complete illusion about that. I repeat: if you really love literature, write *for yourself* at first, and read the classics. You have read too many modern books; one sees them reflected in your work. Practise writing about things that you have felt personally, describing scenes that are familiar to you.

But if Maupassant is unable to expound with any ease or richness what took place *at* lunch, so to speak, he is another man when he tells us of the company that came in afterwards, when he ticks off for us Flaubert's other guests:

He received his friends on Sunday from one to seven, in a very simple fifth-floor bachelor apartment. The

walls were bare and the furniture modest, for he detested
artistic fripperies. As soon as a peal of the bell announced
the first visitor he covered the papers on his work table
with a piece of red silk, thus concealing his tools, sacred
for him as objects of worship for a priest. Then, his
servant always being free on Sunday, he opened the door
himself.

The first to arrive was often Ivan Turgenev, whom
he embraced like a brother. Taller even than Flaubert,
the Russian novelist loved the French novelist with rare
and deep affection. He would sink into an armchair and
talk in a slow, pleasant voice, a trifle low and hesitant,
but giving great charm and interest to his words. Flaubert listened religiously. Their conversation rarely
touched on current affairs, but kept close to matters of
literature and literary history. Often Turgenev brought
foreign books, and translated aloud poems by Goethe,
Pushkin or Swinburne.

Others gradually arrived. Monsieur Taine, with his
timid air, his eyes hidden by spectacles, brought with
him historical documents, unknown facts, an aroma of
ransacked archives. Here come Frédéric Baudry, Georges
Pouchet, Claudius Popelin, Philippe Burty. Then Alphonse Daudet, bringing an air of Paris at its gayest,
its most lively and bustling. In a few words he sketches
amusing silhouettes and touches everyone and everything with his charming irony, so southern and personal;
the delicacy of his wit is enhanced by the charm of his
face and gestures, by the polished perfection of his
anecdotes. Emile Zola comes in, breathless from the
long stairs and always followed by his faithful Paul
Alexis. He flings himself into a chair and looks about
him, seeking to gauge from the guests' faces their states
of mind and the tone and trend of the conversation.
Then still others: the publisher Charpentier, the charming poet Catulle Mendès with his face of a sensual and
seductive Christ, Emile Bergerat, his brother-in-law,
who married the daughter of Théophile Gautier; José-
Maria de Heredia, the famous maker of sonnets who will

always remain one of the most perfect poets of the age; Huysmans, Hennique, Céard, Léon Cladel the obscure and refined stylist, Gustave Toudouze. And finally, almost always the last, a tall, slender gentleman with an air of aristocratic breeding, Edmond de Goncourt.

"I knew Maupassant at Flaubert's about 1874," Zola records, in turn. "He had barely finished college, and no one in our literary circle had yet noticed him. When we arrived on Sunday, about two, we almost always found him already there, often having lunched with the master, to whom he came each week to read what he had written, and who made him entirely rework any phrases that didn't ring true. As soon as we appeared he modestly effaced himself, talked little, and listened with the intelligent air of someone who realizes his own capacities and is taking notes for the future. Later we became friendly with him and he made us marvel with tales of his prowess. Of medium height, sturdily built, muscular and ruddy, he was at that time a terrific oarsman, able to row fifty miles on the Seine in one day for pleasure. Besides, he was a proud he-man, and told us dumbfounding stories about women, amorous swaggerings that sent Flaubert into roars of laughter."

And a letter which Maupassant himself wrote that winter to La Toque is illustrated with a sketch of Flaubert, Turgenev and Alphonse Daudet talking together while he sits in a corner drawing them—a disciple paying homage to his master and his master's guests.

Another glimpse of Flaubert's "little salon, which . . . looked rather bare and provisional," his "small perch, far aloft, at the distant, the then almost suburban, end of the Faubourg Saint-Honoré . . . at the very top of an endless flight of stairs," is given us by a young American writer whose occasional attendance has gone unrecorded by his host or by any of the other guests

but always remained for him a source of vivid recollection, ever richer to him as time went on. This was Henry
James—or, as he then signed himself, Henry James,
Jr.—aged thirty-two, who was spending that winter in
Paris with the thought, at first, that he might live there
permanently, that "there he would find the literary world
with which he had the strongest affinity." He changed
his mind rather rapidly—chiefly, it would seem, as a
result of his Sunday afternoons at Flaubert's, where he
had been introduced by Turgenev. James (whom Turgenev once described as "a very amiable man, who has a
great deal of talent, with a certain tendency toward
melancholy") thought Turgenev "adorable," and in
Flaubert he "saw many reasons for Turgenev's regard,"
though of him he wrote home to his father, "I think I
easily—more than easily—see all round him intellec-
tually"; but he found the rest of the circle not to his
liking. "I have seen almost nothing of the literary fra-
ternity," he wrote his friend Howells, "and there are
fifty reasons why I should not become intimate with
them. I don't like their wares, and they don't like any
others; and besides, they are not *accueillants*. Turgenev
is worth the whole heap of them, and yet he himself
swallows them down in a manner that excites my
extreme wonder."

What was discussed in that little smoke-clouded
room was chiefly questions of taste, questions of art and
form [James tells us], and the speakers, for the most part,
were in aesthetic matters, radicals of the deepest dye.
It would have been late in the day to propose among
them any discussion of the relation of art to morality,
any question as to the degree in which a novel might or
might not concern itself with the teaching of a lesson.
They had settled these preliminaries long ago, and it
would have been primitive and incongruous to recur to

them. The conviction that held them together was the conviction that art and morality are two perfectly different things, and that the former has no more to do with the latter than it has with astronomy or embryology. The only duty of a novel was to be well written; that merit included every other of which it was capable.

There, among the aesthetic "radicals of the deepest dye," James met the young Maupassant. "Distinct to me," he later reminisced, "the memory of a Sunday afternoon at Flaubert's in the winter of '75–'76, when Maupassant, still *inédit*, but always 'round,' regaled me with a fantastic tale, irreproducible here, of the relations between two Englishmen, each other, and their monkey! A picture the details of which have faded for me, but not the lurid impression."*

One can picture the two of them, two of the decidedly lesser figures at the gathering—that is, one can be sure that both were considered among the lesser by everyone present except, perhaps, James himself, who saw "all round" Flaubert—and the young Frenchman talking to the foreign visitor, à propos of English eccentricity (quite possibly he thought James an Englishman) about the visits he had paid to Swinburne and Powell and their monkey in the Etretat villa where the skinned hand had lain with other bones on a table. Heaven knows how he may have piled on the "lurid"—and imagined—detail! That skinned hand had never left Maupassant's mind, and it was particularly in his mind that winter, for he had been writing a tale around it, one of the tales he wrote during the week and brought to Sunday lunch. This one, a tale resembling Merimée's *La Vénus d'Ille*, was the first of his stories ever to be published: it appeared that same winter, entitled *La Main d'Ecorché*

* See Note 2: A Henry James Letter, page 395.

(*The Skinned Hand*), in an obscure provincial almanac
edited by a cousin of Petit-Bleu's.

La Main d'Ecorché was not signed, in the almanac,
with the name Guy de Maupassant, but with the pseudonym Joseph Prunier, which had been bestowed upon
him by his rowing companions on the river; and around
the use of this signature there is an interesting cluster of
reasons.

The name Joseph Prunier has a very lower middle-
class ring, with a hint of absurdity about it, something
like a respectable but very simple English or Yankee
name such as John Higgs or Samuel Small. The name
was doubtless given him ironically, because of his voluble
scorn for the petite bourgeoisie—scorn derived in part
from his family circumstances (his father's name having
a near-aristocratic ring, and his mother being in his
eyes emancipated by her intellect and tastes from even
her high bourgeois background), and probably in part
from Flaubert's incessant anti-bourgeois railings. Flaubert may have advised him to sign such an early, un-
formed story with a pseudonym as a means of indicating
to him his opinion that it was not yet work to be highly
valued; and the use for that purpose of the little river
nickname was natural enough. But, as we shall see, after
abandoning Joseph Prunier, Maupassant was to adopt
another pseudonym, and later still another. So well-
marked a disposition to get away from one's own name
generally has a cause other than mere reasons of practi-
cality: some deeper cause, often unrealized.

In Guy's case the cause is not far to seek. In one of
his letters to his mother during his first years at the
ministry he writes rather proudly of eminent de Maupassant ancestors whom he had come upon in some old
documents; and at times he had a marquis's coronet

engraved on his stationery: consciously he seems to have
had nothing against his perfectly honorable, imposing-
sounding family name, although he did sometimes
jokingly pretend that its derivation was from *mauvais
passant* (evil passer-by) and that it was thus an appropriate name for himself. But the name had a bad defect:
it was his father's—the name of the man by whom (in
her own and Guy's eyes, at least) Laure had been
"crushed, beaten, martyrized." Guy's early and long-
continued dissociation of himself from the name, and
especially this earliest dissociation from it by means of
the very opposite of aristocratic, very plebeian, even
slightly absurd pseudonym Joseph Prunier, indicate how
deeply his spirit had been marked by his parents' dis-
harmony, how violent was his partisanship, his hostility
to his father. It is interesting—even a little frightening,
considering that Maupassant, like many another author
before and after, prided himself on making his writings
"impersonal"—that this very first time he ever published
a story, a feeble, unoriginal story in an obscure almanac,
the pseudonym he signed to it should provide not only
the earliest existing evidence of what was certainly his
greatest emotional obsession, but also a forecast of what
was to be one of the chief general characteristics of his
work.

As the existence of *La Main d'Ecorché* shows, Maupassant was not accurate in saying that nothing survived
of the early writings which he showed Flaubert Sundays
in the Faubourg Saint-Honoré. Much was doubtless
destroyed, but of the poetry written during these years
he preserved enough for a volume which he later published, and there exist also a few more short stories, a

few essays and plays, and a complete fantastic novelette, *Le Docteur Héraclius Gloss*, in which one of the leading characters is a monkey, doubtless a further memory of the visits to Swinburne. Except for the poetry and two of the stories, Maupassant included none of these early efforts in collections of his work published during his lifetime; the rest he preferred to leave either totally unpublished, or unprinted from the obscure periodicals in which they had appeared, and he showed good judgment in doing so.

"I keep working at my rowing scenes that I told you about," he wrote his mother just before the 1875–76 winter began, "and I think I can make a rather amusing, accurate little book by choosing the best of the stories, expanding them, embroidering them, etc." Maupassant never did publish a volume of rowing stories, though those he wrote on the subject would have made a thick book had he ever cared to collect them; but *En Canot* (*In a Boat*), which appeared in another obscure magazine in 1876 and was later rescued and republished by Maupassant under the title *Sur L'Eau* (*On the Water*),* by which it is now known, is apparently one of the scenes mentioned in the letter to Laure. It concerns an oarsman who, after anchoring his boat in mid-Seine one warm night to smoke a pipe in the moonlight, is unable to lift his anchor and has to spend the night on the river. He becomes unaccountably panicky, especially when a thick white fog arises; he senses strange presences and feels that his boat is under a sinister influence; he drinks most of a bottle of rum to give himself courage. Finally he falls asleep, and at dawn a passing fisherman helps him with his anchor: with it they together pull up the heavy

* Quite distinct from his so-called travel-diary of the same title, for which see page 409.

mass in which it had become entangled—the corpse of an old woman with a stone around her neck. Despite the banality of the anecdote, *En Canot* shows Maupassant already master of one instrument: a good *descriptive* style—so frequently the first, and so frequently the only, instrument which a would-be writer learns to use.

> *Je fus ébloui par le plus merveilleux, le plus étonnant spectacle qu'il soit possible de voir. C'était une de ces fantasmagories du pays des fées, une de ces visions racontées par les voyageurs qui reviennent de très loin et que nous écoutons sans les croire.*
>
> *Le brouillard qui, deux heures auparavant, flottait sur l'eau, s'était peu à peu retiré et ramassé sur les rives. Laissant le fleuve absolument libre, il avait formé sur chaque berge une colline ininterrompue, haute de six ou sept mètres, qui brillait sous la lune avec l'éclat superbe des neiges. De sorte qu'on ne voyait rien autre chose que cette rivière lamée de feu entre ces deux montagnes blanches; et là-haut, sur ma tête, s'étalait, pleine et large, une grande lune illuminante au milieu d'un ciel bleuâtre et laiteux.*

Best to leave it in French, since it is an exercise in atmospheric description—a decidedly studied exercise—and little more. But the beauty of that passage and others in *En Canot* descriptive of the night on the river were later to win the praise of Tolstoy, and Flaubert must even as early as this have had occasional reason to be pleased with what his disciple brought with him to Sunday lunch. Indeed, it was a few months after the obscure publication of *En Canot* that Flaubert made up his mind about him. In a letter to a friend on a newspaper, asking that Guy be assigned occasional articles on books and the theater, he finally permitted himself to "cast his poetic horoscope": "This young man whom I am recommending is unquestionably a poet, and I believe that he has a great literary future."

Flaubert's belief must have been strengthened by *Le Papa de Simon*, written in 1877, obscurely published in 1879, and subsequently, like *En Canot*, rescued and republished. Here the interest is dramatic. Little Simon, bastard son of Blanchette, a village girl who has been seduced and abandoned, is tormented by his schoolmates because he has no father. In his misery he is about to drown himself in a brook, when he is rescued by a kindly blacksmith, a newcomer to the village, who takes him home to his mother, realizes the situation, and allows Simon to tell his schoolmates that *he* is his father. That quiets them for a time, but later they return to the attack, jeering that if he really had a father his mother would be married. Simon reports this to the blacksmith, who has meanwhile come to admire and desire Blanchette. He offers to make her his wife, she accepts him, and Simon informs his class that he has a real father at last. "And this time no one laughed, for everyone knew Philippe Rémy, the blacksmith, and knew that he was a father of whom anybody would be proud."

The story is powerfully told. The skillful construction and progression of the scenes, and the merciless choice of the words that Maupassant puts in the mouth of little Simon, force the reader's tears; and it is possible to agree with the publisher of the collection in which it was later re-issued, who called it "quite simply a little masterpiece." It is a very sentimental masterpiece, however, very much in the manner of Daudet, and Maupassant's later stories were to have a different kind of power, less tear-jerking and more original. But *Le Papa de Simon* is an excellent example—the earliest example in Maupassant's work—of what Louis Bouilhet had told him in Rouen about the beneficial results of finding "a subject in harmony with all the tendencies of one's mind." For

in this tale—as in all successful works by all writers—
the roles played by theme and by technique in the formation of the total excellence are inextricably mingled
and inter-active. What could have been more in harmony
with all the tendencies of Maupassant's mind—especially, no doubt, his unconscious mind—than this subject of a boy with a worthless father and a betrayed
mother, who after torment and misery finds a foster-
father "of whom anybody would be proud"? Much of the
story's strength comes from the author's scorn, both
spoken and unspoken, on the subject of fathers: the
name of Simon's real father is never given, he is never
described, barely mentioned—he is considered worthy of
scarcely a word, considered not to exist except for the
biological function he has performed. And Simon's
tormenters in school, we are told, had for the most part
fathers who were "bad, drunkards, thieves, and cruel
to their wives." The schoolboys' jeering cry—"No father!
No father!"—recurs throughout the tale, until finally
the fine, humiliated mother, and the tall, strong blacksmith foster-father with his wavy black hair and beard
and his enormous hands, between them bring Simon
happiness.

For his own foster-father, who so unlike Monsieur de
Maupassant could be respected and loved, for Flaubert,
the master who had come so quickly to believe in his
literary future, Maupassant at times felt a distinct dread.
When an early essay of his on Flaubert—the first of the
many he was eventually to write—appeared in a magazine called the *République des Lettres*, to which Flaubert
had introduced him, he wrote to a friend on the staff:
"This is to tell you that I have not been sent a copy of the

République des Lettres. I have bought one and am sending
it on to Flaubert, but since I have no desire to receive the
dressing-down that he would certainly otherwise give
me, I am being careful to let him know that at the last
moment you made certain changes in my remarks on
Balzac. For I know that Flaubert's opinion of Balzac is
exactly the same as mine—while admiring his incon-
testable genius he considers him not an imperfect writer
but no writer at all."

Maupassant's precautions succeeded, and the article
was well received: "You have treated me with the affection of a son," Flaubert wrote in thanks. "My niece is
enthusiastic about your article. She thinks it the best
ever written about her uncle. I think so too, but I dare
not say so."

The editor of the *République des Lettres*, which was
considered the organ of the parnassian school of poets,
was Catulle Mendès, Flaubert's Sunday guest with the
"face of a sensual and seductive Christ"; and to Mendès
and the others connected with the magazine Flaubert
was at this time the high-priest of French letters, the
recently published final version of *La Tentation de Saint
Antoine* being especially venerated. As his protegé,
Guy was made welcome, and he was soon attending
Mendès's literary dinners, where the guests sometimes
included Flaubert himself and almost always the young
Mallarmé, whose *L'Après-Midi d'un Faune* (detested by
Flaubert) was another object of worship in the little
group. About this time Maupassant began also to go
with a rather different group of literary men of his own
age to Thursday evening gatherings at the home of
another of Flaubert's guests, Emile Zola.

In practical return for the counsels, commissions and
social and literary launchings that the relation with

Flaubert brought him, Maupassant could give little: his services in doing errands in Paris when Flaubert was in Croisset, information concerning the geography of the Norman coast near Etretat that Flaubert needed, or thought he needed, for a chapter in *Bouvard et Pécuchet*. His chief return to the lonely older man was in being there—to distract, to be taught, and to receive and give affection. When the apartment in Paris was empty, Maupassant paid week-end visits to Croisset and wrote letters:

I will write you in a few days to chat a little with you, as I used to every Sunday here in Paris. Our chats have become a habit with me and a need, and I cannot resist gossiping a little by letter; naturally I don't ask you to answer, I know that you have other things to do; excuse my taking this liberty, but in our talks I often felt that I was listening to my uncle, whom I never knew, but of whom you and my mother have spoken so often, and whom I love as though I had been his friend or his son; and poor Bouilhet, too, whom I did know, and whom I also loved.

CHAPTER 3

THE DESTROYER

Meanwhile, as he pursued the training that was to fit him for his career, he contracted the disease that was eventually to destroy the career and him with it.

There was a certain gloomy, almost macabre note that was frequently sounded in the letters that Guy sent, during these early years, to Laure.

You see I don't delay in writing you [he wrote her just after returning to Paris following one of the first Etretat vacations from the ministry], but indeed I can't wait any longer. I feel so lost here, so isolated, so demoralized, that I must ask you to send me one of your good letters. I fear the coming winter, I feel alone in the world, my long solitary evenings are sometimes terrible. Sitting alone at my table I often have moments of such utter distress that I don't know where to turn. And last winter I used to tell myself at such times that you too must feel just as sad during the long cold evenings of December and January. I have resumed my monotonous life—there are three months of it to get through before the next break. The vacation was decidedly too short. You and I had barely time to see each other and exchange a few words: where did all the time go to?

And after leaving her at Etretat another year:

So it's all over: how short it was! I wait eleven long months for those two weeks that are my only pleasure of the year, and they pass by so fast, so fast, that today I wonder how they can really be over. It seems to me that I haven't left the ministry, that I'm still looking forward to my vacation—which ended this morning. What made me even sadder than usual at leaving you this time is my worry about the absolute solitude you'll be in this winter; I keep thinking of the long evenings that you will be spending alone, dreaming sadly of those who are far away, dreams which will leave you ill and despondent; and certainly very often during the long winter evenings when I shall be working alone in my room I will think I see you, sitting in your low chair and staring at your fire as people do whose thoughts are elsewhere. And then despite the terrible heat here and the blue sky, I feel winter today for the first time. I have just had a glimpse of the Tuileries; the trees have lost their leaves, and I suddenly felt a gust of ice and snow; I thought of lamps lit at three, of rain beating against windows, of horrible cold—all of it lasting for months and months. How good it would be to live in a land where there was always sun! It is wrong of me to write you this way—everything that comes into my head. You are only too disposed anyway to see the dark side of things—I shouldn't depress you further with my lamentations. But it is hard to laugh when there's no urge to, and I assure you I have no urge to. We were right in our calculations—All Saints' Day falls on a Monday, so I can come; but unfortunately New Year's is on a Saturday, so that I'll get only three days at the most instead of four like last year. And if next year isn't a leap year it will fall on a Sunday, so that I'll get only two days. . . .

Disquieting letters! Written by a young man of twenty-three and twenty-five, but sounding like the wailings of a child. It is hard to see whether the pity for himself or that for his mother is the stronger, and, beyond

that, whether he relishes more keenly his suffering itself
or the communication of it to her. The letters give
meaning to the phrases which Laure had used about him
when he was fifteen—"his nerves are not strong";
"his impressionable, sensitive nature." Joseph Prunier,
the idler, the rower, the swimmer, with his ruddy face
and his bulging muscles and his girls and his jokes; the
disciple, so deferential and amusing at Flaubert's
Sundays: there was another side to him, it seemed—a
side that takes its rather somber place among his other
legacies from Laure.

"I am not precisely ill, but I feel excessively, frighteningly weak. There are moments when my mind seems
scarcely to function, and I positively wonder whether I
am awake or dreaming." So Laure had written to Flaubert from Etretat in 1872, and it was one of her habitual
ways of writing about herself. A year later she told her
old friend that she had been "very ill with a nervous
fever, which has still not bade me its final farewell," and
replying to still further news of her health Flaubert expressed regret at hearing of her "impoverishment of
blood." About the same time Guy wrote his cousin Louis
Le Poittevin that his mother had been spending some
time in bed—"still with her *crises nerveuses.*" "My
mother has suddenly become very ill," he wrote from
Paris to a friend on another occasion. "I have just spent
ten days with her at Etretat, and despite her extremely
weak state have brought her here to consult some reliable
doctors." She consulted them to no avail: "My dear
mother, I had news of you last night from Léon Fontaine
[Petit-Bleu], who is back from Etretat. He told me that
you are no better—that your eyes hurt you less but that
your heart is worse. I cannot understand why you should
have such violent fainting spells at so early a stage of

heart disease; your heart must be affected nervously as well as organically. I have spoken to some of my young doctor friends about it; they consider your symptoms extraordinary."

And indeed Laure's troubles were so numerous and baffling that other Paris doctors, consulted on her behalf —and in her absence—by Guy and his father, could only suggest the presence of a tapeworm.

I have come to share their belief [Guy wrote her], especially since Hervé had a tapeworm and he could have got it from you—for you have probably had it a long time. Nine times out of ten there is no trace of the worm itself, but it affects the forms of all kinds of illnesses, especially nervous disorders of the stomach and heart. The symptoms are so variable and changing that they baffle all the doctors. These changes of symptom are due to the animal's movements. The patient's appetite, instead of becoming excessive, as is claimed, often disappears. The incomprehensible characteristics of your illness seem to these doctors an almost sure indication of the existence of this animal, whose presence up to now has remained hidden. Do please speak to your doctor about it. Patients have sometimes been treated in vain for ten or fifteen years, and then cured in three months by means of a vigorous vermifuge.

The sufferer from "tapeworm" (one hopes that the poor woman was given no "vigorous vermifuge" to expel it) was shortly thereafter visited in Etretat by Flaubert, who reported to a friend: "The least bit of light makes her cry out with pain. She has to live in the dark. A gay little spot!" And on the basis of what he had seen he asked Guy whether it wouldn't be simplest to put Laure into a nursing home. That fall she came to Paris again and was informed by the celebrated Dr. Potain that she had "nervous rheumatism."

Sick nerves: clearly Laure was suffering mightily from

them during these years. And to a degree that constantly
varied she was to suffer from them for the rest of her
days, always with contrasting interludes of calm and
vigor—now helpless in bed, now fearlessly exploring out-
of-the-way corners of Italy, Sicily and Corsica "alone,
on foot, a large climbing stick in her hand"; now screaming vile names at her daughter-in-law and threatening
to strangle herself with her own hair, now living in melancholy dignity in a villa in Nice—until she attained,
despite all her symptoms, the considerable age of eighty-
two, long surviving both her sons. A *grande hystérique:*
that was what a woman like Laure was called in her day,
and that was what Laure must have been from early in
life. It was probably not for nothing that she had grown
up in such close affection for an older brother who was
romantic and exalted and who ended in melancholia; in
the common background of this brother and sister there
must of course have been something closer and more
personal than merely the romanticism of the age to make
them as they were; and in Laure there must have been
many *crises nerveuses* before those occurring during the
years of Guy's discipleship—*crises* that we know nothing
of but which probably played their role, along with
Monsieur de Maupassant's behavior, in shipwrecking her
married life. Indeed, further acquaintance with Laure
brings with it a certain sympathy for the shallow and
uninteresting creature she married: he can scarcely, as an
attractive, carefree young man, have realized all the
qualities of the bride he was taking unto himself.

It was in 1878, the fifth of the seven years of his discipleship with Flaubert, that Guy began to demonstrate
in letters to others, as he had long been demonstrating
to Laure himself, to what a degree he was, in respect to
sick nerves, his mother's son:

You ask me for news, *mon cher maître* [he wrote Flaubert in July]. It is all bad, alas! My mother is not at all well, my ministry frays my nerves, I can't work, my mind is sterile and tired from the bills I make out from morning to night; and then I have moments of being so convinced of the uselessness of everything, of the unconscious evil of the universe, of the emptiness of the future (whatever it may be), that there comes over me a melancholy indifference to all things and I want simply to be quiet, quiet in a corner somewhere, without hopes or worries. I live completely alone because other people bore me, and I bore myself because I cannot work. I find my own thoughts mediocre and monotonous, and I am so weary in spirit that I cannot even express them. I am making fewer mistakes in my bills these days—thus proving myself stupid indeed. Every day I tell myself, like Saint Anthony, "One more day, one more day gone." They seem long, long and sad, what with an imbecile office-mate and yapping chief. The one I never speak to, the other I never answer. Both despise me a little and find me unintelligent. That consoles me.

Actually, Maupassant's "yapping chief" did not consider him unintelligent, but the rating he gave him at the end of 1877 indicates the doubts he was beginning to have about him: "Intelligent, could have a future here. But indolent, lacks energy. I fear his tastes and aptitudes may lead him away from administrative work."

The chief's fears were scarcely groundless. Maupassant had never wanted to clerk anywhere, and the fact that it was his father who had placed him in the Naval Ministry had always been sufficient reason for him to dislike especially clerking there. Now his association with Flaubert and with the people he met through Flaubert was making doubly uncongenial, by contrast, his work and his colleagues. Another member of the group at the *République des Lettres* records that Maupassant's con-

versation at their dinners was confined to "recollections
of the lessons in literary theology that Flaubert had
inculcated into him, certain admirations more vivid than
profound which constituted his artistic religion, an in-
exhaustible supply of broad stories and savage invective
against his colleagues at the Naval Ministry. Of this last
subject he never tired."

Shortly before this time, a gentleman named Agénor
Bardoux, author (under the pseudonym A. Brady) of a
volume of poems, one of which, *Venise*, was dedicated
to his friend Gustave Flaubert, had been appointed Minister of Education; and Flaubert had mentioned the possibility that he might induce Bardoux to add Guy to his
staff, which was composed in part of literary men. But
Flaubert was not always efficient in such matters, and in
January, 1878, Guy wrote to Laure:

Write him a pathetic letter to stir him up a bit. My
position here is far from easy, but make it seem worse.
Tell him how you pity me, and so forth. Don't ask for
anything immediate, but thank him for what he has
promised to do for me, and tell him how happy I am in
the hope he holds out.

Laure did as he asked:

Since you call Guy your adopted son, you will pardon
me, my dear Gustave, if I quite naturally talk with you
about the boy. Your declaration of affection was so
pleasant to my ears that I have taken it literally and am
pretending that in making it you assumed quasi-paternal
duties. I know that you are familiar with the situation
and that the poor ministry clerk has already told you all
his woes. You were splendid as always, you comforted
him and encouraged him, and your kind words have
given him hope that the hour is near when he will be able
to leave his prison and bid farewell to the charming chief
who guards the door. If you can, my dear old friend, do

something for Guy's future, find him a position that will suit him; you will be blessed a thousand times, thanked a thousand times. But I know there is no reason for me to insist; I know in advance that mother and son can count on your support. Were I not so far from Paris I should have quite simply come and knocked on your door some evening after dinner and asked for a little place beside your fire, and we would have sat a long time talking together.

Flaubert replied that he would speak to his friend the minister, telling Laure, "Your son is the delight of our little group"; but a month later Guy wrote her: "Flaubert has not been very helpful on my behalf. As soon as it is a question of practical matters, the dear master does not know where to begin. His requests are Platonic rather than effective; he does not insist enough. In brief, they fool him, though he will not admit it."

The matter dragged on as bureaucratic matters do, through the spring and summer, and it was that July that Maupassant had written Flaubert his desperate-sounding letter. It worried the older man: he had not previously known his disciple in a mood of such lamentation. "Give me news of Guy," he wrote a common friend a few weeks later. "His last letter was pitiful. I have written him twice since but have had no answer and fear he may be ill. If he is well, you have my permission to give him a good kick on or in the behind."

Guy eventually answered:

I didn't write you, my dear master, because my morale is completely gone. For three weeks I have been trying to work every night, and haven't been able to write a single decent page. Nothing, nothing. The result is that I'm gradually falling into black depression and discouragement and will have a hard time climbing out again. The ministry is gradually destroying me. After

seven hours of administrative work I haven't the resilience to throw off the heaviness that weighs on my spirits.
I even tried to write a few articles for the *Gaulois* in order
to earn a few sous. I couldn't do it, I couldn't think of
a line, and I feel like weeping on my paper. In addition
to that, everything around me is going badly. My mother
is no better. Her heart, especially, gives her much pain,
and she has alarming fainting-spells. She is so weak that
she no longer even writes me; every two weeks at the
most I get a note dictated to her gardener.

And he said that there was only one word of the
French language that he really understood—a word
which he did not identify, but described as "energetically
expressing change, the eternal transformation of the best
things, and disillusion": the word *merde*.

But Maupassant's unhappy letters, which one might
be tempted to think expressive merely of what Freud
calls "a *taedium vitae* probably not entirely genuine," the
result of nervousness, depression, and a longing to change
his job, actually reflect something more, something far
graver. Two years before, when he was twenty-six, he
had written to his friend La Toque a letter that might
almost have been written by Laure about herself:

My heart has been bothering me, and I saw a doctor
and was ordered to rest and to take potassium bromide
and digitalis: late hours were forbidden. This treatment
succeeded not at all. Then I was given arsenic, potassium
iodide and tincture of colchicum: this treatment succeeded not at all. Then my doctor sent me to a specialist,
the master of masters, Dr. Potain. He told me there was
absolutely nothing wrong with my heart but that I was
suffering from the beginning of nicotine poisoning. That
impressed me so that I immediately swallowed all my
pipes in order not to have them around any longer.

Nevertheless, my heart keeps pounding just as hard: it's true that I've only been off tobacco two weeks.

Obviously "the beginning of nicotine poisoning" was not a helpful diagnosis. What *was* wrong with Guy?

A passage in a letter from Flaubert to Zola, written that summer, contains the first hint of what it might be. "I had a most entertaining epistle from our young friend Maupassant yesterday, full of details about his lewdnesses with a fat woman on the river." Concerning this same "entertaining epistle" from Maupassant, he wrote to his niece: "I am going to make my answer severe. The young man gives himself too good a time." His words to the young man himself were: "Your letter rejoiced my heart. But in the interest of literature I urge you to slow down. Watch out! Everything depends on the goal that one wants to attain. A man who has set himself up to be an artist no longer has the right to live like other people."

A few months later Maupassant was consulting a homeopathic doctor, after having had no success with others, concerning both heart symptoms and a skin eruption; and Turgenev was writing Flaubert that "Poor Maupassant says he is losing all the hair on his body. It's due to a stomach ailment, he says. He is nice as always, but very ugly at the moment." Flaubert, about to come to Paris in January, asked his niece to arrange a dinner party for various friends, including "my pupil, Guy the Bald." That summer he wrote to Turgenev about Guy in sentences that have been largely suppressed by editors: * "No news of friends, except young Guy. He wrote me recently that . . . It's wonderful but I'm afraid . . . You and I are no longer up to *that*, my

* See Note 3: Something Very Hard to Believe, page 398.

friend!" And to Guy he wrote, equally unprintably, "Re-strain your . . . !"

That summer Maupassant secured a doctor's certificate to show his chief in the ministry:

This is to certify that M. de Maupassant, employed in the Naval Ministry, has been under treatment for almost two years for a herpetic condition, which manifested itself last year in internal, especially cardiac, symptoms, a month ago in loss of hair on head and body, and at present in herpetic eruptions and numerous symptoms which indicate that M. de Maupassant is still under the influence of the same diathesis. In my opinion it is essential that he undergo a thermal cure, and it is my wish that for this purpose he should go to the baths of Louèche rather than elsewhere. I think that his treatment should last one month.

He spent his month at Louèche, a popular Swiss cure at that time especially for cases of "cutaneous rheumatism"; and on his return Flaubert wrote Zola and Turgenev that the young man had been "befouling Helvetia" with his "obscenities" and his "horrors." The following spring—that is, almost two years after Flaubert had first warned him to slow down—Guy wrote to La Toque: "Three weeks ago I performed an exploit that brought me increased esteem with Flaubert." The next sentences in the letter, describing the "exploit," and an enclosed poem, *Minette*, describing it further, have never been printed.

The fatal word finally appears in one of the gloomy letters to Flaubert in the summer of 1878:

As to me, I am still hairless. The doctors now think there is nothing syphilitic in my case, but that I have a constitutional rheumatism which first affected me in the stomach and heart and then finally in the skin. They are having me take steam baths, which have not helped so

far. But this treatment, together with medicines, mineral
waters, etc., has eaten up the little money I had put
away for my summer. That's at least one result. To con-
found the doctors, I hope it will be the only one.

By the end of the year Maupassant's hair stopped
falling, and eventually it grew again and stayed with
him for the rest of his life; but even that solitary change
for the better cannot be credited to the regime of steam
baths, medicines and mineral waters. For it is clear from
Maupassant's end, that the doctors had been correct in
their original diagnosis, and that sometime during these
years, from some Mimi or Nini at Bezons, from some
"fat woman on the river," from some *marchande de
spasmes*, as he was later to call the species, Guy had
acquired syphilis, for which at that time no cure was
known. There has been speculation as to whether before
very long Maupassant's doctors didn't return to their
original diagnosis and whether Maupassant didn't know
that they did.* His knowledge that he had contracted
the disease, that there was no further risk to be run,
would be a partial explanation of his willingness to continue to lead, as he did for the rest of his days, a life of
quite so many "exploits." But in the case of so nervously

---

* The letter sending him to Louèche is so confused-sounding, even for that
time, that the doctor who wrote it gives the impression of knowing more than he
says; and after Maupassant's death two doctors are said to have stated that he
told them, at the beginning of other "cures" which he took at various times
in his life, that he "had had" syphilis. For what it is worth, there is the testimony
of Frank Harris, also written after Maupassant's death (*My Life*, Vol. 2, Chap.
XX):

   I put the question to Maupassant: "Have you ever had syphilis?"
   "All the infantile complaints," he said, laughing. "Everyone has it in
youth, haven't they? But it's twelve or fifteen years now since I've seen a
trace of it. I was completely cured long years ago."
   I told him what the German specialist had discovered [that syphilis
"often kills its victims by paralysis between forty and fifty when the vital
forces have begun to decline"], but he wouldn't give any credence to it. "I
dislike everything German, as you know," he said. "Their science even is
exaggerated."

sensitive a young man, one who so closely resembled his
grande hystérique of a mother, a diagnosis must have been
particularly full of pitfalls in those days before blood
tests. "Guy probably has the same neurosis as his
mother," Flaubert wrote his niece a year or two later;
and given all the mother-and-son circumstances, and
given the state of medical knowledge, it was possible for
not only Flaubert, but for doctors as well, to identify the
son's suffering with his mother's: "According to my doctor, I have the same trouble as my mother; that is, a
slight irritation of the upper part of the spinal marrow."
But: "I have a paralysis of the accommodation of the
right eye, and my doctor thinks it almost incurable,"
Maupassant wrote Flaubert in that same letter; and that
is but one of the minor indications, before the unmistak-
able end, that "the delight of our little group" was
syphilitic.

Flaubert (who was later, in his worry, to have him
examined by his own doctor, without any definite or
satisfactory results) wrote him sympathetically but se-
verely that summer of 1878:

You complain about *le cul des femmes* being "monotonous." There is a simple remedy—not to use it. "Events
are not varied," you say. That is a stock complaint of
the Realists, and besides, what do you know about it?
The whole thing is to examine events more closely. Isn't
everything an illusion? The only truth is in *"rapports"*—
that is, our ways of seeing. "The vices are paltry" you
say; but everything is paltry! "There are not enough
different ways to turn a phrase!" Seek and ye shall find.
Come now, my dear friend, you seem badly worried,
and your worry distresses me, for you could use your
time more agreeably. You *must*—do you hear me?—you
must work more than you do. I've come to suspect you
of being something of a loafer. Too many whores! Too

much rowing! Too much exercise! Yes, sir: civilized man doesn't need as much locomotion as the doctors pretend. You were born to write poetry: write it! *All the rest is futile*—beginning with your pleasures and your health: get that into your head. Besides, your health will be the better for your following your calling. That remark is philosophically, or rather hygienically, profound.

You are living in an *enfer de merde*, I know, and I pity you from the bottom of my heart. But from five in the evening to ten in the morning all your time can be consecrated to the muse, who is still the best bitch of all. Come, my dear fellow, chin up. What is the use of constantly going deeper into your melancholy? You must set yourself up as a strong man in your own eyes: that's the way to become one. A little more pride, by God! What you lack are "principles." Say what you will, one has to have them; it is a question of knowing which ones. For an artist there is only one: sacrifice everything to Art. Life must be considered by the artist as a means, nothing more, and the first person he should not give a hang about is himself.

Let me sum up, my dear Guy: beware of melancholy. It is a vice. You take pleasure in affliction, and then when affliction has passed you find yourself dazed and deadened, for you have used up precious strength. And then you have regrets, but it is too late. Have faith in the experience of a sheik to whom no folly remains stranger! *Je vous embrasse tendrement.*

"Beware of melancholy"; "Too many whores": Maupassant had neither the ability nor the desire to follow those parts of Flaubert's advice. The disposition to revel in his own melancholy increased, rather than diminished, as time went on; and as for the girls, didn't the all-but-celibate master himself express (to a degree that makes the reader uncomfortable) a vicarious glee, along with his scoldings, in his adopted son's exploits? And excellent as Flaubert's counsels generally were, something he did not know is known today: that by 1878 it was neither

melancholy nor any number of girls that he had reason
to dread as threatening his disciple's artistic existence.
It was the *spirocheta pallida*, already lodged and inexorable, that was to destroy first the artist, then the man.

Doubtless simply to be disagreeable to me [Maupas-
sant wrote Flaubert the following September], my chief
has just given me the most horrible job in the office, a
job hitherto perfectly well done by a stupid old clerk:
the preparation of the budget and the clearing of the
port accounts—figures, nothing but figures! Furthermore, I sit beside him, so that it is impossible for me
to do any of my own work even when I have a free hour.
I think that was his whole purpose. I am surrounded by
dreariness: my mother is very ill, unable even to leave
Etretat.

Tension was mounting in the office, and Maupassant,
who at the beginning was considered by his colleagues as
different from themselves chiefly in the gentlemanly cut
of his clothes and a certain distinction of manner, was
now increasingly disliked for manifestations of superiority and disagreeableness. Fortunately for everyone,
just before the end of the year, the long-drawn-out Flau-
bert-Maupassant-Bardoux negotiations succeeded, and
the "yapping chief" in the Naval Ministry lost his exasperated budget clerk. "Oh, Monsieur, you have nothing
whatever to say about it," Maupassant is said to have
loftily retorted when at the last moment the chief threatened, on some technicality, not to let him go. "This matter is being handled by the ministers themselves—considerably above *our* level."

"There, now, you're a little easier, aren't you?" Flaubert wrote him on New Year's Eve. "Will you get to
work again?"

And during at least part of 1879, a year in which his
physical troubles also seem to have granted him some

respite, he did work again, and better than ever before.
In February Flaubert, angrily kept at Croisset by a
twisted ankle and a broken leg bone, missed his disciple's
debut as a dramatist: the first night of *Histoire du Vieux
Temps*, a brief one-act play in verse, called a "comedy-
proverb" on the play-bill, with which he had helped
Maupassant considerably. The author wrote to Croisset
that the evening had been even more of a success than
he had hoped. (He meant a *succès d'estime;* there was
nothing popular or financial about it, even though the
piece ran several weeks, part of the time as a curtain-
raiser.) "Now editors will read your manuscripts!" Flaubert replied happily, and he said that his disciple's inscription on his printed copy of the play "touched his
heart." The venture cost the young author something
in fees for the claque, the prompter and the stage-setter,
and this, together with the fact that his new job lacked
one of the perquisites of the old—a reduction in the price
of railroad tickets—made it difficult for him to travel
even as far as Croisset. At the beginning of Lent, however, he arrived to spend a few days with his hobbling
master, who now began an apparently unsuccessful campaign to have the play privately performed in the literary
salon of Princesse Mathilde Bonaparte, writing Guy an
introduction to the princess and coaching him as to how
she should be addressed. That summer, while Guy was
walking in Brittany, it was given a production at the
casino in Etretat.

Ma chere Confrère [Flaubert wrote on November 25th
to Madame Juliette Adam, editress of the *Nouvelle Revue*], I am taking the liberty of sending you in this same
mail a piece of verse which I consider very remarkable
and worthy of your magazine. The author, Guy de Maupassant, is a member of the personal staff of the Minister
of Education. In my opinion he has a great literary fu-

ture, and I love him dearly because he is the nephew of
the most intimate friend I ever had—whom he greatly
resembles—a friend dead almost thirty years, him to
whom I dedicated my *Saint Antoine*. In short, I should
be very grateful if you would print his little poem. The
young man had a little play produced by Ballande last
winter with considerable success: *Histoire du Vieux
Temps*. He is known among the parnassians.

"Republicans are generally so chaste that I am not
without uneasiness as to her reception of it," he wrote
Maupassant after sending the manuscript off to Madame
Adam, "but I think that the Goethe-esque side of it will
seduce the lady." His uneasiness was well founded, for
the tone of the "little poem" is fairly accurately suggested by a reference Guy made to it in a letter to La
Toque: "I have almost finished my *Vénus rustique*, and
I'd like to —— her." Madame Adam was indeed so
"chaste" as to decline *Vénus rustique* (it was never published in a periodical), and both the author and his master
lamented. "Life is a heavy load, and today is not the
first day I'm aware of it," Flaubert groaned when Guy
wrote him the news together with an account of some of
Madame Adam's insufferable editorial remarks; and Guy
cried—rather comically, considering his poem's subject-
matter—"Always, always in our country the journalist
tries to lower himself to the level of the public instead
of trying to make the public understand loftier things!"
And it is in this same letter to Flaubert that occurs
the first mention of a work which was to be of considerably greater importance in Maupassant's career than
Vénus rustique—a work that was to determine (until the
spirocheta took over completely) the future course of
his life: "I am working steadily at my long short story
about the Rouennais and the war. From now on, if I
go near Rouen I'll have to carry pistols in my pocket."

CHAPTER 4

FIVE TOGETHER CAN DO
MANY THINGS

I AM CERTAIN that I was not born to write any more than to accomplish any other task. With my obstinacy and my method of work I could just as well have become a painter as a literary man—anything, except probably a mathematician. And that is so true that never in my life, neither today, nor at any time, have I found the slightest joy in work. For me literature has never been anything but a means of liberation.

So Maupassant was later to tell a friend, at the height of his fame. And the friend, in his account of the conversation, published during Maupassant's lifetime and therefore probably not too inaccurate, declared:

It was in order to be able to move about and be free that Maupassant began to write. Accustomed to the open air and open spaces, he felt that he would quickly die if he had to remain in offices, hunched over papers. But how was he to free himself? It was then that the idea of writing came to him, not at all through a vocation, but—the word is his own—through "reasoning." He confided his troubles to Flaubert, who had always been an intimate friend of his family.*

The older he grew, the more cynically—and, frequently, affectedly—Maupassant spoke of his writing as

* Hugues Le Roux, "Guy de Maupassant," *Le Temps*, June 15, 1889; reprinted in *Portraits de Cire*, Paris, 1891.

a mere means of earning a living, like any other trade. He
once spoke of spending most of his time "writing lines
which I sell as dearly as possible, miserable at the thought
of having to practice so abominable a trade"; and on another occasion he referred to himself as a *"marchand de
prose."* And there can be little doubt that the idea of
"liberation"—liberation from his ministry desk (even the
new, less irksome desk in the Ministry of Education),
from the position of civil service clerk, from the inability
to live on any large or free scale—was the chief conscious
motivation for his willingness to serve a writing appren-
ticeship of seven years. From the very beginning financial
considerations were important in his career, and very
early they led him into literary politics, which his master
had always particularly avoided.

"The most faithful of my Sunday visitors," Flaubert
wrote George Sand that winter of 1875–76 when Maupassant's training had become intensified, "are first the great
Turgenev, who is nicer than ever, Zola, Alphonse Daudet
and Goncourt. You have never spoken to me of the first
two: what do you think of their books?" In her reply
(which contained an unfavorable opinion of the books
of all four authors), Madame Sand referred to Flaubert's
Sunday visitors as his "school." He wrote back at once in
protest: *"A propos* of my friends, you call them my
'school.' But I am wrecking my health trying not to
have a school! *A priori* I reject all schools."

Flaubert's antipathy to the concept of literary
schools, and especially to any implication that he belonged to one, is an oft-recurring theme in his correspondence and was related to another of his antipathies. *Madame Bovary* had originally been published serially in a

magazine, where certain of its passages had attracted the
attention of the authorities; Flaubert had been unsuccessfully prosecuted for "offenses against public morality
and religion," and his trial had focussed attention on
the book and brought it a *succès de scandale*. During the
rest of his life, although it was only at moments of the
very deepest melancholy that he lamented the celebrity
which *Madame Bovary* had brought him, he constantly
regretted the role that scandal had played in the book's
success; and he was disgusted that none of his subsequent
books, untouched by such notoriety, ever sold as well.
He had his publisher print the speeches of the public
prosecutor and his own lawyer as an appendix to later
editions of *Madame Bovary*, but forbade the addition
of any comment or the inclusion of any quotations from
reviews; and although he sufficiently resembled other
authors to complain when his publisher allowed his
works to go out of print or when he found a bookstore
out of stock, and to strike back when a critic attacked
Salammbô as inaccurate in its background, he believed
that books should sell on their own merits and that any
kind of personal appearances by authors, any publicity-
seeking except the mere publication of the best work
they could do, was ignoble. "We writers must not exist,"
he said. "Only our works exist."

This dual antipathy, to schools and to publicity-
seeking, brought Flaubert into conflict with his friend
Zola. Each man had considerable admiration for the
other, Zola's for Flaubert being from all evidence un-
qualified: "You are the best of us all," he wrote to
Croisset in 1879. "You are our master and our father."
Flaubert, on his side, considered Zola a genius, a true
artist, but complained that Zola, Alphonse Daudet and
Edmond de Goncourt—all of whom, somewhat to his

discomfort, did look on him as their master—were "not preoccupied *above all else* with what is for me the end of art: namely, Beauty." Unlike Flaubert, Zola had always wanted to become the center of a school of writers, and he once stated that he considered literature a "battle-field"—where a writer should fight with all the weapons at his command, not only his creative work, but also prefaces, letters to newspapers, manifestos, speeches, and other such arms.

"I have just finished your terrible and beautiful book," Flaubert wrote Zola on the appearance of *La Fortune des Rougon* in 1871. "My head is still swimming. It is strong! Very strong! I object only to the preface. To my mind it spoils the book, which is so impartial, so lofty. You give away your secret—you are too candid; and you express your opinion, something which in my own poetics a novelist hasn't the right to do." "Read Zola's Monday articles," he wrote Turgenev in 1876, "and you will see how he thinks * he has discovered 'naturalism' "—a term which Flaubert always insisted no one, not even Zola himself, its "inventor," had ever satisfactorily defined or ever could define. And also to Turgenev he said: "After the realists, we have the naturalists and the impressionists. What progress! They're all a lot of practical jokers, who would like to delude themselves and us too into thinking that they have discovered something that's been known for centuries."

Edmond de Goncourt's journal for February 19, 1877, tells us that at one of Flaubert's Sundays, in the course of the usual literary discussion,

Flaubert began to attack—constantly raising his hat, raising it very high, to Zola's *talent*—Zola's prefaces,

* See Note 4: Flaubert, Naturalism, and Critics, page 399.

doctrines, and naturalist professions of faith. Zola answered approximately as follows: "*You* have a private income, which has made it possible for you to have a large degree of independence. *I* have been obliged to earn my living entirely with my pen; *I* have been obliged to do all kinds of writing—yes, even some contemptible kinds. Let me tell you that I care no more about the word naturalism than you do: nevertheless, I shall continue to use it, because it is necessary to baptize things in order that the public may think them new. Look—my writings are of two kinds: first my works, by which I am judged and by which I want to be judged; and then my articles in the *Bien Public*, my articles in the Russian press, my letters from Marseilles—all of which are nothing to me, which I value not at all, and which serve only to publicize my books. The first thing I did was to set a nail in place and hammer it one centimeter into the public's brain; then, with a second blow, I drove it in two centimeters, and so on. Well, my hammer is journalism—the journalism I write myself about my own books."

Such journalism Flaubert despised, and as more and more noise was made in the press about naturalism after Zola's immense popular success with *L'Assommoir* in 1887 he became increasingly contemptuous, writing to a friend, "My friend Zola wants to found a school. His aplomb as a critic is explained by his unimaginable ignorance"; and to his niece that "Zola is becoming too grotesque. Such bad taste to be always talking about one's self!" To Maupassant he had written in 1876 "How can one give an empty word such significance as is being given to the word 'naturalism'? Why have they abandoned poor Champfleury and 'realism,' which is an ineptitude of the same calibre, or rather the same ineptitude? Henry Monnier [a contemporary 'realist']

is no more true than Racine." And when he was about to
see his disciple in the fall of 1879 he ordered him: "Don't
speak to me of realism, naturalism or experimentalism.
I am fed up with them all. What empty nonsense!"

And empty the nonsense must indeed have seemed to
Flaubert, particularly in the light of the admissions
concerning it which he had heard Zola himself unblush-
ingly make. In the clamor about naturalism his two
antipathies—literary schools and publicity-seeking—
were merged into one.

When his affections were involved, however, when
it was a question of helping someone he loved, Flaubert
had always known how to conquer his repugnance for
promotion. He had intrigued in Paris to secure the
production of Louis Bouilhet's first play, *Madame de
Montarcy*, and after Bouilhet's death he not only went
to fatiguing lengths to secure the production of a posthumous play and the publication of the posthumous poems,
but he even indulged in journalism, publishing in the
Temps the letter to the Rouen municipal council so
enjoyed by Laure de Maupassant in Etretat. We have
seen Flaubert's early words to Laure about her son's
literary efforts—"As to the result, as to his possible
'success,' what difference does it make?"—as well as his
advice to another young writer: "You are lost if you
think of making any profit from your work." But we
have also seen Flaubert—who had never made any great
financial profit from his own books—writing letters to
editors for Guy and importuning the Minister of Education; and if he encouraged him in his writing as a way
of making money, that is but one more indication of the
extent of his confidence and his affection. There is no
evidence that he was anything but indulgent concerning

the flair for self-promotion, particularly by means of participation in a group, which Guy quite early gave evidence of possessing.

The group with which Flaubert's disciple chose principally to associate himself was—ironically enough, considering Flaubert's opinions—the group which began, during that so significant winter of 1875–76, to center itself around Zola.

After becoming acquainted with Maupassant at Flaubert's, Zola had, in the spring of 1875, sent him an inscribed copy of his new novel, *La Faute de l'Abbé Mouret;* and a year later, in addition to seeing Zola at Flaubert's on Sunday, Maupassant was going to his house every Thursday evening in company with four other young literary men of his own age—J. K. Huysmans, Henry Céard, Léon Hennique and Paul Alexis— not one of whom was any less publicity-minded than the man whose openly expressed desire to become the center of a literary group they were (quite consciously) fulfilling by the regularity and respectfulness of their visits. The name of only one member of the group besides Maupassant is well known today—J. K. Huysmans, whose later novel, *A Rebours*, with its celebrated hero Des Esseintes and his organ of odors and other sensual extravagances, brought him reproaches from Zola for its "betrayal of naturalism." Like Maupassant, Huysmans was a clerk in a ministry, and he had published a novel or two; Henry Céard (also a government employee), Léon Hennique and Paul Alexis had published only articles. Alexis had known Zola's family in the south of France, had called on him when he came to Paris for a literary career and had been taken by him to Flaubert's,

where he met Maupassant; Céard had timidly called on
Zola one day without introduction to express his admiration, and to his delight was invited to return and bring
his friends; he brought Huysmans and Huysmans' friend
Hennique, and found Maupassant and Alexis. So the
five young men met, and they began quite quickly to
function together. In the group Maupassant was active,
and, except at certain moments in his relations with Zola
himself, he was also candid.

I have reflected about the manifesto we are considering, and I feel compelled to make you a complete
profession of my literary faith, like a confession [he
wrote to one of the others of the group in a long letter
in which he expresses a Flaubertian non-adherence to any
school, but a love of art in general]. I believe in naturalism no more than in realism or romanticism. Those words
to my mind signify absolutely nothing, and serve only as
quarrels for opposing temperaments. I never discuss
literature or principles, because I think that to do so is
perfectly useless. No one is ever converted, and it is not
to convert you that I am writing you this long letter,
but in order that you should be completely acquainted
with my views and my literary religion. I have stated
them to you a bit heavily, *en bloc*, in a manner that is a
little pretentious and diffuse, but I've had no leisure in
which to study my subject, group my arguments and
present them elegantly. You have it just as it came:
excuse me if it is badly put and poorly co-ordinated. Of
course this letter should not be seen outside our circle,
and I should feel badly were you to show it to Zola, whom
I love with all my heart and admire profoundly, for he
might be offended.

We must seriously discuss *ways to succeed*. Five
together can do many things, and perhaps there are some
tricks that have never been used. What if we were to lay
siege to a newspaper for six months, bombarding it with
articles, with recommendations from our friends, etc.

etc., until one of us was finally taken onto the staff or made a regular contributor? We should think up something unexpected, something that would create a sensation, compel the public to pay attention. Perhaps a joke of some kind? Some really clever trick. We'll see.

And to his rowing friend La Toque he wrote: .

I belong to a literary group that disdains poetry. They will serve me as a foil—rather a good idea. I am supporting naturalism in the theater and the novel, because the more it's done the more people will be irritated, and that's all to the good for the others in my group. Watch out for the reaction, friends!

The first move by a member of the group was made by Hennique, who in January, 1877, delivered a public lecture in defense of *L'Assommoir*, which had been generously attacked on the ground of obscenity and general indecency and around which a violent literary— or rather journalistic—battle was being waged; the next month he was answered from the same platform by a member of the anti-Zola forces; and then came what Maupassant had suggested, the "joke of some kind." On April 13, an unsigned item appeared in the *République des Lettres:*

In a restaurant which is destined to become illustrious, the Restaurant Trapp near the Gare Saint-Lazare, six young and enthusiastic naturalists also destined for celebrity, Messieurs Paul Alexis, Henry Céard, Léon Hennique, J. K. Huysmans, Octave Mirbeau * and Guy de Valmont † recently entertained their masters:

---

* Octave Mirbeau, later known for his *Mémoires d'une Femme de Chambre, Le Jardin des Supplices,* and other works, was briefly a member of the group, but had to leave Paris to accept a political appointment in the provinces.

† This pseudonym now supplanted Joseph Prunier. Valmont had a double significance: it was the name of a Norman village which certain eighteenth-century Maupassants had added to their family name, calling themselves Maupassant de Valmont; and it was the name of the chief male character in Choderlos de Laclos' novel *Les Liaisons Dangéreuses*—an unscrupulous and irresistible villain much to Maupassant's taste.

Gustave Flaubert, Edmond de Goncourt, Emile Zola. One of the guests has told us the menu: Purée Bovary; Salmon Trout à la Fille Elisa; Truffled Chicken à la Saint-Antoine; Artichokes au Coeur Simple; Parfait "Naturaliste"; Vin de Coupeau; Liqueur de l'Assommoir. M. Gustave Flaubert, who has other disciples, remarked on the absence of Eels à la Carthaginoise and Pigeons à la Salammbô.

Many years later Céard also wrote about that dinner. It was in honor of the guests, he said, that it was held in a restaurant as good as Trapp's (an unpretentious place): for ordinarily when the young men met for dinner, as they did every Thursday night before going on to Zola's, it was, because of their financial condition, in a Montmartre restaurant so unappetizing that Zola, who had once joined them there, refused ever to do so again. And, Céard revealed, the alleged menu of dishes named after the works and characters of the eminent guests had existed in one place only: in the imagination of the young naturalist, Guy de Valmont, the author of the article.

That was only the beginning. In June, under a pseudonym, Alexis began a series of newspaper articles which pretended to attack the group, claiming that of the five only Huysmans had a trace of talent, marveling that by simply giving a dinner in a modest restaurant a few unknown young men should succeed in attracting "such attention" to themselves and calling on the public to suppress, before it was too late, these offspring of Zola who threatened to spread the horrors of naturalism. Swallowing this bait, the press began to notice the group; one newspaper remarked that Zola's new school "is spreading like an oil spot; the tail behind the master is growing every day." At all times the possibility of publishing something as a group was kept in mind, and

Charpentier, the publisher of both Flaubert and Zola, was not neglected; he was among those invited to the "naturalist" dinner at Trapp's, and to him Maupassant wrote in the summer of 1878:

Cher Monsieur et Ami: You gave me reason, last winter, to hope that this summer you might spend a day with me in regions which you yourself used to frequent. Next Sunday is the local feast-day at Bezons, and I think there will be amusing things to be seen, all the inhabitants of the village, who hold me in profound horror, being to my mind very comical. With me that day will be Hennique, Céard and Huysmans, and several rowing enthusiasts of both sexes, some of them not too stupid and others not too ugly. I have no novel to propose to you, nor has any of my friends—consequently you have no reason to be afraid of us. I hope that all these considerations will make you decide to join us, in which case here is the itinerary to follow: . . . Try to come in the morning; if you absolutely cannot, I will expect you in the afternoon in any case. We'll row a little, and make the bourgeois gape. Don't worry: no one will recognize you. So: until Sunday.

Maupassant generally preserved a coolness toward *everyone* connected with his chosen group—its central figure included. He did not hesitate to write to Flaubert:

What do you think of Zola? I think he is absolutely crazy. Have you read his article on Hugo? His article on contemporary poets? And his pamphlet, *La République et la Littérature?* "The Republic will be Naturalist or it will not continue to exist." "I am only a scholar." (Nothing but that! Such modesty!)

Zola always professed a personal and literary fondness for Maupassant, but the former, at least, seems not to have been returned. Maupassant wrote admiringly on Zola some years later, and throughout his life sent him each of his books as they appeared, always inscribed *"Au*

Maître et à l'Ami"; but his phrase in the letter containing his profession of literary faith—"Zola, whom I love with all my heart"—was not repeated in later years. And certainly there is much in the bustling, busy, systematic, documentary, public-spirited Zola which could have been only antipathetic to the complicated, inward-turned young disciple of Flaubert's. Similarly with "the tail behind the master." Although Huysmans tells us that Maupassant was the "life and soul" of the group's meetings, bringing to them "the good humor of his comical stories, his easy-going gaiety, and, what was best, under an appearance of not caring a rap about anyone or anything, a very cordial and sure affection," the fact remains that after Maupassant had, by means of participation in the group, achieved a far greater celebrity and success than ever came to any of the others, he ended relations with them rather quickly. Although he affiliated himself with the naturalists, it was his rowing companions that he continued to consider his friends.

To a certain extent, a similar coolness was displayed toward him by the others. His one-act play in verse, *Histoire du Vieux Temps*, was a polished, sentimental little trifle about a count and a marquise at the time of Louis XV—not at all a "naturalistic" work; and when it was produced Maupassant wrote in some annoyance to Flaubert that although Zola and Madame Zola had applauded vigorously and congratulated him afterwards, "Zola's group abandoned me completely, considering me insufficiently naturalist; not one of them came to shake my hand after my success." Flaubert, his opinions being what they were, must have smiled at that. "Naturally the naturalists abandon you," he replied. "I am not surprised. *Oderunt poetas*." The rest of the group had no interest in work which Maupassant produced alone and

which had no reference to the rest of them; their association was a matter of convenience, and their interest
in him was the same as his in them: "Five together can
do many things."

May 1880 treat you kindly, my dearly beloved
disciple [Flaubert wrote on January 2 in reply to a lost
letter of Maupassant's that had obviously mentioned
once again his "long short story about the Rouennais and
the war"]. First of all, no more palpitations, and good
health to your dear mother; a good subject for a play
that will be well written and bring you in a hundred
thousand francs. Wishes regarding the genital organs
come last, since nature herself takes care of them. So you
are going to publish a *volume!* A volume of verse, you
mean, of course? But according to your letter the Rouen
story is to be included. And then you say *our* proofs.
Who are *we?* I have a great desire to see the anti-patriotic
lucubration: it will have to be strong indeed to revolt me.

Mon bien cher Maître [Maupassant replied]: I see that
you have forgotten what I told you on my last visit to
Croisset about our volume of long short stories, and I
hasten to explain. Zola has published, first in Russia and
then in France in the *Réforme*, a story about the war,
called *L'Attaque du Moulin*. Huysmans has had a story
published in Brussels, called *Sac au dos*. And Céard has
sent to the Russian review of which he is correspondent
a very curious and violent story about the siege of Paris,
called *Une Saignée*. When Zola heard about these last
two stories, he told us that in his opinion they would,
along with his, make up into an interesting volume, the
opposite of chauvinistic and rather special in tone. And
he urged Hennique, Alexis and me to write a story apiece
to complete the collection. This has the added advantage
that his name would make the book sell and bring us each
one or two hundred francs. We set to work immediately,
and Charpentier has all our manuscripts. The volume
will appear about March first.

In putting this book together we have no anti-patriotic intention, no intention of any kind; we have simply tried to give our pieces the right note with regard to the war, to strip them of chauvinism à la Déroulède, of that false enthusiasm hitherto deemed essential in every narrative containing red trousers and a rifle. Our generals, instead of being all mathematical geniuses full of noble sentiments and generous impulses, are simply mediocre beings like everyone else, wearing gold braid and getting men killed not by evil intent but out of sheer stupidity. This candor on our part in appraising military matters gives a droll tone to the whole volume, and our deliberate disinterestedness concerning these questions which everyone approaches with unconscious passion will exasperate the bourgeois a thousand times more than any direct attack. It will not be anti-patriotic, but simply true. Indeed, what I say about the Rouennais is considerably less strong than what I could say and still be truthful.

Mon Chéri [Flaubert answered at once], Scarcely had I written you my question when I remembered what you had told me about your story. A thousand pardons! What will be the title of the volume? It seems to me that it will be difficult to find one.

Flaubert was right: a title for the volume by the six writers had not been easy to find. Huysmans had suggested *L'Invasion Comique*, to emphasize the collection's note of anti-chauvinism, its opposition to the retrospective, sentimental patriotism concerning 1870 that was at the moment everywhere evident, from songs sung in the music-halls to the patriotic poems of Paul Déroulède appearing in Madame Adam's "chaste" *Nouvelle Revue*, the organ of the *revanche*. But the others recognized the ugliness of Huysmans' suggestion: the invasion had been comic for nobody in France, and it was not the intention of even this non-patriotic volume to pretend

that it had been. After considerable discussion the group
adopted the title *Les Soirées de Médan*. Médan was the
name of the village on the Seine where Zola had bought
himself a country house with his royalties from *L'Assommoir*, and Céard said later that the title had been chosen
"to pay the group's homage to the dear house where
Madame Zola was a second mother to us all and took
pleasure in making us her spoiled grownup children."
(Actually the name Médan was doubtless used for the
purpose of extracting all possible advantage from the
participation in the volume of the enormously publicized
Zola.) Maupassant disliked the title. He had visited
Médan seldom, not nearly as often as the other members
of the group. He had counseled Zola in the purchase of a
boat, baptized the *Nana*, and he occasionally appeared
at Médan on a week-end in his own skiff, coming from his
own haunts and returning to them rather quickly after a
bit of pistol practice; but he seldom took part in the
literary discussions that seem to have been an incessant
part of the Médan scene. He had a bit of luck in connection with the *Soirées* even before it was printed: he
won in the drawing for first position after Zola's story,
which of course opened the volume. According to Céard,
after the drawing, which took place in Maupassant's
room, the stories were read aloud; Maupassant, as host,
read last; and this revelation of his admirable tale,
Boule de Suif—just finished, and hitherto unknown to
anyone but its author—caused the others, when his
reading was ended, to rise to their feet in tribute.

Boule de Suif: there is little point in Anglicizing the
name to *Ball of Fat* or *Tallow Ball* or *Roly-Poly*. *Boule de
Suif*, being easy to say and to remember, possesses the

two chief requirements of any title. Everyone knows this story about the plump little Rouen prostitute traveling across Normandy from Rouen to Dieppe during the Franco-Prussian war in a stagecoach whose other passengers are Rouennais of great respectability. She alone has thought to bring provisions, and these she timidly offers to share with her fellow-travelers. They are very conscious of their greater moral worth, but they are hungry, and they condescend to accept. At a country inn where the party has to spend the night, a Prussian officer in residence refuses to let them continue their journey unless Boule de Suif comes to bed with him; she indignantly refuses the indecent ultimatum—she is a patriotic girl and hates her country's invaders. The others approve her behavior at first, and for a time treat her with consideration; but after two days of delay they begin to pretend not to understand why, her profession being what it is, she should have scruples. They undertake a campaign of persuasion, and eventually convince her that patriotism demands that she sacrifice herself. While she is in the Prussian's room, they celebrate with champagne. The next morning, timid and ashamed, she enters the coach with the rest of the party whose departure she had made possible. To them, now that they have accomplished their end, her surrender is merely a confirmation of their own moral superiority; no one speaks to her; at noon, she being the only one without provisions, she is allowed to go hungry; and she spends the rest of the journey sobbing in her corner, an outcast once more.

The anecdote on which the story was based is said to have been told Maupassant by his step-uncle, Charles Cord'homme, the second husband of Alfred Le Poittevin's widow, who is himself portrayed as the democrat Cornudet, the only character in the story except Boule de Suif herself who is even halfway sympathetic. Cord'homme is mentioned in a letter from Flaubert to his niece written after the Commune of 1871 as "the communard, communist and common Cord'homme"; and Flaubert also knew about the hazards of the wartime Rouen-Dieppe journey: "Your husband proposed taking us to Dieppe," he had written from Rouen in 1871 to his niece in England, "but your grandmother would be lonely there, and would worry about your uncle Achille; and besides, the trip can be made only under very uncomfortable conditions." The heroine of the original anecdote is supposed to have been a Rouen courtesan named Adrienne Legay, and about her there are various stories: of Maupassant's supposedly meeting her some years after writing his tale, in a Rouen theater, and assuming his most courtly manner with this woman who had brought him, in his immortalization of her, his first success, and taking her to supper; of her denying indignantly that the events in *Boule de Suif* were true; of her dying in misery after Maupassant's own death, and of Laure de Maupassant's comment: "The poor woman died recently in poverty. Some say she killed herself, lacking the courage to endure her wretchedness any longer. I was told too late of her circumstances; otherwise I should have helped her. Some people would have looked at me askance for having anything to do with a creature of that kind, but I would have done my duty. After all, there was a sublime hour in the life of that girl. And my son owed her something."

Wherever the material came from, Maupassant made it into the first of his characteristic works of art. The beauty and power of *Boule de Suif* are the result of the successful combination—by means, of course, of technical narrative skill—of two themes, both close to Maupassant's heart: the theme of the humiliation of a woman, already fruitful in *Le Papa de Simon,* and the theme of the humiliation of France. The national humiliation is painted in the story's opening words:

> For several days in succession remnants of the defeated army had been crossing the city. They were no longer troops, but disbanded hordes. Their beards were long and dirty, their uniforms in rags, they moved slackly. There were no flags, no grouping by regiments. . . .

And the essential attribute of Boule de Suif herself is humiliation: for not only is she hideously treated by her companions as the story progresses, but she is a prostitute to begin with—and it was always Maupassant's belief that a career of prostitution has its origin in a woman's betrayal. Maupassant was subsequently to write numerous stories laid against the background of the Franco-Prussian war—so many, indeed, that the theme of France's defeat can be called one of his predominant themes, almost obsessive. Not only in *Boule de Suif,* but in general throughout his life, it somehow allied itself, almost became fused, with that larger, more fundamental theme that was already, with the double success of *Le Papa de Simon* and *Boule de Suif,* showing signs of becoming the great underlying theme of his work, as it was of his life: the humiliation that had been suffered by Laure.

Flaubert first saw *Boule de Suif* when it had reached its almost final stage:

> I will send you tomorrow or the day after proofs of my long short story, *Boule de Suif* [Maupassant wrote him that January], and I should be grateful if you would

read them. I can change only single words, for we have
all promised not to make any change in the number of
lines, which would upset the entire volume. But an
epithet is an important thing, and can always be
modified.

Flaubert lost no time in letting the young author
know that he realized that something considerable had
happened (though so stubbornly did he continue even at
this late date to think of Guy as primarily a poet, with
his best chance for success lying in the drama, that the
first portion of his letter is devoted to discussion of one
of his plays in verse):

I am impatient to tell you that I consider *Boule de
Suif* a masterpiece. Yes, young man! Nothing more,
nothing less. It is the work of a master. It is original in
conception, well constructed from beginning to end, and
written in excellent style. One can see the countryside
and the characters, and the psychology is excellent. In
short, I am delighted; two or three times I laughed aloud.
I have written my schoolmasterish comments on a scrap
of paper: consider them, I think they are good. This little
story will *live:* you can be sure of it. How beautifully done
your bourgeois are! You haven't gone wrong with one of
them. Cornudet is wonderful and true. The nun scarred
with smallpox, perfect! And the count saying "*Ma chère
enfant,*" and the end! The poor prostitute crying while
Cornudet sings the *Marseillaise*—sublime. I feel like
giving you little kisses for a quarter of an hour! No,
really, I am pleased. I enjoyed it and I admire it and
you. And now, precisely *because* it is fundamentally
strong stuff and will annoy the bourgeois, I would take
out two things which are not at all bad but which might
bring complaints from fools because they give the impression of saying, "To hell with you all." . . . Your
prostitute is charming. If you could reduce her stomach
a little at the beginning you'd give me pleasure. *Je vous
embrasse plus fort que jamais.* I have ideas on how to

make *Boule de Suif* known, but I hope to see you soon.
I want two copies. Bravo again! *Nom de Dieu!*

One can imagine the effect of such a letter as that,
from Flaubert, on a young author.

And it was not only to the author that he expressed
himself. To his niece, the same day, he wrote:

Boule de Suif, the story by my disciple, which I read
in proof this morning, is a masterpiece. I repeat the word,
a masterpiece, of writing, of comedy, and of observation.

At this same time when Flaubert was writing such
praise of his disciple's contribution to the forthcoming
volume (and keeping to himself the opinions he certainly
had concerning the volume itself as a group project), he
was telling two of the other contributors what he thought
of some of the things they were up to.

A volume of three stories by Alexis had just appeared,
and a novel by Hennique, and both young men had sent
him their books. His letters of thanks contained much
praise and encouragement, but neither was without a
scolding.

Last remark: why do you take the public behind
the scenes in your book [he wrote Alexis]? What need is
there to tell them what you think of it? And then, what
is the meaning of the words "the sure triumph of our
struggle," in your dedication? *What* struggle? Realism?
Put aside such puerilities. Why spoil books by prefaces
and libel yourself by a label?

And to Hennique he said:

This mania for thinking that you have just discovered
nature and that you are more true than your predecessors
exasperates me. Racine's *Tempête* is just as true as
Michelet's. There is no such thing as the True. There are
only ways of seeing. Is a photograph a likeness? No more

so than an oil painting. . . . Down with schools, whatever they may be! Down with words empty of sense!
Down with academies, poetics and principles! I am
astonished that a man of your worth should still let
himself fall into such nonsense!

Les Soirées de Médan was published on April 17th. It
bore on its title page the names of all six authors, and
contained a brief preface by Zola, dated "Médan, March,
1880," of the kind so detested by Flaubert:

The stories that follow have been published, some in
France, the others abroad. They seemed to us to proceed
from a single idea, to have the same philosophy: so we
issue them together. We are ready for all attacks, for
the insincerity and ignorance of which the criticism of
the day has already given us so many proofs. Our sole
desire has been to affirm publicly our true friendship,
and, at the same time, our literary tendencies.

On publication day there appeared in the newspaper
the *Gaulois*, in the guise of a letter to the editor, an
article signed by Maupassant and entitled "*Les Soirées
de Médan:* How This Book Came into Being." It began:

To the Editor of the *Gaulois:* Your newspaper was the
first to announce the *Soirées de Médan*, and today you
ask me for some particular details about the origins of
this volume. You would be interested, you say, to know
what it is that we have claimed to do, whether or not we
have wished to put forward the idea of a school and issue
a manifesto. I shall answer these questions. We lay no
claim to being a school. We are simply a few friends,
originally brought together around Zola by common
admiration, and then more and more closely bound by
the affinity of our temperaments, the likeness of our
feelings on all things, and our similar philosophical
tendency. As for me, who as yet amount to nothing as a
literary man, how could I pretend to belong to a school?

I admire without distinction everything that seems to me excellent, of all centuries and of all styles. . . . As to quarrels over the words "realism" and "idealism," I do not understand them. . . .

Those sentences from Maupassant's article were certainly approved by the others in the group—quite possibly they were even written jointly; and we can imagine the joy the young naturalists took in confusing honest readers and solemn critics by now suddenly claiming *not* to be a school, after having put forward innumerable claims that they *were* one—claims that had continued to appear as recently as those prefaces of Alexis and Hennique that Flaubert had so criticized only a few weeks before.

But the quality of their pleasure can only have been naïve beside that which Maupassant himself must have derived from his article. We can only smile at his coolness: his coolness in seizing the occasion of this letter, designed to secure publicity for an enterprise by a group of which he formed one, to announce—now that his story was safely launched—a contrasting position, which for him was the sincere position. "How could I pretend to belong to a school? . . . As to quarrels over the words 'realism' and 'idealism,' I do not understand them." With those words he publicly declared his independence —and he had contrived to do so through means provided by the companions he no longer needed!

After expatiating on his dislike for such words and such concepts as "realism," and stating that he "adored fairy tales," Maupassant devoted the rest of his article to a colorful account of how the stories in *Les Soirées* came to be written. One moonlight night at Médan, he informed his readers, Zola proposed that each of them tell the others a tale; and they agreed that to increase the difficulty, the background used by the first story-teller should be retained by the others. We sat down, and there in the great peace of the drowsy countryside Zola told us that terrible page out of the baleful history of wars called *L'Attaque du Moulin.* When he had finished, everyone cried, "You must write it down, quickly." Zola laughed: "It *is* written." The next day it was my turn.

They told their stories on successive evenings, Maupassant said, except for Alexis,

who made us wait four days, not finding any subject—he wanted to tell us stories about Prussians violating corpses. Our exasperation silenced him, and he ended by imagining the amusing anecdote of a *grande dame* going to recover the body of her husband, dead on a field of battle, and allowing "her heart to be softened" by a poor wounded soldier—and that soldier a priest!!! Zola found these stories interesting, and proposed that we make a book of them.

"It was in such terms," Céard wrote later, "that Maupassant, more astute than accurate, and with the intent to confuse the simple-minded and get them to talk about us, recounted quite fantastically how five not-well-known writers, following in the train of a famous master, decided to appear together simultaneously under the covers of the same book in the windows of the book-shops." And indeed Maupassant's article in the *Gaulois,* with its Arabian-Nights-like account of the oral origins of the collection and its implication that none of the stories had previously been published—whereas Zola's preface had equally untruthfully indicated that they *all* had been published—differs to an amusing degree from the version which Maupassant had given in his letter to Flaubert and from Céard's account of the reading in Maupassant's room. It is very much like that other bit of journalism of three years before: the account in the *République des Lettres* of the dinner at Trapp's, with the "naturalist" menu beginning with "Purée Bovary."

"When our volume arrived from the publisher and I read *Boule de Suif* I was delighted," Zola said later. "It is certainly the best of the six; it has an aplomb, a manner, a precision and clarity of analysis that makes it a little masterpiece. Besides, it sufficed, with the reading public, to put Maupassant in the first rank among the young writers of the future."

Difficult as it is to put one's self in the place of a reader of an earlier generation, the surviving testimonies of two contemporary critics furnish hints as to why *Boule de Suif* should have caught on so particularly well, and why it seemed to the public such a novelty, at the time it appeared.

Oh! What was the charming and comforting and joyful surprise of readers when they saw you make your entrance upon the literary scene, free of all affectation and all pretense, uninterested in trying to make anyone believe that black was white or white black. It was impossible to have enough of your *Boule de Suif*, in which you displayed the ugliness of human selfishness without allowing yourself to be seduced by the sirens of antithesis, without being tempted to make your heroine into a sublime figure.*

And:

The *Soirées de Médan* appeared, and everyone knows about its success. The other authors—except for M. Huysmans—"weren't in it," as the saying goes, in comparison with M. de Maupassant. . . . Since Paris was going through a moment of intense boredom, and since the only fiction it had recently been provided with

* Théodore de Banville, "La Sincerité," *Gil-Blas*, July 1, 1883.

was dreary and pedantic, the fame of *Boule de Suif* was wafted to the skies.*

The day after publication, Flaubert wrote his niece that "Zola, Céard, Huysmans, Hennique, Alexis and my disciple have sent me the *Soirées de Médan,* with a very pleasant collective inscription"; and on the 20th he wrote Maupassant: "I have read *Boule de Suif* again and I maintain that it is a masterpiece. Try to write a dozen like it, and you'll be a man!" It is an additional testimony to the importance of the occasion that in the French the word "try," in that sentence, is in the familiar form, "*tâche,*" instead of the more formal "*tâchez*"—the first time that Flaubert used the intimate form with his disciple.

By the end of the month Maupassant could write to his master:

Boule de Suif is a success. Catulle Mendès came to see me expressly to congratulate me, and he told me, as you did, that in his opinion this story will live, that people will still be talking about *Boule de Suif* twenty or thirty years from now. That gave me great pleasure, for Catulle is a truly well-read man. I am also receiving many compliments from other people whose opinion I value. Give me your opinion on the other stories. Here is mine. . . .

And he proceeded to give estimates of his colleagues' work considerably below those which he had expressed in his letter to the editor of the *Gaulois.* By return of mail Flaubert expressed his low opinions of two of the stories, and did not mention the others. "*Boule de Suif* dwarfs the rest of the volume," he said. "The title of the book is stupid."

Once again, as several years before on the occasion of

* Elémir Bourges, "Un Normand," *Gaulois,* December 5, 1885.

Alexis's pretended attack on the school, the critics swallowed the bait offered them—this time in Zola's preface and Maupassant's letter to the editor. Considerable publicity was obtained, much of it unfavorable (though *Boule de Suif* fared better than the other stories); and in later years Alexis wrote with satisfaction of the critics whom the group had so successfully badgered: "All thanks to our helpful enemies! Didn't they reveal our existence to the public, attract attention to our work, prepare the way for our success?"

On May 3 Flaubert wrote Maupassant in mock envy: "Eight editions of the *Soirées de Médan?* My *Trois Contes* went only to four. I'm going to be jealous!"

CHAPTER 5

FAREWELL TO FLAUBERT

It was appropriate that of all the praise being showered on *Boule de Suif*, Maupassant should in his letter to Flaubert mention with particular appreciation that of the poet Catulle Mendès; for Mendès and what he stood for had played a role in his development.

"What he has shown me is certainly as good as anything published by the parnassians," Flaubert had written to Laure about Guy's verse in his 1873 "declaration of affection"; and although Flaubert's opinion of the parnassian group of poets was not very high—he was of the opinion, shared by many, that their products lacked "soul" and "passion"—it can scarcely have been disagreeable to Laure to hear her son's poetry compared favorably with that of Théodore de Banville, Sully-Prudhomme, Théophile Gautier and Villiers de l'Isle-Adam. These men had been among the contributors to the first so-called parnassian magazine, the *Revue fantaisiste*, which Mendès had founded at the age of eighteen in 1860; and they were later joined by others, notably Leconte de Lisle, François Coppée, Verlaine, Mallarmé, José-Maria de Heredia and Léon Dierx (one of Maupassant's fellow-clerks in the Ministry of Education) as contributors to one or more of the three issues of the *Parnasse contemporain*, a poetry anthology edited by Mendès and Xavier de Ricard in 1866, 1871 and 1876,

and to Mendès's second magazine, the *République des
Lettres*. Mendès was far from being the chief poet among
the parnassians, but he was their chief spokesman; and
he was, as Maupassant correctly wrote to Flaubert, a
man of wide literary knowledge and artistic understanding. He declared the parnassians to be "a group, yes; a
school, no. No countersign, no chief, each individual
absolutely free. Some interested in modern things, others
enamored of religious or legendary antiquity." These
poets of varying tendencies were united chiefly in their
admiration of Victor Hugo and their dislike of such
sentimental romanticism as that of Musset and Lamartine and of such flat modernity as that of Flaubert's
formerly close friend, Maxime DuCamp, with his
apostrophes to locomotives and steam. "Because they
worried about correctness and purity of style, they have
been called 'Stylists' and 'Formists,' " Mendès lamented
in one of a series of delightful lectures, *La Légende du
Parnasse Contemporain*, which he delivered in Brussels;
and he quoted Henry Laujol, one of his assistants on the
République des Lettres, defending the group against the
charge most frequently leveled at it:

I hear sensible, sincere people exclaim: "Oh, yes—the
Parnassian theory? Poetry without passion and without
thought? Scorn for human feelings? The cult of well-
made verse that has no meaning?" No. . . . To be
capable of feeling, and of feeling more deeply than anyone else, but to have also the innate gift, developed by
work, of communicating one's feelings in a perfect form—
that is what is indispensable if one is to be a poet, and
that is also why true poets are so rare! In a word, since
you are a man, love, hope, suffer (the last is inevitable,
in any case!); but think and dream, and know how to
employ all the resources of your art from the most noble
to the most humble, from rhythm to punctuation.

And Mendès commented: "Those last lines actually contain the entire parnassian theory, so often ridiculed."

It is easy to see how a group of literary men professing such high technical standards should admire Flaubert; and yet it is easy to see how Flaubert, hostile to schools and labels, and always concerned to the point of anguish that the formal beauty of his books should be created out of the stuff of human feelings, should, despite what seemed to be an entire concordance between the parnassian "theory" and his own literary aims, look with as critical an eye on the group of poets as he did on that other group who so admired him—the naturalist novelists. Of the two, at least as far as his disciple was concerned, he seems to have had fewer misgivings about the parnassians: he apparently let Maupassant find his way into Zola's circle alone, whereas he took the trouble to send him—or at least to send one of his poems—to Mendès.

In February, 1876 [Henry Roujon, one of the younger parnassians, has recorded], when I arrived at the *République des Lettres* to take up my duties, of which I was very proud, as assistant editor, responsible directly to my master and friend, Catulle Mendès, Mendès handed me a manuscript in which he seemed interested and told me to read it.

It was a poem called *Au Bord de l'eau*, about a shadowy pair of lovers, an oarsman and a washerwoman, who made love until they died of it; an idyll, brutal and sensual, which began like a newspaper item and ended in a nightmare. I was then a very young apprentice, considerably ignorant, and with a full set of intransigent convictions, as is becoming to beginners. An insatiable poetry reader, I distrusted lines that were not chiseled according to formula, and I tended to go even further than the parnassian theories. At first everything shocked me in this manuscript; the vulgarity of the subject, the banality of the metaphors, the looseness of the rhythm, the scattered rhymes, the careless style. This verse was of the type I felt I should disapprove of. Nevertheless, through the rather excessive to-do made by the author about a very banal copulation, there burst the supreme gift of life. I re-read *Au Bord de l'eau*. On second reading, though I perhaps liked the poem even less, I wanted to know something about the author. Brash and opinionated as I then was, I had a presentiment that he was somebody. The manuscript carried the signature "Guy de Valmont."

"Who is he?" I asked.

"A protegé and friend of Flaubert's," Mendès answered. "Flaubert himself sent me the manuscript, urging me to publish it. 'Guy de Valmont' is a pseudonym. Flaubert tells me that his young friend is a clerk in the Naval Ministry, working for a man who dislikes poetry. His real name is Maupassant. He is going to come and see us: beginning today he is one of us."

Mendès, fair-minded and peace-loving, obedient to the principles of literary hospitality which guided his life, immediately sent off to the printer this manuscript by a mere conscript in the army of letters, distinguished by the patronage accorded it by a commander-in-chief. *Au Bord de l'eau* appeared in the next number of the *République des Lettres*, side by side with noble verses by Léon Dierx, the *Marginalia* of Edgar Poe, and an extract from a hitherto unpublished fairy tale for the theater by Flaubert—*Le Royaume du Pot-au-feu*, which, let it be said without blasphemy, added little to the master's glory. The newcomer's verses were read; some of the parnassians, not given to trifling on questions of workmanship, made their criticisms. But in general everyone was in agreement in thinking that the author was a person of consequence. Guy de Maupassant very quickly became a member of our circle.

Mendès was a man of considerable charm and humor, as well as literary knowledge and taste, and not long after the publication of *Au Bord de l'eau* he and Maupassant were friends. There exists an affectionate and humorous letter from Maupassant to Mendès in which he explains, being careful not to offend, just why he is declining his friend's invitation that he become a Freemason: "I am afraid of the slightest chain, whether it comes from an idea or from a woman. . . . I am not yet sufficiently solemn and sufficiently master of myself to be sure of not laughing when making a masonic sign to a 'brother!' . . ." The easy friendship made Maupassant's association with the parnassian band of careful workmen a pleasure; and this association became one more factor, along with his original encouragement by Bouilhet and his training by Flaubert, in his painstaking acquisition of beauty and clarity of style. If the more rigid parnassians found *Au Bord de l'eau* somewhat careless in execution and perhaps made the same criticism of the other Maupassant poems that Mendès published in the *République des Lettres* during 1876, they could scarcely have failed to notice the greater polish of *Histoire du Vieux Temps*, the one-act play in verse of 1879 so disapproved of by the young naturalists. Throughout the seven years of his discipleship, Maupassant continued to chisel and polish one poem after another; and by 1880, when *Boule de Suif* was done, a sheaf of verse was also ready.

I am going to ask you a service [he wrote Flaubert in a letter shortly following the one describing the genesis of the *Soirées de Médan*]. It is to write a line to Charpentier about me, without letting it seem as though I had asked you to. This is what it is about. I have just delivered to said publisher the manuscript of my volume of poetry. To smooth the way for a little play which I plan to submit to the Français or the Odéon in May, it is

most important to me that the volume appear in April.
Charpentier has never had a very high opinion of me,
and I am afraid he may make me wait a long time, or
even refuse the book, for the poetry that he usually
publishes is not at all like mine. You can tell him that
you know I am about to send him a manuscript of poems
and that you know my work. My volume will be very
short. I'd like it to appear quickly. The chief pieces in
it are *Au Bord de l'eau, La dernière escapade, Vénus
rustique,* and my little comedy, *Histoire du Vieux Temps.*

Flaubert did write to Charpentier, and with success;
and Maupassant thanked him in the same letter in which
he announced that he was sending to Croisset the proofs
of *Boule de Suif:* "I have just seen Charpentier, and he
tells me that my volume is accepted, very definitely so,
and that I can count on its being out before spring.
Thank you."

Soon, however, Flaubert was called on to write again:
not a letter to Charpentier, this time, but a letter of the
kind he particularly disliked to write, a public letter, for
newspaper publication.

For *Au Bord de l'eau,* the poem about "very banal
copulation" which had appeared without repercussion
in the *République des Lettres,* had aroused the indignation
of the local authorities of Etampes, a small city near
Paris, when it had recently been reprinted there under
the title *Une Fille:* and Maupassant was threatened with
prosecution for immorality. He called on Flaubert rather
desperately, for he feared that such a suit might cause
him to be dropped from the ministry, and he knew he
was vulnerable. "My poem, chaste in language, is completely immoral and indecent in images and subject
matter," he had written La Toque when it had been
about to appear in the *République des Lettres.* "It's going

some to publish the story of two young people who die from sheer ———ing. I wonder whether, like the illustrious Barbey d'Aurevilly, I may not be called before a magistrate."

Flaubert's aid to his disciple in the crisis cost him three days of work, he told his niece; one day he spent fourteen hours writing letters to influential people and the public letter. In the latter, ostensibly addressed to Guy and appearing on February 21 in the *Gaulois*, where it was preceded by an editorial paragraph referring to Maupassant as "a young poet with a great talent and a great future," he ridiculed the authorities of Etampes as he had previously ridiculed the officials of Rouen about the Bouilhet monument; he described his own courtroom appearance in connection with *Madame Bovary*, "which gave me immense publicity and to which I ascribe three-quarters of my success."

But no! [he ended] Once again, it is not possible. You will not be prosecuted. You will not be sentenced. There is some misunderstanding, some mistake, *something*. The Minister of Justice will intervene! We are no longer in the good old days of the Restoration. Still, who knows? The earth has its limits, but human stupidity is infinite.

He suffered his usual twinges from appearing in print in a newspaper, and he "blushed" for the "mistakes in French" which he discovered, or claimed to discover, in his hastily composed paragraphs, written, he lamented, in "cab-horse style."

The letter accomplished its purpose. The prosecution was dropped after Maupassant, suffering particularly at the time from "paralysis of accommodation of the right eye," had had to make one appearance before the court. "Thank you again, *mon bien cher patron*," he wrote Flaubert gratefully, "for your eloquent letter that saved me, and for your brisk intervention. Those people are wretches and cowards. Their retreat was pretty to watch. Well, it's all over now."

Despite a certain amount of newspaper comment on the affair, Charpentier delayed sending Maupassant proofs of his book, causing the author the annoyance that a publisher does cause when he seems to be letting a particularly golden opportunity slip by; and Flaubert wrote to him again: "What do you think of my disciple Guy being prosecuted for immorality by *the magistrates of Etampes!!!* What is the meaning of it? Do you know that the young man is developing prodigiously? *Boule de Suif* is a gem, and a week ago he showed me a piece of verse that a master could sign. So print his volume at once, that it may appear in the spring. He is dying to be published, and he *needs* to be." Charpentier then did send the poems to the printer, thus avoiding friction with Maupassant that might have spoiled an occasion which several of the people present have described as particularly pleasant: an Easter house-party at Croisset which included Zola, de Goncourt, Alphonse Daudet, Charpentier and Maupassant. ("If you haven't the cash for the journey, I have a superb double louis at your service," Flaubert had written Guy in his invitation. "A refusal on grounds of delicacy would be an unkindness to me. The festival will be lacking in splendor if I don't have my disciple.")

Maupassant's first and only volume of poetry appeared on April 25, 1880, eight days after the publication of the *Soirées de Médan*. While the collection had still been in manuscript, Flaubert had approved the simple

title, *Des Vers*, and when a pre-publication copy arrived
at Croisset he was moved by the dedication:

A
GUSTAVE FLAUBERT
A l'Illustre et Paternel Ami
que j'aime de toute ma tendresse,
A l'Irréprochable Maître
que j'admire avant tout

Young man [he wrote], you are right to love me, for
this old man loves you. I read your volume immediately
—of course I was already familiar with three-quarters
of it. We'll go over it together. What pleases me especially
is that it is personal. No chic! No pose! Neither parnassian, nor realist (nor impressionist, nor naturalist). Your
dedication stirred up in me a whole world of memories:
Your uncle Alfred, your grandmother, your mother; and
for a while the old man's heart was full and there were
tears in his eyes. Save me everything that appears about
Boule de Suif and about your poetry volume.

It was in reply to that letter that Maupassant had
written Flaubert about the success of *Boule de Suif* and
about his pleasure in Catulle Mendès's approval; and it
was certain remarks in this same reply that had drawn
from Flaubert his opinion—hitherto kept to himself—
that "the title of the book is stupid." "In short," Maupassant had written (still speaking of the success of the
volume of stories), "the effect seems to me excellent. It
is a perfect preparation for my volume of poetry which is
to appear on Tuesday and which will put an end, as far
as I am concerned, to all the nonsense about the naturalist school that is constantly being repeated in the papers.
That is the fault of the title *Les Soirées de Médan*, which
I considered bad and dangerous."

Bad and dangerous for himself, Maupassant unquestionably meant. And those sentences throw still a bit
more light not only on Maupassant's cool and careful
planning of his literary début, but also on the position of
literary independence which he was insisting upon now
that *Boule de Suif* was out: the success of his story is
pleasant to him not only because Flaubert considers it
a masterpiece and Catulle Mendès agrees, but also because it will serve to launch another volume—a volume
of poetry, which, in turn, will serve to *dis*sociate him
from the group with which he had so carefully *as*sociated
himself for the sake of the success of his story!

The precaution turned out to be unnecessary, of
course: the originality of *Boule de Suif*, even though it
had appeared in a naturalist collection, did more than
the poems to dissociate Maupassant from the naturalists.

To most readers, Flaubert's approval of Maupassant's title and his emotion at the dedication are more
comprehensible than his admiration of the poems themselves. His high opinion of them was shared by Mendès,
Zola, and a few others, but not very widely. Turgenev,
on the basis of Maupassant's poetry, had declared that
the young man obviously had no literary talent whatever; and Maupassant's later opinion of his own verse
was that it was "the work not of an inspired man, but of
a man who had given thought to what he was doing." In
1881 Maupassant complimented a young literary man
who had sent him some verse by saying: "Here is poetry
that is *clear*. . . ."; and the modern reader is apt to be
dismayed by the rather empty clarity of Maupassant's
largely erotic narrative poems. Although during the rest
of his life he wrote occasional verse, chiefly light, he

published almost none of it. The only poems to appear over his name in a volume after *Des Vers* were three which were included in a satirical and pornographic anthology privately published in Brussels a year later.

In Flaubert's letter of May 3—that in which he pretended to be jealous of the eight editions of the *Soirées de Médan*—he told Guy to "draw up a list of the idiots who write so-called literary reviews for the newspapers. Then we will establish 'our batteries.' But remember that old maxim of the good Horace: *Oderunt poetas.* You will see me the beginning of next week."

For Flaubert, with the end of *Bouvard et Pécuchet* finally in sight, was about to give himself a spring vacation in Paris. During the last years he had been living in straitened financial circumstances due to the bankruptcy of his niece's husband, whom he helped salvage at the cost of much of his capital. Now he was somewhat better off, due to a sinecure which, to his embarrassment, had been secured for him, through the intervention of friends, at the Bibliothèque Mazarine; and his niece, Madame Commanville, had just moved out of and made ready exclusively for him an apartment that they had for a time uncomfortably shared. What happened following his announcement of his imminent arrival is best told in a letter which Maupassant wrote on May 25 to Turgenev in Russia:

Cher maître et ami: I am still prostrated by this calamity, and his dear face follows me everywhere. His voice haunts me, phrases keep coming back, the disappearance of his affection seems to have emptied the world around me. At three-thirty in the afternoon on Saturday, May eighth, I received a telegram from Madame Commanville: "Flaubert apoplexy. No hope. Leave at six." I

joined the Commanvilles at six o'clock at the station;
but stopping at my apartment on the way I found two
other telegrams from Rouen announcing his death. We
made the horrible journey in the dark, sunk in black and
cruel grief. At Croisset we found him on his bed, looking
almost unchanged, except that his neck was black and
swollen from the apoplexy. We learned details. He had
been well the preceding days, happy to be nearing the
end of his novel, and he was to leave for Paris Sunday
the ninth. He looked forward to enjoying himself, having,
he said, "hidden a nest-egg in a pot." It wasn't a very
large nest-egg, and he had earned it by his writing. He
had eaten a very good dinner on Friday, spent the evening reciting Corneille with his doctor and neighbor M.
Fortin, slept until eight the next morning, taken a long
bath, made his toilet and read his mail. Then, feeling a
little unwell, he called his maid; she was slow in coming,
and he called to her out the window to fetch M. Fortin,
but he, it turned out, had just left for Rouen by boat.
When the maid arrived she found him standing, quite
dizzy but not at all alarmed. He said, "I think I am going
to have a kind of fainting fit; it's fortunate that it should
happen today; it would have been troublesome tomorrow, in the train." He opened a bottle of eau de Cologne
and rubbed some on his forehead, and let himself down
quietly on to a large divan, murmuring, "Rouen—we
aren't far from Rouen—Hellot—I know the Hellots. . . ." And then he fell back, his hands clenched,
his face darkened and swollen with blood, stricken by
the death which he had not for a second suspected.

His last words, which the newspapers interpreted as
a reference to Victor Hugo, who lives in the Avenue
d'Eylau, seem to me unquestionably to have meant: "Go
to Rouen, we are not far from Rouen, and bring Doctor
Hellot, I know the Hellots."

I spent three days near him; with Georges Pouchet
and M. Fortin I wrapped him in his shroud; and Tuesday
morning we took him to the cemetery, from which one
has a perfect view of Croisset, with the great curve of
the river and the house he so loved.

The days we consider ourselves happy do not counterbalance days like those.

At the cemetery there were many friends from Paris, especially his younger friends, *all* the young people he knew, and even some whom nobody knew; but not Victor Hugo, or Renan, or Taine, or Maxime DuCamp, or Frédéric Baudry, or Dumas, or Augier, or Vacquerie, etc.

That is all, *mon cher maître et ami*, but I shall have many more things to tell you. We shall attend to the novel when the heirs have settled their affairs. You will be needed for everything.

I wrote the very day of the calamity to Mme. Viardot, asking her to tell you, for I didn't know your address in Russia. I preferred that you should learn this sad news from friends rather than from a newspaper.

I shake your hands sadly, *mon cher maître*, and I hope to see you soon. *Votre tout dévoué.*

Sometime in May Maupassant wrote to Zola to announce a forthcoming second edition of *Des Vers*, to ask him to mention the volume in one of his weekly newspaper articles, and to tell him of his own and Huysmans' appointment to the contributing staff of the *Gaulois:*

I cannot tell you how constantly I think of Flaubert [he said]. He haunts me and follows me everywhere. The thought of him seldom leaves me, I hear his voice, I see his gestures, I see him every moment, standing before me in his long brown robe, raising his arms as he speaks. It is as though a solitude has suddenly set in around me, the beginning of the horrible separations which will continue now from year to year, carrying away the people one loves, the people with whom one shares memories and speaks of intimate things. Such blows ravage the spirit and leave us with a permanent pain in all our thoughts.

And to Madame Commanville he wrote of Laure:

My poor mother, in Etretat, was shattered by the news. It seems that she remained locked in her room for

two whole days, weeping. For her, it is the last of her
old friends gone; from now on her life will have no echo
of the happy memories of her youth; never again will she
be able to recite with anyone the litany of the "Do you
remember's. . . ."

It is difficult, however, not to smile at Maupassant's
first public manifestation of his devotion to Flaubert. In
June a third edition of *Des Vers* was called for, and in
addition to the dedication this new edition contained a
so-called "Letter-Preface":

Since this book first appeared (barely a month ago),
the marvelous writer to whom it was dedicated is dead.
Gustave Flaubert is dead.

I do not wish to speak here of this man of genius
whom I passionately admire, and of whose daily life,
intimate thoughts, exquisite goodness and admirable
greatness I shall later tell.

But at the head of the new edition of this volume,
the dedication of which, he wrote me, "made him weep,"
(for he loved me, too), I wish to reproduce the superb
letter which he wrote for me in defense of one of my
poems, *Au Bord de l'eau*, against the public prosecutor of
Etampes, who was attacking me.

I do this as a supreme tribute to the man who is gone,
who took with him certainly the keenest love I shall ever
have for a man, the greatest admiration I shall ever feel
for a writer, the most absolute veneration with which
any human being will ever inspire me.

And in doing so I once again place my book under
his protection, which once covered me, when he was alive,
with a kind of magic shield, against which the decrees of
magistrates dared not strike.

And then follows the "superb letter": a slightly
shorter version of Flaubert's letter to the *Gaulois*, with
some of its "mistakes in French," or at least its evidences

of hasty composition, corrected—probably by Maupassant himself.

It was indeed a striking and touching tribute from the poet to his dead master: and yet, was it the **very** greatest tribute he might have paid?

"As to my letter for the *Gaulois*," Flaubert had written him immediately after sending it off, "I incline more and more to think that it would be useless. In any case, if you think it should be published, re-copy it for me and send it to me so that I can revise it." But it had appeared without Flaubert's being given a chance to correct it: "What was my astonishment to find your letter in this morning's *Gaulois!*" Guy wrote him, embarrassed. "They had formally promised to publish nothing without my order. . . ."

Now, even without Flaubert's clear though delicate expression of preference that the letter not be used, Maupassant well knew his master's dislike of publishing anything except his imaginative work, his aversion to appearing in print with anything resembling a manifesto, the rarity of the occasions on which he had allowed himself to do so. He realized the greatness of the service Flaubert was doing him. Probably, if asked, Flaubert would have consented, because his affection would have overcome his reluctance, to allow the letter to appear as a preface to his disciple's volume just as he had consented to write it in the first place. But although there had been plenty of time, between the publication of the letter in the newspaper and the printing of the first edition of the volume, for the letter to have been set up and included, Maupassant did not ask Flaubert's permission to make use of it; nor had he asked his permission to use it in the second edition. The third edition gave him an opportunity to include it, without asking, as a memorial to the man he loved and admired: but would not its continued

exclusion have been, perhaps, a more whole-hearted tribute? Can one be blamed for smiling a little to see the
deep and genuine devotion to the master thus combined,
in the "Letter-Preface," with another of the traits which
we have seen so deeply engrained in Maupassant—the
care which he devoted to his own career?

"We didn't even wonder whether Maupassant had
talent," Zola wrote in an account of his first acquaintance
with Guy. "We had seen certain of his poems, written
for men; but it is easy to have vigor in that kind of
thing. Thus we were astonished, when he published a
little poem, *Au Bord de l'eau,* which contains qualities
of the highest order. Another surprise, another revelation, was *Boule de Suif.*" Alphonse Daudet admitted that
"If that sturdy, ruddy-faced young Norman had consulted me, as did so many others, as to the chances of
his vocation, I should have answered without hesitation:
'Do not write.' " And we have seen Guy's fellow-mem-
bers of the Médan group, unprepared for the "revelation," so impressed at the reading of *Boule de Suif* that
they rose in tribute.

But unlike those others, Flaubert had believed in
Maupassant's talent for some time. He had come to believe—about three years after writing to Laure in his
"declaration of affection" that he was unable to "cast
his poetic horoscope"—that Guy had ahead of him, as
we have seen him tell an editor, "a great literary future."
What had Flaubert seen in the young man that no one
else had seen?

Here, once again, as so often during any consideration of Maupassant, one's thoughts go to Laure. After
detaching Guy from his father, she had found him Flaubert as a foster-father. This she effected in part by means

of the boy's own charm and accomplishments, and in
part because of Flaubert's lonely state at the time; but
her favorite and most effective device was her invoca-
tion, oft-repeated, of the memory of her brother, and
her constant reiteration to Flaubert that her son resembled Alfred. The answer to the question about what
it was that Flaubert, and no one else, had seen in Guy is,
of course, that he had seen his adored Alfred. Guy took
Alfred's place; and anyone who could do that must, in
Flaubert's eyes, have, like Alfred, genius.

Whether or not Alfred Le Poittevin, who died at
thirty-two, had the genius that Flaubert thought, Guy
de Maupassant did have it. And though it is a commonplace that genius cannot be accounted for, there is less
wonder about the *flowering* of Maupassant's genius than
about many another. It would be naïve to suppose that
during the years of her discordant marriage the aggres-
sive Laure did not employ strategy and tactics to make
Guy her ally. And, loving her brother, venerating his
memory, and despising her husband, she must constantly
have held up the one as an example to her son, in brilliant
contrast to the other. With a considerably artistic and
imaginative family tradition, with so intelligent and cultivated a mother so constantly invoking the example of
so brilliant and literary an uncle, and invoking it so aggressively as to quite eclipse the poor little bit of amateur
painting that was quite literally all that Monsieur de
Maupassant had to offer; with nothing, then, in his father
to emulate, and with a foster father "of whom anybody
would be proud" in the person of Flaubert, one of the
great novelists of the world, who offered him personal
and professional devotion; and with a living to earn. . . .
Such circumstances were a hot-house, a forcing-bed, for
genius.

PART TWO

ARTIST
AT
WORK

CHAPTER 1

NEWSPAPERS: THE *GAULOIS*
AND THE *GIL-BLAS*

Perceptive readers of *Boule de Suif* predicted the greatest success for Maupassant as a writer of short stories—a journalist later wrote *—so to prove them right Maupassant immediately began to turn out newspaper articles!

That is not as paradoxical as it may sound.

He immediately stopped work at the ministry that May of 1880, not resigning, but cautiously going on leave of absence (subsequently prolonged until 1882, then cancelled by the ministry); and on May 21 the beginning of his journalistic career was proclaimed. Arthur Meyer, editor-in-chief of the *Gaulois*, in an article detailing the summer treats in store for his readers, announced that the paper would publish several series of pieces by new writers, among them, "*Contes de Navarre*, by Margot, a Parisienne witty to her rosy fingertips; *Les Mystères de Paris*, by M. Huysmans, a realist of the new school; and *Les Dimanches d'un Bourgeois de Paris*, by M. Guy de Maupassant, the young writer whom Flaubert considered his successor."

* Elémir Bourges, *op. cit.*

The *Dimanches*, a series of ten Sunday outings in the life of a government clerk, appeared with almost weekly regularity from the end of May to mid-August.

Cher maître et ami [Maupassant wrote Zola], For the past two weeks Meyer has been pestering me to take my character Patissot to call on artists, and he wants me to begin with you. I resisted, telling him that the idea might very well not meet with your approval, but he says that you have had so many articles written about you already that one more or less won't much bother you. Since that seems to me to be true, I consented. I tell you this so that you may know how I came to write this article, in which I have been very careful not to include anything intimate.

It is not known how many of the *Dimanches* were written as closely to Meyer's order as that one in which Maupassant took his clerk on a visit to Médan; but in any case, unlike another somewhat similar series of sketches, written to editorial order by another young man, *The Posthumous Papers of the Pickwick Club,* these were no literary or popular triumph.

They were followed in the autumn and throughout the next two years by almost weekly, largely ephemeral, articles on a variety of subjects: Flaubert and other literary men, old and new books, old china, travel, politics, society, wit, and women. These articles have long since been lost sight of; only recently was the first approximately complete list of their titles compiled *; and only a few, chiefly on literature and travel, have ever been republished. Some are interesting for what they tell of the author and his opinions and attitudes, often confirming what is to be sensed more delicately in his later

* Edward D. Sullivan and Francis Steegmuller, "Supplément à la Bibliographie de Guy de Maupassant," *Revue d'Histoire Littéraire de la France,* Octobre–Décembre, 1949. See Note 1: Note on Bibliography, etc., page 393.

fiction; those on Flaubert are valuable because they are
first-hand documents relating to a great man (despite an
ever-present air of exploitation, reminiscent of the "Letter-Preface" to the new edition of *Des Vers*); and the
weakest (apart from the purely political, which now lie
in that particularly deathly death reserved for political
newspaper pieces) are those in which Maupassant reflects
with rather pretentious and awkward inadequacy on
life and its futilities, usually echoing one or both of his
admirations among the philosophers, Herbert Spencer
and Schopenhauer, and usually including a lament on
the inferiority of his age, particularly as exemplified in
the democratic imbecilities of the Third French Republic.

The anti-egalitarian sentiments which Maupassant
expressed in his articles were in key with the rest of the
Gaulois. In the same issue which contained the announcement of the *Dimanches*, Arthur Meyer stated his paper's
principle:

The *Gaulois* belongs to no party, to no coterie, to no
school of government, art or literature. It is open to
everything that is young, to everything that has talent
and ideas. It has but one principle: respect and love for
authority. We are authoritarians. But political forms
matter little to us.

Actually, under Meyer the *Gaulois* was royalist, devoting much of its space to the activities of the pre-
tenders to the French throne, attacking the institution of
civil marriage in France, the expulsion of religious orders
from the country, and other republican measures. Maupassant continued to write for the paper, with no change
in his tone, during the year or more when Meyer was
temporarily ousted and replaced by an editor of republican sympathies. Meyer later boasted in his memoirs of
having published Maupassant's early work, and from

the beginning he treated his young author with respect, printing his articles almost without exception on the front page, often in the leading position, and making no changes or cuts in his text without his permission.

More amusing, less political, and more important in Maupassant's career than the *Gaulois* was the other daily newspaper for which he wrote.

This was the *Gil-Blas*, founded in 1879 by Auguste Dumont to exploit, so said his rivals, the vogue for articles and short stories already launched by other editors. Showing a rare spirit of teamwork, a number of established Paris papers, many of them none too clean themselves, had during the summer of 1880 published simultaneous attacks on the newcomer for filling its columns with obscenities—apparently an organized invitation to the authorities to prosecute.

Zola, several of whose later novels were to be serialized in the *Gil-Blas*, has given a description of the paper and its attackers:

We have just been witnessing a singular occurrence. Paris has been seized with a fit of virtue. I speak of a fit in its acute sense: one of those fine crises which spread out to full view all the ignorance and foolishness of a public. The press has made the startling discovery of what it calls, in its indignation, "obscene literature." The story is so droll that I feel I must tell it in detail. A newspaper had been started, the *Gil-Blas*, which at first sold very badly. Once in a while I questioned, through curiosity, the editors of rival sheets as to the chances of the newcomer's success, and these editors, shrugging contemptuously, declared that they had no fears, the paper would never sell. Then all at once I saw the editors' noses lengthening; the *Gil-Blas was* selling;

it had adopted a specialty of light stories which gave it a
certain public. I mean, if you like, the public at large—
men and, above all, women, who did not dislike questionable stories. From this in a few weeks arose this great
storm of virtuous indignation on the part of the press.

I do not wish to defend the *Gil-Blas,* but it seems to
me that it is a case which can very easily be analyzed.
Certainly the paper was not founded with the avowed
intent to corrupt the nation. It simply felt its way with
the public; new newspapers all know this period of
hesitation. Success does not come; everything is tried
until something is found which makes the public bite.
Well, the *Gil-Blas,* having ventured among other things
a few coarse articles, realized that the public had bitten;
and it continued to give its readers the dish that was to
their taste.

"Ignoble speculation! School of perverted tastes!"
cry its indignant colleagues. *Mon Dieu!* I should like to
see the paper that would refuse its subscribers what they
clamored for!

I subscribed to the *Gil-Blas* to find out what there
was to it. I found some charming articles: sketches by
M. Théodore de Banville, for example, full of poetic
charm; little novelettes, fine and spirited in their style,
by M. Armand Silvestre; highly colored studies by M.
Richepin. Here are three poets whose company is highly
honorable. It is true that the rest of this issue was of a
lower literary order. Indeed, some of its stories were
positively gross. Not that I have anything against this
source of inspiration, for I should have to condemn on
such a ground Rabelais, La Fontaine, and still others
whom I esteem. But these stories were too badly written.
That is my whole quarrel. You are highly blameable
when you write badly. That is the only crime which I
can admit in literature. I do not see where else "morality"
enters the picture. A well-made phrase is a good action.*

The campaign against the *Gil-Blas* fizzled out, and it

---

* "Obscene Literature," in *Le Roman Expérimental.* (Belle M. Sherman's
translation, slightly revised.)

was soon able smugly to announce that its circulation
was increasing daily.

The paper has been called "a sort of *Heptameron*,"
in which, every day of the week, the staff storytellers
took turns telling stories; and it does seem a trifle strange
that even in France at that time it should have been
considered a *news*paper. It looked like one, but inter-
national and even national news was almost entirely
absent from its pages. Except for a column or two, each
issue was devoted to entertainment: articles, stories, and
more or less scandalous gossip items known as "*échos*"
and "*le courrier mondain.*" It also engaged in activities
unknown to modern journalism, such as the launching of
de luxe courtesans, picturesquely known as *horizontales:*

At the *Gil-Blas*, then occupying quarters behind the
Opera, reigned the debonair epicureanism of the literary
world, as well as a mysterious activity which derived
profits from several schemes under the general heading
"Society Chronicle." At its head was a former master of
the foils, the Baron de V[aux], who organized fencing
exhibitions and champagne parties; and his assistant was
a pleasant young fellow who had baptized himself "The
Intrepid Bottle-Opener" and was a champagne salesman
in addition to being the newspaper's gossip editor.

This last role included the mission of "rescuing"
young creatures who were beautiful but penniless: freeing
them, first of all, from the clutches of their unreasonable
mothers (who foolishly nourished for their daughters the
"vain, obsolete and immoral hope of marriage"), and
then launching them as stars in the music-hall firmament,
or in what the younger Dumas had christened the demi-
monde. They were plucked like violets, taught to walk,
to eat, to talk (for they were ignorant of all these things),
to dance, to dress, and to insist on being given a great
deal of money. They had to know how to choose a house
and run a household, to know about horses and servants.

Even some slight acquaintance with generally known facts was desirable (though here one didn't demand the impossible): if they could avoid confusing Manon Lescaut with Madame de Pompadour, so much the better. Once emerged from obscurity into celebrity on the Paris scene, the violet was christened Comtesse de Belgranitos or Baroness Montefiora. This nobility, baptized with torrents of champagne, thus became a priceless source of material for the newspaper's gossip columns—that Gotha of the boudoir, which in the elegant circles of the Third Republic had taken the place of the Gotha of the divine right.*

In its issue of October 29, 1881, this rather weird-sounding sheet announced a "considerable strengthening and improvement of its staff for the winter season." In addition to weekly contributions by René Maizeroy, Catulle Mendès, Jean Richepin and Armand Silvestre, it said, there would be one by a writer whom it called simply and without introduction "Maufrigneuse." That same day appeared Maufrigneuse's first article, *Les Femmes,* describing various types of Parisiennes and promising in subsequent issues to take readers into a number of Paris salons. Maufrigneuse's next, *Politiciennes,* treated of women's hidden role in politics; a week later *Galanterie Sacrée (Holy Dalliance)* dealt with women's sentimental attachments for priests; and throughout the winter and the next few years Maufrigneuse wrote almost weekly in the *Gil-Blas.*

Maupassant's adoption of a pseudonym for the *Gil-Blas* doubtless had some practical reason behind it: an agreement with the *Gaulois,* a fear that his own name

---

* From *Intimités de la IIIme République,* by Ferdinand Bac, an illustrator of many books of the period, including several of Maupassant's. "The Intrepid Bottle-Opener," Charles Desteuque, is said elsewhere to have been the *son* of a champagne dealer, and to have been able himself to drink nothing but milk. (Charles de Saint-Cyr, "Qui fut le véritable Bel-Ami?" *Toute l'Edition,* January 30, February 6 and February 13, 1937.)

might lose journalistic value if used too often, or something of the sort. Maufrigneuse is the last of his pseudonyms, taken from the *Comédie Humaine*, in which the Duchesse de Maufrigneuse, later the Princesse de Cadignan, is successively the mistress of twelve of Balzac's characters. Maupassant's choice of the name of the gay duchess is a comment on the character of the paper for which he chose it; and so, invariably, are references to the *Gil-Blas* that appear throughout his works. In one of the *Dimanches* a prostitute reads the *Gil-Blas* on the train and offends a bourgeois family by offering it to them; in the short story *La Revanche* (*Revenge*) a pretty young divorcée reads the *Gil-Blas* in the lounge of a Cannes hotel, and from her choice of paper one knows that her ex-husband's designs on her have a good chance of success; in *En Wagon* (*In the Train*) the whole ludicrous story of the abbé and the childbirth rises out of the announcement in the *Gil-Blas* gossip columns that "all the *horizontales* known and unknown" were flocking to the neighborhood. Mention of the *Gil-Blas* invariably creates an atmosphere of titillation.

But the chief interest in the dozens of articles that Maupassant wrote for his two newspapers in the years immediately following *Boule de Suif* is their gradual evolution into something else. The French newspaper article, the *chronique*, allowed and still allows greater discursiveness than its American or British counterpart; and from the beginning Maupassant's articles frequently contained anecdotes. Gradually Maupassant introduced more and more anecdotes into his articles, or stretched his central anecdote longer and longer: almost imperceptibly, what began as articles pointed up by anecdotes became lengthy anecdotes with a thin surrounding text of general matter; and eventually the general matter was to drop off entirely, and the result was stories.

Thus, in retrospect, the chief function of Maupassant's articles in his career is seen to be their provision of a setting for anecdotes, which gradually developed, more and more skillfully written, into many of the short stories that we know. Their character was related to the character of the papers in which they appeared; and their function was to entertain the readers of those papers. Maupassant once said that the qualities essential to a good writer of newspaper articles were "good humor, lightness of touch, vivacity, wit, and grace"; and with the evolution of his articles those qualities were to pass into large numbers of his stories.

CHAPTER 2

LA MAISON TELLIER

DURING HIS FIRST TWO YEARS of newspaper work
Maupassant was so busy that his friends complained;
and one of them, his rowing friend, Petit-Bleu, finally
wrote to Laure, now established on the Riviera. She
replied from Menton in March, 1882:

Rest assured that your old friend loves you as much
as ever, but I think at the moment he is the busiest man
in France and Algeria. Even I, his own mother, am made
to feel it—his letters are short and few. But we must not
reproach him, for we know that we cannot doubt his
affection. When he is less preoccupied, less caught up in
things, we shall find him his old self. I wish above all that
he would give up journalism—his serious work would be
the better for it; but young men need money, and one
would have to be very sober-minded indeed to neglect so
easy and quick a way of earning it. Let's leave him alone,
and hope the day may not be far off when our young
writer will rid himself of a few of his commitments and
find time to look about him.

What Laure called "serious work" (she did not mean
writing on "serious," that is, solemn, subjects, but fiction
as opposed to newspaper articles) had continued, with
Flaubertian carefulness, along with the journalism, from
the very moment of Maupassant's liberation from the
ministry.

Since the end of his daily drudgery had coincided with the onset of warm weather, he had lost no time in getting out of Paris for the summer. He moved not very far from the offices of the *Gaulois:* at Sartrouville, a village on the Seine a few miles below Paris, he rented what Petit-Bleu describes as "an apartment in which each of us had a bedroom, with a writing-room for the 'Master' in between. Needless to say, the house we chose was on the river, just across the quay from our laundress-landlady's floating wash-house. We looked out on the Seine, winding its way so charmingly between the park of Maisons-Laffitte, the forest of Saint-Germain and the hills of Cormeilles. This was no longer the immediate suburbs; the river banks were less noisy and crowded, the country was greener and more smiling." * Maupassant was in high spirits on moving day, scandalizing passers-by by shouting lines from his poem *69* (one of those soon to be privately published in Brussels) as he installed his possessions.

He had told his friends that he was moving to Sartrouville to work with concentration, and that his only interruptions, in addition to articles, were to be swimming and rowing—he and Petit-Bleu kept their skiffs on the quay outside the house. But, unfortunately, interruptions of a different kind made their appearance: here in Sartrouville, at the very beginning of his liberated existence, he began to suffer atrocious head pains. They were to recur throughout his life; and although he always called them migraines, doctors think that they were syphilitic symptoms, that already his brain had been marked out as the part of his organism to be destroyed. Henry Céard, arriving from Paris one day for a visit, found him in agony, and spent much of his time rowing

* Pierre Borel et Léon Fontaine, *op. cit.*

back and forth between Sartrouville and Maisons-Laffitte
bringing him phials of ether. From now on ether-inhaling
was to be one of Maupassant's habits; he began it as a
pain-killer, but came to enjoy its relaxing and hallucina-
tory effects, like those sought by reefer-smokers today.*

That summer he visited Etretat only long enough to
write what would be called today an "Etretat Letter"
for the *Gaulois*, and in August he made the first considerable trip of his life. It is not surprising that it should
have been to Corsica: "How good it would be to live in a
land where there was always sun!" he had written his
mother from the ministry; and this was but the first of
many sun quests. He reveled in the heat and the color.
"My arrival in Ajaccio was a triumph," he wrote to
Louis Le Poittevin's wife, Lucie. "All the newspapers of
the city announced my coming in magnificent terms. But
I have just upset the republicans by my rough handling
of the local prefect in one of my articles. He is furious, I
hear. Beware the vendetta! I have been making superb
excursions into the mountains. I hunt, fish, sail on the
Mediterranean, etc." Laure was with him, and spent a
week in bed as a result of following him as closely as she
could by carriage along mountain roads.

He cut his trip short in reply to a telegram from
Huysmans, Hennique and the other members of the
Médan group. He had agreed, before leaving France, to
collaborate with them in the founding and editing of a
weekly newspaper of literature and art, to be called the
Comédie Humaine; Huysmans, who was to be editor-in-
chief, said that the paper's only politics would be "the
nihilism of Herzen, embellished with a charming skepti-
cism." Maupassant promised to reserve for the new

---

* See his story, really little more than an article, *Rêves* (*Dreams*), part of
which he used again in his so-called travel diary, *Sur l'eau*.

paper a story which he was just finishing and which had already been asked for by two editors—Laffitte of the *Voltaire*, who had backed down, however, when on Zola's advice Maupassant had demanded a stiff price, and Madame Adam of the *Nouvelle Revue*, who had previously been so chastely inhospitable to *Vénus rustique*. He would give Madame Adam instead, he wrote Hennique from Corsica, one of the travel pieces he had written there, which was "good enough for her boring magazine." But despite Maupassant's return to Paris to help with preparations, the *Comédie Humaine* never appeared. "Difficulties with the printer" caused its abandonment; and it was, after all, in Madame Adam's "boring magazine," the issue of March 1, 1881 (containing also the concluding installment of Flaubert's posthumous *Bouvard et Pécuchet*, which had been running serially since December 15), that the story appeared.

This, Maupassant's first piece of "serious work" in the year that had gone by since *Boule de Suif*, was a strong performance: *En Famille*. Its hero, or victim, is a government clerk—and we know what good reason Maupassant had to feel strongly about *that* group of society.

Of all classes of individuals [he wrote in one of his 1882 *Gaulois* articles, *Les Employés*], of all categories of workers, of all men engaged in the desperate struggle for existence, they are the most pitiable, the most devoid of advantages. Do you know what they earn, these wretches with their diplomas and their law degrees, these young fellows who find themselves, as the result of their ignorance of life, the guilty negligence of a father, and the protection of some important functionary, working as special assistants in a ministry? They start at fifteen or eighteen hundred francs! Certain ministries are veritable penal colonies. I have already mentioned the Naval

Ministry, and in this connection I mention it again. I worked there; I know it well. There the tone is the tone of command commonly used by officers aboard ship.

Excoriation of "the guilty negligence of a father" is the drive of *En Famille*. The "humble attitude and sort of nervous stammer" of Caravan, clerk in the Naval Ministry; Madame Caravan's "chronic cleaning-sickness," her mania for scratching herself that is "almost a tic"; the anxiety and frustration and pettiness that lie thick over the Caravan household; the tragi-comic events of the day Caravan does not go to his office; his cold sweat when he thinks of facing his chief in the morning: in all those Guy's resentment pours out, and the acid with which they are depicted is the acid of his bitterness at the father who had been quite willing for his son to become another Caravan.

Three weeks later, on March 26, in the *Revue Politique et Littéraire* (also called the *Revue Bleue* from the color of its cover), appeared another Maupassant story, the famous *Histoire d'une Fille de ferme—Story of a Farm Girl*. Here the theme is again, as in *Le Papa de Simon*, a woman's humiliation and the finding of a foster-father for her son: the real father is a disappearing ne'er-do-well. In its freshness and seriousness, its classic feeling and modernity, this tale can be likened to one of Pissarro's blue and green Norman peasant paintings of the 1870's or 80's. It is the first of Maupassant's stories of Norman peasant and farm life, a long series that was eventually to include the even more celebrated *La Ficelle* (*The String*) and *Toine*.*

Back in January, Maupassant had visited Etretat, probably to enjoy the country in the snow and to take a

* See Note 5: Maupassant and Normandy, page 400

look at Les Verguies, now inhabited only by servants and
dogs; and from there he wrote to his mother:

Ma bien chère Mère, I am writing you on a corner of
the table in our little salon. The two dogs are thin but
happy and well. They are here at my feet; Matho keeps
disturbing me by rubbing against my leg. Daphne is
entirely cured. As for me, I sniffle and sneeze in the grip
of a terrible head cold, for I traveled all night in a below-
freezing temperature and cannot get warm in this icy
house. The cold wind blows under the doors, the lamp
keeps threatening to go out, and my chief light comes
from the bright fire, which scorches my face but heats
the room not at all. All our old things are around me,
cheerless and depressing; not a sound comes from the
village, which seems to have died under the snow. I
cannot hear the sea. I feel even more chilled by the
solitude of life than by the solitude of the house. I sense
that all human beings are blind wanderers, that everything is a void. And amidst this disorder my brain
functions lucidly, exactly. I have almost finished my
story about the brothel women at the First Communion.
I think it is at least as good as *Boule de Suif,* if not better.

That story was *La Maison Tellier—Madame Tellier's
House.* The idea was given Maupassant by a friend who
had noticed, while passing a Rouen brothel, a sign saying
"Closed because of First Communion"; and readers who
get added pleasure from a tale by picturing its author at
work can particularly enjoy *La Maison Tellier,* for its
imagined details and their build-up around the sign are
beguiling to a degree. Maupassant constructed an excursion of feather-brained outcasts to the very shrine of
village respectability, the church, and his scenes include:
the consternation among the male population of Fécamp
when the brothel is found to be closed; the train journey
of the prostitutes, with a disturbance caused by a
presumptuous garter-salesman; their gaily-clad march

down the village main street (an old woman mistakes them for a religious procession); the gratitude of the priest for their sobs in church; the unseemly behavior of Madame Tellier's brother, a respectable carpenter; the beginnings of boredom; and finally the all but hysterical delight of returning home to the brothel, with the resulting benefit to the male population of Fécamp, who are rewarded, at the end of the carefully built story, for their deprivations so vividly portrayed at its beginning.

It is the first of Maupassant's stories to contain touches of his personal humor—a wildish, fly-away, fantastic, non-respectable humor which to those who care for such things is like the taste of a favorite wine. A French photograph of the time, which purports to be that of "the Rouen brothel on which Maupassant based *La Maison Tellier*" and which in any case does depict the staff of *a* Rouen brothel, a provincial establishment of the kind described in the story, illustrates both Maupassant's material and what he did with it. He well knew any brothel's combination of grimness and gaiety, both of which are clearly visible in the faces and gestures of the originals in the photograph: but whereas in the raw material grimness rather dishearteningly prevails and a capacity for comedy and farce barely suggests itself, in the story those suggestions blossom into Maupassant humor and even the grimness of the women's existence is comically (that does not mean unsympathetically) conveyed by means of the sobbing in church.*

The three stories—*En Famille, Histoire d'une Fille de ferme,* and *La Maison Tellier*—along with four others including *Le Papa de Simon,* were published in May,

* See Note 6: Maupassant and Degas, page 402.

1881, in Maupassant's first volume of fiction, entitled *La Maison Tellier*. Its reception was one which, with minor variations, was to greet Maupassant volumes for years to come: sales were good (there were eleven reprintings in two years), and there were enthusiasts among literary men—in this case especially Pierre Loti and Théodore de Banville; but critics and others attacked the author for choosing to depict lowlife. "In ten years M. Guy de Maupassant, who has, I suppose, a literary conscience, will regret having put this repugnant book into circulation," said the critic on the *Evénement;* and the *Figaro*, which refused even the publisher's paid advertising, put up a strong defensive and delaying action when handed a favorable review by Zola, whose contract with the paper obliged it to print whatever he might submit.

Two months after publication, Maupassant was in Africa.

I left Paris on July 6, 1881 [he wrote in a later account of his trip]. I wanted to see the land of sun and sand in midsummer, under the weight of its greatest heat, in the most furious resplendence of light. Another reason, too, made Algeria particularly attractive at this moment. The elusive Bu-Amama was conducting that fantastic campaign which inspired the utterance, writing and commission of so many stupidities. It was also rumored that the Mohammedans were preparing a general insurrection, that they were about to make one last effort, and that after Ramadan war would break out in all parts of Algeria simultaneously. I was extremely curious to see the Arab at that moment, to try to understand his soul— something seldom attempted by our colonials. Flaubert used to say: "It is possible to imagine the look of the desert, the pyramids and the Sphinx before one sees them; but the sort of thing one cannot imagine is what a Turkish barber looks like, squatting before his door."

Would it not, it occurred to me, be even more interesting to know what was going on inside that Turkish barber's head?

Maupassant caught never a glimpse, during his Algerian journey, of Bu-Amama, a marabout who had recently been encouraging his followers to murder European colonists and who soon thereafter disappeared from view in Morocco; but a number of the articles which he sent from Algeria to the *Gaulois* are devoted to the Bu-Amama insurrection and to other aspects of French administration in Algeria. He was immediately popular with French army officers in Algiers, and accepted an invitation given him by two young lieutenants who were about to head an expedition into the interior, charged with charting the springs on which French troops would be dependent if the expected post-Ramadan uprisings took place. With his pleasant companions he made his way on horseback over the desert from oasis to oasis, native riders being sent ahead to prepare the next oasis for their evening arrival; the trail was read by guides from the whitened bones of long-perished camels of earlier caravans. He "often longed for the Café Anglais when mealtime came," but he enjoyed the feasts in the tents and oasis homes of sheiks, and the party ran into a sandstorm and saw adders, scorpions, tarantulas and jackals. From the oasis of Saïda he wrote his mother: "An officer in the Zouaves, whose detachment we met in the middle of the desert, told me that Zola has written an article about me in the *Figaro*."

Zola's fight with the *Figaro* over his review of *La Maison Tellier* had lasted two months, but he had finally won it, as he almost always won any fight in which he engaged, and the piece appeared on July 11 as half of a double article entitled *Alexis et Maupassant*. It defended

Maupassant's choice of lowlife subject matter and
particularly praised *La Maison Tellier* and *Histoire d'une
Fille de ferme*. In his temperament, Zola said, were
combined a "breadth of shoulder" and a "ruddy sturdi-
ness" that were typically Norman and

the style of a born writer. He certainly owes much to
Flaubert, whose adopted son he was during the last
years. But he brings an originality, which was evident
in his verse and affirms itself today in his prose, virility,
and a sense of physical passion that blazes from his best
pages. There is no neurotic perversion, there is only a
healthy, strong desire, free earthly love, life widely
spread out in the sun. That gives a very personal accent
of fecund good health and rather braggartish good humor
to everything he writes.

In sum, Maupassant continues in his new book to be
the penetrating analyst, the solid writer, of *Boule de Suif*.
His is certainly one of the sanest and healthiest temperaments of the younger generation. Now he must write a
novel, a long work to show us his full capacity.

From the Zouave encampment where he happened on
the article, Maupassant wrote gratefully to Zola at once:

Your voice, so unexpected here, and so kind, coming
from so far away across this horrible, burning, desolate
solitude of the high Algerian plateaus, has given me the
deepest pleasure. I had given up hope, I confess, that you
would be able to force the resistance of the *Figaro*. But
you succeeded: thank you a thousand times. This copy
of a newspaper is the only one that I have seen in two
weeks. No mail reaches me in the desert, and I do not
know whether my letters reach France. I am finally
satisfying my vagabond instinct, and this country,
abominable to inhabit, is really thrilling, especially at
this moment of general warfare, when one is likely at any
moment to meet a party of enemy Arabs. . . .

Turgenev, who had helped Maupassant with a detail in *La Maison Tellier* ("The song that your English sailors would sing is *Rule Britannia, Britannia Rules the Waves*— the first two words are enough," he wrote in reply to the author's query) and to whom the volume was dedicated ("*Hommage d'une affection profonde et d'une grand admiration*"), had received his copy in Russia; now he was back in Paris, and there Maupassant found a letter from him waiting when the African journey was over:

Your name is making a stir in Russia. We have translated what is translatable, and I have brought back with me a devilish big article about you in the *Golos*, very well done and very enthusiastic.*

* See Note 7: Turgenev, Tolstoy, and *La Maison Tellier*, page 403.

THE CUCKOLDS

In the three chief stories in *La Maison Tellier* Maupassant had obviously been following, and following successfully, the course charted for him by Flaubert at the time of *Boule de Suif:* "Try to write a dozen like it and you'll be a man." As Zola indicated in his review, the stories were indeed like *Boule de Suif;* they were of the same general character, the same weight and pace; even *La Maison Tellier,* for all its humor, is full of the grave and measured influence of Flaubert. They were infinitely superior to Maupassant's newspaper work, and it is easy to understand that Laure might wish her son to give up journalism because "his serious work would be the better for it."

But Laure had reckoned without the influence of the *Gil-Blas.*

At the time she expressed her wish, her son was still writing chiefly articles for his newspapers, and the few tales that he had published in them could not compare with those that he had written for his volume. In the months immediately following, however, he began to write for the *Gil-Blas* a series of very different tales, tales characterized above all by the article-writer's qualities of "good humor, lightness of touch, vivacity, wit and grace": *Un Coq Chanta (A Cock Crowed)*, with its

huntsman too sleepy for love; *Farce Normande,* with its
wedding-night horseplay; *Mon Oncle Sosthène,* about the
Freemason converted by the Jesuit sent him as a joke by
an unlucky nephew; *La Rouille (Rusty),* whose title
describes the condition an old bachelor finds himself to
be in when belatedly contemplating marriage. These
stories and the others like them which appeared in the
Gil-Blas during the months just after Laure wrote her
letter all partake pungently of the newspaper's character;
they are of far greater interest than the stories appearing
in the *Gaulois* at the same time; they mark the triumphant climax of the evolution of Maupassant's anecdote-
studded articles into stories. The raffishness of the
Gil-Blas had led him to discover one side of his genius:
his supremacy in the light, risqué story.

This is the type of story that has come to be known as
Maupassantian, and that comes to mind as soon as his
name is mentioned; the type that caused the critic Jules
Lemaître to call him an "almost irreproachable author
in a genre that is not"; that made Henry James, obliged
in an essay on Maupassant to call these stories "indecent," lament that "we suffer in English from a lack
of roundabout names for the *conte leste*—that element for
which the French, with their *grivois,* their *gaillard,* their
égrillard, their *gaudriole,* have so many convenient
synonyms"; and that caused Lemaître to write of Maupassant:

In France the short story *(conte)* is a national type.
Under the name of *fabliau,* then of *nouvelle,* it is almost
as old as our literature. It is a French taste, the taste of a
people that loves stories, but likes them to be lively and
light in touch; and, though it can sometimes stand their
being long, at other times prefers them short; and, al-

though it likes them to be moving, does not despise them
for being merry. The *conte* was a contemporary of the
chanson de geste, and existed before the prose novel.

Naturally it was by no means the same in all periods.
Very diversified in the Middle Ages, by turns licentious,
religious, moral or fantastic, in the sixteenth and seven-
teenth centuries it is chiefly licentious, sometimes
"tender." In the eighteenth century, "philosophy" and
"sensibility" appear, and also a more profound, more
refined libertinage. . . . M. de Maupassant seems to me
to have the temperament and the taste of the French
conteurs of old; I imagine that had he lived at the time of
Louis XIV he would have told stories like those of La
Fontaine.

Some of the public's pleasure in Maupassant's tales
must have been due to this realization, made articulate
by Lemaître, that while the tales were new and modern,
they were not strange or discordant; that while they
were, as Zola said, "original," they were also in a great,
familiar French tradition.

Very quickly, this new, lighter style blending beautifully with his own temperament, Maupassant began to
use it also in stories that were not risqué; and soon not
only little comedies and farces, but also little tragedies,
dramas and satires were appearing at the rate of one a
week. They were presented in a variety of forms with
apparently equal ease: straight third-person narrative,
monologue, reminiscence, conversation, entries in a
diary, exchange of letters. Frames are absent, simple,
elaborate, or over-elaborate; consisting most frequently
of conversation at dinner in a house, a club, or a hunting
lodge; or perhaps at a funeral. Sentences flow, crackle,
glitter or sparkle, at the author's desire; characters make
their entrances gracefully, though often with a certain

daring and violence; they induce, suffer, or react violently
or subtly to situations from the most delicate to the
most baroque; and closings range from quiet fade-aways
to brutal shocks.

These stories, the direct outcome of the journalism so
despised by Flaubert, make it seem likely that not only
Flaubert's life, but also his death, contributed to Maupassant's maturing into artistic "manhood." Along with
the grief, which was certainly deep and sincere—after
Flaubert's death Maupassant was never again so close to
anyone, always excepting Laure—the foster-father's
disappearance must have brought with it a sense of
hitherto unknown independence. During his eleven-year
writing career Maupassant was to obey Flaubert and
produce a dozen or more tales "like" *Boule de Suif*. But
he was also to produce dozens more *unlike* it, many
of them very unlike it indeed, and numbers of them
considerably superior to it. And notable among the non-
Flaubertian traits which he developed were the rapidity
and ease with which he learned, from his work for the
Gaulois and the *Gil-Blas*, to write—a faculty which
resulted, when everything turned out well, in a fluidity
and freshness that make his style the perfect expression
of the extreme vivacity of his imagination. That Flaubert
himself possessed imaginative vivacity is evident from
his letters; but supreme as is Flaubert the artist, there is
nevertheless truth in the words of Henry James about his
novels that "it was as if he had covered them with
metallic plates." From the fiction of Maupassant, whatever its other faults may be, "metallic plates" are
delightfully, utterly absent.

Maupassant's shift from articles to stories was
amusingly described a few years later in the *Gaulois:*

A newspaper is like the ceremonial float of the great
Indian hero Rama—a float capacious as a city, filled with
people, almost a god itself. It makes its way through the
thickest crowds, and as it moves those aboard shoot
arrows. He is king among them who shoots his arrows the
farthest.

A sterile trade, surely! For all the arrows are lost.
Try to read a newspaper article six months after it has
appeared! Thus it was that Maupassant . . . had an
idea of the greatest good sense, consequently, an idea of
genius. He thought of writing short stories, not more than
two or two and a half columns long. These stories were
certainly "journalism," and yet at the same time they
were not. All he had to do, at the end of the year, was to
gather all these pieces together and have them bound up
in a volume. "I, a journalist? Indeed! I am a bird—see
my wings!" So La Fontaine put it, of old.*

That points up not only Maupassant's evolution, but
also the chief source of his financial prosperity, which was
now not long in coming: double sale—in newspapers and
in books. Volumes of short stories by living authors
were in those days free of the disfavor with which the
public regards them today; their sale was frequently
large; and quite apart from translations, which were to
become an ever-increasing source of revenue, Maupassant was handsomely paid twice over in his own
country for every tale he chose to reprint. There were
also special, illustrated editions of single stories or
collections of stories in volume form; and toward the end
of his life many of the stories were republished in the
Gil-Blas Sunday supplement, illustrated with the celebrated colored lithographs by Steinlen. An anecdote was
often the source of considerable income: first used as part
of a newspaper article, it would then be expanded into a

* Elémir Bourges, *op. cit.*

newspaper story, and then, if Maupassant thought the story capable of further possibilities, he would rewrite it and enrich it, republishing it (usually in the *other* newspaper) under some other title, or, under its old title but in its new form, in a volume.

The first such volume following *La Maison Tellier* was *Mademoiselle Fifi,* whose title story (first published in slighter form in the *Gil-Blas*), is so like *Boule de Suif* even in subject matter that the French makers of the motion-picture *Boule de Suif* had only to tack *Mademoiselle Fifi* onto it to get their required length. René Maizeroy, one of Maupassant's associates on the *Gaulois* and the *Gil-Blas*, wrote in his review of *Mademoiselle Fifi* that the author was

also himself in those stories which seem to date from the eighteenth century, and which combine the mocking, airy pirouette of that age, its subtle perfume of powder, the disdain (skin-deep only!) of its women, with a touch of truly modern Parisianism that seasons them like a pinch of red pepper in a cup of tea.

Next was *Contes de la Bécasse* (*Snipe-Shooting Stories*), of which Maupassant, asked by the publisher to write a blurb, said its particular distinction was its "gaiety and amusing irony." "Only two or three of the stories," he said—thus indicating where the public's Maupassant tastes had come to lie—"introduce a dramatic note into the collection."

And then, at the rate of two or even three a year came *Clair de Lune* (*Moonlight*), *Les Soeurs Rondoli* (*The Rondoli Sisters*), *Miss Harriet,* and the other famous little volumes that mention of Maupassant's name evokes, all of them illustrated, all of them selling largely in a dozen languages. Reasons of national prudery obliged

English and American readers to wait longer for some of
them than most of the rest of the world.

The raffishness of the *Gil-Blas* brought onto the scene
the famous Maupassant cuckolds: those husbands with
horns who are almost a Maupassant trademark.

In *Un Réveillon (Christmas Eve)*, the second story he
ever published in the *Gil-Blas*, Maupassant gave a comic
twist to his hitherto grimly serious destruction of father-
figures: a peasant grandfather who dies on Christmas
Eve is unceremoniously got out of the way by being put
into the bread-bin for the night, and the author's pleasure
in the indignity is reflected in the narrator's "laughing
till he cried." And in others of the first *Gil-Blas* stories
the cuckolds immediately appeared. Someone has said
that "a sound was audible in France in the 1880's—the
sound of husbands squirming as they read Maupassant";
and it was with their reading of those issues of the
Gil-Blas that their squirming began. A wife is cheerfully
ready to slay her cuckolded husband with a hatchet in
Marocca; in *La Bûche (The Burning Brand)* a husband is
saved from cuckoldry only by chance; a woman from the
provinces cuckolds her husband with a famous writer in
Une Aventure Parisienne.

More clearly than ever, the humiliation of Laure de
Maupassant is the general, underlying theme; but with
his cuckolds her son turns the tables; instead of lamenting her fate, he avenges her. Indeed, of all wronged wives
in the annals of literature, Laure is perhaps the most
voluminously and variously—farcically, comically, tragi-
cally—avenged: in her son's more than two hundred
stories, all manner of disasters happen to fathers; and as
for husbands, they are often brutes, knaves or fools—
and almost always cuckolds.

Two Maupassant stories of this time tell with particular eloquence how far he had by now advanced in his art.

His first mention of trying his hand at short stories had been in the letter to his mother from the ministry back in 1873: "To try to cheer myself up a little I have just written something in the style of Daudet's *Contes du Lundi.*" Now Daudet's *Contes du Lundi* contains Christmas stories; and if one compares with them the two excellent Christmas stories which Maupassant had professionally ready for his two newspapers at the end of 1882, a drama for the *Gaulois* (*Conte de Noël:* a possessed peasant woman is exorcized at midnight mass) and a farce for the *Gil-Blas* (*Nuit de Noël:* a plump lady guest behaves inconsiderately in a bachelor's bed), it is apparent to what extent he had left Daudet and everyone else behind and found himself.

CHAPTER 4

FIRST NOVEL: *UNE VIE*

About sixty Maupassant-Maufrigneuse short stories had appeared in the two newspapers, when on Monday, February 12, 1883, and for several days thereafter the *Gil-Blas* carried an announcement of a forthcoming lengthy attraction:

Immediately following M. Emile Zola's splendid novel, *Au Bonheur des Dames*, we shall publish:

UNE VIE

by

Guy de Maupassant

The young novelist is not unknown to our readers, who are proficient at lifting veils and who have not forgotten that *Mademoiselle Fifi* first appeared in this newspaper under a pseudonym.

In *Une Vie*, the first novel by M. Guy de Maupassant, which he wrote especially for the *Gil-Blas*, our contributor has depicted the life of the provincial gentry. It is the story of a woman, from the hour of her heart's awakening until her death.

Actually, when the first installment of *Une Vie* (*A Life*) appeared on the front page of the *Gil-Blas* on February 27, *Au Bonheur des Dames* (a novel about a department store) had not quite ended, and its last installments were relegated to an inner page, crowded off page one by the younger man's book. *Une Vie* does not carry its heroine to her death. And Maupassant had not written it "especially for the *Gil-Blas*": vague references to a novel are to be found in his correspondence over the previous several years, and there exists an incomplete old manuscript of *Une Vie* in primitive form which seems to date from 1878. Otherwise—as is the way with publishers' blurbs—the announcement of the novel was quite accurate.

As the installments succeeded one another, certain episodes were recognized by readers of the Maupassant-Maufrigneuse newspaper tales. Much as in *Le Saut du berger* (*Shepherd's Leap*), a short story which had appeared in the *Gil-Blas* a year before, an adulterous couple in *Une Vie* is pushed over a cliff in a shepherd's hut; and *La Veillée* (*The Vigil*), about the discovery of an old lady's love secret, and *Par un soir de printemps* (*A Spring Evening*), about a maiden aunt's emotion at the sight of young love, and several other *Gil-Blas* and *Gaulois* tales now made reappearances as episodes in *Une Vie*. Maupassant had extracted them from his novel for advance separate publication, and in doing so he had betrayed his as yet inadequately developed sense of some of the subtle but innate differences between long and short fiction: not one of those episodes makes a strong independent story, whereas, strengthened by their attachment to the rest of the text, they take their places well as portions of the novel. He learned quickly: of only one more novel was he to sell a few episodes separately.

The last installment appeared on April 6, and almost immediately the book was published. It bore a dedication to an old friend of Flaubert's: "To Madame Brainne,

homage from a friend who is devoted, and in memory of
a friend who is no more." Not only the dedication invokes
the memory of Flaubert: the style, the general plan and
the setting are all reminiscent of works by the master,
and instead of its actual subtitle, "The Humble Truth,"
Une Vie could bear that of *Madame Bovary: "Moeurs de
Province."* The class that Maupassant portrays is higher
in the social scale than Emma Bovary's, but one book is
as Norman as the other. Except for brief glimpses of
Paris and Corsica the entire action of *Une Vie* is confined
to Normandy. As the title indicates, there is no "plot."
After leaving her convent school, the heroine moves with
her parents from Rouen to an isolated old chateau; she
dreams of love and romance and marries a local vicomte;
he proves to be worthless, and she suffers a series of cruel
disillusionments; and she is last shown living modestly
(the chateau having been sold for debts), bringing up a
grandchild with her maid, who had been her *soeur de lait*
and her husband's mistress. By the time the reader
reaches the closing words—"Life, you see, is never as
good or as bad as one thinks"—he has been well drenched
in Norman rain, Norman sea air and Norman country
smells. Maupassant once told his valet that he had
written much of it—he perhaps meant that he had
thought it out—sitting in his boat off the Etretat cliffs,
with his dog Matho.

Just as stylistically and otherwise the book is so very
close to Flaubert, so thematically also it marks a retrogression from the most recent tales: it is the closest of all
Maupassant's writings to the facts of his mother's life, his
largest-scale straight depiction of humiliation. Jeanne in
the novel is a less intelligent, less intellectual, less independent Laure—a young woman of good Norman
family who does *not* insist on a separation, but allows her

husband to continue his humiliating escapades until he
has wrecked her life, the lives of others, and his own. (His
destruction, at the hands of a neighbor whom he has
cuckolded, is one of the most savage husband-father de-
structions in Maupassant.) But Jeanne is approximately
of Laure's generation, like Laure she travels to Corsica,
suffers nervous disorders and fainting spells, has *"un
coeur égoiste de mère"* and loses her religious beliefs. Her
maltreatment by her son Paul is a reference to Guy's
younger brother Hervé,* and her home, the Chateau des
Peuples, is Miromesnil. Maupassant made two pilgrim-
ages to his probable birthplace while he was writing *Une
Vie.* He had no memory of it, but he recognized the background value of the picturesque old mansion, and besides, to visit the scene of sufferings as legendary (for
him) as Laure's, must have been an emotional bath, a
source of enrichment to his creation.

Maupassant's retrogression, in *Une Vie,* to earlier
stylistic and thematic levels than he had reached in recent short fiction (in the novel there are even retrogres-
sions to the early imitation of Daudet) was the result of
the strain imposed by this first experience with the longer
form; the heroine's simplified character and the lack of
plot also indicate his need to make things as easy for
himself as possible in the unfamiliar undertaking; and
within those self-imposed limitations the book can be
said to succeed. It is always alive, and the grace and
charm of its movement bring to mind the silvery, green-
ery-bowered flow of some shining Norman stream.

The book had the ironic good fortune (ironic because
of all Maupassant's works it is the most sympathetic
portrayal of suffering virtue) to run into censor trouble.
A critic in the *Revue Bleue* warned the public, in his re-

* For Hervé de Maupassant see page 278 et. seq.

view, that although *Une Vie* contained many charming pages which a mother might safely show her daughter, the book as a whole could not be recommended for family reading; and the publishing and bookselling firm of Hachette, which had the monopoly of the bookstalls in French railway stations, refused to stock it. Against this private censorship, potentially so disastrous to any author, Maupassant composed a strong petition to the Chamber of Deputies which was published in the *Figaro* and aroused comment in other journals.

And thus we ask you, gentlemen [the petition ended], in the name of simple liberty, liberty of thought, that this monopoly be destroyed; that the railway stations once again become public places not subjected to any moral control whatever, so that as travelers we may be able to buy the publications that appeal to our tastes, so that as authors our books may be sold there exactly as elsewhere, without distinctions and categories.

Such arbitrary action by a "eunuch in an office at Hachette's," Maupassant wrote Zola, was worse than the old governmental system of the *estampille*, or official licencing of books, which the Republic had abandoned. With Georges Clémenceau, then deputy for Paris, he went to the Chamber of Deputies and discussed the matter privately with Reynal, Minister of Public Works, whose jurisdiction included the railroads. When no progress was made, he wrote a long letter to the *Figaro* on the legal aspects of the question, and finally the petition, signed by about twenty writers, was presented to the Chamber and there briefly discussed on May 28, with some of the titillation proper to such occasions:

Minister Reynal: It is true that Hachette has refused to sell M. de Maupassant's novel.

[Cries of "*Ah! Ah!*" from the floor.]

Deputy Lorois: Do not read us any extracts!

Minister Reynal: Gentlemen, the Chamber need not be alarmed. I shall not express an opinion concerning the refusal to sell this book. It is not my function to investigate whether Hachette has acted properly or improperly. I shall be all the more impartial since I will confess to the Chamber that I have not read the book, but have merely been shown certain passages, which are indelicate, to put it mildly. But M. Hachette, with whom I discussed the question unofficially when I was endeavoring to act as friendly intermediary between the parties, told me that he felt himself bound to exercise a certain caution, that very often he received complaints from heads of families concerning the books carried by the station bookstalls.*

Following that bland lead by the Minister, and after a certain amount of "*hilarité générale*," the Chamber voted 334 to 116 not to act; and the matter of *Une Vie* and Hachette was dropped. (Hachette to this day has the monopoly on the sale of books in French railway stations.) But considerable publicity had been obtained, including an amusing set of humorous verses in a magazine,† and sales were satisfactory. An English translation was immediately made, and others followed.

Une Vie has never lacked for appreciative readers. Tolstoy declared it to be "perhaps the best French novel since *Les Misérables*," and said that in it Maupassant was "a serious man whose gaze penetrated deep into life." A few years ago it was consecrated by a group of French writers consisting of André Gide, Jean Giraudoux, Edmond Jaloux, François Mauriac and André Maurois, who placed it on their list of "France's ten greatest novels."

* *Annales de la Chambre des Députés*, 1883, page 473.
† See Note 8: "Silvius" in *La Jeune France*, page 404.

For *Une Vie* Maupassant received from the *Gil-Blas* eight thousand gold francs. If he were to present them at a French bank today (1948–49), he would receive approximately 1,670,000 present-day French paper francs. And if he were able to exchange that sum for American currency at the legal rate, it would bring him today approximately $5,500. That payment was for newspaper publication only (figures for royalties from the volume are not available), and it will serve as a gauge of some of his other earnings. His royalties were forty centimes a copy on the first two thousand copies of each of his books, and one franc a copy thereafter. (His contracts were for six years only, and he retained the right to bring out special illustrated or de-luxe editions whenever he wished, with any publisher of his choice. For a de-luxe edition of five hundred copies he asked two thousand francs.) The Russian translation of *Une Vie* brought him two thousand francs. A long short story in a newspaper brought him at least fifteen hundred francs, and a short article five hundred. Small though the amounts may seem today, they enabled him to lead a life of considerable luxury. With *Une Vie* appearing at a time when he was publishing at least a story a week, and articles besides, he was busy and prospering.

Two months after the book publication of *Une Vie*, there appeared the volume of collected short stories called *Contes de la Bécasse*, and four of these were dedicated to Maupassant's young collaborators on *Les Soirées de Médan*—Huysmans, Hennique, Céard and Alexis. The dedications were a kind of farewell. "It would be most unpleasant for me to appear in a volume signed by several names," Maupassant told a publisher who shortly before *Une Vie* had asked him to contribute to an an-

thology; and just as he now felt himself above, or at
least beyond, literary collaboration, he had no urge to
continue seeing the men with whom he had made his
debut. Even Zola he was to see little of from now on:
his sparse correspondence with him consists chiefly of
apologies for unpaid visits. And as for the others: *"Cher
maître et ami,"* he wrote Zola the next year, "I am full
of remorse, terrible remorse. Here I have been back in
Paris two months, and haven't found time to come see
you at Médan. . . . Nor have I had time to see Huysmans or Céard. I have seen Hennique, and Alexis I ran
into very late one night, on the street. . . ."

Except for Huysmans, none of the other young contributors to the *Soirées* was ever to display any considerable degree of creative originality in literature; and even
Huysmans, despite his interesting evolution, was to remain a very limited literary artist—and a ministry employee for thirty years. Maupassant's destiny differed
from theirs.

CHAPTER 5

PROSTITUTES, ACTRESSES, LITTLE WORKING GIRLS, AND WOMEN OF THE WORLD

THEY WENT THERE every night about eleven, as to a café. They were always the same six or eight, not rakes, but respectable men, merchants and younger men of the town; and they drank their chartreuse, teasing the girls a little, or talked of serious things with Madame, who was universally respected. Then they went home to bed before midnight. Occasionally the younger men stayed on.

Those opening sentences of *La Maison Tellier* are a reminder that visits to brothels, until recently in France as legally and freely accessible as cafés, did not necessarily always mean "business." In the speakeasy French brothel of today, as always in England and America, the casual dropper-in is less welcome; but in those days a visit could very well be, and frequently was, a merely sociable pastime, a genial, only mildly erotic hour's distraction from the humdrum and the respectable. Maupassant was well acquainted with this casual role often played by brothels and prostitutes, and as a writer he was adept at describing it. But it was not the role that they principally played in his own life.

For several years following his arrival in Paris, the

years of his greatest fair-weather activity among the
riverside Mimis and Ninis, he had remained in his dingy,
gloomy, ground-floor, courtyard room on the lower slopes
of Montmartre, 2 rue Moncey. It was so small that
guests, upon arrival, were handed folding chairs which
were at other times kept in a closet; and about the time
of his change of ministry he moved into two rooms and
kitchen in the same neighborhood, 17 rue Clauzel. (There
is a commemorative plaque on the *next* house, number 19:
plaques often go astray.) Here his guests met a different
reception. When they rang his bell, doors throughout the
house were flung open and more or less charming voices
called down the stairs inviting the visitors up: apart from
Maupassant the place was inhabited exclusively by prostitutes. With them he was on cordial and familiar terms,
calling them his seraglio, and it was among them that he
wrote *Boule de Suif*. With its success and his engagement
by the *Gaulois* he changed neighborhoods, moving to a
larger apartment with a cook at 83 rue Dulong, which
commanded an extensive view of railroad tracks. (The
choice of location seems odd: perhaps he made it because
the trains he saw were the trains serving his beloved
Normandy, leaving and approaching the Gare Saint
Lazare!) During his stay in Sartrouville, a friend records,
a happy quartet set out from Maupassant's house one
evening, treated most of the villagers to drinks at a café,
and about midnight left by skiff for Saint-Germain,
where they stayed until dawn in "a local Maison Tellier."
In the spring of 1883, when Maupassant had written
Une Vie and was Tolstoy's "serious man whose gaze
penetrated deep into life," there appeared in the *Gil-Blas*
a rollicking Maufrigneuse article about a four-day rowing
trip with a friend down the Seine from Paris to Rouen,
which also ended in a brothel. Later, even after Maupas-

sant had moved away from the railroad tracks into a
fashionable quarter, as he was soon to do following the
success of *Une Vie*, and accompanied this move with a
corresponding change in the character of many of his
associates, persons close to him tell of his continued frequenting of prostitutes, and of one of his more prolonged
relationships being with a waitress in a sordid restaurant.

In a scene from another Maupassant story, *Un Fils*
(*A Son*), a senator and an academician are discussing
human seed under a laburnam tree, whose golden pollen
is being blown through the air about them:

"Ah, my dear fellow," the senator said, "if you had
to make a list of your children you would be hard put
to it. This tree here breeds its children without effort,
abandons them without remorse, and concerns itself
with them not at all."

The academician replied, "We do the same, my
friend."

"Oh, I don't deny that we sometimes abandon them,"
the senator said, "but at least we are conscious of doing
so. That constitutes our superiority."

But the other shook his head. "No, I mean something
quite different. There is scarcely a man who is not the
father of children of whose very existence he is ignorant,
children whose birth certificates read 'father unknown,'
children he has engendered almost without knowing it,
like this tree. If we had to make a total of the women
we have possessed, you'll agree that we should be as
perplexed as this laburnam tree if it were asked to list
its descendants. Between the ages of eighteen and forty,
if we include passing encounters, contacts of an hour,
we'd have to admit to having had intimate relations
with two or three hundred. . . ."

The mention of those figures—high, low, or normal
as they may strike the reader—probably gave Maupassant a malicious pleasure, in indicating his estimate of

the degree of hypocrisy represented by the ultra-respectable academic and senatorial façades of his characters: *Un Fils* is an utterly serious story, devoid of any hint of farce or burlesque, and he clearly considered the figures realistic. And since his own frequent boasts of being outside any definition of respectability in such matters are more credible than most people's, the figures also provide a faint indication of the size of the throng of women in Maupassant's life. "Never shall I be able to understand that two women aren't better than one, three better than two, and ten better than three," he wrote in a preface to a colleague's book. In an article, he advised an imaginary young friend:

"When you've had enough of a woman, why—keep her."
"Keep her? But what about her successor?"
"Keep them all!"

"I feel myself incapable of loving one woman," says a character in the story *Lui* (*Him*), "because I shall always love the others too much. I wish I had a thousand arms, a thousand lips and a thousand—temperaments, in order to be able to embrace, at one and the same time, an army of these charming and unimportant creatures." And a person long close to Maupassant has described his feminine company as "flocking into his homes through the windows and through the doors."

Such promiscuity might seem on first view to amount to a taking over of his father's way of life, to a betrayal of his mother; actually, the promiscuity and the degradation in his life are as great a tribute to Laure as the cuckoldries and the father-destructions in his fiction—or rather, they *are* the tribute, of which the stories are but an expression. His is the classic situation of excessive

mother-adoration forcing a young man to go to inferiors
for the satisfaction of his sensual needs. Because of the
incest-taboo * these needs seem too gross to be associated
with anyone comparable to her in class, refinement or
"virtue"; but while all his sensuality goes to the one
type, all his tenderness remains with the other; and unable to find complete gratification anywhere, he keeps
seeking it everywhere and always, in a series of encounters that are like a child's ceaseless questioning. In Maupassant's case the situation was aggravated by Laure's
complete marital dissatisfaction (which was doubtless
partially the result of the French system of arranged
marriages), by the sound of Laure's laments and recrimi-
nations. For him, marriage was unthinkable because of
her; and his drive to injure the man who had first possessed and then betrayed her resulted in his great pro-
pensity to cuckold others. Maupassant's cuckoldings
were by no means confined to his stories. "I am in Rouen,
but not alone," he wrote Robert Pinchon from a hotel
room, in the midst of a typical adventure. "Don't tell
anyone of my being here. Everything has to be very
mysterious, for she has a troublesome husband." For
Maupassant, the existence of a husband was all but pre-
requisite to an enjoyable affair. "The wife didn't please
me particularly," a character reminisces in *La Porte* (*The
Door*), "but her husband's probable jealousy was a great
temptation"; and throughout Maupassant's life there are
husbands in the background.

Maupassant was well aware that the kinds of love
which he was able to experience were, despite his joyous
escapades, fundamentally inadequate; as we shall see,

* Maupassant is one of the rare writers to have written a story not only
portraying but defending an incestuous relationship that is conscious on one
side—*Monsieur Jocaste*, which appeared in the *Gil-Blas* in 1883 but was not
reprinted in a volume until after his death.

even the hand-pressings, deep looks and grand passions against fashionable backgrounds depicted in his later work are indications of his dissatisfaction. There was a human relationship that he did not know; and on this score his writings are full of his unrest and confusion.

If the French Academy really wished to be useful to humanity, he suggests in one of his articles, it would offer a prize of five thousand francs for the best treatise on how to "break decently, properly, politely, without noise, scene or violence, with a woman who adores you and with whom you are fed up." "Do you know what I'd do in your place?" he asks elsewhere of a young friend whom he is advising on how to rid himself of an unwanted, aging mistress. "What I am going to tell you is infamous, but everything is permissible in self-defense. I should try to make her pregnant, if that is still possible at her time of life. She'd be so furious that she might leave you." Constantly in his articles as in his stories he proclaims the incompatability of love and marriage; the inevitability of being cuckolded and the futility of a husband's taking offense; * the absurdity of considering marriage a serious matter as far as the affections are concerned— "As to fidelity, as to constancy, *quelle folie!*" "Love, simple love that attaches two people one to the other is too bourgeois, too reasonable, too common, humanly speaking, in short, too stupid, for those privileged beings, the poets. They need more. They cannot be satisfied with the *little* that love is." And he announces: "Spring is officially with us. Odious season, ruined by that scourge known as lovers! Blessed season, bringing that divine bounty known as spring vegetables!"

Only one of all his stories, *Le Bonheur* (*Happiness*),

---

* Did dread of cuckoldom play a role in Maupassant's perennial bachelorhood? No one knew better than he the extent of the danger.

shows a marriage happy in the fullest sense that includes mutual fidelity; and four years after its original publication he rewrote it, first adding a touch of scorn for the woman who had found such complete happiness in her husband, and then allowing her to discover that it had been an illusion—he had long been betraying her. She kills herself: so ends the single Maupassant example of a perfect marriage. Of the sexual act he writes according to his mood either voluptuously and in glorification or with disgust, using the scornful *inter urinas et faeces* reflection of theologians concerning the position of the genital organs. A woman's awakening to sexual pleasure, her sexual enjoyment, is to him as important as a man's, and he considers it a subject as appropriate as any other for repeated literary treatment, from the seriousness with which he handles it in *Une Vie* to the comedy of *Enragée?* (*Mad Dog?*) in which a young bride diagnoses her bewildering new physical sensations as the results of a dog-bite. Maupassant was a "good lover" in that sense of the term. And yet his stories, abounding in physical consideration for women and in other tributes, abound also, at this period of his life when he was producing so much of his best work, in brutality, in savage attacks on women, the result of his constant frustration in his search for satisfaction and his frequenting of the kind of woman whom he could only despise. Maupassant, the writer of fiction, is usually able to keep his obsessions from running away with him to the detriment of his art; or, to put it more properly, it is, of course, his obsessions plus his art which make the best tales the masterpieces they are. Occasionally, however, the brutality, instead of remaining inherent in characters and situations, becomes gratuitous, and the reader becomes uncomfortable, as in *Le Verrou* (*The Lock*):

It was a dinner of bachelors, hardened old bachelors. They had inaugurated the strange feast twenty years before, baptizing it "The Celibates' Dinner." They were then fourteen, definite in their resolution never to take a wife. Now four remained. Three were dead, the other seven married.

These four had held firm; and to the extent that was in their power they scrupulously obeyed the rules laid down at the time of the founding of their curious association. Placing hand in hand, they had sworn to turn from what is known as the straight and narrow path all the women they could, especially their friends' wives, most especially the wives of their most intimate friends. Also, it was their duty to indulge, at each of their dinners, in mutual confession, recounting their latest adventures with all details, names, and the most precise information. Whence an expression they commonly used: "To lie like a bachelor." Furthermore, they professed the most complete scorn for woman, whom they considered a mere animal for their pleasure. They constantly quoted Schopenhauer, their god; they longed for the reestablishment of harems and medieval keeps; and on the table linen used at their dinners they had embroidered the ancient precept *Mulier perpetuus infans*, and beneath it the line from Alfred de Vigny: *La femme, enfant malade et douze fois impure.*

Elsewhere he quotes Rousseau, Byron, and Herbert Spencer against women, and the pessimism that infuses so much of his work is surely in part the result of his hopeless, frequently disheartening quest.

When, however, he came upon a woman who combined some of Laure's refinement with other qualities, qualities of a non-intimidating kind—an invitingly free-and-easy manner, or a reputation for being willing to embark on adventures—Maupassant could be gallant and charming. Such a woman was Madame Bizet, the delightful and witty widow of the composer of *Carmen*,

daughter of Fromental Halévy, composer of *La Juive,*
and later one of Proust's models for the Duchesse de
Guermantes. Madame Bizet had something of the name
of a *coureuse,* and although she probably never became
for Maupassant anything "more than a friend" (in 1887
she married his lawyer, Emile Straus), it was not for lack
of gallant trying on his part:

Madame, would it not occasionally be possible for me
to call on you at times other than your regular hours for
receiving friends? If you find this request displeasing, tell
me; I will not take offense. At bottom it is a very modest
one, and its only fault lies in its not being made in verse.
Is it not natural to ask to see more often, and to see
alone, for the sake of acuter pleasure, the better to savor
their charm and their grace, women under whose spell
one has come?

The day and the hours for everybody are not to be
borne, for the constant expectation of others half spoils
one's pleasure. The door is a menace, the bell a torture.
I like to come when I know that I alone am expected,
that I alone am to be paid attention to and listened to,
that only I, that day, shall find my hostess beautiful and
charming. And I do not stay too long, I promise.

You will doubtless think that you still know me very
slightly, and that I am quick to claim the privileges of
intimacy? What would be the purpose of my waiting
longer? Why should I? I know your charm now, and I
know now how much I love the nature of your mind and
how much more I shall love it every day. These are not
compliments, but simple facts. It remains to be seen
what you think, what you will reply. Concerning this,
one request. If I bore you, if you foresee that I shall bore
you, if you feel that it would be mere politeness and the
desire to be kind that would determine you to grant me
what I ask, I prefer that you tell me or let me know that
I am, or would become, intrusive.

I consider (in prose) that a woman is a *sovereign,* with
the right to do only what she wishes, to obey all her

caprices, impose all her fancies, and tolerate nothing that
would be a burden or a bore.

Few men capable of writing such a letter would also
express themselves as in the passage from *Le Verrou:* but
the erotic core of Maupassant's personality was particularly convoluted, and it had tentacles that reached in all
directions.

In one of his letters to Zola, apologizing for not coming to see him, Maupassant wrote: "I have had to turn
out so much copy to pay for a house that I've built in
Etretat that I really couldn't find two hours." This new
house at Etretat, a gay little half-timbered affair with
yellow plaster and red shutters that he was dissuaded
from calling La Maison Tellier and called, instead, La
Guillette (Guy's House), takes its place along with the
success of *Une Vie* and the volumes of stories, and the
avoidance of Zola and the other Médanistes, as marking
Maupassant's transition from one way of life to another.

Other such events are his hiring of a valet, and his
move, the following spring, out of his flat overlooking the
railroad tracks to the ground floor of a house built by his
cousin Louis Le Poittevin (who occupied the other floors,
the top floor being his studio) at 10 rue de Montchanin,
near the fashionable Parc Monceau and Place Malesherbes.

All these can be considered symptoms of his principal
desire of the time, a desire which he describes in his
article offering advice to a young friend: "After running
about in the streets and among the women of the streets,
you began to feel the desire we have all felt—the desire
for *amours plus élégants.*" Similarly in the story *Imprudence,* a young husband, pressed by his wife to speak of

his pre-marital affairs, tells her that they were with four kinds of women—*filles, actrices, petites ouvrières,* and *femmes du monde* (prostitutes, actresses, working girls and women of the world), a gradual ascent in the social scale. The hero of Maupassant's next novel, *Bel-Ami,* was to feel embarrassment when one of the elegant ladies he had recently met asked to come to his flat (which, like the author's, looked over the railroad tracks): "He felt himself blushing. 'It's just that it's . . . very modest,' he said, 'where I live.' " Maupassant's own move was so inspired.

His valet, who came to him, recommended by his tailor, during his last months near the railroad tracks, was a young Belgian named François Tassart, who combined independence of spirit (he refused to enter Maupassant's service until the requirement that he wear livery was withdrawn) with a stylized and attentive *serviabilité* that deepened over the years into adoration. The memoirs which he later wrote of his master are prefaced with the words:

All great minds have been unanimous in proclaiming M. de Maupassant a *Master among literary men;* I, very humble, who have lived long years at his side, knew him better than anyone else, and I am taking the liberty, with all the sincerity of my heart, of publishing these few modest memories in order that it may be known that my Master, who has been recognized as a *Man of great talent,* was something better: for he was in the supreme degree *Good, Just and Loyal.**

Early in his memoirs, François tells of how very quickly, after being engaged, he was drawn into participation in his master's adventures. Almost immediately

---

* See Note 9: The Memoirs of François Tassart, page 406.

they went to Etretat, to spend ten days at the newly
completed La Guillette:

The second day of our visit, about seven o'clock in
the evening, I took a lantern and accompanied my master
to the garden gate. A carriage soon arrived. Out of it
stepped a lady, enveloped in wraps. Monsieur took her
hand and we returned to the house, I walking backwards
and giving them as much light as possible with my lantern. In the antichamber my master relieved the lady
of a whole series of shawls. He was very attentive and
courteous, and I noticed how very charming his way of
speaking could be when he wished. When they were at
the end of their dinner I went to the kitchen, where the
cook had a meal ready for herself and for me. "Well?"
she demanded. "Is the lady beautiful or isn't she?" I
replied laughing, "She certainly is; and she has the manner of an empress." "Don't laugh," Désirée told me,
seriously. "That lady was Napoleon's mistress; everyone
in Etretat knows it. Napoleon was mad about her and
gave her a title. She has her arms engraved on all her
jewels, on everything she owns." At ten o'clock the carriage returned, once again I took my lantern and accompanied Monsieur and his guest. My master got into
the carriage with her, saying, "Don't wait up for me. I
have my key."

Any uncertainty as to what it meant in those days for
a lady to dine alone with a gentleman in his home can be
dissipated by a reading of Edith Wharton's *House of
Mirth;* in accompanying his guest to *her* home, Maupassant was but dotting an i. It was considered daring even
to invite an unattached lady to come with others, as is
made clear in another of his letters of about this time to
Madame Bizet:

Madame: would it be very improper of me to ask
you to dine at my house next Saturday with the Porto-
Riches who have accepted, with Meilhac who has also

said yes, and perhaps with Straus to whom I am now writing?

I know that it is not usual for a lady to dine in the home of a bachelor. But I cannot see why it should be at all shocking if the guests include other women, whom she knows. And then if I were to show you the list of ladies who have dined with me in Cannes, in Etretat, or here, you would see that it is long, and *full of distinguished names! ! ! !*

So, you would make me very happy, Madame, by accepting; and I promise not to send an "echo" of this dinner to the *Gil-Blas.*

To the person in charge of the *Gil-Blas* "echoes," Baron Ludovic de Vaux, Maupassant had occasion to write as soon as he and François returned from Etretat:

Thanks for the warning. Don't let the item appear. It was indeed I at Triel, but I wasn't with a "white negress." I was with two white women. You know one of them by name, the one I ran into there by chance. I will tell you who she is. Incidentally, one of your recent items got me into serious trouble. I don't mind when you write only about me; but this one involved a woman, and everything almost went wrong. I'll tell you what it was all about when we meet.

And François (noting that at this time as many as seventeen dinner invitations poured in on his master in one day) records another episode:

On December 15 I was looking at a calendar when my master opened the door of the salon. His face was cloudy. The night before he had gone to a party at the home of some Highness and had brought a lady home with him, a foreigner, reddish blonde, not pretty, but young and quite appetizing. After lunch she left, but not for long; at four o'clock she was back. She had to wait for him until six, and then at seven-thirty she left again, for my Master was dining out. The next morning at nine she reappeared. That lasted four days, at the end of which my master said: "Do whatever you want to with her—I don't want to see her again. She keeps telling me that she's leaving for Vienna, but she always comes back. *Kick* her out, if you have to."

Later that same winter, while he was in Cannes visiting Laure and Hervé, a lady sent him from Paris a gift of half a dozen dolls dressed as widows—doubtless to indicate the number of bereft intimates whom he had left behind; and he returned them to her after stuffing old handkerchiefs under their clothes—giving them, as François notes, "a very prominent abdomen, which would leave no doubt as to their interesting condition"— and accompanying them with a note saying "All in one night!"

Early in the spring (1884) he and François returned to Paris and moved into the new apartment in Louis Le Poittevin's house, and then in June they went to Etretat, to spend their first season in La Guillette. There was a study with door-panels painted by Louis, poplars had been planted, and an apple orchard, a strawberry bed, vegetable and flower gardens and lawns for bowls and croquet; there were goldfish, chickens, dogs, cats, and a parrot, Jacquot, who was trained to greet ladies by shrieking, "*Bonjour, petite cochonne!*"

Here, between June and October, while Maupassant was working on *Bel-Ami*, can be glimpsed a few of the figures in the parade of *amours plus élégants* that was from now on to pass through his life. Only glimpses can be had: Maupassant was discreet about his guests.

First, because she was the first occupant of the guest-room at La Guillette, there was Blanche Roosevelt.

Blanche was an American who had come abroad to Milan to study singing [Frank Harris tells us in *My Life*]; she was extraordinarily good looking, a tall, well-made blonde with masses of red-gold hair and classically perfect features. . . . She wrote a novel in English called *The Copper Queen*, and on the strength of it talked of herself as a *femme de lettres* and artist. She evidently knew Maupassant very well indeed and was much liked by him. . . .

Her full name was Blanche Roosevelt Tucker Macchetta, Marchesa d'Alligri; and the Marchese, whom she had married in Milan, had somehow acquired the habit of remaining in the distance. She studied singing in France for a time with Pauline Viardot, Turgenev's beloved, and it was perhaps through Turgenev that Maupassant met her.

François describes his master, before Blanche's arrival at La Guillette that summer of 1884, "listing with a meticulousness worthy of an expert housekeeper the things the guest-room still needed: powder, perfume, triple mirror, pin-cushion"; and the valet quickly took a liking to the American beauty's free and easy ways. "She was as intelligent as she was beautiful," he says. " 'Come in, François, and put the tray on the table,' she encouraged him one morning when the maid who usually served her had failed to arrive and he stood respectfully on the threshold with her breakfast. 'It's quite all right; I'm covered with bedclothes.' "

The Marchesa had been born at Sandusky, Ohio, and brought up at LaCrosse in the new state of Wisconsin (her father had been Wisconsin's first senator to Washington). After studying in Italy she had made her debut as Violetta in *La Traviata* at Covent Garden, but her voice was too small for grand opera, and she subsequently

appeared in both England and the states as Josephine in
Pinafore and as Mabel in *The Pirates of Penzance*. Some
of her friends called her Pandora, for she had attempted,
not very successfully, to produce Longfellow's *Masque of
Pandora* as an opera comique in New York. She met the
poet, however, and spent some time with him and his
family at their Massachusetts seaside home in Nahant;
and it was apparently he who had turned her to literature. The year before she occupied Maupassant's guest-
room she had published *The Home Life of Henry W. Longfellow*, in which the poet was displayed drinking a toast
to the absent Marchese, describing his own inability,
for moral reasons, to finish reading *La Dame aux
Camélias*, and declaring of Alfred de Musset, "As a
student I read, but as a God-fearing man I lament."
Everything about the authors of *The Masque of Pandora*
and *La Maison Tellier* would seem to be richer in differences than in similarities; but the authoress, who had
visited Etretat before, found a likeness in their surroundings:

> Etretat, on the coast of Normandy, is not unlike
> Nahant in its retirement and natural beauty. We miss
> in our American resort the enormous *falaises* (cliffs)
> that clasp the French village in their embrace and stand
> boldly out to sea. . . . Nahant, without the cliffs, is
> none the less inviting, and although the tableau is dif-
> ferent, its quaint grace still reminds one of Etretat.

The tableau is indeed different—Etretat without its
cliffs would be far from being Etretat at all—and it is
easy to understand why a contemporary American
literary gossip-columnist should have recorded that "The
critics are poking no end of fun at the silly book about
Longfellow."

But Blanche was splendid—when she was seventeen

Victor Hugo called her "the beauty and genius of the
New World"—and she was indeed wonderfully beautiful.
Browning is supposed to have said, "What a pity Raph-
ael is not living to see her! There would be a new Ma-
donna!" And Arsène Houssaye, in a tribute which
Blanche graciously allowed to be printed as a preface to
a book she wrote on Gustave Doré, described her as

lovely with every loveliness; her fair hair rippling with
sunshine; her blue eyes as deep as the sky beneath their
dark lashes; tall, slight and supple as a reed; her profile
one that might have been designed by Apelles or Zeuxis.

She was dynamic—after her death in her forties (she
was killed in a carriage accident in Monte Carlo) a
member of the New York Women's Press Club wrote
that "a more fascinating woman I never came in contact
with, and if she had lived in this country she would have
been an inspiration to all thinking American women.
Madame Macchetta was an indefatigable worker and
always declared that her best thoughts came after
midnight." And her book on Victorien Sardou bore as a
motto one of her own poems:

> *Some lives in peaceful meadows flow;*
> *Like brook that steals from hidden glen,*
> *Their tranquil days ebb to and fro,*
> *Their actions " 'scape the mark of men."*
> *Far more would I the fiercest strife*
> *Engage, and strike for good or ill;*
> *Who has not warred knows naught of life:*
> *Fate conquers man, man fate through will.*

Blanche's first novel appeared in New York the year
of her first visit to La Guillette: *Stage-Struck; or, She
Would be an Opera Singer*, dedicated to "Uncle Ferdinand" (F. C. Roosevelt, of Fort Benton, Montana)

and depicting the sufferings and miserable end of a girl
from LaCrosse who made the mistake of going to Europe
to study music. In addition to other novels and the books
on Doré and Sardou, she wrote letters from Europe,
chiefly on musical subjects, to the *Chicago Times*, and
books on Elizabeth of Roumania (Carmen Sylva) and
Verdi. In an article for Oscar Wilde's magazine, *The
Woman's World*, she wrote in 1889 the first description of
Maupassant and his homes in English:

M. de Maupassant lives in Paris with his cousin, De
Poitevin [sic], a fine landscape-painter, at No. 10, Rue
[de] Montchanin, Quartier Malesherbes. His house is
charming, luxurious, and artistic. While the exterior is
very simple, the interior is a wilderness of Genoese
tapestries, Louis XV furniture, sculptured cabinets, and
rare porcelain. In the drawing-room are an admirable
head of Flaubert, some charming Normandy studies
by M. de Poitevin, well-lined bookshelves, and an immense bear-skin, which stretches its white length over
the entire parquet. Beyond are the poet's bed-chamber, a
splendid but sombrely furnished apartment, and, further
on, a sort of writing-room and conservatory in one—a
perfect museum of rare and interesting objects; amongst
others, the author's MSS., piles of autograph letters
from some of the greatest living and dead celebrities,
and a magnificent statue of Buddha, representing the
high priest of this religion with so benign an aspect that,
were the original at all like the effigy, none could resist
being a follower of this teacher and faith. Our author's
favorite home is Etretat, the well-known sea-side resort
in Normandy.

In personal appearance Guy de Maupassant is of
medium height, solid, well-built, and has the bearing of a
soldier; he has a fine characteristic Norman head, with
the straight line from neck to crane which we see in the
medallions of the old Conquest warriors; his forehead is
low, rather too heavily lined; and his hair, brown and

wavy, is now combed straight back in the fashion of the
modern Roman youth. In short, M. de Maupassant has
such a look of cheeriness that he reminds one of a clear
autumn day—an agreeable harmony in russet colours
and russet tints: dark brown laughing eyes, a shapely
mouth, half concealed by a heavy brown moustache, an
olive skin mantled with red and a general healthy
ruddiness, give this character and warmth to his physi-
ognomy. In France they call him a "très joli garçon,"
and I presume he might pass for that anywhere. With all
that, one is most pleased with the expression of his countenance, which indicates simplicity, intelligence, and
great good-nature. Dress this gentleman in a tweed
suit—do not start!—also of russet tints, and you will see
him as he stands on the balcony of La Guillette, or as I
saw him one summer day at the gate, waiting for a friend
who was coming down the road to the cottage. "La
Guillette," the name "Guy" feminised, is a pretty place,
and the author has made it a delightful residence. Here
he spends several months in each year, and here he has
written the greater number of his books.

Blanche's inauguration of the guest-room at La
Guillette is only the first of her appearances. François
tells of her talking with Maupassant on one occasion
about "how hard it almost always is for two people to get
along well together when they love each other completely
—you know what I mean—two people able to give each
other the maximum of sensual pleasure. Once that happens, an abyss immediately opens between them." And,
a few years later, "my master sent me to get news of this
lady in the Hotel Meyerbeer, at the Rond-Point des
Champs Elysées. A groom took me to her room; I was
scarcely on her doorsill when she cried, 'Come in,
François, come in! Come close; you know I'm not silly
about such things. Tell me all about your master—you'll
never weary me with that subject.' " She was in bed

again, this time resting before a serious operation; Maupassant had spent the afternoon with her two days before; and now she told the valet how greatly she loved his master. " 'You know,' she said, 'I don't love him merely as a writer, I love him for himself: as we say in my country, "for his good heart, for his extreme loyalty, and his great kindness." Be sure to tell him that if I don't come out of the chloroform my last thought will be of him.' "

Happily Blanche did emerge from her chloroform, radiant as ever, and we shall meet her again.

Unlike the footloose Blanche, who came and went, Hermine Lecomte du Nouy occupied her own tiny villa, La Bicoque (The Shanty) behind the Etretat casino.

She was the daughter of Eugène-Stanislas Oudinot, an artist in stained glass, who designed and made windows for the Parisian churches of Sainte-Clothilde, Saint-Augustin and the Trinité (there is a small window by him in La Guillette), and she was a woman of cultivation and large acquaintance; but like Laure—with whom she alone among Maupassant's women friends seems to have been on terms of friendship—she considered herself not strong (she suffered heart attacks), and she preferred largely to forego the strenuous pleasures of Paris and to spend most of the year in the country, devoting herself to her young son. Her husband, an architect, spent only about a month a year in Etretat; the rest of the time he lived in Roumania, where he was a favorite at the court of the literary queen—the same Carmen Sylva written about by Blanche.

In *Decoré* (*Decorated*), one of his cuckold tales, Maupassant tells of a member of the Chamber of Deputies

who rewards his mistress's obliging husband by securing
for him the cross of the Legion of Honor; and it is amusing to find in Maupassant's correspondence a letter to
the Minister of Foreign Affairs on the same subject:

Monsieur le Ministre, I am writing you on behalf of
M. André Lecomte du Nouy, a French architect employed during the past several years by the Roumanian
government for the execution of important artistic
projects. The King of Roumania, through your minister
to Bucharest, M. de C. . . ., has recently requested that
M. Lecomte de Nouy be awarded the cross of the Legion
of Honor. It would be unbecoming of me to put forward
the qualifications of this artist and scholar, who is the
greatest living authority on byzantine architecture and
who has restored in a manner gloriously flattering to
French pride the most beautiful monuments of that style
in the Roumanian kingdom. I wish only to ask you,
Monsieur le Ministre, to have the kindness to see that
special attention is given the request concerning him.
He is one of my good friends. . . .

There is no record, unfortunately, that Monsieur
Lecomte du Nouy was ever decorated, despite the eminence of his sponsors; but he continued for many years to
live chiefly in Roumania, while many miles away in
Etretat relations between La Bicoque and La Guillette
pleasantly flourished.

In the unpublished portion of his memoirs, François
calls Madame Lecomte du Nouy one of his master's two
"body-guards":

I shall give her the name of Hermine,* because she
had that white, faintly glistening skin that asks to be
caressed, like the fur of the little ermine that creeps along
the edge of the wood. She was blonde, very fair; her
slightly crinkly hair threw off sparks at the slightest

* François is being coy: her name *was* Hermine.

touch of the comb; her ears were rather large and flat; her forehead high and rounded; her eyes blue, with rainbow-tints passing through them at certain moments. I have heard people say that she had the eyes of a lynx, or of Argus; she had a strong, aquiline nose, naturally rosy lips; her chin jutted roundly over her alabaster neck as though it were trying to match the roundness of her breast. Everything about her was full of grace.

As to her voice, M. de Maupassant used to say that it would give pleasure even to the most insensitive, and would move the most stubborn. "Her diction is perfect," he used to say. "She reads poetry with a mastery far beyond the average; whether it is by Molière, Lamartine or Racine, she is in possession of her subject, she infuses you with it, impregnates you with it to the depths of your being." How often she used to recite the classics in the rose-arbor at La Guillette!

And at night, when the little white ermine crept out to seek its prey around the wood-shed and the chicken house, *Hermine la grande* continued her poetic recitals to the gods of love on the soft pillows of the sofa in the salon. . . .

For Hermine was like Laure not only in enjoying poor health and living in retirement with her son: she was also literary.

We were in Etretat [she says in her memoirs].* Guy, already ill, was having trouble with his eyes. He disliked going to bed early, however, fearing insomnia; and he often came to pass the evening with us. He liked me to read aloud while he lay stretched out in a dark corner. We were studying the eighteenth-century writers, and had read Diderot's letters to Mademoiselle Volland and the letters of Mademoiselle de Lespinasse, the Marquise du Chatelet, and Madame d'Epinay. Now we were reading the correspondence of Madame du Deffand. . . .

* *En regardant passer la vie* (written in collaboration with Henry Amic; Paris, Ollendorff, 1903).

A poem quoted by Madame du Deffand in one of her letters inspired Guy to write, one night after going home to La Guillette, a set of verses that he sent Hermine in the morning. Like Blanche, she lacked prudery, and she included the verses in her memoirs.*

The easy friendship continued for years. The two friends met also on the Riviera, and when they were apart they corresponded. There was never a question of exclusivity on either side. Each well knew that the other had other intimates, and that was the way they preferred it.

Princess Peglioso had married at sixteen. Born in Seville, daughter of the Polish Count Sabrinski and a Greek ex-dancer at La Scala in Milan, her paternal grandmother had grown up in Washington, where her father had been minister plenipotentiary of the young Queen Victoria. Madame Peglioso thus had Slav, Hellenic and English blood in her veins.

With her mat skin, her red-blond hair curled over the forehead and drawn tightly back from the temples, in the style made popular by the Princess of Wales, this cosmopolitan combined the rich aroma of an oriental with the refined distinction of an Anglo-Saxon: it was difficult to tell which predominated, except in her accent, which was heavily British. Her murderous sayings made the round of the salons. "Free as air" was the way she described herself, but she was the willing prisoner of a circle of adorers, at least one of whom society would have been very glad to be able to designate as her lover. But this was impossible. She asked to be amused—no more.

Mme. Peglioso lived alone in her husband's mansion. He allowed her free use of the carriages and servants, as long as she allowed him to remain in his villa in Florence with his pianists: he considered himself a composer, and sang his own abstruse operas.

If she had been more capable of standing the boredom

* See Note 10: *Mars et Vénus*, page 407.

of those society people whom she called "the unendurables," the Princess, one of the queens of Paris, could have served as a link between the elite of the Faubourg Saint-Germain dowagers and her American friends, many of whom had only their dollars to speak for them.

Those attributes of the Princess Peglioso (thus described in *Aymeris*, a *roman à clef* by the French painter and writer Jacques-Emile Blanche) are said to be, in slightly altered form, those of another good friend of Maupassant's, Emmanuela, Countess Potocka, née Pignatelli, the lady to whom he returned the dolls in interesting condition; and on other pages of *Aymeris* Jacques-Emile Blanche tells of how the lady attended Renan's lectures at the Collège de France, loved to watch surgeons perform operations, took pleasure in seeing the philosopher Caro crawl around her salon on his hands and knees in search of a pearl she pretended to have lost, worshipped in her private chapel, used crude and obscene language, and surrounded herself with nobility, painters, writers, priests, rich Americans, poor relations, secretaries, lady-gymnasts (she herself performed on the trapeze), liveried servants and magnificent dogs, one of them named Nick for her often absent husband—who was also a friend of Maupassant's.

She well fulfilled Maupassant's husband conditions. Proust, who knew her later, when she had moved out of her husband's twelve-million-franc mansion on the Avenue de Friedland with its staircase "as big as the one in the Opera House" into a remote house with a garden in Auteuil (where, she said, human beings might refuse to come to see her, but where she could look after her dogs), reveals the size of her husband's role in her life in an article he wrote for the *Figaro:*

One will understand that she could be seductive, with her antique beauty, her Roman majesty, her Florentine grace and her Parisian wit. As for Poland, which was also her country (since she is married to that good and charming man Count Potocki), she herself once revealed how much she retains of it, in one of those street-urchin remarks that so contrast with her statuesque beauty and her purling voice. . . . One day when she was cold and was trying to warm herself, making no reply to the greetings of visitors who kept arriving and who, a little intimidated by this absence of welcome, kept uttering monologues in insistent, embarrassed voices and respectfully kissed the hand she gave them without seeming to know they were there, she suddenly pointed . . . to the stove beside which she was standing, and cried, whether in melancholy or joyful recollection I cannot say, "My Choubersky stove! The only bit of Poland I have left!"

A fantastic figure, the Countess—and Proust, speaking of "her white beauty, like that of an indifferent Artemis," is echoed by Jacques-Emile Blanche, who tells of her being thought to be a virgin. Nevertheless, a group of her particularly favored men friends (Maupassant was one) were known as her Macchabées (corpses) because they considered themselves as lifeless, their lives belonging no longer to themselves, but to her. Jacques-Emile Blanche declares that her intelligence was keen, and that when one was alone with her fascinating conversation was possible; and Proust says that for those who could take her unpredictable temperament her friendship was full of delights.

Following the episode of the dolls, Maupassant wrote her from Cannes, thanking her for not taking it amiss, and expressing his surprise at the sparse mental furnishings of some of the dukes and princes he was now meeting for the first time:

They make me feel that I am the prince, and that I am talking with a lot of very little children, who have been taught nothing as yet except their Bible History. I keep thinking of other people, people with whom I like to talk. Do you know one of them? She is completely lacking in respect for these "masters of the world," and she is frank in her thinking (at least I believe she is), in her opinions and in her dislikes. That is probably why I think of her so often. Her mind gives me the impression of brusque frankness, free and bewitching. It is a constant surprise, full of the unexpected, of strange charm. Unfortunately, I cannot believe (I don't know why) that her friendship is lasting. That is what I should like to know, to find out. Does the friendship that she is capable of feeling for people come from her being momentarily distracted or amused by them, or does it come from something deeper and more human—that bond of intelligence that makes for durable relationships, that inexpressible harmony of minds that infuses even a handshake with a subtle mental and physical pleasure? I am expressing myself badly. You often understand me when I say nothing—do you also understand me when I speak in words that are poorly chosen?

In some way, possibly weird or possibly quite simple —for the Countess was above all bewildering—she convinced him that her friendship could be lasting. They saw each other constantly, they corresponded—in one letter he signed himself "honorary husband and true friend"—and it was to her, fantastic as she was, that he was to write at one of the worst moments in his life.

Blanche, Hermine, Emmanuela. . . It is interesting to think of what they had in common, these three *amours plus élégants*. Not only their husbands—the absent marchese, the absent architect, and the absent count with the dog named after him—but also a quality of remoteness from the humdrum, from the respectable, from the

possibly adhesive, the "normal." Blanche was a beautiful, easy-going bohemian from a distant land; Hermine's attractive resemblances to Laure were mitigated
by her other, less rigid qualities. (Hermine, one feels,
must have been as close to perfect as it was possible for
any woman to be for Maupassant, and indeed his relations with her seem to have been the most satisfying
and continuous. "You have a genius for friendship," she
says he once told her: and there was a harmony between
them that may well have inspired the words.) Countess
Potocka is the extreme illustration of his need, in his
intimacies, for a distance from what he called "bourgeois" love: her fantastic kind of highlife often removes
women (and men too) almost outside the human species
itself, and perhaps his relations with her were purely
"honorary"; but we know that he found comfort in her
affection.

And during these three long intimacies, the passing
encounters continued innumerable. One is almost
tempted to find in them an analogy with the short stories
that continued so profuse during the writing of the
novels!

But perhaps more fruitful in any consideration of
Maupassant's works—fruitful in giving an indication as
to why some of his stories portray women as they do—is
a glimpse of one more long, little-known intimacy: the
fourth, and apparently the last, of the continued relationships in which he came as close as it was possible
for him to come to finding satisfaction.

Late one night or early one morning—"at an embarrassing hour," François says—Hermine suffered a
heart attack at La Guillette; and when master and valet

had exhausted their resources to no avail "Madame Clem" was hastily sent for. She quickly came, and with almost magic remedies, including "a sort of metal ring that she rubbed on her friend's skin over the heart," she restored the sufferer. This valuable acquaintance, mistress of another near-by villa, François calls his master's second "body-guard":

She was named Clémence, but among her intimates was known as Clem. She was of middle height and had chestnut hair; there was an air of gaiety about her that held one's attention; she enjoyed excellent health, the result of long sojourns in the center of Burgundy, where wine takes the place of milk even for babies.

She had known Monsieur de Maupassant at least two years before I entered his service. In summer she lived in her villa at Etretat and spent part of her time at La Guillette, playing bowls, tennis, and, in the evening, handkerchiefs. Her vivacity at games infected everyone with gaiety, and whenever she succeeded at something she would scream like a bird. In the autumn she organized comedies—subjects, costumes and everything else were attended to by her. In Paris, things were more serious: she would throw pillows at her friend until he lay completely invisible under them on the sofa, and then she would tell his fortune, for she was a good chiromancer. . . .

And François goes on to tell of how she was constantly with Maupassant, how he allowed her to read and answer his mail, and hid nothing from her.

Clem, Madame Clémence Brun (sometimes using the name Brun-Chabas), is only a silhouette; a charming one, a little touching. Unlike the other ladies she had no socially exalted or even artistically interesting background: François says she was the widow of a well-to-do wholesale coffee merchant. The more respectable families of Etretat—who avoided dropping in at La Guillette for fear of what they might find there, and came only when specifically invited to garden parties—were not on visiting terms with her. If her attitude toward her husband was the usual one in the Maupassant circle, his trade may partly explain her enjoyment of the company of artists and writers. Maupassant's friends liked her pert wit, and called her **La Gamine de Paris** (guttersnipe). Her devotion found practical outlets: her good nature made her willingly help the suffering Hermine, and her secretarial help spared Maupassant's eyes, so often ailing. She astounded François by the speed with which she took his master's dictation. In Etretat, in Paris, and later on Maupassant's yacht, she amused everyone (there were usually people around) by her free comments on his correspondents as they revealed themselves in the letters she helped answer. She also aided him in his dealings with publishers, perhaps even suggesting the contents of some of the collected volumes; more than one of the letters to Maupassant from his publisher Havard contain greetings for her.

But Clem suffered, as is revealed in the memoirs of one of Maupassant's friends:

The lady who for some time acted as his secretary when he was suffering from his eyes had reason to consider herself indispensable, to think that she had attached him to herself by two strong bonds: habit and a kind of gratitude. She was sadly undeceived when she learned one day that Maupassant had gone off on his yacht. He didn't return for some time. It was his way of avoiding "clinging," as he called it.*

Poor Clem! Not as safely removed as the others, apparently, from "bourgeois" or "simple love." Not

* Charles Lapierre, "Souvenirs Intimes," *Journal des Débats*, August 10, 1893. Reprinted in Albert Lumbroso, *Souvenirs sur Maupassant* (Rome, 1905).

exotic, fantastic, or a Laure-with-a-twist. Practical, good-hearted, direct—and probably, from the little we know of her, a good deal simpler than the others in the expression of affection. Those were bad handicaps, leading straight to the suspicion of "clinging," whether justified or not, when the object of the affection was the young man who was first and foremost the son of Laure de Maupassant.

CHAPTER 6

THE NECKLACE

AT THE SMILING MOMENT of his life when he was thirty-four, had built his house at Etretat, hired François, and begun to enjoy his *amours plus élégants*, Maupassant did some of his best and his best-known work. In both these categories can be placed *La Parure* (*The Necklace*), one of the most famous short stories in the world, described by Henry James when it was new as "a little perfection."

Although everyone knows the plot, not everyone knows James's resumé of it:

> In "La Parure" a poor young woman, under "social" stress, the need of making an appearance on an important occasion, borrows from an old school friend, now much richer than herself, a pearl [sic] necklace which she has the appalling misfortune to lose by some mischance never afterwards cleared up. Her life and her pride, as well as her husband's with them, become subject, from the hour of the awful accident, to the redemption of this debt; which, effort by effort, sacrifice by sacrifice, franc by franc, with specious pretexts, excuses, a rage of desperate explanation of their failure to restore the missing object, they finally obliterate—all to find that their whole consciousness and life have been convulsed and deformed in vain, that the pearls were but highly artful "imitation" and that their passionate penance has ruined them for nothing.*

* Preface to Vol. xvi of the New York Edition.

The particular brilliance with which *La Parure* is written triumphs over a number of improbabilities. (The lack of insurance on the necklace, sometimes mentioned by critics, is not among them: insurance of jewelry in France began to be common only a few years later.) But even a halfway careful reading of the famous tale shows the relationships between the two women and between the heroine and her husband to be vague and unconvincing; and the purchase and successful substitution of the new necklace are of dubious verisimilitude. But the shock of the shattering, crushing end has always endeared the story to the multitude. The common tribute of nonliterary readers of *La Parure*—"It shouldn't have been written! It makes you feel too bad!"—is phrased as a reproach; but actually it is an expression of the intensest pleasure, the ability to be made to "feel bad" by a story being prized by most readers beyond rubies.

Maupassant would have enjoyed that tribute. For he liked very much to make people "feel bad"—to give them, at least, a few bad moments, to shock them and surprise them. The perpetration of what the French call *farces* and we call practical jokes was one of his favorite forms of amusement, and the memoirs of François and of Maupassant's friends are full of examples of the elaborate lengths to which he was willing to go to secure a victim's momentary discomfiture. In addition to *Farce Normande*, the story about wedding-night horseplay, he wrote another, *La Farce*, which contains two practical jokes, one of them involving an old lady's chamber-pot, and innumerable other tales about victimizations; and in life he enjoyed inviting people to dinner under false pretenses (pretending to be launching an investment scheme, to furnish a needy courtesan of his acquaintance with a wealthy protector in the form of a "Spanish marquis,"

actually a friend in disguise, to introduce to a group of
ladies a charming college boy whom they allow to take
certain precocious liberties, not realizing that he is a
woman); having François deliver to a lady in her salon
a basket full of live frogs, making his dinner guests at
Chatou, when he took an apartment there one spring,
miss the last train back to Paris; turning mice loose on
his boat among lady guests; using filthy language in the
hearing of stuffy people; assuring acquaintances that he
had once eaten "roast shoulder of woman" and so enjoyed it that he had taken a second portion, and so on.
This rather infantile love to shock is a mild expression of
the sadism which finds further outlet in his frequent and
usually artistically superfluous descriptions of blood—
such as the hideous abortion in *L'Enfant,* and, in his
travel sketches, a sanguinary fight among Mediterranean
fishes and a description of the red flesh of watermelons.
A brutal, shocking ending like that of *La Parure* is another expression of the tendency.

Maupassant has an immense reputation as a specialist
in stories that end in this way—stories with "trick" or
"twist" endings. Considering how deeply engrained in his
nature was the desire to shock, he might be expected to
have written numerous such stories; but the fact is that
he did not. It is impossible to mention a precise figure,
since between shock and non-shock there is no clear de-
marking line, but of Maupassant's more than two hundred short stories a mere handful have endings that can
properly be called trick or shocking.

The legend of his being a specialist in this kind of
story did not exist during his lifetime. His work was re-
peatedly and rigorously analyzed by such contemporary
critics as Jules Lemaître and Anatole France, men who
despite the differences in their approach to literature

from that of present-day critics were keenly discriminating and perceptive; and they would without mercy have pointed out the aesthetic inferiority—the drastically diminished pleasure of re-reading—inherent in a large body of Maupassant stories with trick endings, had such a body existed. Present-day critics who make the charge reveal that they are repeating what they have heard or read, that they are not well acquainted with Maupassant. Indeed, the statement that Maupassant's work is generally characterized by trickery can usually be considered a warning: a warning that other inaccuracies are hovering near. When a critic reviewing Henry James's notebooks, for example, says, "One sees that the example of Maupassant—more frequently invoked, I think, than that of any other writer—with his plots that depend on pure trickery, has had much more influence on Henry James than one would ever have expected," * he betrays not only a faulty memory of Maupassant, but also a careless reading or interpretation of the work in hand: examination of James's notebooks shows that it is not Maupassant's trickery or plots that Henry James keeps invoking, but Maupassant's enviable ability to write with brevity and compactness.

In exactly one recorded instance Maupassant's "trickery" did influence Henry James and influence him concretely; and on this unique occasion the trickery was that of *La Parure*. The origin of his short story *Paste*, James tells us, "was to consist but of the ingenious thought of transposing the terms of one of Guy de Maupassant's admirable *contes*"—*La Parure*.

It seemed harmless sport simply to turn that situation round—to shift, in other words, the ground of the horrid mistake, making this a matter not of a false treasure sup-

* Edmund Wilson, *The New Yorker*, Dec. 13, 1947.

posed to be true and precious, but of a real treasure
supposed to be false and hollow: though a new little
"drama," a new setting for *my* pearls—and as different
as possible from the other—had of course withal to be
found.*

Paste—in which James pays Maupassant more or less
conscious tribute by naming one of his characters Mrs.
Guy—is an excellent tale; and in indulging in what he is
certainly right in calling the "harmless sport" of turning
Maupassant's situation around, James provides the
reader with considerable entertainment—more, perhaps,
than he realized. For, as James either did not know, or
had forgotten that he knew, or merely did not mention,
La Parure is itself a transposition: a year before writing
it Maupassant had published a tale called *Les Bijoux*
(*The Jewels*), in which a bereaved government clerk discovers that his late lamented wife's supposedly false
jewels are real. Thus James's *Paste*, transposing or
rather re-transposing *La Parure*, tells the same story as
Les Bijoux; and the reader can enjoy the spectacle of
two masters busy "transposing terms," two masters dealing with the same situation. *Paste*, with its very Jamesian
"effaced" governess and its "honest widowed clergyman
with a small son and a large sense of Shakespeare," con-
trasts with the very Gallic, and considerably inferior,
Les Bijoux in a manner not to be missed by any lover of
fiction.

Les Bijoux is without a shock ending (although there
is a laugh in the last line), and it is considerably more
typical of Maupassant's work than *La Parure* in that the
chief moment of drama—the discovery of the value of
the jewels—comes in the middle of the tale, and the remaining pages are devoted to the protagonist's behavior

* Preface to Vol. xvi, New York Edition.

in the new circumstances in which he finds himself. *Les Bijoux* fails: for the account of that behavior, which the reader has looked forward to savoring after the excellent opening and halfway-point shock, is slighted by the author; but in Maupassant's many successful tales cut to this excellent pattern—in *La Rouille* (*Rusty*), to cite but one example—the reacting protagonists, animated by the imagination of the author, provide a gallery of delights.

This pair of Maupassant tales, *La Parure* and *Les Bijoux*, is thus an interesting example of something more than merely transposition: an interesting example of the success of a story which, although inherently inferior, and flawed by improbabilities, happens to be done with particular brilliance; and the failure of an inherently superior tale due to lethargic execution. In *La Parure* Maupassant the superb technician working at the top of his powers carries all before him; in *Les Bijoux* he misses an opportunity.

Maupassant's work contains many missed opportunities like *Les Bijoux*. Any writer as prolific as he, particularly any writer so constantly productive of short stories,* each one of which represents a fresh approach, a new attack, without the gradually accumulating drive and unity that can make more uniformly successful an equal number of pages in a novel, must be expected to fail some of the time, to produce pale approximations or foolish burlesques of his best work, or departures from it that arrive nowhere; and his reputation suffers accordingly. But the strange feature of Maupassant's case is that his considerable number of failures has done very

---

* It has been estimated that in 1884, the year of *La Parure*, Maupassant produced 1500 printed pages, about 1000 of them in short stories.

little harm indeed to his reputation as compared with the damage dealt it by one of his greatest successes—*La Parure*.

For *La Parure* has been *too* successful—too popularly successful. From the "little perfection" which it seemed to Henry James, it has become, in the eyes of the contemporary cultivated reader, an "overworked hack of the anthologies," a "skillful conjuring trick," which "has served far too long as a model for the commercial short-story writer." * Weary of its ceaseless reappearance, disgusted by its hundreds of imitations, the inherent inferiority of its form becoming unbearable with repetition, highbrow and middlebrow readers have long since had more than enough of it. Unquestionably it is the extreme familiarity and popularity of this single story, gradually built up over the years, that has resulted in Maupassant's unjustified reputation as a specialist in trick endings. And many critics and readers, perceptive but not quite *sufficiently* perceptive or familiar with Maupassant's work, have in their irritation been even more unjust: the immense lowbrow popularity of the tale † has resulted in the assumption that Maupassant is a writer for lowbrows only, that he has little or nothing to offer the more discriminating. This identification of the author with his most popular tale, plus the swing of the highbrow pendulum away from tales with surprise endings, has resulted in the dismissal of a large body of Maupassant's work: not only his many successful tales on the superior pattern of *Les Bijoux*, but also those of his tales which are plotless or all but plotless, whose patterns are so loose and unobtrusive as to be all but

* These phrases, typical of those commonly employed, are from an article by V. S. Pritchett in *The New Statesman and Nation*, Sept. 18, 1943.

† Along with the general vulgarization and commercialization of Maupassant in English translation. See Sixty-five Fake "Maupassant" Stories, page 353.

imperceptible, and which are pungent and iridescent with character, atmosphere, sentiment, and subtle comment on human life both individual and collective.

Although even middlebrows and highbrows reading *La Parure* for the first time are still apt to be caught by its power, and can well understand why Henry James should have praised it as he did, it would be fruitless to suggest that it be reappraised, "read with fresh eyes": its damning career of lowbrow popularity continues too unabated; only recently it was televised.* Rather, let it be suggested that some one of the other, contrasting tales be tried instead—for example *La Reine Hortense* (*Queen Hortense*). Read if possible in the original French, it emerges another and quite different "little perfection" from the obscurity in which it has been preserved.

* This was Maupassant's debut in television (January 21, 1949). Introduced by an actor with an Irish brogue (Arthur Shields), and punctuated by advertisements for a well-known brand of cigarettes, the made-in-Hollywood television version of *La Parure* took its place with the Hollywood moving picture version of *Bel-Ami* [see next chapter] at the bottom of the Maupassant heap. The brutal shock of the end—the *raison d'etre* of the story and hitherto the chief reason for its popularity—was removed, and the couple, instead of being ruined for nothing, was shown to have found happiness—i.e., "each other"—as a result of their prolonged scrimping! "The story ended on a ray of hope which, I'm sure, De Maupassant never intended, but which isn't as bad as it sounds," the usually more sensitive radio critic John Crosby wrote on February 3 in his review in the *New York Herald Tribune*. "I have a hunch all these classics will be rather substantially revised in tone, if not in content, to suit the sentimental tastes of the movie-going and radio-listening public." Material for sociologists! I have tried to engage in correspondence with the Hollywood authors of the castrated television version of *La Parure*, hoping to gain some insight into the motives and entertainment-ideas of such practitioners. But my interested queries, perhaps naïve, have remained unanswered.

CHAPTER 7

BEL-AMI

Bel-Ami, THE NOVEL of newspaper life, filled with echos of the *Gaulois* and the *Gil-Blas*, on which Maupassant worked during the months when he was receiving his first series of guests at La Guillette, has been seen by so many people on the American screen, in such ineptly distorted form, that the text as it appeared serially in the *Gil-Blas* and then between covers in various languages has been somewhat lost sight of. The story, with its sharply period air, its peculiarly Parisian types, its triumphant villainies and blackmails, its adulteries and assorted promiscuities, is like most French fiction magnificently unsuited to present-day Hollywood; and it is regrettable to have to say that a pre-1940 German film of the story, also distorted, but this time with nefarious skill into savage anti-French propaganda, is a considerably better job. Nevertheless, the text as Maupassant wrote it summer and fall mornings of 1884 at Etretat remains quite decidedly the best version of *Bel-Ami*.

Paris is the artist's dunghill [Maupassant wrote in one of his essays on Louis Bouilhet]. It is only there, with his feet on its pavements and his head in its exhilarating, tangy air, that he can come to fullest flower. And it is not enough merely to *be* in Paris: you have to become part of it, quickly get to know its houses, its people, its

ideas, its ways and intimate customs, its banter, its wit.
Great, strong, full of genius though you may be, if you
cannot become Parisian to the marrow you retain a certain awkwardness of talent, a certain something of provincialism.

In those sentences, written to explain some of the
awkwardness and provincialism that always, despite his
talent, clung to Bouilhet, Maupassant was referring also,
by contrast, to himself. He maintained a home of one
kind or another in Paris from his twenty-second year;
and with his talent fertilized by the glorious dunghill
many of his stories are as recognizably and inimitably
Parisian as the products of the Rue de la Paix. *Bel-Ami*
goes one step further: it is the story of a vulgar cad from
the provinces who makes himself into one of the denizens
of the dunghill in the most unfavorable sense of the word.

At the time of its publication the novel aroused a good
deal of indignation among Parisian journalists. Some believed that they had been depicted, and others that in
describing the *Vie Française*—the newspaper on which
Bel-Ami rides to fortune—Maupassant had cruelly syn-
thesized the Parisian press. In a Zola-like reply to such
critics he retorted that his hero-villain was not a journalist at all, but merely a low adventurer who happened to
get a job on a newspaper; and that he had chosen journalism as his scene simply because the kaleidoscope of
the Parisian newspaper world was the most convincing
background for so Parisian a success story. (Actually it is
fairly obvious that he had chosen to write about the
newspaper world because it was one that he knew and
thought entertaining, and that had not previously been
exploited by a novelist.) The charge that he had depicted
actual people he answered virtuously, to his own pretended satisfaction: "Can anyone recognize himself in a

single one of my characters? No. Can it be said that I
had actual people in mind? No. I was alluding to no
one."

This question of the portrayal of actual, living people
in novels, he had discussed in *Gil-Blas* the year before, in
an article called *Les Masques.* "The artist has the right
to see everything, to use everything," he wrote. "But
his characters must be carefully masked so that they are
not recognizable." A glance at the names and attributes
of some of his characters will indicate to what extent he
observed that precaution in *Bel-Ami.*

Bel-Ami himself (the nickname means sweetheart),
who begins his newspaper career as assistant to a gossip
editor, is named Georges Duroy; as he rises in his profession he rebaptizes himself Du Roy de Cantel; and the
director of his newspaper, whose wife he seduces and
whose daughter he marries, is named Walter. Now it
seems fairly safe to assume that a certain trio of flesh-
and-blood individuals, today forgotten but at that time
prominent in the Paris newspaper world—Georges
Duprey, gossip writer on the *Gil-Blas*, Arthur Cantel,
theater gossip writer on the *Gaulois*, and Jehan Valter,
one of the assistant editors of the *Gaulois*—did not feel
masked, precisely, as they read about those characters in
Bel-Ami, even though in their cases it may have been
only their names that Maupassant used! And Baron de
Vaux, the former fencing master, the organizer of fencing
exhibitions, who as we have seen was head of the Society
Chronicle on the *Gil-Blas*, probably did not feel totally
masked when he read in *Bel-Ami* about "Jacques Rival,
the famous *chroniqueur* and duellist." * And Bel-Ami's

* Baron de Vaux is sometimes credited with being Maupassant's chief model
for the character of Bel-Ami himself. The Baron was, like Bel-Ami, a brutal
former *sous-officier;* he was a great bluffer, and his title, like Bel-Ami's, was more
than suspect; he signed his gossip columns Asmodée—that is, Asmodeus (the

charming and devoted little mistress, Clothilde de
Marelle, nicknamed Clo and described as a *gamine:* "She
possessed a droll sense of humor, a wit that was charming
and unexpected—that of an experienced gamine with a
carefree outlook on life and a kindly, light-hearted skep-
ticism. . . ." Did Clémence Brun, Maupassant's devoted "bodyguard," secretary and friend, known among
her friends as Clem, or *"la gamine de Paris,"* feel masked
as she read about Clo?

Laudable though it may have been for Maupassant
to intend to mask his characters carefully, he failed to
do so; and it is well that he did fail, for in writing a novel
like *Bel-Ami,* which is so completely what the French
call *un roman vécu*—a novel that has been lived—an author who worries overmuch about masking his characters
is apt to take the life out of his book. Many unfavorable
things have been said about *Bel-Ami*—that it is sordid,
disgusting, hastily written, uneven, shallow—but it has
never been called lifeless; and in this case the liveliness
is due in part to careless masking. "He gave himself the
cruel pleasure of including among his characters two
women who more or less danced attendance on his growing reputation," a friend has recorded; and the advance
announcement of *Bel-Ami* in the *Gil-Blas* on January 17,
1885, declared: "This very lively novel contains several
accurate and charming silhouettes of Parisiennes, taken
from life itself."

Bel-Ami's duel with a rival journalist in the Bois du
Vésinet has a background that is very much *vécu.* Such
duels were then—and still, to a small extent, are—part
of the Parisian scene. The *Gil-Blas* for August 11, 1880,
contains a satirical *"écho"* about the editor-in-chief of a

demon of matrimonial unhappiness and jealousy); some of his journalism was
written for him by others. (Charles de Saint-Cyr, *op. cit.*)

rival newspaper who had insulted the *Gil-Blas* in print, and who, challenged to a duel by one of the *Gil-Blas* assistant editors, haughtily refused the challenge because of his higher rank; and the *Gaulois* for November 16, 1881, printed the account of a duel in the Bois du Vésinet between the journalist René Maizeroy and the editor of a rival sheet. On this occasion Maupassant was one of Maizeroy's seconds; and three weeks later, in the *Gil-Blas*, in an article expressing his preference for boxing and swimming over fencing, and his utter contempt for duelling, he wrote:

There remains one variety of duel which I accept, the industrial duel; the duel for publicity, the duel between journalists.

When the circulation of a newspaper begins to drop, one of its editors bestirs himself and in a scathing article insults one of his rivals. The rival replies. The public watches as it would watch a wrestling match. And a duel takes place and is talked about in the salons.

This procedure has one excellent thing about it: it will make more and more unnecessary the employment of editors who know how to write French. They will merely have to be accomplished at duelling. . . .

And out of the Parisian, or rather journalistic, dunghill Maupassant plucked other living ingredients for his book. The prevalence of ghost-writing, for example. Bel-Ami begins his career on the *Vie Française* with an article on Algeria written for him by someone else; when he is asked for a second article he finds himself helpless; and other journalists in the book are shown having their copy written for them. The journalist René Maizeroy (whom we have seen reviewing *Mademoiselle Fifi*) was well known as an employer of ghosts. In the *Gil-Blas* there appeared over Maizeroy's signature an endless flow of articles, short stories and novels, surpassing Maupassant's own output in quantity; and the serialization of the longer Maizeroy pieces was occasionally interrupted when a ghost inconsiderately went on strike between installments. Reminiscent of the *Gil-Blas'* traffic in *horizontales* are the pretty young woman "who looked like a cocotte," and her companion, the "old actress," whom Bel-Ami sees waiting in the reception room of the *Vie Française* and who are spoken to mysteriously in a low voice by one of the editors—who was apparently in the violet-plucking business.

Maupassant also utilized the vulgarity of Arthur Meyer, his editor-in-chief on the *Gaulois*—a vulgarity which betrayed itself in connection with the Jewish question. Meyer frequently mentioned his Jewish origin, but always in the same breath as his conversion to Catholicism; and he was capable of printing in his own newspaper an item about himself beginning, "You were born a Jew, as you yourself recently reminded us; and you have become a royalist. Certain humorists are beginning to ask whether you may not soon have yourself decircumcized." A vulgarity like Meyer's is attributed in *Bel-Ami* to Walter, the Jewish editor-in-chief of the *Vie Française*, who is said to have undergone a Catholic baptism. But Maupassant goes further, and in attributing to Jews in general the traits of avarice and ostentation he falls into stereotypes. Here he is not an artist who sees for himself, but a member of conventional "good society," adopting that society's convenient *parti-pris*, oblivious of actuality; and his language in these passages is typical society language on the subject—that is, it is composed of clichés, most of them sadistic and more vulgar than anything they describe. This is the first example of Maupassant's capacity for committing the great artistic sin: being willing on occasion to abdicate his artist's vision in favor of an easy, false society judgment. In his case, as in so many others, the descent to anti-Semitic stereotypes was symptomatic of a broader evil.

A glimpse of another deeply engrained characteristic of Maupassant is afforded by examination of his hero, for into Bel-Ami he has put more of himself than merely such details as his newspaper career, his Norman origin, his room overlooking the railroad tracks and even his delight in cuckolding. Bel-Ami is a blackguard, and we have seen how Maupassant liked to pretend that his own name was derived from *mauvais passant* (evil passer-by). Inscribing a copy of his novel to a lady, he wrote "*Hommage de Bel-Ami lui-même*" ("Greetings from Bel-Ami himself"); and burlesquing Flaubert, who used to say "*Madame Bovary, c'est moi!*" he was in the habit of saying "*Bel-Ami, c'est moi!*" That was a joke; but in Maupassant's life the prominence of Bel-Ami as the name of his novel is rivaled by its prominence as the name of his two yachts, which were for him real and beloved homes, in which he spent large portions of his last years. Constant association with the name and with the thought of the *mauvais passant* he had created were anything but displeasing to him. And it can scarcely be denied that someone possessing Maupassant's savagely utilitarian approach to most of womankind, with all the brutal details of relationship which it implies, must necessarily have certain traits included in any definition of the word blackguard.

However, in Bel-Ami's blackguardism there is a certain special shading which Maupassant puts there delicately, with considerable skill. For all his vitality and swagger, for all his adventures in bedrooms, boudoirs

and *garconnières*, there is something feminine, or at
least non-masculine, about Bel-Ami. Maupassant indicates his character's lack of a certain fundamental male-
ness chiefly by details concerning money: his general
failure to do anything *for* women, his willingness to take
money from them, and especially his stinginess with
women who make their living from their bodies. This
last is scathing, for throughout Maupassant's fiction is
found the assumption that any man worthy of the name
who has enjoyed a woman's "love" feels that he has in-
curred an obligation: "It is admitted in our society," he
says in *La Confession*, "that the love of a woman must
be paid for, with money if she is poor, with presents if
she is rich." And in Bel-Ami there are traits which go
beyond his mere lack of that basic male instinct. During
the course of the novel he likens himself to two persons,
both of them women: a successful courtesan whom he
sees driving a smart carriage in the Bois de Boulogne—
"he sensed, perhaps vaguely, that they had something
in common"—and his "worldly vagabond" of a mistress,
Clo de Morelle.

Maupassant had previously remarked on the presence of feminine traits in his own sex in an 1883 *Gil-Blas*
article called *L'Homme-Fille* (*The Man-Tart*), which
amounts almost to a preliminary sketch for the character
of Bel-Ami:

How often we hear people say "That man is charming, but he's like a girl, a real tart." They are alluding to
the man-tart, the bane of our country.

For all Frenchmen are men-tarts, that is to say, we
are fickle, temperamental, innocently perfidious, without
consistency in convictions or will, violent and weak as
women are.

The most irritating of the men-tarts is surely the
Parisian and the boulevardier, in whom the appearances

of intelligence are more marked and who combines in himself, exaggerated by his masculine temperament, all the attractions and all the defects of charming harlots.

Our Chamber of Deputies is filled with men-tarts. They form the greater number of those amiable opportunists who might be called "The Charmers" . . . . The newspapers are full of men-tarts. That is probably where one finds the most of them, but that is also where they are most needed. A few papers must be excepted, such as the *Débats* or the *Gazette de France*. Certainly every good journalist must be something of a prostitute. . . .

The feminine characteristics with which Maupassant endows Bel-Ami, the extended attribution of these characteristics in *L'Homme-Fille*, and his joking *"Bel-Ami, c'est moi!"* make it impossible not to cast another glance at his choice of the pseudonym Maufrigneuse—that name which he was still, as he wrote *Bel-Ami*, occasionally signing to short stories and articles in the *Gil-Blas*. There was something of a vogue among journalists of the time for pseudonyms taken from Balzac, and the name Maufrigneuse has the first three letters and the aristocratic or near-aristocratic ring of the name Maupassant. Perhaps that is sufficient explanation of his choice. But something more comes to mind. Although despite the ending in *euse* there is nothing intrinsically feminine in the name Maufrigneuse (actual French family names of geographical derivation, such as that of the Ducs de Joyeuse, have ended with the same syllable), and although in the *Comédie Humaine*, from which the name is taken, it is borne not only by the Duchesse de Maufrigneuse herself but by two men, her husband and her son, nevertheless the immediate reference of the name in the mind of anyone acquainted with Balzac is to the courtesan-like Duchess, much the most prominent of all the Maufrigneuses. Why should Maupassant have been the only male journalist of his day to take a Balzac name that immediately evokes a woman? Did he seriously recognize in himself those feminine traits which artists are apt to possess in profusion, and which, in his case, he-man though he prided himself on being, came perhaps all too profusely from Laure? His possession of them is probably one of the explanations of his extraordinary genius for depicting feminine types, for drawing innumerable shades of feminine character—a genius so great that there has come to exist in France, among the semi-literate who nonetheless know his tales, the legend that the author using the pseudonym Guy de Maupassant was a woman.

Bel-Ami is at the present time the most widely read of Maupassant's novels in France. In it he came closer than anywhere else to creating a type—as Flaubert did in *Madame Bovary*, causing the word *bovarysme* to pass into use as a common noun. Bel-Ami is the type of ambitious, unscrupulous man in any field; and his ruthlessness, plus the feminine subtleties of his character that are particularly evocative for those familiar with the Parisian "dunghill," has a special appeal for the present generation of French readers.

Bel-Ami and the notorious *La Parure* are not the only striking products of the year 1884. It is the year of *Garçon, un bock!* . . . (*Waiter, a Beer!*), the tale of the childhood memory of father striking mother; of *Châli*, about the eight-year-old mistress (sic), which would come near the top of any list of stories compiled to show the extraordinary freedom of publication that Maupassant was permitted by his editors; * of *Un Lâche?* (*A*

* Only occasionally did an editor beg him to tone something down. Free as many of his stories are, none ever attracted the attention of a French court like

Coward?), the famous sketch of the man who shoots himself because he is too frightened to face a duel; of one of the most comic of the Norman tales, *Tribunaux rustiques* (*Rustic Tribunals*); of one of the most touching of the encounters with prostitutes, *L'Armoire* (*The Closet*); and of *L'Héritage* (*The Inheritance*), outstandingly strong and savage because it combines the themes of paternity and government clerking.

It is also the year of *Yvette*, the superb novelette about one of the most adorable young girls in fiction, the courtesan's daughter who reads and remains naïve and innocent in her mother's household until her eyes are opened at eighteen. Once again Maupassant is at the top of his form in writing about outcasts; this account of a girl's discovery that she will always be an outcast—a further variation of the humiliation theme—is marked by marvelous narrative skill, the timing of the constant changes of scene being particularly dexterous. The book contains the famous description of La Grenouillère, the floating café on the Seine, and a picture of the now-vanished world of the great courtesans, the fashionable demi-monde. Maupassant once spoke, in a letter to Baron de Vaux, of "the world of the *grandes cocottes*—a world into which I do not go, where I have never been." That was not quite accurate; he had visited the salons of at least two very superior courtesans—superior, that is, in the sense that they maintained salons attended by literary men: Jeanne Detourbey, the daughter of a stonecutter and a laundress who became Comtesse de Loynes and one of the great literary hostesses (her copy of *Madame Bovary* was inscribed "*A la très belle et très*

---

the poem *Au Bord de l'eau*. Prosecution for "immoral" writing was, then as now, spasmodic and capricious. In this very year 1884 Maupassant defended in print one of his literary friends, Harry Alis, charged with pornography.

cruelle Jeanne de T. Le plus soupirant de tous ses adorateurs, Gustave Flaubert); and Nina de Villard, friend of the parnassians and the symbolists, some of whom usually used her salon as a dormitory after her parties. And probably he knew the even more celebrated, somewhat older, ex-model, Madame Sabatier, called La Présidente, beloved of Flaubert, Baudelaire, Victor Hugo, Sainte-Beuve and Théophile Gautier. The brilliantly characterized mother of Yvette, the beautiful former cook who calls herself Marquise Obardi, is not one of those literary demi-mondaines; she is closer to Zola's Nana and her friends; and if Maupassant really did not know her world his description of it is one of the greatest indications of his power of imaginative construction.

Like most authors, Maupassant did not always have a proper appreciation of the quality of his own work. He disparaged *Yvette*—"It is a bright trifle, but not a study," he wrote his publisher. "It is adroit, but it isn't strong"— whereas it is an undoubted masterpiece, a marvel of storytelling.

Tolstoy, who abominated *Yvette*, calling it "horrible in its immorality," declared: "The author should have ended his narrative with the beautiful young soul's meeting with the perverse world, a profoundly touching and admirably rendered situation, instead of continuing— quite unnecessarily from the standpoint of action or general idea—by having the gentleman in question enter the girl's room and violate her." The words show that Tolstoy had badly mis-read the ending of *Yvette:* actually its closing situation is what he says it should be. He continues: "In the first part of the book, the author is evidently on the side of the young girl; but in the second, he has suddenly gone over to the side of the débauché. Thus one impression destroys the other and the whole book falls to pieces." The objection is, as usual with Tolstoy, exaggerated; but it does touch upon the book's weakest element: Maupassant's delineation of the leading male character, Jean de Servigny, the man of the world who will not marry Yvette, who is the cause of her awakening to her social situation, and who is about to become her lover as the book closes. The refusal of a man of good family to marry a lowly-born girl whom he claims to adore was not as grotesque in the eyes of Maupassant's French readers of 1884 as it is in ours; but even then the value of the book lay in the delicacy of the situation, and even then the story's closing scene, with Servigny on the balcony, *"l'âme radieuse, la chair émue,"* humming

> *Souvent femme varie,*
> *Bien fol est qui s'y fie*

only a few feet from the poor child still lying weak from her suicide attempt, must have been brutally jarring, artistically speaking. Much as the reader would like to, it is impossible for him to feel that this ending is a scathing comment by Maupassant on Servigny's hardness and egotism; rather, it must be recognized as another indication of Maupassant's own uneasiness in the realm of sex and love. In his mind the man of the world must at all costs be, on that subject, ironical and superior; and probably without being fully conscious of what he was doing, he sacrificed the end of his masterpiece to that morbid conviction.

The stories of this year are frequently swifter than their predecessors. *Bel-Ami* moves twice as fast as the beautiful but deliberate *Une Vie;* and some of the others

make even the masterpieces among the earlier work—
Boule de Suif and *La Maison Tellier*—seem like studies
in slow-motion. Laure, to whom Maupassant showed
much of his work before it was printed—she often read
his proofs and offered criticisms, and the mother and son,
François records, always had a great deal to say to each
other about Guy's work and other subjects when they
were together—warned him about this time that the beginnings, at least, of his stories were becoming *too* fast.
Not all of Maupassant's work from now on was to have
this quickness of pace, but greater and greater speed was
to characterize some of it. Since during 1884 he wasted
less of his time than previously on articles and gave
more of it to fiction, perhaps the more rapid movement
in some of the fiction is merely an indication of increased
technique. It has frequently been noted by non-scientific
commentators that Maupassant, infected by his fatal
disease, seemed to write faster and faster both in certain
individual works and in general, as he "felt" or "sensed"
his time growing shorter and shorter. A similar statement is made less mystically by doctors, who state that
a brain attacked by the *spirocheta pallida* does frequently
work with increased speed, due perhaps to irritations set
up by the germ, during the years preceding its destruction. (Maupassant, François tells us, wondered on one
occasion whether his capacity for such rapid production
was due to the Norman doctor's birth-time massage!)

The medical statement makes tantalizingly dramatic
—because of our ignorance as to how aware Maupassant
was of his own condition—the fact that it was precisely
this year (during which, furthermore, he suffered a particularly severe recurrence of his syphilitic eye troubles)
that he wrote the only two of his stories which mention
syphilis, and that both references to the disease should

be characterized by fear. In *Les Soeurs Rondoli* (*The Rondoli Sisters*) a young Frenchman who has picked up a pretty Italian on a train is invaded by the "nagging fear that pursues us after dubious embraces, and spoils our charming encounters, unpremeditated caresses, and kisses that are garnered at random." And in *Le Lit 29* (*Bed 29*) a captain abandons his dying ex-mistress, one of Maupassant's heroic and patriotic prostitutes, who in order vengefully to infect Prussians had deliberately not sought treatment for the syphilis which a Prussian had given her. The captain's chief reason for abandoning her is the jeers of his comrades; but Maupassant also describes his disgust and fear at the thought of her *"mal ignoble et terrible,"* her "ignoble and terrible disease."

François's memoirs give a picture of his master's life in Etretat that summer of *Bel-Ami:*

He rose in the morning about eight and took no breakfast; he claimed that eating before work was bad for his writing, and that morning coffee was a woman's habit. He strolled around his garden several times, paid a visit to his goldfish, and came back to the house to bathe his eyes; often he wrote until eleven, then took his cold tub, dressed and lunched. After lunch every day he took forty or fifty pistol-shots at his target.

Afternoons there was also bowling, swimming or sailing with house-guests and other friends, and in the evening parlor games after dinner. And François tells of carrying offerings of pears from his master to "the ladies in the post-office"—a certain part of whose daily chore consisted in handling the voluminous mail of this local boy who had made good—and to "Madame C. . . . , Offenbach's daughter." This year they remained at Etretat until well into the autumn, and a dramatic finish was given the season by the midnight cremation, on the beach below the towering cliffs, of a Hindu prince who had died while vacationing. The pyre blazed, the prince's attendants sat about "like Buddhas," and the Etretat fisherfolk and tradesmen were agitated by the heathen strangeness of it all. Maupassant sent an account to the *Figaro*, earning his customary five hundred francs.

Back in Paris, social agitation set in again. He continued working hard on *Bel-Ami*, and he paid his respects to his old masters, writing an essay on Bouilhet and one on Flaubert to serve as introduction to an edition of the letters to George Sand; but on December 24 Edmond de Goncourt noted in his journal:

Maupassant, who came to see me today about the bust of Flaubert, told me a number of things typical of high society. At the present moment fashionable young people are taking lessons from a writing instructor *ad hoc* in modish handwriting, a handwriting divested of all personality, looking like a string of m's. Another bit of chic: Since the Rothschilds have gone through all the various kinds of hunting and there is no longer any animal on the face of the earth that interests them, they have the skin of a deer dragged through the woods in the morning, and in the afternoon they follow, with special dogs, this scent of a non-existent animal, like the pursuit of a shade. And since Mme. Alp[honse] de R[othschild] is a very good jumper, obstacles are prepared for her in advance, and the grass near them is watered, so that should the huntswoman fall she would do herself no injury. Maupassant tells me that Cannes is a marvelous spot for the documentation of elegant society.

To have become an authority on highlife for Goncourt marked a rather rapid progress on the part of one who less than a year before had been living in a flat overlooking the railroad tracks. As usual, a move of Laure's—in this case her settling on the Riviera—was in part responsible for her son's development; and his increased worldliness was as significant, was to be as far-reaching in its effects, as his increased literary pace.

The year 1884 was one of the high spots of Maupassant's career. *Bel-Ami*, which stands impressively with a very personal bearing of its own, a kind of non-meditative document, a masterly arrangement of facts and events, steady-paced and colorful; the bravura of *La Parure*, the strength and delicacy of *Yvette*, the brilliant mosaic of the other tales. . . . The fine variety and carelessness and self-confidence exhilarate the reader. Maupassant took pains, of course, with his work, but at this time it seems to have caused him no suffering. Someone has said that he produced his stories as a Norman apple tree bears its fruit. Despite the pessimism and misanthropy underlying much of the work, the aesthetic effect of this rich bearing, this easy, full production, is one of joy.

A tribute to the impression of joyfulness made by Maupassant's work of the period of *Bel-Ami* is found in a letter written some years later by one of his fellow-artists—Vincent Van Gogh, writing to his brother Theo about the beauty of the women of Arles:

The best thing to do here [Van Gogh wrote] would be to paint portraits of women and children. But—I do not feel that this is my allotted task—I am not enough of a "Bel-Ami" for the work. But I should be mightily glad if [a] Bel-Ami of the South . . . if an artist could be born among painters, such as Guy de Maupassant was among writers, who could joyfully paint the beautiful people and things which are to be found here.

"What I seek above all is *beauty*," Flaubert had written to George Sand in an 1875 letter discussing the naturalist novelists who were his Sunday guests ". . . and that is something that my companions look for but half-heartedly." Flaubert's quest for beauty had played a major role in the formation of his disciple's art, which had happened to spring into first prominence amid the naturalists and their indifference (as Flaubert considered it) to beauty; joyous as the beauty of the disciple's work was, rather than somber like his own, it is impossible not to think of the pride Flaubert would have taken in it.

CHAPTER 8

"QUITE UNLIKE *BEL-AMI*"

W<small>HILE</small> *Bel-Ami* appeared serially in the *Gil-Blas* in the spring of 1885, Maupassant traveled for the first time outside French territory. Laure had always talked to him of Italy, and now he toured it from Venice to Sicily with two painter friends, Henri Gervex and Georges Legrand. Like his cousin Louis, they were academic painters: Maupassant was never an admirer of the Impressionists and Post-Impressionists, the only French painters of his period who were his equals as artists. He visited the galleries of Venice, Florence and Rome, climbed Vesuvius and Etna, enjoyed Italian girls and the behavior of Neapolitan pimps, saw Wagner's former home and the Capucin catacombs in Palermo, and some Sicilian sulphur mines. During his travels and after his return to France he wrote travel articles for the *Gil-Blas* and the *Figaro*.

Flaubert had always held a low opinion of travel-writing, claiming that a writer worthy of the name incorporates his travel experiences, like any other experiences, into imaginative works. Maupassant's travel pieces are not such as to challenge his master's condemnation of the genre, and yet neither did foreign scenes ever inspire any of his best fiction. His only story laid in

Italy, *Les Soeurs Rondoli*, was written before he ever
went there; and none of his African stories is the equal
of a good French one. His travels, at first enjoyable
superficial holidays, gradually turned into compulsive
symptomatic wanderings; in neither guise did they ever
awaken the magic of his art.*

Back in Paris, he wrote to Laure on July 7:

Nothing new about *Bel-Ami*. It has kept me from
going to Etretat so far, as I have been busy trying to do
something to help sales—without great success. Victor
Hugo's death was a terrible blow to the book.† It is in
its twenty-seventh edition—that is, thirteen thousand
sold. As I told you, it will go to twenty or twenty-two
thousand: a very respectable sale, but no more. I am
leaving for Etretat on Friday at one. I will stay only
three days, then come back here and set out for Châtel-
Guyon on the eighteenth. Do join me there—I'd so enjoy
having you with me for my twenty-five days. If you
would consent, I would rent a little house (which I
wouldn't do if I were alone), and would bring François
to serve us. Please send me an answer to Etretat immediately, so that I can make plans.

Two years before, in the summer of 1883, Laure and
Guy had spent some time together at Châtel-Guyon, a
watering place in Auvergne; but this time she did not
join him for the twenty-five days of his cure. He went in
other company, and toward the end of his stay, in
August, he wrote her:

There is quite a crowd here, for Potain has adopted
the place, but everything is so horribly boring that most
of the patients will never come back despite all the good
they get from the waters. I am doing nothing except preparing my novel very slowly. It will be a rather short

---

* See Note 11: Maupassant's travel writings, page 408.
† Truly one literary man's lament on the death of another!

and very simple story, laid in this calm landscape. It will be quite unlike *Bel-Ami.*

That letter has never been printed by Maupassant's editors in its entirety, and the rows of dots which are found in the printed text are, as usual, tantalizing, arousing curiosity as to the omissions. In this case, however, it is fairly certain—despite the close confidence existing between mother and son—that the missing passages do not contain a complete description of Maupassant's life that summer in Auvergne.

The tone of that existence seems to be rather accurately rendered in a story called *Mes 25 jours* (*My 25 Days*), which he sent during the summer from Châtel-Guyon to the *Gil-Blas.* This is in the form of a journal (which Maupassant pretends to have found in his hotel room) kept by a high-spirited, hare-brained bachelor, desperate at the prospect of spending twenty-five days in the insufferable watering place. Boredom turns to gaiety, however, when amid the invalids he makes the acquaintance of two frolicsome self-styled "widows," who are as charmed to find him as he them. They make excursions, they swim nude in "an admirable little lake, perfectly round, utterly blue, clear as glass, lying at the bottom of an extinct crater," and they cause tongues to wag. Even after the widows' departure—to the bachelor's regret they are called for by two gentlemen, "widowers, no doubt"—the memory of their company benefits him; he continues to enjoy himself, and when he leaves at the end of his twenty-five days he calls Châtel-Guyon "a charming little place."

The manuscript ends there [Maupassant concludes his story]. I have no desire to add to it, my impressions of the place not having been exactly the same as my predecessor's. But then I didn't meet the two widows!

Actually, there had been no need for Maupassant to meet two widows in Auvergne. Laure having declined to accompany him, he had supplied himself with other companionship, and the raffish tone of *Mes 25 jours* is an echo of its character. One of his companions was none other than his father, Monsieur de Maupassant, who on this occasion makes positively his first appearance since obtaining for his son the detested clerkship in the Naval Ministry back in 1872. "One sheds one's sicknesses in books," D. H. Lawrence once said—"repeats and presents again one's emotions to be master of them"; and apparently in the dozens of stories of cuckolds, of miserable or contemptible husbands and fathers and government clerks Guy had shed sufficient of his father-hatred to be willing to spend some time in that unreformed gentleman's company. Monsieur de Maupassant did not stay very long in Auvergne, and the only record of his sojourn there is that he "painted some bad pictures and led a gay life." *

The latter was made easy for him by the rest of the company his son had brought with him: a pair of women characterized by Maupassant as *moukères* (tarts), one tall, dark and distinguished, the other blonde and mischievous. The two *moukères* got along well together: indeed, their relation seems to have been that of the female characters in Maupassant's story, *La Femme de Paul* (*Paul's Wife*). This did not prevent them from being satisfactory companions for the gentlemen, and the tone of the foursome is one more indication of Maupassant's degree of filial respect as far as his father was concerned.

After his twenty-five days were over and Monsieur de Maupassant had left, Guy and the two *moukères*

* Gustave de Maupassant is said at one time to have threatened to leave an inn at Pont-Aven in Brittany unless certain paintings by Gauguin were removed from the walls of the dining-room.

moved into a guest-house on the grounds of a chateau
near Châtel-Guyon belonging to a friend of Guy's named
Durand de Rochegude. The property included the Gour
de Tazenat, an extinct crater containing a clear blue lake
apparently ideal for nude bathing. Here the bigamous
household devoted itself to all kinds of *"eccentricités,"*
and were generally so far from respectable that Rochegude's mother, nominally their hostess, refused to receive
them at the chateau and had servants carry their meals
to them in baskets.

A year later, when his novel was almost done, Maupassant returned to Auvergne and spent some time
with Rochegude in Riom. Only one *moukère* was with him
this time, and he and Rochegude allowed her to accompany them and other friends on their visits to a local
Maison Tellier where they enjoyed drinking beer.

All these details, and especially the quality of *Mes 25
jours,* make it a little surprising that the novel laid in
Auvergne should, as the letter to Laure said it would,
"be quite unlike *Bel-Ami."* Nevertheless, such is the
case. *Mont-Oriol,* the novel of a watering place, differs
from *Bel-Ami* in tone and very much indeed in excellence.

Maupassant had first sketched what became the
background for *Mont-Oriol* in an 1884 *Gaulois* article,
Malades et médecins (Patients and Doctors):

In every one of the thermal stations that spring up
around every tepid stream discovered by a peasant, a
series of wonderful scenes takes place. First the peasant's
sale of his land, the forming of a corporation with a
fictitious capital of several million, the miracle of the
construction of a bathing establishment with these
imaginary funds and real stone, the installation of the
first doctor, with the title "Medical Inspector," the appearance of the first patient, then the eternal, the sublime
comedy between the patient and the doctor.

That comedy of the development of a watering-place and of the relations between doctors and patients forms the background of *Mont-Oriol.* Guy's and Laure's long frequenting of doctors made him well qualified to handle the subject, and his sadistic strain made him enjoy writing of sufferers, stomach-pumpings and violent, absurd gymnastics. Unfortunately the background is overwritten and intrusive (so unlike the case of *La Maison Tellier,* where Maupassant's control of a very strong background was unerring); and to make matters worse, a love affair is arbitrarily pasted against it—a solemn infatuation quite unrelated to it, involving vapid worldlings, people of a kind Maupassant had not previously written of with solemnity, and having for its cuckold a Jew whose stereotyped portrayal confirms the forebodings aroused by the portrayal of the editor Walter in *Bel-Ami.* This Jewish stereotype is the chief thing the two books have in common: but whereas in *Bel-Ami* the Jew's vulgarity is part of the general disreputability of the scene, in *Mont-Oriol* he is a contrasting, ludicrous victim amid a group of the well-born. It is only a guess, but perhaps a suggestive one, to relate this bit of casting to Maupassant's new toleration of his father. With the well-born Monsieur de Maupassant partially forgiven, someone else, different in type and yet sufficiently despicable, had to be found to fill the cuckold's role; and, adopting the values of the society which he was now for the first time seriously and sympathetically portraying, Maupassant made his victim a Jewish parvenu.

The obtrusiveness of the background, the choice of victim, the vapidity of the sympathetically portrayed characters, and the almost complete absence of the raffish disreputability that is the joy of *Bel-Ami* and also of the shorter Auvergne story, *Mes 25 jours,* combine to spoil *Mont-Oriol.*

The culprit is Maupassant's increasing worldliness. He was well aware of the dangers he was running in his new associations, the associations that Goncourt had recorded in his journal. Early in 1886, while *Mont-Oriol* was in process of composition, he wrote Hermine Lecomte du Nouy from Antibes, and after telling her of the number of counts, dukes and princes he had been seeing, and of his "stupor" at discovering that "royal distinction and bourgeois vulgarity" could not always be told apart, he said:

In any case, all this has served to formulate for me a principle which is more true, you may be convinced, than the existence of God:

Every happy man who wishes to preserve his integrity of thought and independence of judgment, to see life, humanity and the world as a free observer, above all prejudice, all preconceived belief and all religion, must absolutely keep himself removed from what is called Society; for universal stupidity is so contagious that he cannot frequent his fellow-creatures without, despite his best efforts, being carried along by their convictions, their ideas and their imbecilic morality.

Teach that to your son instead of catechism.

His exposition of that principle to Hermine was apparently unaccompanied by any realization of how his own failure to observe it was affecting his novel; but in the same letter he touches more consciously on another troubling aspect of *Mont-Oriol:*

I am writing a very exalted, very alert, very poetic story of passion. For me this is a change—and it embarrasses me. The chapters about the feelings are much more scratched out and rewritten than the others. It is coming along anyway—one adjusts to anything with patience; but I often laugh at the sentimental ideas— very sentimental and tender—that I find if I look hard enough. I fear that all this may convert me into the lover-type, not only in books but also in life; when the mind takes a new crease it keeps it; and really, some-times when I am walking on the Cap d'Antibes, a cape as solitary as a Breton heath, preparing a poetic chapter in the moonlight, I find myself imagining that that kind of experience isn't as stupid as one might think.

Was this another case of "shedding one's sicknesses in books"? Like the dozens of fictional father-destruc-tions resulting in the new toleration of Monsieur de Mau-passant, had the dozens of brutal, erotic, cynical, gay little stories brought about at least some slight suspicion in their author's mind of what the advantages of another kind of affair might be? So far, apparently, the suspicion was dim; or in any case it had not brought with it literary mastery of new subject-matter. For the inanities of the infatuation in *Mont-Oriol* make painful reading, and one longs for the widows and the bachelor in *Mes 25 jours*, for the Maupassant of *Bel-Ami* and the little stories in the *Gil-Blas*.

Mont-Oriol caused Maupassant more trouble than any of his previous works. After having begun his manu-script in Auvergne in the summer of 1885, and taken it to Paris and then to Antibes, he took it back to Au-vergne again, and then, after a brief holiday visit to England, once again to Antibes. From there, aboard his newly acquired yacht *Bel-Ami*, he wrote to Louis Le Poittevin on November 7, 1886: "Nothing to tell you. I work and sail, sail and work; my novel is almost fin-ished, but I don't count on returning to Paris before December 15. Excuse this short note, but I am being careful of my eyes." By November 21 the book was finally completed and sent to Paris, and he wrote Lucie that he was making *"superbes promenades"* on the *Bel-Ami* in May-like Mediterranean weather.

His publisher, Havard, wrote him on December 10 that he thought the book excellent, and it ran serially in the *Gil-Blas* from December 23 to February 6. When it appeared between covers the reviews were mixed: one critic dismissed it as a mere "guide-book to Auvergne," others found it flat, and still others welcomed the new "note of tenderness." It is pleasing to be able to report that in later years Maupassant himself described the book as being "not worth very much." That phrase occurs in a letter to Havard, disagreeing with the latter's opinion of certain later stories. "Remember," Maupassant urges him, "your enthusiasm for *Mont-Oriol*, which I myself disliked." That is one of the differences between *Mont-Oriol* and the best of the earlier works: in it, the author communicates his own lack of enjoyment; in them, his buoyancy and self-confidence are infectious.

From *Mont-Oriol* it is a relief to turn to another unit in Maupassant's fiction: a small group of short stories which, like *Mont-Oriol*, deal with highlife, but deal with it very differently: four particularly frothy tales whose leading characters are two little baronesses, a little countess, and a little marquise.

The earliest Maupassant predecessor of these lighter-than-air narratives is probably the 1883 *Aux Eaux* (*At the Waters*, or *Taking the Waters*), in which a young marquis, dreading the boredom of a cure at Louèche (Maupassant's first watering-place, visited during ministry days), takes with him an actress whom he passes off as his wife. Her success among the assembled nobility who adore her, the marquis's wistful thought and quick rejection of marriage, the actress's delight in being treated like a respectable woman and her despair in returning to her usual life—all, handled with Maupassant's surest and slightest touch, make it one of the smaller masterpieces. Another predecessor is *Rose*, recounted during the flower festival at Cannes, in which the perfect lady's maid, whose intimate cares and massage had been enjoyed by her mistress, is revealed by the police to be not only a man but a rapist. The series proper begins in July, 1885, with *Joseph*, about the man-servant of the little countess Noëmi de Gardens, and continues with *La Confidence*, about the little marquise de Rennedon's revenge on her husband, with *Sauvée (Saved)*, about her securing of evidence for her divorce, and with *Le Signe*, about her friend the little baroness de Grangerie, who adores living near a railroad station but gets herself into trouble by sitting in her window and imitating the tactics of a professional neighbor.

For those whose tastes include light fun and who are not offended by the literary equivalent of a good champagne (it is remarkable how many readers *are* offended by that sort of thing, or dismiss it with contempt or condescension), these stories are among Maupassant's most masterly accomplishments. For his powerful and emotional stories he devoted himself seriously (usually bitingly) to the chief themes that came to him from Laure; and even in the realm of light comedy and farce there are those who prefer his peasant scenes, full of the aroma of Normandy—"I like *La Bête à Maître* [sic] *Belhomme, La Ficelle, Le Petit Fût, Le Cas de Madame Luneau, Tribunaux rustiques*, and many others of this category much better than his anecdotes of the mutual

confidences of his little *marquises* and *baronnes*," said
Henry James; but the *marquises* and *baronnes*, too, are
miracles of craftsmanship and fun, every line of their
"mutual confidences" evoking the Gallic comic god. How
preferable this laughing treatment of highlife inanities is
to the searching of empty souls in *Mont-Oriol*, and how
much more at home Maupassant is among what James
calls the *saletés* (indecencies) than among the *grandes
passions!* This little series is the finest, most delicate fruit
of his erotic confusion.

Sauvée and especially another, slightly less successful
story of the same general type, *La Revanche* (*Revenge*),
are interesting because they are Maupassant's first uti-
lization of new situations created by the institution, or
rather re-institution, of divorce in France in 1884. On
July 31 of that year the news of the promulgation of the
divorce law was blazoned in the newspapers. In the
Figaro, under the large headline *MANUEL du DI-
VORCE,* half the front page was given over to the provisions of the law and a discussion of this "greatest moral
revolution in France in sixty years":

You henpecked husbands, you husbands of the category that has always been laughed at, you martyrized
wives who have seen the false caresses of the honeymoon
disappear with the dowry money, and most especially
you, oh lawyers, whose practices will now double their
value—mark with a red letter this great day of the courts,
this blessed day which brings liberty to the galley-slaves
of marriage.

The pros and cons of divorce had been thoroughly
debated in the Chamber of Deputies during the previous
few years, and the newspapers had not been shy about
expressing their opinions. In the *Gaulois* for June 27,
1882, Maupassant had written an article stating that the

sensibilities of almost any Frenchman, he was sure, were too delicate to allow him to marry a woman whose ex-husband was alive; and shortly before the promulgation of the law he returned to the subject in the *Figaro*, prophesying all kinds of farcical situations in forthcoming books and plays. In the consequences of the new marital freedom, he said, the playwright and novelist would dis-cover "a California of situations never before dreamed of." The kind of situation he had in mind he himself utilized in *La Revanche*, in which M. de Garelle embarks on a new relationship with his ex-wife, now Mme. de Chantever—thinking gleefully, of course, of the role to be played by M. de Chantever. But the new law is re-flected in very few of his pages. Divorce, although legal, long remained in most French circles so unthinkable that even its literary possibilities were little exploited during Maupassant's lifetime. Laure and Gustave de Maupas-sant, among many other estranged French couples of good family, preferred to remain merely separated for the rest of their days.

CHAPTER 9

ENGLAND AND OTHER EXAGGERATIONS

My dear henry james [Paul Bourget wrote the summer of 1886, when Maupassant was writing *Mont-Oriol*], It is to Maupassant that I am giving this brief word for you. He is going to stay with Ferdinand de Rothschild, where you will perhaps see him. In any case, I have told him that you were the only man in London with whom it is possible to talk as with the Gallo-Romans. It gives me great pleasure to send him to you, and I am melancholy at the thought of the dinner you will have together in smoky but nonetheless beloved London. See that he meets Burne-Jones and Rossetti—in short, watch over his exile as you once watched over that of your constant friend, Paul Bourget.

The following January Bourget wrote to James again: "Last summer I gave Maupassant a letter for you when he was on his way to London. Did he deliver it? I have never heard, either from him or from you."

The letter had apparently been delivered, for there exist letters from James written in August, 1886, to Gerald du Maurier and Edmund Gosse, inviting them to dinner to meet Maupassant. A more or less dependable account by Oscar Wilde of that or another dinner indicates that Maupassant had understood, or chosen to understand, in a very "Gallo-Roman" sense Bourget's word that James was the only man in London with whom one could talk as with a Frenchman:

Wilde told me that when Maupassant visited London he was the guest of Henry James. James took him to the exhibition at Earl's Court and they dined in the restaurant. Maupassant said, "There's a woman sitting over there that I'd like to have. Go over and get her for me."

James was horribly shocked.

"But, my dear friend, I can't do that. She may be perfectly respectable. In England you have to be careful."

After a few seconds Maupassant spotted another woman.

"Surely, you know her at least? I could do quite well with her if you'll get her for me. Ah, if I only knew English!"

When James had refused for about the fifth time, Maupassant observed sulkily: "Really, you don't seem to know anybody in London."

That James had refused to do what he asked from motives of prudery and respectability never occurred to him.*

That Maupassant may well—if the story has any truth in it—have been subjecting Henry James to one of the *farces* in whose perpetration he took such pleasure apparently occurred to no one.

In a letter to Madame Straus, written from Waddesdon, the Rothschild country house, Maupassant describes another kind of farce in which he was indulging— the farce of virtuous behavior:

As I told you at the beginning of this letter, I have been in England for the past fortnight, and in the Rothschild manor I have watched a whole procession of illustrious personages, beginning with the son of the Prince of Wales. But the men interest me little, and the

* Vincent O'Sullivan, *Aspects of Wilde*, Henry Holt and Co., New York, 1936; p. 206; Constable and Co., London.

women here haven't the charm of ours—I mean of the
women of France. People claim that only their appearance is severe, but when one confines one's self to appearances—and that is my case—one has the right to ask that
they be a little less forbidding. However, I rather imagine
that before my arrival I was painted as enjoying a terrible reputation, and that I therefore find myself in the
presence of strongholds which have been heavily fortified
out of fear of immediate and impetuous assault by this
French *débauché*. I therefore behave like a little boy who
is anxious to be very good and who probably seems very
timid. And after my departure everyone will talk about
the sexual modesty of Frenchmen, as we talk—without
believing a word of it—about that of the English.

In one way or another, the spirit of much of the
English visit was fairly slapstick. Blanche Roosevelt,
who was traveling with Maupassant at least part of the
time, wrote in her article in Wilde's *The Woman's World*
an account of other episodes of the excursion:

M. de Maupassant has travelled widely, but never
visited England till the summer of 1886. He was invited
specially as guest of Baron Ferdinand de Rothschild,
and it was at the magnificent seat of Wadesden [sic] that
he was introduced to the charm of English country life.
His cultured host had made up an unusually distinguished party to meet him, and, according to the French
author, this visit was "one of the most interesting events
of his life." After the stay in Hampshire he returned to
town, and, to the general surprise, said he would not
"do" London, but desired to go the next morning to
Oxford. "My friend Paul Bourget" (the gifted young poet
and novelist), he said, "writes me: 'You must see Oxford,
the only genuine mediaeval town in the world; it will
charm you. Don't fail to see it.' " The following day we
took an early train thither, and, although in August, the
air was raw, the wind high, and the weather atrocious.
Before we arrived an accident delayed the train, a

terrific storm arose, and we reached the mediaeval town
in anything but a cheerful humour. De Maupassant was
shivering from cold, and, to quote his own words, "fainting from hunger." "I am fond of antiquities," he observed, "but first of all breakfast! breakfast! breakfast!"
This meal was admirable and prolonged. In the meanwhile the rain fell with torrential fury, and the entire
town seemed one vast wreckage of Nature. In spite of the
discouraging aspect without, our author cried, "Ah, now
for some sight-seeing I promised Bourget, etcetera!"

A guide informed us that, although the colleges were
closed, neither wind, weather, nor circumstance could
alter the beauty of this mediaeval town. Our selection of
a cab was unfortunate: the driver was intoxicated and
the vehicle shattered. But we drove boldly forward. De
Maupassant, with his back to the horses, was trembling
and regretting Africa, when he was startled by a terrific
rap at the window. The carriage stopped, and the driver,
dripping, gravely opened the door. Shaking his head with
one maudlin and unparalleled human gesture, he hic-
coughed, "This—is—the Shel—donian!" M. de Maupassant did not understand English, but the accents
threw him into fits, and I thought the rest of our party
would simply go into convulsions. The classic Jehu,
although not understanding the cause of our mirth,
smiled responsively, waived ceremony, and began the
stereotyped history of the institute.

At other stopping-places other histories were repeated
in a similar manner. Finally, between laughing and choking, De Maupassant got into such a state that I feared
we should be arrested for lunatics, and proposed returning to town. At the station a facetious telegram was
despatched on the spot to M. Paul Bourget, and we
swung into the train just as the guard was closing the
doors.

Arrived at the London terminus, we informed M. de
Maupassant that, having "done" Oxford, one great
historical place yet remained to be visited. He was
carried without demur to Madame Tussaud's. After

finishing the afternoon in the Chamber of Horrors, the
day was concluded by a dinner and a visit to the Savoy
Theatre. Although aware of M. de Maupassant's antipathy to singing drama, we felt that, in justice to England,
he must hear a genuine English operetta. At its close he
professed himself really charmed. The next morning I
received the following: "I am too cold; the city is too
cold; I am leaving for Paris. Au revoir! many thanks, &c.
—De Maupassant."

And this is the way one French author saw England!
I gave a celebrated poet a description of how he at least
saw Oxford. "Was it not comic?" I added.

"Comic!" he cried; "I think it was most tragic."

Comic or tragic, the spirit of this brief and never
repeated visit to England was the spirit of almost everything that Maupassant had ever written about the
English. His vision of them was a very conventional
French vision, what Flaubert would have called *une idée
reçue*, doubtless "received" in Etretat, when he had seen
English tourists arouse the laughter and wonder of the
inhabitants, when he himself had dressed in girl's clothes
to shock an English old maid, and when he had visited
the English eccentrics at the Chaumière Dolmancé. The
excellence of his chief story containing an English character, *Miss Harriet*, is not due to his portrayal of Miss
Harriet herself, who remains little more than a caricature
with her appearance of "a red herring in curl-papers";
and others of his tales abound in "those good-hearted but
unbearable old maids who haunt all the hotels and
pensions of Europe, ruin Italy, poison Switzerland,
render uninhabitable the charming towns of the Riviera,
carry with them everywhere their bizarre manias, their
behavior of petrified vestals, their indescribable clothes,
and a certain odor of rubber that makes one think that
at night they are slipped into a case." Only occasionally

is justice done to English beauties, "with their exquisite freshness, their delicate coloring of sea-shells and mother-of-pearl"; usually Maupassant's Englishwomen have *"les dents au vent"* (buck teeth). Although he is usually classified as a literary "realist," Maupassant is by no conceivable definition realistic when he thus writes about the English: his English tour and his English writings are alike fantastic.

It is interesting that the same charge of false representation has been made against him in other, French fields: he has been ridiculed for his picture of impecunious Faubourg Saint-Germain nobility in such a story as *A Cheval (On Horseback)*; condemned by doctors for his description of attempted suicide by chloroform in *Yvette*, and for other medical details; and even one of his great specialties, the portrayal of the Norman peasantry, although it has received and continues to receive much praise for veracity in many quarters, has also been violently attacked, especially by Normans.

The English caricatures and the French complaints raise the question of Maupassant's value as a portraitist of his own society. Was the world he lived in as he describes it? When, for instance, he says in *Une Surprise* that the feet of pupils at the Yvetot seminary were washed only three times during the school year, and in *Blanc et Bleu (White and Blue)* shows a fashionable bachelor walking barefoot in the snow at night to give himself a foot-bath (having unexpectedly just made a conquest at a party and wanting to freshen himself a bit before his rendezvous), and in *La Bête à Maît' Belhomme (Belhomme's Insect)* describes the interior of a peasant's ear, is it necessary to accept the generality that comes to mind? In *La Maison Tellier* he declares that "The stigma of dishonor attached to prostitution, which is so strong in the cities, does not exist in the Norman countryside. The peasant says, 'It's a good trade,' and allows his daughter to tend a harem of prostitutes as he would allow her to direct a young ladies' boarding-school." In *Un Fils* (*A Son*) the narrator rapidly forgets the hotel maid with whom he spent several nights, "hotel maids being generally expected thus to entertain travelers." And Maupassant's whole general picture of French married life, with cuckoldry rampant, full married happiness non-existent—is all this "the truth?"

A partial answer can be found in a number of articles by Zola, originally printed in the *Figaro* and later collected under the title *Une Campagne* (*A Campaign*), in which he discusses such matters as prostitutes, respectable women and adultery among the bourgeoisie. As he describes French middle-class family life of the time, it seems to have been much as it is in France—and in England and America—today. For all his sensationalism, Zola was soberer than Maupassant in his documentation.

In Maupassant's work, when women of the world get drunk it is on champagne; when a peasant or working-girl is debauched, it is almost never by a social superior, but by one of her own class; aristocrats bear such names as Gontran or Roland, dogs Mirza or Sam; a married woman makes a better mistress than a single woman, one of her advantages being that her husband makes a convenient friend for her lover; peasants are merciless to their animals and to incapacitated non-productive members of their own families; Parisian men about town use a toilet water with an English label—"New-Mown Hay"; illegitimate children are brought up by peasants, and usually, even though their parents are aristocrats or otherwise attractive, grow up to be uninteresting peasants or petty bourgeois themselves; France is a glorious

land, supreme especially in its wit and its women, but
the French Republic is a ridiculous institution, a ship of
fools; if a girl of the people is in some admirable way out-
standing, she probably has some "better blood" in her
veins; men make formal love declarations; and except
for the crews of transatlantic liners, Frenchmen who
visit America do so as one might venture to the other
side of the moon.

Such are some of the conclusions concerning Maupassant's society that a reader of his works is likely to arrive
at; but caution is advisable, for very often, as in the case
of the English, he was quite uninterested in presenting
things as they were. His stories are so crammed with
social "facts" that a large number of them are inevitably
"true"; in his later society novels he indulged in rather
painstaking documentation; and even in his early and
middle works, when he thought it advisable, he made
an effort in that direction: he consulted Turgenev as to
what song British sailors might sing outside the Maison
Tellier, he returned to Auvergne a second summer to
immerse himself in the atmosphere of the place he was
describing, in *Mont-Oriol* he portrayed with care a
peasant family in the process of social transformation.
But in general his purpose was even less "realistic"
than that of Flaubert, who said:

God knows how scrupulous I am in the way of consulting documents and books, collecting information,
traveling, etc. Well, I consider all that very secondary
and inferior. Material truth or what is called that should
be but a springboard, to raise one to something higher.

For every artist that "something higher" is his personal vision of that part of reality which he has chosen
to explore. In Maupassant's case the vision inspired him

with a sense of farce, absurdity, irony and horror; and
his communication of those feelings in his stories gave
him his chief satisfaction. Certainly one of the reasons
for such satisfaction as he experienced must have been
the fact that his work gratified his audience, the readers
of the newspapers for which he wrote; and to the extent
that readers were gratified his writings can be called representative of his society—in the sense that his audience
is mirrored in the popularity and wide acceptance of his
stories.

> Imagine my state of happiness [wrote Henry Adams
> from Paris in 1891], surrounded by a pile of yellow litera-
> ture, skimming a volume of Goncourt, swallowing a vol-
> ume of Maupassant with my roast, and wondering that
> I feel unwell afterwards. These writers have at least the
> merit of explaining to me why I dislike the French, and
> why the French are proper subjects for dislike.

Some of Henry Adams's indigestion was perhaps the
result of swallowing the "facts" in Maupassant stories.
And yet the very fact that, whether "factual" or not,
published Maupassant stories took the form and character they did, does explain something of "why the
French are proper subjects for dislike"—or the opposite.
If Henry Adams read *Châli*, with its French naval officer
and his eight-year-old Indian mistress, or *L'Enfant*, with
the bloody self-abortion by an aristocratic French widow,
or *Duchoux*, with its cruelly named bastard child, or even
La Fenêtre (*The Window*), in which a French man of the
world lifts his fiancée's skirts and kisses her on the buttocks, having mistaken her for her maid, or *L'Inconnue*
(*Unknown Woman*), his indigestion is understandable.
Whether or not the "facts" in those stories are "true,"
they certainly suggest a good deal about France and
Frenchmen and Frenchwomen of that time: if not about

what they actually did, then about what they would
have liked to do, about the way they thought of themselves—perhaps unconsciously, perhaps despite the official opinions they expressed concerning themselves. In
this sense, Maupassant's exaggerations may afford a
deeper, more poetic truth—Flaubert's "something
higher"—than would soberer documentation.

CHAPTER 10

THE HORLA: STORY AND BALLOON

Now comes *Le Horla,* the famous story of a terrified madman who burns his beloved house to destroy an evil presence.

Le Horla is as universally known as *La Parure,* but its excellence is of a subtler kind. In it Maupassant's skill is devoted to gradually communicating a sense of fear, rather than leading brilliantly up to a brutal shock; and the greater dependence on subtleties of language in achieving the effect causes the story to suffer more gravely in translation. In certain English versions it reads like one of the less successful products of a pulp-writer; in the original it is an absorbing and exciting study of insanity, with the beauties of Maupassant's language unobtrusively fulfilling the task imposed by the subject.

Its success is all the more remarkable in that it is not a "psychological" story: that is, little if any explanation for its supernatural events can be sought in traits or actions attributed by the author, more or less as clues, to his characters—the kind of explanation or solution that can be suggested, for example, in the case of Henry James's *The Turn of the Screw.* In *Le Horla* the supernatural is imposed from without—it comes from Brazil, on a ship; all we know about the protagonist is that he

lives near Rouen and that he is, or is going, crazy. Such
a lack of *"human* interest" usually makes for dull story,
or rather—since almost no story seems to be dull to
everyone—for a story interesting only to undemanding
audiences, such as perpetual radio-listeners. The fact that
Le Horla impressed the most discriminating readers of its
time (it caused Anatole France to call Maupassant
"prince of storytellers"), and especially that it still im-
presses some in the psychologically more sophisticated
present, is a tribute to technical skill (emphasis on everyday detail, punctuation, etc.) and hard work (the commonly known version of the story is the third of three
published versions).*

The external aspect of *Le Horla*—the imposing of the
supernatural from without—is exemplified in the title
itself. The French word *hors* means outside, without; in
Une Vie and *La Bête à Maît' Belhomme* there are characters named respectively Horslaville and Horlaville
(outoftown); and Horla, a word invented by Maupassant, combines that sense of *hors* with a suggestion of the
first syllable of *horrible—L'Horrible* being the title of one
of Maupassant's earlier horror tales. ("On certain days,"
he once wrote a friend, "I experience the horror of everything that is, to the point of longing for death; on other
days I enjoy everything like an animal.") *Le Horla* therefore means "the horrible thing out there." †

Also pertinent to the without-ness of *Le Horla* is the

* *Lettre d'un Fou* (*Gil-Blas*, February 17, 1885; see Four Hitherto Unreprinted Maupassant Stories, page 383); *Le Horla* (*Gil-Blas*, October 26, 1886;
reprinted in Volume VI of Librairie de France edition of Maupassant's works);
and *Le Horla* (in volume of the same name, first published May 1887).

† There have been two other guesses about the derivation of the name. It
has been suggested that Maupassant may have adopted it as the result of hearing
some of the many Russian residents of the Riviera use the Russian genitive of
Oriol, which is said to be *Orla* or *Horla*. (Impossible suggestion in any case, for
the second version of *Le Horla* appeared before *Mont-Oriol* even began to be
serialized.) And it has been proposed that the name may have been suggested

statement made by Axel Munthe in *The Story of San Michele* that Maupassant did not write the story entirely from within himself, but sought outside documentation:

> I seldom failed to attend Professor Charcot's famous *Leçons du Mardi* in the Salpêtrière, just then chiefly devoted to his *grande hystérie* and to hypnotism. The huge amphitheatre was filled to the last place with a multi-colored audience drawn from tout Paris, authors, journalists, leading actors and actresses, fashionable demi-mondaines, all full of morbid curiosity to witness the startling phenomena of hypnotism almost forgotten since the days of Mesmer and Braid. It was during one of these lectures that I became acquainted with Guy de Maupassant then already famous for his *Boule de Suif* and his unforgettable *Maison Tellier*. We used to have endless talks on hypnotism and all sorts of mental troubles, he never tired of trying to draw from me what little I knew on these subjects. He also wanted to know everything about insanity, he was collecting just then material for his terrible book 'Le Horla,' a faithful picture of his own tragic future. He even accompanied me once on a visit to Professor Bernheim's clinic in Nancy which opened my eyes to the fallacies of the Salpêtrière school in regard to hypnotism.[*]

Subjects like that of *Le Horla* were in the air in the 1880's. In an 1882 *Gil-Blas* article, *Une Femme*, Maupassant had written:

> *Hystérique*, Madame—that is the great word of the day. Are you in love? You are a hysteric. Are you in-

---

to Maupassant by the pen name (Jean Lahor) of one of his friends, Doctor Cazalis. In this case the name would be associated with duplication of personality in life as in the story. (See B. M. Woodbridge, *Modern Language Notes*, January, 1921, pp. 51–52.) But the derivation from *hors* and *horrible* seems fairly obvious.

[*] *The Story of San Michele* (New York, E. P. Dutton & Co., Inc. 1930. Copyright, 1929, by Axel Munthe). See Note 12: The Credibility of Axel Munthe, page 410.

different to the passions that sway your fellow-creatures?
You are a hysteric, but a chaste hysteric. Do you sometimes deceive your husband? You are a hysteric, but a
sensual hysteric. Do you steal bits of silk in a shop? Do
you tell lies at every turn? Are you a glutton? Nervous?
Hysteric, hysteric. . . . We are all hysterics; we have
been ever since Dr. Charcot, that high priest of hysteria,
that breeder of hysterics, began to maintain at great
expense in his model establishment in the Salpêtrière a
horde of nervous women whom he inoculates with madness and shortly turns into demoniacs.

Today one has to be truly very ordinary, very commonplace, very reasonable, not to be classed among the
hysterics. Academicians are not, senators are not . . .

It has been remarked * that a considerable number of
works on hypnotism, suggestion, obsession and neuroses
appeared at this time; *Les Leçons de Charcot sur les maladies du Système nerveux faites à la Salpêtrière* were published by Féré in 1884, and Ribot's work on *Les Maladies
de la Personnalité* the year following. All Paris was talking
about the phenomena of duplication of personality, of
possession. So commonly discussed were such matters
that credit for "giving" Maupassant the subject was
disputed by several of his friends. And Maupassant himself was acquainted with a Belgian hypnotist, Pickman,
saw something of him, sponsored him in certain salons,
and wrote about him in one of his newspaper pieces.

Despite all that, however, the particular success of
Le Horla is due to one of the conditions made long before
by Louis Bouilhet: the subject was in particular harmony
with the tendencies of Maupassant's mind. From the
vantage point of *Le Horla* the prevalence of madness and
mental agitation in his work from the beginning stands
up in striking prominence. Madness strikes the hero of

* By René Dumesnil, in the *Notice* to Volume VI of Librairie de France
edition of Maupassant's works.

La Main d'Ecorché, the first story he ever published; Dr. Heraclius Gloss in the early novelette of the same name is taken to an asylum and given cold douches; the oarsman in *Sur l'Eau* comes close to madness on the Seine; *Terreur,* one of the poems, contains a mysterious, unseen presence. And after *Boule de Suif* the titles themselves are revelatory: three stories are called *Fou (Mad)*; two *La Peur (Fear)*; and others *L'Apparition, Magné-tisme, L'Horrible, Lettre d'un Fou* and *La Nuit—Cauche-mar (Night: A Nightmare)*. And in still others of his works, works of predominantly different character, such as *Bel-Ami,* deep mental disquietudes play their role. What, within his own experience, had caused Maupassant to be so preoccupied with terror, madness and the supernatural? His long familiarity with Laure's *grande hystérie* and her *crises,* his probable knowledge of the melancholia of his uncle Alfred, his own illness, depression and feeling of spiritual solitude, so evident in the letters to Laure from the ministry and later infused into such stories as *Solitude*—these are scarcely sufficient explanation.

Because *Le Horla* is the culmination of his tales on morbid themes, because his syphilis was eventually to drive him insane, and because he first showed signs of serious mental confusion about a year after he wrote *Le Horla,* it is often assumed that the story itself is one of the earlier symptoms of his own illness and that the manner in which its hero is portrayed reveals Maupassant's awareness of his own approaching fate. And it is just as frequently objected that such cannot be the case; that the artistic excellence of the story nullifies such an assumption; that insane people cannot write like Guy de Maupassant; that the story was written dispassionately, as a literary tour de force.

Probably the truth about Maupassant's obsession lies in the midst of these various claims. On the one hand, the subject was current, Laure had made him familiar with mental stress and strained nerves, and it is known that he was amused by the success of his story in horrifying readers; furthermore, it was followed by numerous works utterly unconcerned with horror, including some of the most masterly of the comic stories, *Le Rosier de Madame Husson* (*Madame Husson's May King*) among them.* On the other hand, syphilis probably did have something to do with it. His first story, *La Main d'Écorché*, which heads the morbid list, was written about the time he contracted the disease (it appeared in 1875, and the doctor who certified him for Louèche in 1877 said that he had been under treatment for almost two years); and earlier than the writing of *Le Horla* he told Paul Bourget: "Every other time I come home, I see my double. I open my door, and I see him sitting in my armchair. I know it for an hallucination, even while experiencing it. Curious! If I didn't have a little common sense, I'd be afraid." (The possibility of his perpetrating a hoax, saying something to shock, must always be kept in mind, though he was probably less likely to do so with Bourget than with others.) In his moments of mental distress he quite possibly had some kind of presentiment, at this time still unformulated, of all not being well with himself; and his presentiment he tried to "shed in books." In *Le Horla* Maupassant is probably the opposite of a sufferer from a stroke, who, understanding others perfectly, nevertheless cannot express himself: in the story he gives disciplined, perfect expression to hallucinations

---

* *Le Rosier de Madame Husson* seems to be the only one of Maupassant's stories to have inspired an opera libretto—Eric Crozier's book for Benjamin Britten's *Albert Herring*. In France it has been the basis of a film and of an operetta, both starring Fernandel.

and fears which he does not understand, and which have not yet troubled him to the extent of making him incapable of his own, superior, artist's utterance. Once again, Laure's words to Flaubert about Guy at fifteen, "His nerves are not strong," and Flaubert's and the doctor's words about his suffering the same "neurosis" or "trouble" as his mother, and the disease which he called "*le mal ignoble et terrible*," all form a confused, far from completely disentangleable knot of causal factors.

Two months after *Le Horla* appeared in its definitive form, Maupassant made his first balloon ascension. On the Riviera he had become acquainted with an aeronaut named Jovis, who was a favorite with the smart set; on his return to Paris he joined the *Union Aéronautique de France;* and François reports that he had a balloon especially constructed for his own use. This is unlikely, since he seems to have made only two ascensions; but in any case formal engraved cards, bearing the club's motto, "*Quo Non Ascendamus*," were sent out inviting friends to be present at the take-off at the La Villette gas-works at five o'clock in the evening of July 8, 1887. There was, of course, no definite destination. "I am leaving by balloon on Thursday for ———," he wrote Madame Charpentier, leaving a space blank. "From wherever we land I expect to return to Paris slowly, stopping here and there on the way." After a snack in the gas-works canteen everybody shook hands all round in French style, and the balloon, bearing, in addition to Maupassant, two other passengers, Paul Bessard and Eugene Beer (presumably fellow club-members), and a crew consisting of "le Capitaine P. Jovis et le lieutenant Mallet," rose into the air to the accompaniment of applause.

They took off from La Villette about five in the afternoon in superb weather [François says], and for more
than an hour the balloon moved slowly over Paris in an
easterly direction. Then, in response to the desire expressed by Princesse Mathilde to see the aerostat above
Saint-Gratien, the captain maneuvered it in that direction, and from nine o'clock until eleven the princess and
her numerous guests had the satisfaction of seeing the
balloon floating over the chateau.

The weather was so calm that the voices of the
princess's guests on the dining-room terrace of Saint-
Gratien were clearly audible to the balloonists. But then
a wind sprang up, and as they passed over the estate of
another of Maupassant's friends they heard nothing,
even though the people on the ground were ringing bells
and firing rifles. The wind bore them "rapidly" north
through the moonlight, they crossed the Belgian border,
replied with their siren to the carillon of Bruges, and at
dawn landed at Heyst-sur-Mer, whence telegrams were
sent to friends and an early train was taken directly
back to Paris.
The sequel to the trip is amusing.

The flood of gossip items in the newspapers concerning my balloon trip [Maupassant wrote from Etretat on
July 15 to his new publisher, Paul Ollendorff], has subjected me to much joking and considerable inconvenience. I beg you to stop this torrent. It was not my idea
to baptize a balloon with the name of my book, and now
everyone thinks I made use of the balloon for publicity
purposes.

Maupassant had given some of his books to Ollendorff, François says, because he considered him more
publicity-minded than his other publisher, Havard;
perhaps it was the new publisher who had had the idea of
calling the balloon the *Horla*. However, not only is there

no evidence that Maupassant had ever opposed the project, but the very day after the letter was written there appeared in the *Figaro* an account of the excursion written by Maupassant himself—an article called *Le Voyage du Horla*. Despite his complaints when the effects of publicity became excessive, he was clearly no more publicity-shy than ever. A year later he made a second ascension in the *Horla*, remaining aloft a shorter period because a lady was along. This time, instead of a bite in the gas-works canteen, there was a picnic-basket prepared by François, containing "*filet de boeuf du Horla*, a chicken in jelly, and everything that makes a very comfortable cold dinner." They went only as far as Beauvais, and Maupassant was back in the rue de Montchanin by eleven o'clock the same night.

Although these balloon episodes in Maupassant's life are perhaps not of vital import in any account of his literary development, one biographical detail does emerge from them. They show fairly clearly that whether or not *Le Horla* contains any indication of deteriorated mental condition, Maupassant was not, either at the time of publishing the story or a year later, consciously aware of any such indication. It seems almost unbelievable that he would have allowed a balloon to be christened *Le Horla* for publicity reasons, written an article in which the name was given still further publicity, and gone up again in the *Horla* the next year, had the story held for him that painful significance.

CHAPTER 11

PIERRE ET JEAN

THE MOST ELOQUENT ANSWER to the assumption that *Le Horla* reveals a writer with a brain already deteriorated is the existence of another of Maupassant's works, written after that story, a work that is probably his finest and that Henry James pronounced "faultless": the short novel *Pierre et Jean*.

During the spring of 1887—the spring of the publication of the volume *Le Horla*—there was the usual Parisian parade of social events and lady visitors.

One afternoon when he was out [François records] a little yellow English gig stopped in front of the house, and out of it stepped a young lady in a tightly fitting tailored costume of a pretty shade of gray and a hat of the same color. I opened the door and she asked me curtly whether M. de Maupassant was at home. "No," I told her, "Monsieur is out." "Then I'll come in," she said. "Give me some writing paper and a pen." And on a sheet of ordinary paper that was lying on the desk she wrote in huge letters, covering the entire sheet, the one word PIG.

When my master returned he saw the paper, read it and laughed heartily. Then he suddenly cried: "The devil take them all! That young marquise, who writes so beautifully, is the daughter of a former minister of the

Empire. But I don't want to see her. I'm fed up. And let me tell you right away, François, I can't stay any longer in Paris; people don't let me breathe; it's impossible. I've just rented a place in Chatou. . . ."

With François, Maupassant stayed in the apartment he had rented in Chatou, on the Seine, for the rest of the spring. He did not shut himself off completely from friends—at one of his dinner parties nine of the twelve guests were ladies, and seven of the nine countesses—and François tells of the arrival of another lady during one of his master's absences, a lady who, François had been warned, was in a vindictive mood and armed with a revolver:

"François, is M. de Maupassant in?" "No, Madame, my master is in Paris." "No! No!" she cried, raising her voice. "I wanted to . . ."

And suddenly she stopped, turned white and started to fall; I had barely time to catch her in my arms and prevent her from hurting herself. I carried her to a willow chaise longue in the dining-room, stretched her on it, rubbed her hands and put vinegar compresses on her temples; there was no result. Then I had recourse to smelling-salts, holding a phial under each nostril alternately. She still didn't regain her senses, she seemed not to be breathing, and she was so extremely white that I began to wonder whether she wasn't dead. . . . Finally, little by little, she recovered. After resting for a moment she seized both my hands, wept passionately, and said: "François, I beg you, give me M. de Maupassant, give me M. de Maupassant, or I shall die! I want him! I tell you I want him! I'll not harm him, believe me, I promise —but give him to me!" I calmed her as best I could, promising to look for my master at once. I went out, but no one had seen him; then, when I was back with the lady I heard a door open and it was he. "I know all about it," he said at once. "I'll take care of it." He was as calm as if it were the simplest thing in the world.

That evening, Monsieur, accompanied by the lady, came to the door of the kitchen, and with the greatest easiness, as though nothing had happened, he said, "François, everything is taken care of." And the lady added: "Yes, we're good friends now."

At Chatou the thirty-seven-year-old Maupassant discovered that his physical prowess was not what it had been. After a four-hour rowing bout he returned exhausted, and despite cold showers and massage did not recover his strength. Intestinal symptoms manifested themselves, and after several weeks of discomfort and depression he left Chatou, whose location he pronounced too damp, unfavorable for his well-being, and installed himself for the summer in Etretat.

There, in improving health and spirits, though somewhat sobered by the revelation of his limited endurance, he began to write again.

Maupassant read me the first pages of his new novel, *Pierre et Jean* [Hermine Lecomte du Nouy noted in her diary for June 22, 1887]. It promises well; an actual happening gave him the idea for writing this book. One of his friends has just * received a legacy of eight millions, left him by a friend of his parents. It seems that the father of the young man was old, the mother young and pretty. Guy has tried to discover how the bequeathing of such fortune could be explained; he has made a supposition that imposed itself on him; he is going to develop it, and we are to go together to Le Havre so that he may get the landscape, the docks and the activity of the harbor thoroughly and accurately into his mind.

Except for the interruption of the balloon trip from Paris to Beauvais in July, the novel steadily progressed, Maupassant thinking it out as he walked up and down

---

* This is unlikely. *Pierre et Jean* is clearly developed from a short story. *L'Attente (Waiting)*, published in the *Gaulois* in 1883 and not reprinted until after Maupassant's death.

his alley of young ash trees,* and writing it at his desk on which every morning François arranged a bouquet of fresh flowers. He went in for astronomy a little that summer, looking at the stars with a local astronomer from the top of one of the cliffs; he learned why the chocolate that François served him was so particularly good (François cooked it in a double boiler for twelve hours, with a piece of vanilla in it all the while); he had guests almost every evening; and in September he went hunting, although a little less energetically than usual. The novel was finished by October, and that month he went to Africa with a party of friends, remaining until January, making "a superb excursion" in Algeria "in a wild country that looks like a lion-skin rug," going to Fez with the new French ambassador who was presenting his letters to the Sultan, and continuing to Tunis, where he visited Carthage and thought of Salammbô (that novel whose presentation by Flaubert to Laure de Maupassant had reopened, with such consequences, their old friendship).

From Africa he wrote one of his charming letters to Madame Straus, and in it he said:

We must *feel*—that is everything. We must feel as a brute beast; filled with nerves, feels, and knows that it has felt, and knows that each feeling shakes it like an earthquake. But we must not say, must not write—for the public—that we have been so shaken. At the most, we can let it be known to a few people who will respect the confidence.

* From the unpublished portion of François' memoirs:

"In two months [a slight exaggeration] he wrote *Pierre et Jean*, walking up and down his alley of young ash trees—not very tall at the time, since one day M. René Maizeroy had his beautiful pearl-gray felt hat snatched off by their branches, and another day Professor Pouchet, that faithful lover of Etretat, his navy-blue beret."

Maupassant once said, "I enjoy thinking my stories out, but not writing them."

Those lines are a key not only to the personality, but to the art, of Maupassant; and nowhere are more of the finest and most characteristic elements of his art more richly distilled, more intensively present, than in *Pierre et Jean*, which appeared in the December and January issues of the *Nouvelle Revue* and in book form on January 8, 1888, just after his return from Africa.

A petit-bourgeois couple keep a small shop in Paris; the wife, five years after bearing her husband one son, bears a second, who grows up radiant, blond and smiling, whereas his dark-haired older brother, jealous of the newcomer, develops a character that is somber and morose. Both young men study for professions, the older, after many false starts, for medicine, the other tranquilly for the law; and when both are about ready to begin to practise, the shop is sold and the family retires to the provinces—to Le Havre, where in French style the parents will live out their days modestly on their savings, the father finally able to indulge his lifelong love of sailing. Suddenly comes news: an elderly friend of the family has died in Paris, and has left all his fortune to the younger son. The older son's jealousy flares, and with it his suspicion; and the drama, played against the middle-class background, is one of filial accusation from the older son, maternal suffering and confession, filial love from the younger son, fraternal conflict, and paternal obliviousness.

As usual, the husband is dismissed—"*Le bonhomme comptait si peu,*" Maupassant says ("The good man counted for so little")—but this time the wretch is at least given the good-natured tag of "*bonhomme*" and not depicted too cruelly: he benefits from that new tolerance that had allowed Maupassant to take his father with him to Châtel-Guyon. And the theme of a woman's

humiliation is also directly present, but in richly developed form; the woman who cuckolds her husband is
humiliated by her suffering son: by now Maupassant
has moved from Laure's humiliation, through her
avenging, to something more impersonal: the consequences of a mother's adultery. Thus, here in *Pierre et
Jean* are found, but enriched and transformed by mature
art, many of Maupassant's usual ingredients: love-
making behind a dull husband's back (so amusing in the
earlier *Gil-Blas* stories), maltreatment of a mother by
her son (so gratuitous in *Une Vie*), whip-lashes of cruelty
(here supplied by the sudden, crude legacy, by Pierre's
torturing of his mother, by his own final exile), mental
torment, the sea: the whole suffused with a beautiful,
poised gravity that takes the place of—and in a sense
contains—the ingratiating raffishness and ebullience of
the earlier fiction.

The intensity with which the characters are felt, or
"seized," by the author, and the reserve and economy
with which he depicts them and tells their story (*Pierre
et Jean* is only about fifty pages longer than the novelette
Yvette), are the essence of the best of Maupassant's art;
and to anyone who sympathizes with his words to
Madame Straus about "feeling" and about reserve, that
art, as illustrated particularly in *Yvette* and in *Pierre et
Jean*, will always have extraordinary appeal. *Pierre et
Jean* is the longest piece of fiction in which Maupassant
is all but uninterruptedly in top form; it is the first—and
alas, the only—completed novel which equals the best
of his tales, and in which he gives promise of becoming
a novelist to rival the storyteller.

A young and little known author, Edouard Estaunié,
just after completing his first novel, found on reading

Pierre et Jean that Maupassant had used the same subject matter. He wrote his far more celebrated fellow-
writer of his dismay, and Maupassant replied:

Why should you think it surprising that the same
subject should have attracted us at the same time? You
have had the bad luck to see my book come out ahead of
yours, although both were ready at the same time. That
is a misfortune for you, but it takes away not at all from
the excellence of your book. Unquestionably you were
ignorant of what I was writing, just as I was ignorant of
what you were writing, all during the time when, far
apart and unknown to each other, you were composing
Stéphane * and I *Pierre et Jean.*

But in the frequency of these coincidences—which
are called plagiarisms when the authors' ignorance of
each other and each other's works is not definitely
established, as it is in our case—is there not some un-
perceived cause, unobserved and mysterious? How does
it come about that two men of the same profession often
finish the same task the same day, bring to birth two
books so alike that they seem to have intercommunicated
their thoughts and their subjects?

Isn't it that without suspecting it they have both
picked up the same germ of emotion? It was an item in a
newspaper that gave me the first idea for *Pierre et Jean.*
May not you have read the same item, the same day as
I? And how many times some striking event, widely
discussed and commented upon, produces in two minds
similarly attuned the same disturbance, then the same
series of reasonings and deductions, and engenders
parallel undertakings, leading to the same logical consequences. Let one of these minds produce more quickly,
for some reason, the work born of the same seed, and the
other will almost inevitably accuse him of being a
plagiarist.

Let me assure you of my deep sympathy for you in
this troubling circumstance. And let me congratulate

* Retitled *Un Simple* when it was published in 1891.

you on this first book, which I scarcely dare praise since it resembles my own. I wish it great success, and beg you to accept my sincere good wishes.

Without being asked, Maupassant through a common friend gave Estaunié permission to use his letter as a preface. The younger novelist did not use it, but he dedicated his novel to Maupassant.

Printed as a kind of preface to *Pierre et Jean*, and still usually reprinted with the volume, was Maupassant's essay, *Le Roman* (*The Novel*). On January 7, 1888, the day before its publication in the volume, it had appeared in the literary supplement of the *Figaro* in a considerably cut and mutilated version. Writers on Maupassant have usually, for sensational or sentimental reasons, been overeager to place the beginnings of his madness as far back in his career as possible; and some, artistically too perceptive to join the ranks of those who have placed them as far back as *Le Horla*, have found the earliest manifestations in his extreme irritation and threatened lawsuit concerning the *Figaro* cuts. His belligerence in the matter has been charitably explained on the grounds of mental deterioration.

This assumption, however, is no more valid than that concerning *Le Horla*.

There are in existence several letters which show that Maupassant did not refuse to listen to, and to take, editorial advice concerning cuts or changes in his stories; but he did insist on being consulted; and during the past few years he had contributed much less often than formerly to the *Gaulois* "because," as he wrote his lawyer, "of a change, or rather a cut, made *in my absence* to an article on *Manon Lescaut*." Now the *Figaro*, in printing the essay on the novel, not only made extensive cuts without consulting the author, but did its cutting in such a way as to gravely distort, indeed make all but incomprehensible, the sense of certain passages. Maupassant received numerous letters from literary men expressing surprise or bewilderment following their reading of the article, and one from his friend the critic Jules Lemaître indicates the gravity of the *Figaro's* offense:

I have just read your preface in the supplement of *Figaro*, and must ingenuously ask you for some explanations of your meaning [Lemaître wrote, preceeding then to quote, among other passages, one made ridiculous by the cuts]. In short, I can make nothing of it, and am thus writing to you in complaint. You—ordinarily so lucid! What in the world has happened to you?

Now that I have made my little protest, I can comfortably tell you that *Pierre et Jean* (which I piously read in the *Nouvelle Revue*) is one of the most beautiful things that you have written. It is cruel, but full of verisimilitude; that is to say, true. And as for its execution, nothing you have done is sharper, better planned, better composed and arranged, more masterly. But I hope soon to see you and to give voice to all the admiration—and all the rancor!—that are in my heart.

When an influential critic is led to ask a writer, "What in the world had happened to you?" partly as the result of unauthorized cuts made by an editor, vigorous action by the writer against the editor is clearly indicated; and Maupassant's indignant, explicit letters to his lawyer, Emile Straus, and his equally eloquent letters to the *Gaulois*, to the *Gil-Blas*, to the *Figaro* editors and to others were but necessary parts of that action.

The case never went to court, and eventually the

Figaro published a note that had been composed by Maupassant and Straus:

Monsieur Guy de Maupassant, following explanations offered him concerning cuts made without his authorization in an essay appearing in these columns—cuts which were the occasion of the institution of legal proceedings against the *Figaro*—has withdrawn his suit. We are happy to announce this amicable solution, which makes it possible for Monsieur de Maupassant and the *Figaro* to resume their old relations.

Despite the "amicable solution," Maupassant never wrote again for the *Figaro*. But to secure by means of waspish letters an *amende honorable* from a culpable editor is no more indicative of mental deterioration than to write a story in which mental deterioration is portrayed.

As for the essay itself,* so widely read by students of literature and so generally regarded as the classic disquisition on the "realistic," "naturalistic," or "objective" novel, Henry James expressed an opinion shortly after its appearance which is something of a counterbalance to the high esteem in which it has since come almost universally to be held:

The first artists, in any line, are doubtless not those whose general ideas about their art are most often on their lips—those who most abound in precept, apology, and formula and can best tell us the reason and the philosophy of things. . . . I may as well say at once that in dissertation M. de Maupassant does not write with his best pen; the philosopher in his composition is perceptibly inferior to the story-teller. I would rather have written half a page of *Boule de Suif* than the whole of the introduction to Flaubert's *Letters to Madame*

* Some of its contents have been noted on pages 60–61.

Sand; and his little disquisition on the novel in general, attached to that particular example of it which he has just put forth, is considerably less to the point than the masterpiece which it ushers in. In short, as a commentator M. de Maupassant is slightly common, while as an artist he is wonderfully rare. Of course we must, in judging a writer, take one thing with another, and if I could make up my mind that M. de Maupassant is weak in theory, it would almost make me like him better, render him more approachable, give him the touch of softness that he lacks, and show us a human flaw.*

Indeed, despite the glimpses of his teachers Bouilhet and Flaubert which Maupassant's essay affords, and except for its few moments of revelation, its commonness —by which James doubtless meant its inadequacy—is such as to make one almost wish that its author had not chosen to go beyond a statement he once made in the *Gaulois* (*Question Littéraire*, March 18, 1882): "Art is art, that is all I know about it. *Opium facit dormire quia habet virtutem dormitaven.*" But it is impossible to wish that wholeheartedly, for due to its wide circulation— wider than that of most treatises on the subject because of the fame of the novel to which it is attached—the inadequate essay has at least performed one office: it has given many a reader his first hint of the selection and distortion of material that go into any act of artistic creation. And even artists have taken courage from it. Once again it is Vincent Van Gogh, writing to his brother from the hospital in which he was confined at Arles, who reveals with particular poignancy how one creative spirit can give another the nourishment it needs:

I am just reading Guy de Maupassant's *Pierre et Jean*. It is very fine. Have you read the preface to it, in

* From the essay "Guy de Maupassant" (in *The Fortnightly Review*, March, 1888; *Partial Portraits*, Macmillan and Co., 1888; *The Art of Fiction and Other Essays*, Oxford University Press, 1948).

which he declares the artist free to exaggerate and to
create a more beautiful, more simple, and more comforting life in the novel, and explaining what Flaubert wished
to express with the words "talent is a long trial of patience," and originality an act of will-power and of most
intense observation?

CHAPTER 12

SHOCK

THE YEARS of Maupassant's great output of short stories were now over. Between 1882 and 1887, inclusive, he had written almost two hundred and fifty; in 1888, the year of the publication of *Pierre et Jean*, he wrote only six—almost as few as in 1881, the year of *La Maison Tellier*. The reason and the circumstances in the later year were different, however: several of the 1881 stories were long and rich, and he gave them his best attention, taking far greater pains with them than with his other, simultaneous productions—"journalism," that is, articles, of which in 1881 he had been writing one a week. In 1888 he wrote almost no articles at all, and his stories were not his best. His attitude toward his work at the time of the completion of *Pierre et Jean* is expressed in a letter to his mother:

Times are very bad for us writers: nothing is selling. As for me, I am broke, and if I don't want to have to ask for a librarian's job I mustn't lose any time, for I can no longer write journalism.

Pierre et Jean will have a literary success, but not a commercial success. I am sure that the book is good—I have always told you so; but it is cruel, and that will prevent its selling. Therefore I must see about earning my living without counting too much on the booksellers, and I am going to try the theatre, which I consider a trade, in order that I may be able to write my books exactly as I please, without the slightest thought of what happens to them. If I can succeed in the theatre I will be easy in my mind—and don't think that I would devote too much of my time to that pseudo-literary branch of business.

The fact that Maupassant proclaimed himself "broke" did not prevent him from shortly thereafter going off to Africa for three months; the "librarian's job" is probably a reference to the sinecure that had been found for Flaubert in his needy old age; and since he does not mention short stories as a means of earning a living he had perhaps by now come to consider them, along with articles, as "journalism." As usual with a writer, his pronouncements concerning his own work were subject to change—he was still to write several of his best and best-known short stories, such as *Boitelle, Le Champ d'Oliviers (The Olive Field)*, and *L'Inutile Beauté (Useless Beauty)*—but the emphasis on novels, with commercial theater on the side, marks a difference from Laure's wish in 1882 that he would give up journalism in favor of "serious work" which very definitely included short stories.

Also, Maupassant had by now come to take less pleasure than formerly in Paris, the "dunghill" which in earlier days he had said was so necessary to an artist. "I am preparing myself for Parisian life," he wrote Madame Straus on his way back from Africa. "It would make me melancholy in advance if it weren't for the thought of a few people, very few but very longed-for, whom I will find there." More and more he stayed away from the city. "At the moment I am planning a long cruise for this summer," he wrote in the same letter. "I am going to sail around Spain in a new yacht which I have just bought. Thus I will combine my two chief passions, travel and navigation." He never made the cruise around Spain, but from now on he was constantly aboard the new and larger *Bel-Ami*.

His income, which had formerly come chiefly from newspaper stories, articles and serialized novels, now came increasingly from French and foreign book sales. There was constant correspondence with Havard and others about translations; certain rights to various stories belonged to various publishers, who had brought out the volumes in which they appeared; unauthorized translations and reprints appeared and had to be checked; publishers from all lands wrote for rights to this book or that. Maupassant was hard in money matters: "You are tyrannizing me about your account with unheard-of cruelty," Havard wrote him on one occasion; the correspondence between them is full of references to his demands for advances and accountings; and in the *Petit Bottin des Lettres et des Arts* (*Little Directory of Arts and Letters*), which was published anonymously in 1886, he was one of three authors, out of four hundred listed, after whose names were appended the letters N.C.: "*Notable Commerçant*" (*Notorious Businessman*). He lived expensively, with the apartment in the rue de Montchanin, an additional small apartment, or *garçonnière*, nearby for clandestine meetings, the house at Etretat, and usually an apartment somewhere on the Riviera near Laure in the winter, with François as cook and valet and with two southern French sailor brothers-in-law, Raymond and Bernard, as skipper and mate on the *Bel-Ami;* and in his homes and on the yacht he constantly entertained at dinner and lunch. (Following one lunch party aboard the *Bel-Ami* in the bay of Agay, given in honor of a visiting Cambodian potentate, mice,

which had been dyed various colors, were let loose among
the guests; and when the ladies stopped screaming they
[the ladies] grouped themselves around the king and
entertained him with French songs whose character can
be imagined. The king had continued unperturbed, to
eat his sandwiches, pronouncing mice "inoffensive.")

He was generous with Laure, whose income had
steadily dwindled (Les Verguies in Etretat was for sale,
as she never left the Riviera but for an occasional summer visit to central France), and François tells of his
gifts to less prosperous literary men whom he admired,
among them Mallarmé and Leconte de Lisle. Along with
the advantages of fame he suffered some of the draw-
backs: his celebrity and his erotic adventures combined
to bring about a steady stream of true and false gossip
items in the papers and rumors that circulated by word
of mouth, and there were cases of impersonation and of
forgery of his signature on letters and other documents.

The year of *Pierre et Jean* was the year of Maupassant's English and American canonization—in Henry
James's essay already mentioned, a study notable for its
characterization of Maupassant's writings, its placing of
Maupassant in the French tradition, and its exposition
of differences between French and English fiction.

Using the preface to *Pierre et Jean* as a starting point,
James proceeds to discuss the keenness of Maupassant's
physical senses as revealed in his work, and his almost
exclusive concern with the very lively physical senses of
his characters, especially "the sense *par excellence*, the
sense which we scarcely mention in English fiction, and
which I am not very sure I shall be allowed to mention
in an English periodical." He then mentions that sense
anyway, at length, and points up certain national differences. He exaggerates, forgetting such a story as

Yvette, when he concludes that "M. de Maupassant has simply skipped the whole reflective part of his men and women—that reflective part which governs conduct and produces character." He speaks of Maupassant's best short stories as "a collection of masterpieces," "gems of narration"; "The author fixes a hard eye on some small spot of human life, usually some ugly, dreary, shabby, sordid one, takes up the particle, and squeezes it either till it grimaces or till it bleeds. Sometimes the grimace is very droll, sometimes the wound is very horrible. . . . M. de Maupassant sees human life as a terribly ugly business relieved by the comical." And he expresses the transforming magic of Maupassant's art when he says of *L'Abandonné* (*The Abandoned Son*), "The manner in which this dreary little occurrence is related makes it as large as a chapter of history." And his discussion of the novels concludes that "*Pierre et Jean* is the best of M. de Maupassant's novels mainly because M. de Maupassant has never before been so clever. It is a pleasure to see a mature talent able to renew itself, strike another note, and appear still young."

One wonders whether Maupassant knew of this excellent essay, which remains the best discussion of his fiction in English, and, if he did, how much it meant to him, accustomed as he was by now to praise and analysis by the leading critics of his own country. Perhaps he did know of it, for he was acquainted with Theodore Child, the Paris representative of Harper and Brothers, and it was Harper's, perhaps stimulated by James's essay, who the next year published in New York the first collected volume of Maupassant stories in English, *The Odd Number*. This contained a short preface by James and thirteen tales, translated by James's friend, Jonathan Sturges, the young man whose repetition to James of a

few chance words by Howells was the first faint beginning of *The Ambassadors*. Sturges' translations are
excellent (though no better than those which Lafcadio
Hearn had made of fifty or more Maupassant stories for
the *New Orleans Times-Democrat* between 1881 and
1887), but the collection is a pallid one, composed entirely
of tales which are not concerned with "the sense *par
excellence*," and thus scarcely representative of their
author. It was to be a little while yet before Maupassant
broke with his full production—and even something
more than his full production—into a portion of the
English-language market.*

Now, weary of journalism and not yet launched in
the theater, he began a new novel—the one type of work
he wanted to do.

I am very slowly preparing my new novel [he wrote
his mother from Paris in May, 1888] and I am finding it
very difficult—there have to be so many shadings, things
suggested and not said. It will not be long, and I want it
to pass before the reader's eyes like a vision of life,
terrible, tender and desperate.

Give me news of yourself as often as you can. If you
would like me to send you some books, tell me, and I will
choose the least irritating of those that I receive. I know
you read but little, but perhaps you could look through
a few pages. I am so unhappy at the thought of your
feeling so alone, so tormented and so ill, that I constantly
try to find some little distraction for you. Alas—it isn't
easy.

The tone of that is the tone of one of the letters from
the ministry; and in reading it one suddenly remembers

* See: Sixty-five Fake "Maupassant" Stories, page 353.

that there have been no such letters from Maupassant
since *Boule de Suif*. He has been marvelously fertile,
busy with his fiction, "shedding" his depressions and
disquietudes in many of his stories. But now here is the
old note back in the correspondence again, after eight
years. Why is it there?

    Hervé de Maupassant, Guy's younger brother by
six years, had always been something of a problem.
    Things had gone badly with him from the beginning.
His birth was presided over by the same doctor who had
given Guy his round head and with it his "active brain
and first-rate intelligence," but the potter's art failed
with Hervé. "Whether the six years that separated us
had weakened the doctor's hand," Maupassant told
François, "or whether he simply was not in form that
day, he was unable to give my brother's head the shape
he wanted. It kept slipping out of his hands, and he was
so irritated that he swore a Norman oath." Like Guy,
Hervé was educated chiefly at home, but though he
shared his brother's athletic tastes (he was a fencer and
a boxer, and enjoyed scrapping with dockhands along
the waterfront), he was a retarded student and shared
Guy's literary tastes not at all. Gardening was his most
elevated pleasure, and passages in Laure's letters to
Flaubert show her chagrin that a son of hers should be
such a rustic. But she saw the folly of expecting him to
follow any indoor career, and it was with her encouragement that he joined the army and became a junior
officer, a quartermaster sergeant in the cavalry. But he
kept getting into fights and duels with his fellow-officers,
and into other predicaments made easy by his charm
and good looks, and soon he was loudly calling on his

mother and brother for help. "Hervé has been acting
like a scoundrel with my mother," Guy wrote his cousin
Lucie from Corsica in 1880, "demanding money by
telegraph to pay his debts, refusing to re-enlist, going
further into debt in Paris, and making conditions. He
is a complete skunk. I've sent him three hundred francs
that he hasn't thanked me for or even acknowledged.
He has only one idea—to borrow from everybody. I'm
much afraid that this last blow may be fatal to my
mother and that she'll never get over it. She would be
cured by now were it not for Hervé's stupid, hateful
conduct of the past two years."

By this time Hervé had gone to live with his father
in Paris, and Guy and his mother, after paying his debts,
resolved to wash their hands of him. But their affection
caused them to keep trying to help him out of his difficulties, which seemed never-ending. At one moment Guy
tried in vain through a friend to get him a position with
Lesseps in Panama; and later he asked Louis Le Poittevin, also in vain, to recommend him for a position
in the Crédit Lyonnais. During these years he expressed
his opinion of him quite plainly in the character of Paul
in *Une Vie*.

About 1885 Hervé went to live with Laure in the
South, and early in 1886 he married Marie-Thérèse
Fanton d'Andon, a young girl of good family but without
dowry, and Guy bore the chief expense of establishing
him in the nursery business near Antibes. A daughter,
Simone, was born to the couple, and for a time things
promised well. "I think that Hervé will have many
customers among Cannes society this winter," Guy wrote
his mother in the fall of 1887, just before leaving for
Africa after completing *Pierre et Jean*. "But everybody
is going south late this year. Yesterday I lunched with

Madame de Sagan, and she told me that she and her friends aren't going before January 15."

By that date, however, January 15, 1888, Hervé no longer had the prospect of a good season that winter or any winter. On that very day Guy wrote Emile Straus from Cannes: "My brother's condition makes it impossible for me to leave him, especially since my mother is absolutely crazy with grief. As soon as I receive Dr. Blanche's advice concerning a sanitarium we mustn't lose a day in taking him there; and I am the only one who can accompany him to such a place."

Hervé had become dangerously insane. The family always claimed, and perhaps believed, that he went mad as the result of a sunstroke, suffered as he lay in the full sun for several hours after fainting in his fields. "My brother has a pernicious fever with meningeal symptoms —symptoms which are persistent and greatly worry us," Guy wrote at the time to Petit-Bleu. Hervé's madness manifested itself a few days later, when he attempted to strangle his wife. His end was to be such as was never caused by sunstroke alone: he, too, like his older brother, had during his youth become infected by the *spirocheta pallida*, which attacked his brain, and he was the first to be destroyed. Guy did accompany him to the place where he was to be confined. According to the only account which survives, he took him to a house near Paris which he pretended belonged to one of his friends, and where Hervé was to "convalesce." With the supposed friend—the doctor in charge—Guy accompanied him even to his room, "to see whether it pleased him":

"Look out the window" [the doctor said]. "See what a fine view you'll have."

Hervé went trustingly to the window, and the doctor signaled to Guy to move quietly toward the door. And

when the patient turned around and made a move to
accompany them, two athletic attendants suddenly
appeared. But they could not prevent him from stretching his arm out the door and crying: "Ah! Guy! You
scoundrel! You're locking me up! But it's you who are
mad, do you hear? You're the crazy one of the family!"*

That account of the scene may be apocryphal, but
by Guy the heartbreaking mission was in some manner
performed. And it can be imagined with what horror the
fate of Hervé filled his artist brother, who without (so
far as is known) being aware of his own impending fate,
was sufficiently familiar with mental disquietude to have
"shed" it to the extent that he did in his writings. Hervé
lived a little less than two years; first in the institution
at Ville-Evrard near Paris, and then in one at Bron,
near Lyons.

Late in her life Laure herself spoke of the effect of
Hervé's madness on Guy:

I swear [she told one of Guy's friends who asked
about first signs of his mental trouble] that Guy experienced no confusion before the illness of his brother
Hervé. Hervé had suffered a sunstroke, which brought
on cerebral disorders. Guy followed the progress of his
disease, which was purely the result of an accident. When
Hervé died he was very affected, and fell into a somber,
discouraged state of mind. People have claimed to see
in *Le Horla* the first manifestation of his madness. That is
an error: *Le Horla* is only the fancy of a powerful imagination, and Guy was in completely good health when
he wrote it. On the other hand, his volume, *Sur l'Eau*,
which followed his brother's illness, reveals a great
uneasiness.†

* Maurice de Waleffe, quoted in Georges Normandy, *Guy de Maupassant*
(Paris, 1926).

† Right as Laure was about *Le Horla*, she was apparently unaware that
Sur l'Eau could scarcely be symptomatic of any new uneasiness, since (although
it was published at this time) it had chiefly been written in previous years. See
Note 12: Maupassant's Travel Writings, page 408.

So that the depressed and concerned letter to Laure of May, 1888, written as he was beginning the new novel into which he was to put all his serious effort, that letter so reminiscent of the letters from the ministry, has specific reference to what had happened to Hervé, and its effect on Laure and himself. There is a curious near-repetition of pattern here. Just as the high point of *Boule de Suif*, his first considerable accomplishment, had been quickly followed, almost accompanied, by the sudden death of Flaubert, so now the achievement of *Pierre et Jean*, that high point among his novels, which displayed "a mature talent able to renew itself, strike another note, and appear still young," was accompanied by another shock. There is little doubt that the madness of Hervé was indeed a severe shock, one that helped to precipitate Guy's own long-maturing disintegration.

The following September, after four months of what should have been (since he was writing almost nothing else) steady work on the new novel, he wrote to Madame Straus from Etretat:

I am so ashamed that I scarcely dare write you. My only excuse is the state of constant suffering in which I am living; my migraines now never leave me, neither by day nor by night. For this reason I have done nothing, absolutely nothing, and my novel is at the same stage as when I left Paris. I am passing through distressing, empty days, waiting for the end of this state which plunges me into such a torpor that I no more have the energy to write a letter than I have to leave this place. I undoubtedly owe the prolongation of these troubles to my stay in Paris, which always has the same effect upon me.

And three days later he wrote Havard:

I am not at all well. For the past two months I have

not been able to work an hour. I am leaving tomorrow for Aix, to try to get some relief from my terrible migraines.

The impaired capacity for work marked the onset of the end.

PART THREE

THE
END

CHAPTER 1

PAUL BOURGET, HIGHLIFE, AND OTHER CALAMITIES

ONE OF THE CHARACTERISTICS of Maupassant's fiction from the beginning, its preoccupation with the lower strata of society, had been attacked, as his books appeared, by almost every conservative French literary critic.

People will ask [wrote Zola in his review of *La Maison Tellier*], "Why choose such subjects? Can't writers write about respectable people?" Of course. But I think Maupassant chose this subject because he felt that it struck a very human note, a note which stirred the very depths of his own creative powers.

Among the people who, after reading *La Maison Tellier*, asked the very questions that Zola said they would ask was a person of considerable distinction: Hippolyte Taine, scholar, historian, critic, and friend of Flaubert's (although Flaubert had frequently complained about his imperfect understanding of art and about the conservatism that had overtaken him after 1870). Taine had been welcome at Flaubert's Sundays and Maupassant had been taught by his master to respect him. In a letter which begins on a touchingly humble note— for Taine himself had once unsuccessfully attempted the writing of fiction—the scholar communicated to Maupassant his thoughts inspired by *La Maison Tellier*:

Flaubert and I used to have tête-à-têtes five hours long, during which we talked of nothing but literature. I should need such a tête-à-tête with you to tell you all the ideas that your book suggested to me. In many respects it is you who are the true and only successor of my dear Flaubert. You have the essential gift that we so admire, we dissectors and analysts, precisely because we lack it and because it reveals a mind of the opposite pattern to ours; this gift consists in natural fullness of conception, ability to see the whole, and extreme abundance and richness of impressions, memories, and psychological ideas; besides an accumulated store of half-realized perceptions that underlie and support every sentence, every word that you write. When one has that gift, one can create; when one does not have it, one can only enjoy, analyze and understand the creations of others.

In this second role, I can only beg you to increase the range of your observation. You portray peasants, the lower middle class, workers, students and prostitutes. Some day you will doubtless portray the cultivated classes, the upper bourgeoisie, engineers, physicians, professors, big industrialists and men of business. In my opinion, civilization is an asset; a man born into comfortable surroundings, the product of three or four honest, industrious and respectable generations, has a greater chance of being upright, refined and educated. Honor and intelligence are always more or less hothouse plants. This theory is certainly aristocratic, but it is based on experience, and I shall be happy when you devote your talent to men and women who, thanks to their culture and fine feelings, are the honor and the strength of their country.*

* Taine's letter continued: "Another remark I might make is that the critical and pessimistic point of view is, like any other, arbitrary. I often discussed this thesis with Flaubert. *En Famille* is cruelly true, but were we to read it on returning from a visit to Bulgaria, or even Sicily, our horror and disgust would

Maupassant candidly quoted Taine's letter, saying that he disagreed with it completely, in two *Gaulois* articles replying to attacks on *Mademoiselle Fifi* by two critics: Albert Wolff (called by Flaubert a eunuch), who had labeled Maupassant a "sewer-man," and Francisque Sarcey (called by Flaubert a bourgeois), who had warned: "Let him beware! The public is beginning to have enough of these ugly pictures. It is not the magistrates by whom the author will be fined or imprisoned: M. Guy de Maupassant should fear the sentence of a judge infinitely more dangerous." Maupassant's replies were, as was usual with him, not masterpieces of critical analysis. He contented himself with denying the validity, especially among women, of Taine's human differentiations according to class, and declared that, "The writer is and must remain the sole master, the sole judge, of what he feels capable of writing."

Then he continued to write as he chose. Criticized for being too much a son of Zola, he wrote a laudatory article on Zola; praised for having reformed and become a "serious man" because he made *Une Vie* a novel definitely not about lowlife, he published a series of the rowdiest stories about all classes of society, but especially the lower classes, ever written in France: about a petit-

---

yield to respect and perhaps admiration; we should think in the highest terms of a family whose members steal so little from each other and in which murder is unknown. Our judgments depend upon our ideals; yours are very high—hence your severity. Our great master Balzac was more indulgent because his method was based on sympathy—as in *La Vieille Fille* [*The Old Maid*]; such was also the case with the minor Flemish painters, Teniers, Van Ostade, Adrien Brauwer; one can feel even with the petit bourgeois, even with peasants clinging to their soil, or workers bound to their bench; you have done this in *Histoire d'une Fille de ferme* and in *Le Papa de Simon*. Such sympathy is generous and comforting, and I wish for the sake of the enjoyment of all of us that you would display it more often.

"I shake your hand and thank you. There is nothing more pleasing at my age than to see the dawn of a great talent."

bourgeois wedding lunch in the apartment of the bride's
unmarried but lavishly kept sister (*Le Pain Maudit—
Accursed Bread*), about a middle-class couple whose
passions are rekindled by the exploits of their maid
(*La Serre—The Greenhouse*), about the strategic pinching
of a notary's baby by a cuckolding captain (*Le Mal
d'André—What's the Matter with André?*), about a
peasant's suit for damages against the woman who had
hired him to perform a specific personal service (*Le Cas de
Madame Luneau—The Case of Madame Luneau*), about
the old school friend whose flourishing brothel had begun
with a staff consisting only of his wife and sister-in-law
(*L'Ami Patience—My Friend Patience*). Chided for lack
of sympathy, he wrote *Mon Oncle Jules* (*Uncle Jules*) and
other heart-wrenching tales about victims of the hypocrisy of "respectability." And in among all these he
interspersed, as he wished, a number of pieces sufficiently
gentle for family reading.

Among these quieter stories, not concerned with lowlife, is one called *Menuet*, a sentimental scene in a hidden
corner of the Luxembourg Gardens, where two aged sur-
vivors of the eighteenth century, one of them a famous
dancer in her time, perform a stiff-jointed minuet.
Charming though it is, it could have been written by
many another writer, especially Daudet, and its greatest
Maupassant interest lies in its dedication—to Paul Bourget.

Maupassant had met Bourget before the appearance
of *Boule de Suif*, in the office of the *République des Lettres*.
He was a very serious young man, two years younger
than Maupassant, the son of a professor of mathematics
at Clermont-Ferrand. He had recently abandoned a
teaching post in Paris to devote himself entirely to writing, and had published a volume or two of verse, and,

in a magazine, a story whose hero was depicted as having been preserved from passion and debauchery by his absorption in scientific studies—Bourget himself was always interested in scientific studies, especially the new "science" of psychology. The two young writers saw something of each other: at the *République des Lettres* (it was walking home from that office one cold spring evening, Bourget later reminisced, that they first became acquainted; Maupassant recited Bouilhet as they walked), at Zola's, and later at the *Gaulois*, where Bourget was for a time in charge of special articles. But Bourget soon found more congenial surroundings in the chaste company of Madame Adam and her *Nouvelle Revue*, and it was there that he published his most durable work: a series of penetrating essays on contemporary writers, *Essais de psychologie contemporaine*, which he described as "studies of the literary manifestations of contemporary sensibility." It was about the time these were collected in a volume, in 1883, that he received the dedication of *Menuet*.

Maupassant was tactful in his dedication of stories, offering in every case a story somehow appropriate to the person honored, and usually leaving undedicated any story which might unfavorably associate the name of a dedicatee with a character. That he should dedicate a story to Bourget at all testifies to his admiration (only about forty of the more than two hundred are dedicated, very few to literary men of any prominence); and the appropriateness of his choice of *Menuet*, with its absence of lowlife and its nostalgia for the *ancien régime*, became increasingly apparent as Bourget published a series of analytical, "psychological" novels, all of them concerned with varieties of purity and all of them characterized by the fervent hope that society would continue to maintain

its existing pyramidal form, with its broad base tapering
gradually up to the pinnacle of high society.

Bourget enjoyed writing about the piously conservative, but above all he preferred his characters to be
fashionable and wealthy; and when he described the latter he adopted their own tone. His novels are filled with
a parvenu obsession with the trivia of highlife, with a
reverence for the more fashionable outer manifestations
of Catholicism, with a stereotyped anti-Semitism (Bourget was opposed to any attempt to right the injustice
done Dreyfus), with a lip-service to something called
"Art," all of which suffocate as one reads. His novels
became the vogue, he was accepted by the classes which
he so reverenced, and his life was one of fashion and
immense respectability, including election to the French
Academy.*

Bourget, whose grandfather was an Auvergne peasant, was occasionally troubled by his own *mal d'élégance,*
by the intensity of his own snobbery. He once wrote to
Comte Robert de Montesquiou: "I wish I had the blood
of a savage, so that I might not have this catch in my
throat at sunset in the Bois de Boulogne, at the sight
of all the coupés and victorias. The feeling is utterly
plebeian, and I hate myself for it—but what can I do?"

Maupassant and Bourget wrote complimentary articles about each other, and they remained friends

---

* Few unpleasantnesses marred Bourget's serene existence. Among them was
a brush with Mark Twain. Bourget traveled to America and wrote the inevitable
book, and his friendship with the expatriated Henry James and Edith Wharton
had done nothing to prepare him for Twain's reaction to some of his published
remarks. One of his quips about the absence of portraits of grandfathers from
American homes (the implication being that grandfathers were unknown)
brought a retort from Twain in a magazine article to the effect that Frenchmen
probably spent their leisure moments seeking their *fathers'* identities. Bourget
and his supporters were pained by what they considered that "gross reply to a
good-humored bit of chaffing." (See Twain's essays: "What Paul Bourget thinks
of Us," and "A Little Note to Paul Bourget.")

throughout the years of Maupassant's career. Bourget
gave Maupassant the 1886 letter of introduction to
Henry James in London, in 1889 he visited a Roman
brothel with him (Bourget was a spectator only), and
later he was a guest on one of the last outings of the *Bel-
Ami*. One of the occasions on which they saw each other
was the beginning of *Mont-Oriol:*

> One evening when I went to dine with him—it must
> have been in the summer of 1885—how near that is and
> yet how far! [Bourget wrote later]—I found him in a
> state of gaiety which by this time was becoming rare.
> He was beginning to write *Mont-Oriol.* "I've got forty
> characters in motion," he told me. "Forty—that's quite
> a number. Forty people, going and coming in the first
> two chapters!"

Bourget admired the vapid, worldly *Mont-Oriol*, especially the "conflict of races," as he called it, which the
book depicted, and on the appearance of *Pierre et Jean*
he regretted that Maupassant had not continued to write
about the upper classes:

> Maupassant is publishing in the *Nouvelle Revue* [he
> wrote to Henry James in December, 1887, from Corfu]
> a long *nouvelle* of which I greatly liked the first part,
> published December 1, on the eve of my departure. What
> extraordinary gifts that man has, and if he had a strong
> and noble society to depict, how he would tower! Un-
> fortunately he has before his eyes these insipid petits-
> bourgeois of whom Flaubert said that their stench rose
> to his nostrils as he wrote about them. Even so, Maupas-
> sant's talent is so strong that he finds tragedy in this
> wretched milieu.

Now Maupassant himself was far from being a "man
of the people." He had (or had almost) begun his days
in a chateau rented by his mother for the purpose, and
he had been raised in one of the upper levels of a heavily

stratified society, always a member of the gentry while
he played in Etretat with the children of peasants and
fisherfolk. Now, in later life, he continued to enjoy such
people's company—especially that of Bernard and Raymond, his sailors on the *Bel-Ami*—but with his own
position always clear in everyone's mind. In September,
1875, returning to Paris and the ministry from a vacation
in Etretat, he had written his mother, "Paris is empty,
empty, empty. I haven't seen a single man who looks as
though he had ever been in a salon, even to pass the re-
freshments"; and his early articles in the *Gaulois* and the
Gil-Blas constantly lament the increasing obliteration of
old distinctions, the rise of popular education, the institution of universal suffrage and the like. In his fiction he
portrayed lowlife because he knew it, because it was
picturesque and effective, no doubt in part because naturalism had made fashionable its literary use, and because it lent itself to his themes. But as far as his own
social life was concerned, we have seen how—apart from
his need for sexual degradation—he sought his associates
in increasingly exalted social strata, until Goncourt was
impressed with his knowledge of *chic*.

That entry in Goncourt's journal is the first indication
that Maupassant's highlife was to impinge on his art, as
it so shortly thereafter did in *Mont-Oriol*. Probably Bourget played a role in this. Convinced himself of the superiority of highlife as literary subject matter, he must at
the very least have expressed to his friend the approval
he felt of *Mont-Oriol* *; and no doubt his regret at the
descent to lower social levels in *Pierre et Jean* was ex-

* The peculiarly faulty structure of *Mont-Oriol*, unusual in Maupassant,
the cleavage between background and foreground, and Maupassant's previously
expressed interest in the background comedy only, make one wonder whether the
highlife foreground may not have been the result of outside suggestion, perhaps
Bourget's. Bourget's own Auvergnat background also tempts one to link him
with *Mont-Oriol*.

pressed not only to Henry James but to Maupassant as
well. Furthermore, Bourget's books were selling increasingly well. During Maupassant's visit to Africa, following
the completion of *Pierre et Jean*, he said thoughtfully to
François after an evening spent with French officers: "I
noticed that most of those soldiers were admirers of Paul
Bourget." So that it seems likely that his friend Bourget's example, and Bourget's success,* were in part responsible for Maupassant's now proceeding, at this same
time when he was shaken by his brother's madness, to
transfer the scene not only of his own life, but of his
principal works, to high society.

A position in society, Henry James once said, is a
legitimate object of ambition; and so, perhaps, it is. But
in that ambition there are dangers, and more dangers
for some than for others. We have already seen Maupassant writing from Antibes to Hermine Lecomte du Nouy,
urging her to teach her son, "instead of catechism," the
dangers of society to a man who "wishes to preserve his
integrity of thought and judgment"; and on another occasion he wrote that, "High society makes a failure of
every scholar, every artist, every intelligent man whom
it captures. It destroys every sincere feeling by its way of
frittering away taste, curiosity, desire, the little flame
that burns within us." In one's regret that Maupassant
did not heed his own warnings, one can only be grateful
that he had not made his literary shift to higher circles
eight years before, when Taine had urged it. How much
of his best work would have been lost! For now when he
did make the change it was immediately disastrous to his
art.

---

* See Note 13: *Articles de Commerce*, page 411, for testimony to the triple
success at this time of Bourget, Maupassant and Pierre Loti—and incidentally
for evidence that Hachette's ban on the sale of *Une Vie* in railway stations had
not been extended to Maupassant's other books.

His rowing friend Petit-Bleu later lamented his altera-
tion: "Those who knew Guy only toward the end of his
life had no idea of his real character and temperament.
In his later years a darkness came over his spirits. He
was captured by society: it afforded him no real enjoyment, but he was susceptible to its praises." The change
that came over much of his art was similar: the joyous-
ness that had characterized it disappeared, for his easy
familiarity with the milieus which he depicted no longer
existed. After *Pierre et Jean,* his principal work consisted
of two novels about highlife—*Fort Comme la Mort (Strong
as Death)* and *Notre Coeur (Our Heart,* or *A Woman's
Heart)*—and both are lamentable.

Bourget also made Maupassant self-conscious about
what was then called the "psychological" element of the
novel—analysis of character and motive.

The success of Bourget's first novels [wrote Léopold
Lacour, dramatic critic of the *Nouvelle Revue,* who saw
something of Maupassant in Etretat], that is, the psychological and analytical novel, caused him to reflect a
good deal. Not, certainly, that he felt the slightest jealousy—he did not consider Bourget a born novelist, and
to his talent as a psychologist he was happy to do justice
—but he was eager to demonstrate, at least to proclaim,
in a sort of little manifesto, the superiority of his own
method, his own art—the method and art of the original
disciple of Flaubert.

The "little manifesto" was of course the essay on the
novel, published in the *Figaro* and as a preface to *Pierre
et Jean;* and in it Maupassant expressed his preference
for revealing character in fiction by action rather than
by explanation and analysis. But he also had the candor
to point out that *Pierre et Jean* itself is not a complete

illustration of that preference, that it is a "psychological study." No one can regret the passages of analysis contained in *Pierre et Jean*—whose author, having previously written *Yvette*, needed lessons from no one in "psychology"; but the two novels that follow it contain less and less action, more and more tedious analysis of characters who offer little to an analyst. In these books, to quote the metaphor of one commentator, Maupassant, "wearing patent-leather evening pumps, stays close to Paul Bourget's hunting preserve."

The unsuitability of that preserve for Maupassant's talent must be added to the precipitant effect of Hervé's madness on his mental state as explanation of the slow progress of his new novel, his diminished ability to work, in 1888.

And there was still another element in the confusion.

Hervé's tragedy and Laure's grief seem to have intensified, if such a thing were possible, the attachment between the mother and her older son; and it was during this year that Maupassant wrote one of his greatest tributes to Laure, a tribute more outspoken and explicit than *Le Papa de Simon* or *Une Vie* or the cuckold tales: *Un Portrait*, the story in which the narrator, seeking an explanation for the irresistible charm of one of his fellow men-about-town, suddenly finds it in a portrait hanging in the friend's drawing room—a portrait of his mother.

And yet it was at this same time that Maupassant seems to have embarked upon what for him could only be a folly, a kind of crazy, forced imitation of the real thing—a relationship that he wanted to believe was a *grande passion.*

Partly, perhaps, because he had to a certain extent

(but of course far from completely) "shed his sickness in
books"—that is, in the present instance, somewhat
purged himself in his stories of his compulsion to engage
in purely physical, often degrading, encounters—he had
portrayed a high-society *grande passion* in *Mont-Oriol*,
one of his most painful performances. While portraying
it, he had written to Hermine Lecomte du Nouy that he
found himself imagining that "that kind of experience
isn't as stupid as one might think." And apparently the
next step, once he had glimpsed the richness that such
an experience could hold for others, was to desire to try
it for himself.

Mystery surrounds the affair—and one is thankful
for the darkness, since what it hides can only have
been hollow, frustrated, ludicrous and tragic.

In the *Grande Revue* for 1912 and 1913 there appeared
a series of articles entitled *Guy de Maupassant intime*,
signed X . . . , whose author claimed to be the woman
who was the great love of Maupassant's last years. Details of their meetings are given, and several letters, of
which the following, dated "Tunis, December 19, 1887,
eleven P.M.," is typical:

Since last night, X . . . , I have been longing for
you, desperately. A mad desire to see you again, to see
you at once, right here, before me, suddenly entered my
heart. And I should like to cross the sea, cross mountains
and cities, solely to put my hand on your shoulder, to
breathe the perfume of your hair.

Do you not feel it hovering about you, this desire,
this desire coming from me who seek you, this desire
imploring you in the silence of the night?

I long especially to see your eyes, your tender eyes.
Why is our first thought always for the eyes of the woman
we love? How they haunt us, how happy or unhappy
they make us, those clear, impenetrable, deep little

enigmas, those tiny bits of blue, black or green, which without changing form or color express in turn love, indifference and hate, soothing sweetness and freezing terror, more eloquently than the most profuse words or the most expressive gestures.

In a few weeks I shall have left Africa. I shall see you again. You will join me, will you not, my adored? You will join me in . . .

The identity of Madame X . . . has always remained a mystery. The dates and references in her articles read convincingly,* but none of Maupassant's passionate letters which she prints have ever been seen in their original form. It has been said † that the whole series—letters, text and all—are a complete forgery, a joke perpetrated by a French literary man who was impeccable in his documentation and ingenious in his imitation of Maupassant's turgid late style. The only chance of proof would seem to lie in the existence and discovery of the letters themselves.

But whether or not the throbbing articles in the *Grande Revue* are genuine, a *grande passion* of some kind apparently did exist—between Maupassant and one of the greatest beauties of Paris society, Marie Kahn. *"La femme remarquable qu'est Mme. Kahn,"* and her sister Loulia, *"l'exquise Mme. Cahen* [d'Anvers],*"* are two of the many elegant Parisiennes celebrated by Marcel Proust in his letters and early articles. Loulia, says a member of her family now living in Paris,

married, while very young, Count Albert Cahen d'Anvers, whose favorite occupation was the writing of

* Except for the statement which she attributes to Maupassant that of all his stories he preferred *Le Père Amable (Old Amable)*. That story, not a particularly remarkable one, seems a strange choice for a favorite—even though it does contain the suicide of a father-figure! As noted on page 313, Maupassant told Havard that he considered *L'Inutile Beauté* his best story.

† Aurèle Patorni, "Julien Le Corbeau" (*L'Esprit Français*, July 10, 1932).

operas, some of which were played in Paris and elsewhere. The Countess, née Warshawski, was of Russian
origin, without great fortune but of dazzling beauty and
extraordinary personality. There are no words to describe
her: her humor, her intelligence and her elegance made
her a person of a kind rarely encountered, who never
failed to impress and dazzle even the most indifferent.
No one could resist the charm that emanated from her
entire person.

Her sister, Madame Marie Kahn, was even more
beautiful and just as intelligent, *d'une allure royale*. She
was less aggressively virtuous than her sister, but there
was never any scandal concerning her lovers. Her adventures were not innumerable, and her two greatest
and best-known lovers were Maupassant and . . .

Personally, I doubt [Mme. Kahn's relative adds, in
English] that she had any physical propensities, so much
so that there is a very great possibility that her relations
with men, and more particularly with Guy de Maupassant, were solely based upon the mysterious charm which
emanated from her immensely "brainy" personality.
That she was a drug addict is a fact and that she under-
went cures on that behalf was commonly known.

Such is the somewhat erratic bit of light—if light it
is—that can be cast on the beautiful Warshawski sisters,
both of whose sumptuous houses were frequented by
Maupassant. Marie is said to have inspired the heroine,
Michèle de Burne, of his last novel, *Notre Coeur*, and
to have received from him more than two thousand letters (none of which have come to light) during the course
of whatever their relationship may have been. By some
she is thought to be "the lady in gray" whom François
depicts in vampirish light in the last chapters of his
memoirs.

The worldly, artificial, unsatisfying character of the
affair can be partially gathered from the novels; and the

novels, deformed by "psychology," highlife and mental depression, are further marred by what can only be called the pitiable farce of the affair.

All those elements were behind Maupassant's "migraines" that summer of 1888, the head pains that kept him from working. In September, after a summer in Etretat so cold that he resolved to sell La Guillette and "never return to that horrible Siberia," he met his mother in Aix-les-Bains, where he hoped for relief from his suffering; but despite waters and mountain-climbing relief came only with ether and antipyrine. He was close to despair about his health:

All summer [he wrote Mme. Straus] I have been in a state of suffering which has kept me from doing the slightest work and makes my life intolerable. After a late season at Aix I am now fleeing to Africa, where I shall look for some warm and quiet spot. I may even stay there if I find it suits me.

So, these are almost my farewells. . . .

I hope very much, however, to return for a while in the spring and spend a month or six weeks in Paris. This resolution to leave must seem very strange to you, Madame, who love society, or who at least endure, with smiling resignation and surely also with a certain pleasure, people and the things they say. As for me, I should gladly live in Paris four months each winter if it were possible for me to see a dozen people at the most. But the others prevent me from attaching myself to that dozen sufficiently closely never to leave them.

On his way to Africa Maupassant stopped on the Riviera to see Laure and to call on his father, who was now also installed beside the Mediterranean, having re-accumulated sufficient capital to live modestly in a "villa"—an exceedingly plain little house—in Sainte-Maxime. He also saw, at dinners and lunches, something of the society he claimed to be fleeing, whose company in Paris he considered partly responsible for his "migraines." That opinion was apparently partially correct, or, to put it differently, periodic escape from his environment had by now become a necessity—a necessity as compulsive as the choice of the environment itself—if he was to find any relief from the mental and physical complexity of his troubles. "More and more," he wrote Princesse Mathilde Bonaparte, "I feel myself a peasant and a vagabond, made for the shores and the woods, not for the streets"; and he told Hugues Le Roux:

Nothing gives me greater pleasure, on a spring morning, than to arrive with my boat in some unfamiliar harbor; and I love to walk about all day amid new scenes, rubbing elbows with men whom I shall never see again, and of whom I will take leave the same evening to sail away, sleep at sea, hold the tiller as I choose—with no longing for houses where lives begin, continue, cramp themselves and come to an end, with no desire to cast anchor anywhere, no matter how soft the sky, how smiling the land.

In Africa, amid the primitive and exotic Arabs and in the dull, provincial French society of Algiers, his head pains soon disappeared and he finished *Fort Comme la Mort*. Edmond de Goncourt, who had taken personally and was never to forget or forgive some remarks which Maupassant had made about over-elaborate writing in his essay on the novel, wrote in his diary for Wednesday, March 6, 1889:

Maupassant, back from his trip to Africa, dining with the Princesse [Mathilde Bonaparte], says that he is in perfect health. And indeed he is animated, lively, talkative; and with his face thinner and bronzed by his travels he looks less common than usual.

Fort Comme la Mort ran serially in the *Revue Illustrée* in February and March and was published in book form by Ollendorff immediately after the appearance of the last installment. This novel, whose theme Jules Lemaître accurately described as "*l'immense douleur de vieillir*" (the immense sadness of growing old), is scarcely, for us, the "marvelous book" it was found to be by those critics who saw it as going beyond the materialism and brutality of naturalism. Its story of the hopeless love of a worldly, successful academic painter who is growing old (he is almost fifty) for the young daughter of the vapid, fashionable countess who has long been his mistress, brought joy to the hearts of those who loved highlife in books, and made it seem that the terrible, cynical Maupassant was mellowing:

A breach has been made in the novelist's indifference [wrote Hugues LeRoux in the *Temps*]. Pity for mankind has entered into him by way of some tiny wound that quickly closed over. Will this dew of tears dry up? Or will it rise and gush forth? The latter, I hope, much as I love Maupassant. His frankness, his sincerity, his straightforwardness, his probity of thought, have given us great joys. But we are thirsty from walking behind him in the desert [of his delight in man's stupidity and brutal instincts]. Blessings on the miraculous hand that will strike water from the rock.

To us the "pity for mankind" seems rather a displeasing self-pity on the part of the hero, and the mellowness smells like decay. For all the correctness of the "psychology," and telling as numerous passages are—

descriptions of an artist's creative day, of the beginning
of a love affair, of an infatuation with a young girl,
glimpses of restaurants and boulevards reminiscent of
Bel-Ami—the work suffers from a most pernicious form
of anemia. It is especially Maupassant's failure to leave
anything unsaid, any action unexplained, any thought
unrecorded, that causes the loss of energy and life; and
that failure is due to his over-estimation of the characters
and world that he portrays.

Very shortly after the completion of *Fort Comme la
Mort* Maupassant remarked to François one morning,
"I stayed in bed an hour longer than usual, getting under
way in my mind the story I want to write today."

Was this *Boitelle*, the particularly excellent, richly
symbolic story about what happens to a Norman farm
boy whose mother forbids him to marry the Negress he
loves—a story that was badly mis-read by no less
eminent a critic than Benedetto Croce, who in an otherwise understanding essay on Maupassant * praised it as
being all "frank and happy laughter"? Or was it *Hautot
Père et Fils* (*Hautot and Son*), also excellent, about a
son's respectful assumption of his late father's mistress
and child? It could have been either—both appeared in
the *Echo de Paris* during January. Or it may have been
Allouma, a longer, inferior, African tale, or *Le Port*,
particularly liked by Tolstoy. Maupassant wrote only
about half a dozen short stories in 1889, of varying
quality, one of them being *Le Rendezvous*, which contains
an amusing anticipation of the modern "Won't you come
up and see my etchings?": "You know," says Baron de
Grimbal to the pretty Madame Haggan, whom he meets

* "Maupassant," *London Mercury*, May, 1923. Trans. by Douglas Ainslie.

in the street, "you are the only one of my—friends, I hope you will allow me to say—who has never come to see my Japanese collection."

Unfortunately, before the year was out he was busy at another novel of the type of *Fort Comme la Mort*.

The head pains returned in April, and stomach troubles with them; and now Maupassant began to wear black glasses.

CHAPTER 2

LAST WRITINGS

THAT SUMMER was a rather special one in Paris—it was the summer of the Exposition Universelle of 1889, complete with the newly finished Eiffel Tower. Two years before, when the construction of the "high, thin pyramid of iron ladders," the "metallic carcass," as Maupassant variously called it, was first announced, he had been one of a group of writers, painters and musicians to sign a protest, published in the *Temps*, against the disfiguring of the Paris sky-line; he hated the thought of the tower's long shadow being cast "like an ink-spot" over the beauties of the city; and soon after the Exposition opened he moved out of town, taking a villa at Triel on the Seine for part of the summer. (He would not return to Chatou, his previous refuge, he told François, because it was too full of *demi-mondaines*, whose presence would be embarrassing to his new friends.)

Before leaving, he entertained in his apartment a troop of Arab dancers, acrobats and musicians who were in Paris for the Exposition—four men, twelve women (one of whom threw herself on the embarrassed François, claiming to have known him in Algiers), and their manager, or "barnum." Stomach dancing, oriental cacophonies, and champagne (served not as wine, forbidden by the prophet, but as a special beverage in-

306

vented in honor of the guests, and as such accepted and
much appreciated) made up into a wild evening which
François, recording it later, could describe only as *"un
mêli-mêlo fantastique."*

The huge handbook of the Exposition contains, along
with essays on most other subjects by a great many
people, one by Maupassant on "The Evolution of the
Novel in the Nineteenth Century," and from time to
time he came in from Triel to visit the Exposition with
friends. But:

. . . it had not occurred to me what Paris would be
like, invaded by the universe.

From the first hours of daylight the streets are full,
the sidewalks flooded like swollen rivers. Everything
moves toward the Exposition, or from it, or back to it.
In the streets the carriages are like the cars of an endless
train. Not one is free, not a coachman is willing to take
you anywhere except to the Exposition or back to his
stables when he goes to change horses. No coupés at the
clubs—they are all engaged by flashy foreigners. Not a
table in the restaurants, and not a friend who dines in
his own home or is willing to dine in yours. When you
invite him, he accepts on the condition that you banquet
on the Eiffel Tower. It's gayer there. And everybody, as
though obeying a watchword, invites you there every
day of the week, for lunch or for dinner.

It seemed to me legitimate that one should go once
or twice, with disgust and curiosity, to eat the canteen-
like food served up by those wretched aerial cooks, in all
the heat, the dust, the stench, amid the crowd of the
common herd celebrating and sweating, and the greasy
papers littering the scene and flying everywhere, and the
smell of delicatessen and wine rising from the tables and
wafted by three hundred thousand breaths exuding the
stale smell of meals, amid the elbowing, the close contacts, the mass of heated flesh, and the mingled sweat of
people scattering their fleas. But it seemed to me as-

tounding to dine amidst that filth and that mob every
night, as had become the custom of good society,
refined society, the society of the élite, which is ordinarily
nauseated by the spectacle of people who labor and the
smell of human fatigue.

All this is a definitive proof of the complete triumph
of democracy.

There are no more castes, races, aristocratic natures.
There are only rich people and poor people. No other
classification can be made of the strata of contemporary
society.

Thus did the Exposition inspire one of Maupassant's
strongest expressions of distaste for his fellow-creatures
en masse—the opening pages of his last travel book,
La Vie Errante (*The Wandering Life*) .* For, before the
summer was over, he fled from the entire Parisian region,
and even from France, "because the Eiffel Tower finally
became unbearable."

He went first to Etretat, where he worked on *Notre
Coeur* and gave a large garden party which included a
country band, dancing, a lottery, a fortune-teller, and the
viewing by his guests of a Grand Guignol drama, *Le
Crime de Montmartre*, complete with a bleeding corpse,
the arrest of the murderer, and a real fire, during which
the actor-firemen, overstimulated by Normandy cider,
directed their hoses on some of the lady guests. Hermine
Lecomte du Nouy presided over the buffet. The guests
included the fashionable passengers of somebody's yacht,
the *Bull-Dog*, anchored off Etretat, and people from
Fécamp, Dieppe, and neighboring chateaux; and the
roads and slopes surrounding La Guillette were crowded
with noninvited villagers, staring through and over the
hedges. Successful though the affair was, François records, Maupassant told him he was not satisfied: "If I

* See Note 11: Maupassant's Travel Writings, page 408.

had a very large house, and an estate that was well shut
in, I would do better, I promise you. And it wouldn't be
twelve or fifteen people that you'd have to find room for
overnight, but eighty or a hundred." There was a
feverish note, now, about some of the things he said and
did.

Then he went south, to cruise to Italy on the *Bel-Ami*.

I curse the social conventions that forbid me to ask
you to come with me [he wrote Countess Potocka]. It
must be a dream to travel with you. I am not speaking of
the charm of your person, which I can enjoy here, or of
the pleasure of looking at you, which is as great in Paris
as elsewhere—but I do not know any other woman in
whom I see, as in you, the ideal traveling companion. Let
me add that if you were to say *Yes* tomorrow, I should
perhaps reply *No;* for in climbing the heaths with you
and running on the sandy beaches I should court a
danger so strong that prudence would advise me to avoid
it. This is not mere banter, but I regretfully resign myself
to your not believing a word of it.

But on the way, there was a visit to be paid.

The last time he had seen Hervé in the sanitarium
near Lyons he had found him so lucid-seeming that his
chief feeling had been one of irritation at the patient's
brutal, violent behavior; but by now things were different:

He so tore at my heart [he wrote Countess Potocka]
that I suffered more than I ever suffered before. When
I had to leave, and they refused to let him go with me to
the station, he began to wail so frightfully that I could
not keep back my tears as I looked at him—this condemned man whom Nature itself is killing, who will never
leave his prison, never see his mother again. He feels
something frightful, irreparable within himself, but he
does not know what it is.

Ah! The poor human body, the poor mind, what an

obscenity, what a horrible creation! If I believed in the
God of your religions, what limitless horror I should feel
for him!

· If my brother dies before my mother, I think I will
go mad myself from thinking of her suffering. Ah, the
poor woman, how she has been crushed, beaten, martyrized without respite since her marriage!

And to Lucie Le Poittevin he wrote from Santa
Margherita:

I found Hervé absolutely mad, without a glimmer of
reason, leaving us without the slightest hope of cure—
something that my mother does not know. The two hours
that I spent with him in the asylum at Bron were terrible,
for he recognized me perfectly, wept, embraced me a
hundred times, and wanted to leave, raving all the while.
My mother herself can no longer walk, and she scarcely
speaks: you see how badly everything is going.

After seeing Genoa and some of the smaller Ligurian
coastal towns, and after visiting the scene of Shelley's
cremation on the beach of the Bay of Spezia—which
reminded him of the Hindu funeral pyre in Etretat—
Maupassant went on by rail with François to Pisa and
to Florence, where he suffered an alarming intestinal
crisis, with hemorrhages and high fever. When he was
able to move, he cancelled plans to proceed as far as
Naples and hastily returned to Cannes. They arrived on
October 31, and François records that

Madame de Maupassant was at the door of the apartment to greet her son. As soon as she saw him she became
very emotional, her voice contracted, she could scarcely
utter even the words "My dear child!" . . . Before
leaving for her own house, Madame came to the kitchen
and thanked me very much for the care I had taken of
her son since our departure from Cannes. Great tears fell
from her poor sick eyes, and her maid led her

away weeping despite all her efforts at self-control. After ten days of rest M. de Maupassant was much better, and had regained his usual healthy color.

Hervé died in his asylum on November 13, 1889, two weeks after the emotional reunion between Guy and Laure.

I saw him die [Maupassant told François]. According to science, his end should have come a day sooner; but he waited for me, he did not want to go without seeing me once again, without saying adieu. . . . When I kissed him he twice called loudly: "Guy! Guy!" just as he used to call me to play games in the garden of Les Verguies. With my handkerchief I wiped his poor veiled eyes, from which all the beautiful blue color had gone. From a sign that he made, I understood that he wanted me to lower my hand a little, and he touched it with his lips. My poor brother! His friendship for me was sincere, and he has been taken from us very young.

It was about this time, or a little earlier, that Laure began a health-ritual that continued until her death in 1903: every day, whatever her immediate condition, she received the always professional, though increasingly friendly, visit of a Nice physician, Dr. Balestre.

For some time Maupassant had been finding his ground floor in Louis Le Poittevin's house in the rue de Montchanin unpleasant and noisy, with an ugly vacant lot across the street, and the clatter and rumble of horses and wagons on the paving stones outside his windows. François agreed with him, and had long urged a move to a quiet, high floor in an apartment house; but when Maupassant did move, about the time of Hervé's death, it was to an *entresol*—a mezzanine. The street, the Avenue Victor-Hugo, was fashionable, but the ground floor of

the building was occupied by a baker; and too late—
after a long lease had been signed, six thousand francs
spent on decoration and all moving completed—sleep
was found to be impossible due to the nocturnal noise of
the baker's kneading-machine in the basement, which
the renting agent had sworn was inaudible. A city official
was brought in to spend the night and certify to the
nuisance, a doctor's certificate was obtained, and after
threatening suit Maupassant was allowed to break his
lease as of the following October. He spent the rest of the
winter in Cannes, writing and sailing, returned in bad
shape to Paris in March, found a new apartment (in the
rue Boccador, near the present Hotel Georges V—unfortunately with a view of the Eiffel Tower, but with a
garconnière conveniently situated in the same street),
and finished his novel.

It is a tribute to the mysterious force of the creative
process that during these very months, when he was
stricken by his brother's fate and his mother's increasing
invalidism, himself almost constantly ill, harassed by
the baker's noise and the necessity of moving, and
engaged on a novel beside which *Fort Comme la Mort* is a
masterpiece, Maupassant should write four short stories
that are a kind of swan-song—the last stories of his life,*
none of them negligible and two of them among the best:
Mouche, Le Champ d'Oliviers (The Olive Field), Qui Sait?
(Who Knows?) and *L'Inutile Beauté (Useless Beauty)*.

Each was published in the *Echo de Paris* or the *Figaro*
in February or April, 1890, and each is an example of a
different, contrasting, Maupassant genre. In *Mouche*,
which he is said to have written in three hours, he returned to the rowdy days of the '70's beside the Seine;

* One story, *Les Tombales (Tombstone Ladies*, or *Graveyard Sirens)*, was
published later, but seems from internal evidence to have been written earlier.

there is not the slightest lessening of verve, but the style
is marvelously changed, free, impressionistic, non-
naturalistic, its structure almost not to be analyzed.
Le Champ d'Oliviers, with its unforgettable figures of a
passionate priest and his criminal son, is one of Maupassant's or anyone's noblest productions; Taine pronounced it worthy of Aeschylus. *Qui Sait?* is the last of
the supernatural stories, and *L'Inutile Beauté* the best
serious work with a highlife background.

L'Inutile Beauté perhaps illuminates, or rationalizes,
the nature of Maupassant's relations with so elegant and
"useless" a society beauty as Marie Kahn; the long
disquisition which interrupts, and by modern standards
mars, the story, contains the essence of his great obsession in the famous "Do you know how I conceive of
God? As a monstrous creative organ . . ." and in the
violent disgust with which the sexual organs are displayed as being *"inter urinas et faeces."* Maupassant
considered *L'Inutile Beauté* the best of his work. The
publisher, Havard, to whom he had given none of his
recent books, wrote him during 1889, "Are you working
a bit for me, as you promised? You know I am waiting for
that as for the Messiah, to restore the fortunes of my
firm a little," and, when Maupassant gave him for
publication a collection of stories including those four,
he wrote again, expressing his particular admiration of
Le Champ d'Oliviers.

As for your volume [Maupassant replied], you may
rest assured that *L'Inutile Beauté* is worth a hundred
times more than *Le Champ d'Oliviers*. The latter will be
more pleasing to bourgeois sensibility, but bourgeois
sensibility has nerves in the place of discrimination.
L'Inutile Beauté is the finest story I ever wrote. It is
nothing but a symbol.

The hero's self-commitment to a mental hospital in *Qui Sait?* is of dramatic biographical interest; and indeed, for any writer, and for anyone at all who has followed Maupassant's career from the beginning, this cluster of four final tales can only hold tragedy and wonder, and make possible deep appreciation of a few words uttered by the other great storyteller of the modern world, Chekhov: "In the face of the demands imposed by the art of Maupassant, it is difficult to work. But we must work anyway." The collection in which they appeared, *L'Inutile Beauté*, published by Havard that April, was the last collected volume of short stories to appear during Maupassant's life.

Partially basing himself, perhaps, on Flaubert's dictum following the government's refusal to decorate Zola with the cross of the Legion of Honor—"Honors dishonor; a title degrades"—Maupassant once declared to a friend:* "I will not write for the *Revue des Deux Mondes*. I will not be a member of the Academy. I will not be decorated. I will not marry."

Maupassant did decline the Legion of Honor (he felt that government officials were incompetent to decide which artists should receive its various grades) and he declined to put himself up for election to the Academy (candidature involved the obligation to solicit votes, a procedure he found abhorrent). His avoidance of the *Revue des Deux Mondes* was due to its semi-official connection with the Academy.

The *Revue des Deux Mondes* is the road to the Academy [Théodore de Banville had written in a laudatory *Gil-Blas* article addressed to Maupassant in 1883]. It leads to the Academy as directly as a straight line goes

* Charles Lapierre, *op. cit.*

from one point to another. These two institutions are founded on the same principle: that a distinguished education, good connections in society, and a certain respectability should take the place of genius. Thus they complement and support each other. You have noticed that as soon as a writer begins to aim at the Academy his first thought is to give the *Revue des Deux Mondes* some novel in which each character is ideal, in which people who find a pocketbook in the street, far from taking money out of it, put some in! The true artist cares nothing for all that. . . . So it is with you, my dear poet. No prize for good behavior has ever been awarded to the pupil Guy de Maupassant; but the innumerable readers sitting at the banquet you provide have felt that they were drinking the bitter, bracing wine of truth.

The editor of the *Revue des Deux Mondes*, Ferdinand Brunetière, had been one of the critics most persistently hostile to naturalism, but in Maupassant's early stories and novels he had, almost against his will, admitted the presence of high possibilities, and the later novels made him an admirer. Recanting from one of his four "I will not's," Maupassant sold Brunetière *Notre Coeur*, his last and his weakest novel. Brunetière guaranteed him an income from the magazine of 22,500 francs a year in return for an option on future novels, and he published *Notre Coeur* in the issues of May and June, 1890. It appeared in book form in July.

The thesis of *Notre Coeur* is stated by one of the characters:

The only women still capable of attachment are shop-girls or unhappily married, sentimental little women of the lower middle class. They are overflowing with sentiment, but a sentiment so vulgar that to give them ours in return is to give alms. In our young, rich society, where women want nothing and need nothing except a little safe amusement, where men have regulated their pleasures as they have regulated their work, the old, charming and powerful natural attraction between the sexes has disappeared.

The cultivated hero, hopelessly in love with a modern Parisienne of the salons, a woman incapable of deep affection, is forced in the end, even while continuing to adore her, to keep—on the side, so to speak—an affectionate little waitress, in order that his simpler needs may be satisfied.

Only biographically is the novel interesting. For one thing, it is not truly creative fiction, with the novelist creating by means of characters a world of his own and their own, impinging on the real world in some way of his choosing or non-choosing; it is a more common and considerably less pure literary form, a social thesis illustrated by more or less lifelike puppets—a sad decline for Maupassant. It is self-consciously "modern," aiming to record an aspect of society as it was at a given moment: but its careful documentation and the very resemblances between that society and ours—the superficial, physical, "modern" touches such as the mentions of photography, railroads, telegraphy and central heating—have the effect of making the more fundamental concerns dated and ludicrous—unlike *Bel-Ami,* whose imaginative vigor gives its characters timeless life despite their costumes. And in this novel, almost for the first time, there are clumsy repetitions of words and phrases that contrast painfully with the obvious care of the writing—for this is no strong, flowing work like *Bel-Ami,* whose blemishes are lost in the dash of the narrative.

Perhaps the most interesting passage in *Notre Coeur* is one about a writer:

As to Lamarthe, Gaston de Lamarthe, the *de* in whose name had inoculated him with certain pretentions to

being of noble birth and high social position, he was first
and foremost a writer, a pitiless and terrible writer.
Armed with an eye that recorded images, attitudes and
gestures with the rapidity and precision of a camera,
and endowed with penetration and a novelistic sense
that was as natural as the scent of a hunting dog, he
accumulated professional information from morning to
night. With these two very simple senses, a clear eye for
outward forms and an instinctive intuition of the under-
side of things, he gave his books—which contained none
of the ordinary intentions of the psychological writers,
but which seemed to be pieces of human existence torn
from reality—the color, the tone, the aspect and the
movement of life itself.

Paul Bourget was the greatest admirer of *Notre
Coeur*, saying that it showed as did no other of Maupassant's books his growing realization of the importance
of a book's subject; the reviews by Anatole France and
Jules Lemaître, usually quoted by commentators as
being laudatory, will be found on careful reading to be
more complimentary to Maupassant in general than to
the novel.

It was well received by the subscribers to the *Revue
des Deux Mondes*, but because of its very appearance in
that magazine the sale in book form was cut down. "The
Revue des Deux Mondes," Maupassant wrote his mother,
"has taken from me as buyers of my book everyone in
Paris society, and the official society of all the provincial
towns—the society of professors and magistrates. According to Ollendorff and the booksellers, this amounts
to twenty-five to thirty thousand buyers at the least."

"Everyone in Paris society . . . The official society
of all the provincial towns . . . professors and magistrates . . ." Despite all the changes and developments
that had taken place, those words and the *Revue des*

Deux Mondes make a strange note on which to end the
short story and novel-publishing history of the escaped
colt of Etretat, the writer of *Bel-Ami* and the stories in
the *Gil-Blas*.

Once again I will write you a very short letter [Mau-
passant wrote his mother on May 20, 1890, while *Notre
Coeur* was appearing in the *Revue des Deux Mondes*], for
my eyes are completely bad again. I had to stop Bouchard's treatment completely—it was putting my nerves
in a terrible state and thus harming my sight. I no longer
know to whom to turn. My friend Grancher has given
me his advice. He prescribes especially Plombières as
does Bouchard also—and mountain air in a warm
climate. I shall leave for Plombières about the 20th or
25th and then probably go to finish the treatment in the
Pyrenees.

My new apartment will be very pretty, with only
one inconvenience: the dressing room is too small and
badly arranged. But I have to give François the pretty
room that would have been my dressing room, in order to
have him near me at night, for the doctors prescribe
dry-cupping the length of the spinal column for all cases
of insomnia accompanied by nightmare. That quiets me
instantly, and is such a light treatment that it can be
repeated the next day. Actually I have a Norman
rheumatism, an advanced and total case, which paralyzes
all my functions. The mechanism of my eyes changes
according to the condition of my stomach and intestines.

François was usually called three or four times between eleven at night and two in the morning, either to
do the dry cupping or to brew some calming camomile
tea; and Maupassant's diet these days was a complicated
sequence of eggnogs, rare meats, puréed vegetables,
cheeses and custards. He was becoming more solitary,

seeming (like the hero of *Qui Sait?*) to be often unable to
stand the company of others; and he was growing more
violent-tempered. He flew into a rage when Charpentier
issued a new edition of the *Soirées de Médan* embellished
with etched portraits of the six authors, demanding that
the entire edition be withdrawn and his portrait removed,
and threatening otherwise to sue Charpentier and the
etcher who had engraved his portrait without permission.
It was an undoubted cause for irritation—Maupassant
had long had a detestation of having his likeness published, and since the first edition of *Mademoiselle Fifi*,
which had contained an unflattering etched portrait, he
had allowed none to appear—but this time, unlike the
matter of the *Figaro* cuts in the essay on the novel, the
degree of his anger seems exaggerated. There was also
confusion and near-lawsuit with a team of playwrights
over an abortive adaptation of *Pierre et Jean.*

The summer was a wandering one. He did not go to
the Pyrenees after all, but visited the Vosges, staying
part of the time at Plombières and part of the time with
the Cahen d'Anvers at their chalet in Gerardmer, saw
his parents on the Riviera, attended to the erection of a
tombstone for Hervé at Lyons, and went to Aix-les-
Bains, where he took the waters and began a new novel,
L'Ame étrangère. It was abandoned after twenty pages—
put aside, it is said, because Maupassant felt insecure
in his portrayal of the Roumanian heroine and intended
to accept an invitation tendered him by the Roumanian
queen, Carmen Sylva, to visit her court for purposes of
documentation. The hero, in the fragment that survives,
bears the same last name as the hero of *Notre Coeur*—
confusions in Maupassant's life and writings now become
more numerous. He paid a brief visit to La Guillette,
which he was increasingly determined to sell, the cold

Normandy weather being less and less to his taste, and installed himself in his Paris apartment, planning a novel, writing a play based on a combination of two of his tales—*Au Bord du Lit* (*The Edge of the Bed*) and *Etrennes* (*New Year's Presents*)—and collaborating with a literary man named Jacques Normand on another play based on his story *L'Enfant*, about a young man's mistress who dies giving birth to his child on his wedding night. On November 23 he went to Rouen to attend the unveiling of a monument to Flaubert, and Edmond de Goncourt noted in his journal:

> I was struck, this morning, by how badly Maupassant looks, by the emaciation of his face, his brickish color, the elderly aspect that his whole person has assumed, and even the unhealthy fixedness of his stare. I do not think that he is long for this world.

If ever I could speak freely, with no feeling of there being a barrier between me and the person I was addressing [Maupassant wrote sometime this year to an unidentified woman],* I would expel all the unexplored, suppressed, desolate thoughts that I feel within me. I feel them swelling and poisoning me, like bile. If one day I could spit them out, perhaps they would evaporate, and I would find myself with a light and joyful heart—who knows? Thinking becomes an abominable torment when the brain is but a sore. There are so many bruises inside my head that my ideas cannot stir without making me want to scream. Why? Why? [Dr.] Dumas would say that I have a bad stomach. I think, rather, that I have a heart that is proud and ashamed, a human heart—that old human heart that we laugh at, but which beats and aches, and whose ache is also felt in the head. I have the Latin soul—which is very much the worse for wear. And then there are days when I do not think these things,

---

* Not the perhaps non-existent Madame X of the *Grande Revue*, but a bona fide correspondent whose name has been suppressed by French editors.

but suffer anyway, for I am one of those who have been
skinned alive. But I do not say that and do not show it;
indeed, I think I hide it very well. People probably think
me one of the most indifferent men in the world. I am a
skeptic, which is not the same thing, a skeptic because
my eyes see clearly. And my eyes say to my heart: "Hide,
old man; you are grotesque." And it hides.

And on January 7, 1891, he wrote to his cousin Louis:

My doctor has just left. He forbids me to go out, and
for a long time to come he does not want me to venture on
the streets at night. It is my same old trouble, a neurosis
which requires many precautions.

Despite the constantly increasing troubles, he finished
both plays. One, *La Paix du Ménage*, was not performed
for several years, but the one written in collaboration,
Musotte (so called because the model-mistress has a
charming little *museau*—face), was immediately sched-
uled for production. Although Maupassant was tense,
touchy, and constantly on the verge of exploding in the
face of the opinionated director, he controlled himself—
he knew that he was entering a new field for what money
he could find there—and the play opened at the Théatre
du Gymnase on March 4, 1891. It was dedicated to the
younger Dumas, and with reason: it was a Dumas play,
with all the appropriate discussions of the hypocrisies of
conventional society and a death scene strongly reminiscent of the last act of *La Dame aux camélias*. The
first-night audience sobbed and applauded, the notices
were good, and *Musotte* ran for seventy performances at
the Gymnase and more elsewhere. "*Musotte* is going very
well," he wrote his mother on March 14. "The theater is
always full. Four Parisian companies are going to play it
in the provinces—we have contracts especially with
Rouen, Lyons, Bordeaux and Lille. Abroad it is going to

be played at Brussels, Berlin, and Vienna, in Italy, Por-
tugal, Sweden, Denmark, and at St. Petersburg. The
foreign productions bring in little money, but such
publicity!"

Maupassant could perhaps have made a fortune in
the theater. Earlier in his life he had, like Flaubert,
steadily refused permission that his stories and novels be
dramatized—the artist in him recognized that theatrical
adaptations of prose fiction are almost invariably mere
travesties of the originals—but now he enthusiastically
told his collaborator that what had been done with
L'Enfant could be done with hundreds more of his tales—
they were a gold mine.

Of the new novel that he was planning, *L'Angélus*,
only about fifty pages were ever written, the opening
pages showing a countess in her Norman chateau during
the Franco-Prussian war: Maupassant's writing career
ended as it began, with a story describing the humiliation
of his country and of a woman. These pages are beautiful
to read, and the extraordinary richness of the biographical and symbolic interest of the book's plan can be
gathered from the memoirs of a friend * to whom Maupassant told the whole story that summer:

He told it with extraordinary lucidity, logic, eloquence and emotion. It was the story of a woman, about
to become a mother, whom her husband, a soldier, has
left alone in the family chateau during the terrible year
of 1870–71. One winter night, Christmas Eve, the Prussians invade the house; because she resists or complains,
they put the unhappy woman in a stable, after having
mistreated and even injured her; and on the straw, while
the church bells ring in the distance, she brings into the
world a son, as did the Virgin Mary. But what a son! A

* The poet Auguste Dorchain, quoted in Lumbroso, *op. cit.*, pp. 63–5.

child malformed, maimed forever by the blow given the
mother, its legs crippled so that it will never walk, never
be a man like other men. The years pass; he is not cured,
but by his mother's infinitely tender love his soul is made
fine—as though to make him capable of still more suffering. For—did Jesus really come into the world to
bring joy? One day, when he has become a young man,
a young girl appears, and the cripple adores her with
his great and tender heart, but he cannot tell her so, and
she cannot love him. It is his older brother, his strong,
handsome brother, whom she loves; and he is tortured
by the spectacle of their happiness.

"Come, my sweet," his mother says, cradling him
in her arms like a little child. "I will take you to a
beautiful country and will read to you from beautiful
books, you will forget, you will be happy, too. I want you
to, I want you to."

But the young man shook his head. They traveled.
And everywhere and always he was to see passing before
his eyes, until the day he was to close them forever, that
charming phantom that he would never hold in his arms
—a young girl.

And Maupassant wept as he ended his recital, which
had lasted two hours; and we too wept, for we could see
all the genius and tenderness and pity that still remained
in that soul, which would never again express itself and
reach out to other souls.

Well may Maupassant have wept as he told that
story, with its moving allusions—of how many was he
conscious?—to his own crippling, his own quest. By the
time he told it, that summer of 1891, he was capable
only of weeping over it, not of continuing it. The manuscript, containing in its few pages a beauty that the last
novels and the plays do not even suggest, containing a
promise of a new novelistic richness that might have
equalled the mature richness and nobility of *Le Champ
d'Oliviers*, had been put aside, never to be taken up.

And the priest replied:

"Poor child, pitiless destiny has decreed a sad fate for you, also. But at least you will have, I think, in compensation for all the physical pleasures, the only beautiful things that are allowed to men: dreams, intelligence, and thought."

Those words, on one of the last pages of the manuscript of *L'Angélus*, are close to the last, if not the very last, that Maupassant wrote in fiction.

In its eloquence and richness and pity, what exists of *L'Angélus* is, like the final cluster of short stories, a swan song. But it is a fragment, a promise, whereas the superb final tales were completely realized—they exist totally. In that difference, perhaps, can be found a reaffirmation, if any is needed, of the supremacy of the short story as the vehicle for Maupassant's genius. With the novel he progressed, then retrogressed, then gave sign of rich promise—and collapsed. With the short story he began, and with it he continued through countless variations, giving it a stature that it had never known before.

Only with Chekhov (as has so often been said) has the short story reached comparable heights. For some reason none of the many gifted writers of the present century has been able to renew and transform it as radically and vitally as Maupassant and Chekhov did. Hemingway's short stories, probably the most creative body of short pieces by one man since those earlier masters, remain—for all their freshness and their technical innovations—very definitely within the classification of "objective" short fiction (to use the term largely) which includes both Maupassant and Chekhov. Adventurous twentieth-century writers have inevitably grown impatient with the limitations of "objective" writing, and there has been constant search for radically new approaches and uses of language—for thorough-going renovation of the art of fiction. Joyce succeeded, and he possessed the technique and the human qualities to consolidate his discovery in a novel; but there is no body of twentieth-century short stories which displays that combination of major discovery, rich humanity, and technical power contained in *Ulysses*.* In the opinion of some critics the form has become unprofitable, and is incapable of much more development. The glory of Maupassant and Chekhov would shine all the brighter if it were possible for present-day short-story writers to demonstrate that that is untrue: if they could discover and carry richly through as the older men did in their day, and as Joyce has more recently done with the longer form.

In thus being with Chekhov a culmination (unfortunately) in the development of the short story—a block, since no one has been able to go beyond the power and life with which he endowed the form—Maupassant well merits the epithet applied to him by Henry James in the *Partial Portraits* essay: "a lion in the path." James was referring to something else when he used the phrase: to the fact that Maupassant's purely sensual point of view made him a "case" that was "embarrassing and mys-tifying for the moralist." Perhaps James's phrase can be used to carry, today, a third meaning: that "M. de Maupassant, who is at once so licentious and so im-peccable," is a highly imposing figure in the literary path, considerably more imposing than many critics since James have been inclined to admit.

* For an interesting discussion of the limitations of naturalism and the role of technique, see Mark Schorer, "Technique as Discovery," *The Hudson Review*, Spring, 1948.

CHAPTER 3

FIRST DEATH

His eyes and other organs disordered, his memory failing, his brain confused, his spirits wildly fluctuant, Maupassant now presents the picture of a genius in full disintegration. In eleven years he had written, in addition to articles, close to three hundred stories and six novels; now, following the fragment of *L'Angélus*, he fought and struggled to continue to produce—and occasionally, by tremendous force of will, he achieved the dictation of a simple article.

He wrote constantly to Laure, no longer lamenting his condition, but, as it became steadily worse, concealing his bewilderment and desperation and reassuring her— admitting little more than eye troubles and headaches and toothaches:

Don't be too worried about my health. I think simply that my eyes and head are tired, and that this abominable winter has made a frozen plant of me. I consulted a man said to be very superior to Charcot about my nervous state. He examined me carefully, listened to my whole history, then said: "You have all the symptoms of neurasthenia (as Charcot now calls it: it used to be known as hysteria). It comes from intellectual overwork: every other writer and stockbroker is in your condition." It is certain now that my new novel will not appear in the fall, but the success of *Musotte* makes it possible for me

to wait. The improvement I told you of continues—not
that I am entirely well, but I am gaining weight, my
face is fuller again. I walk every day in the Bois de
Boulogne—certain corners are absolutely quiet and
pretty. I'm not allowed to walk too much, just enough to
rest me. Even my eyes are a little better—you have proof
of that in this letter, which is much longer than I dreamed
I could make it. And then I feel the good feeling of returning health.

What was really taking place, and the self-control
demanded by the writing of such letters to Laure, are
revealed in letters to others, often confused, misspelled,
and all but illegible.

To an unidentified woman:*

My state is well expressed by the howling of certain
dogs—a lamentable complaint addressed to nothing,
reaching nowhere, saying nothing, but flinging into the
night the cry of chained-up anguish that I should like to
utter. If I could wail like them, I should sometimes go
out onto a great plain or into the depths of a wood, and
I should howl for hours on end in the shadows. That, I
feel, would relieve me.

My mind is following dark valleys, that lead me
I know not where. They open one into another, merge,
and are deep and long, impossible to escape from. I leave
one only to find myself in another, and I cannot foresee
what will be at its end. I am afraid that weariness may
make me decide, later on, not to continue along this
senseless road.

He visited the Riviera again that summer of 1891,
but there his troubles increased, and its strong summer
sun was pronounced harmful by his doctors—exactly
which doctors it is hard to say, for in his letters from
1889 through 1891 he speaks of no less than twelve. He

* Cf. note on page 320.

wrote to his friend Dr. Henry Cazalis (the poet Jean Lahor):

I don't think that I will hang on much longer, either on shore or at sea, sicker and sicker in brain and body. I am at Divonne [in the Jura], which I am also going to leave, because of the incessant storms, rain and dampness. I am at the end of my strength, not having slept for four months.

I need exercise, and I cannot take any with this feeling of despondency into which I have fallen. Besides, what kind of exercise? Walking? Travel? Where to? I have seen everything, and refuse to start all over again. The body is strong, the head sicker than ever. There are days when I am strongly tempted to put a bullet into it. I cannot read; every letter I write is a terrible effort. God, but I have had enough of life.

There were also external irritations.

Between March 3 and July 5, 1891, there ran in the *Echo de Paris*, a newspaper to which Maupassant was a contributor, a series of interviews with writers under the general title *Enquête sur l'évolution littéraire* (Inquiry into Literary Trends). The author of the series, a journalist named Jules Huret, had been given the idea of the project by Zola, and the interest aroused by his articles resulted in their being issued later the same year in a volume. In his preface Huret told a little about his aims, methods and results, and he listed the writers interviewed under five headings: Full of Fair Words, Boxers and Prizefighters, Vague and Morose, Ironic and Cynical, Theoreticians. Maupassant was listed in the third category. In the interviews he was mentioned respectfully by Edmond de Goncourt, Anatole France, and a few others; but a number of younger writers, allied with the symbolist school, spoke of him with scorn. Paul Adam

said that he had been transformed into a storyteller for
the salons, and Charles Morice declared: "Let us say to
Maupassant, 'One trade for another, why don't you
work in the Stock Exchange instead of in literature?' "
Gustave Kahn called him "a former business man, who
has as much talent as anyone else; he reads *La Vie
Parisienne* a good deal; you can see him in the country
in sports clothes writing Norman stories; he knows about
process-servers and notaries"; and Charles Vignier
declared, "Certainly it is easy to state that M. Zola no
longer holds the attention of the public; and neither does
M. de Maupassant, who occasionally used to give the
illusion of being a great writer."

Most unpleasant, however, was Huret's interview
with Maupassant himself:

Maupassant has the reputation of being the hardest
man to see in Paris. That made me all the more eager to
see him—this man who had embodied for me, when I
was twenty, the most complete expression of truth, to
whom I had felt closer at that time than to Flaubert
himself. In my provincial town I had thought of him,
with his aristocratic names, the easy, slightly scornful
swagger of his style, the perspicacity of his psychology,
his insistence on exactitude, his reputation as a beloved
pupil of Flaubert's, as a Balzac hero, something like a
quintessence of Rastignac and d'Arthez combined. Those
strong youthful imaginings had not been shaken by the
sort of thing one constantly hears about M. de Maupassant in literary circles: "He is a snob; in his opinion
the most practical procedure for a writer would be to
have the Louvre and Bon-Marché department stores as
his publishers; he has his tailoring and his laundry done
in London; 'Every evening,' he says, 'my valet hands
me my evening shoes on shoe-trees and my evening
trousers on their stretchers.' "

I wanted to see. Besides, his opinion in this inquiry

interested me especially. And unresponsive though he might at first be, the famous names of those who had consented to answer me would make him decide to be willing to talk.

I rang. A servant—a flunkey, rather—opened the door. You know that insolent face one sees in the front hall of every haughty bourgeois? "Monsieur is not at home."

I wrote a few words on my card, and was admitted after all. I crossed a reception room hung with Arabian stuffs and entered a luxurious drawing room which I have no time to describe in detail; soft colors predominated, and my general impression was one of rather bad taste.

The master entered. I looked at him with curiosity, and stood there amazed: Guy de Maupassant! Guy de Maupassant! During the time it took to exchange greetings, choose a chair and sit down I kept mentally repeating the name and looking at the short man in front of me, with his middling shoulders and his two-toned moustache, chestnut with certain hairs that looked bleached. He asked me politely to sit down. But at the first words about literature, interview, etc., he took on a surly air as though he were suffering from a headache, and seemed to be really discomfited.

"Oh, Monsieur," he said, and his words were languid and his manner very morose, "I beg you—don't speak to me of literature. I have violent neuralgia, I am leaving in a day or two for Nice on doctor's orders; this Paris air disagrees with me completely, this noise, this agitation . . . I am really very ill here."

I expressed sympathy, and speaking hesitantly and delicately tried to extract from him at least some vague opinion.

"Oh, literature, Monsieur—I never speak of it. I write when I feel like doing so, but I never talk about it. Besides, I don't know any literary men. I have always been on friendly terms with Zola, and with Goncourt despite his *Memoirs*, but I rarely see them, and never see

any others. I know only the younger Dumas, but we are
not in the same trade . . . and he and I never speak
of literature—there are so many other things to talk
about."

My eyes were open like port-holes. "Yes," I said,
knowing his taste for sports, "yachting . . ."

"So many other things! Look, Monsieur, the proof
that I am not lying is that I was recently offered member-
ship in the Academy; I was promised twenty-eight certain votes; and I refused; and the Legion of Honor, and
all that. . . . No, really, I am not interested. . . .
Don't speak to me any more about it, Monsieur, I beg
you."

Such was the very languid and very morose opinion
of M. de Maupassant on literary trends.

On one of his worse days Maupassant had run into
a pitiless reporter, whose interest was in getting a good
story, and who got one. . . .

And from Divonne he had to write to Francis Mi-
gnard, editor of the *Figaro*, to ask him to deny a story
that was being circulated by a writer named Nicolas
Brousse, who claimed that Maupassant had stolen *Fort
Comme la Mort* from a philosophical short story by him
that had been printed the previous year in a minor
newspaper. "My novel, *Fort Comme la Mort*, whose title
is taken from the Bible (Song of Songs), was published
four years ago by Ollendorff," Maupassant wrote inac-
curately. "Thank you for what you can do. Brousse's
accusation is merely funny—so funny that were it not
for the hostile articles in newspapers accusing me of
plagiarism, I would only laugh."

Then an American newspaper added itself to the
exacerbators.

A New York sheet of the period, the *Star*, was in the
habit of advertising that in each issue of its Sunday self,

the *Sunday Star*, "the best Sunday paper published,"
would be found "A Complete Novel by some famous
writer." During 1890 the paper specialized in French
writers, and among the Sunday "complete novels" were
tales purporting to have been "written for the New York
Star" by Jules Verne, the younger Dumas, Zola, and
Georges Ohnet. Tolstoy's *Kreutzer Sonata* also appeared,
"translated especially for the *Star*." In the issue of July
13, 1890, appeared "*The Last Will and Testament of Madame de Courcils*, Written for the *Star* by Guy de Maupassant." This was a lengthy short story based on Maupassant's *Le Testament* (*The Will*), which had originally appeared in the *Gil-Blas* in 1882, the story of a woman who
disinherits her husband and legitimate sons in favor of
her lover and their child. But *Le Testament* is only the
jumping-off place for the *Star* story: the anonymous
adapter, apparently desirous of using a famous name but
needing to fill a certain number of columns, departed
wildly from Maupassant's tale and invented a new,
trashy sequence of his own. The story was tagged "Copyright, 1890, by the Authors' Alliance. All rights in this
English version reserved"; but neither Maupassant nor
any of his publishers had been consulted.

Six months later, on January 25, 1891, in the last
issue of the *Sunday Star* (by the following Sunday, February 1, it had become the *Daily Continent*), appeared
another so-called Maupassant tale: "*Father and Son*, or
An Inherited Love, written for the New York *Star* by
Guy de Maupassant. English adaptation by Philippe
Prevost." This was a lengthy and thoroughgoing mutila-
tion of *Hautot Père et Fils*, to whose cast of characters
Philippe Prevost—whoever he may have been—had
coolly added a scornful noblewoman, making her reject
the younger Hautot and thus causing him to find solace

in his late father's mistress. As in *The Last Will and Testament of Madame de Courcils*, the result was trash.

There is no evidence that Maupassant ever learned of the existence of *Father and Son*, but someone, perhaps Theodore Child, the Paris representative of Harper's, told him about *The Last Will and Testament of Madame de Courcils*, and on November 5, 1891, he wrote to his lawyer—not to Straus, but to an attorney named Jacob— asking for advice:

I accuse [the *Star*] of theft and forgery. It is a clear case of swindling. I have written more than three hundred stories, but not that one. My name is sufficiently valuable in Paris newspapers—since the slightest article by me brings five hundred francs—to be respected by those American crooks.

With such external irritations added to the relentless internal disintegration, the summer and fall were atrocious. At Divonne, where he wept when telling friends the story of *L'Angélus*, he assured them that if the book were not done in three months he would kill himself; at another watering place—by now doctors recognized his state and merely calmed him as best they could, prescribing sedatives and "cures"—he talked wildly about once having bought a batch of three hundred umbrellas and about having successfully fought off, with a cane, three pimps who were attacking him from the front and three mad dogs attacking him from the rear. He wrote in pathetic confusion to editors and publishers about literary plans:

I have reflected, and I have absolutely decided not to write any more short stories or novelettes. The form is overdone, finished, ridiculous. Besides, I have written too many. I want to work only at my novels, and not let little stories distract me from the only task for which I have enthusiasm. When the book on which I have been working for two years is finished, I will be able to give you some lively travel pieces. I have received a mass of propositions and have accepted none. All futile work fatigues me mentally. I will also give you some little-known portraits of Bouilhet and Turgenev. But I want to live absolutely quietly at this moment, and for that reason I am leaving Paris.

I must see you tomorrow. I am going to have a volume ready almost immediately—not my novel, but a book of criticism and portraits. . . .

For the "book of criticism and portraits" he intended to use and re-cast his earlier articles on Flaubert, Bouilhet, Turgenev and Zola; but it came to nothing.

Shortly after writing his lawyer about the American piracy, he went to the Riviera for the winter, and in a letter to Dr. Cazalis, mentioning among other things Laure's pleasure in one of the doctor's poems, he wrote:

When my mother saw me she cried, "My poor boy! Your eyes are so sick! You'll not be able to work this winter . . ." Now I am almost blind. I shall pass a winter like last, in some solitary, out of the way spot, for I can no longer stand the slightest light at night, not even a candle. I am thoroughly melancholy and wretched. A mistral that has been blowing since my arrival is forcing me to leave here. The mosquitoes are devouring me. Where shall I go? I have no idea.

He found, in Cannes, a pleasant, sunny, sheltered house, the Chalet de l'Isère, where for a brief moment he felt more peaceful. But soon violent letters began to pour out. The man who a few months before had told Jacques Normand that his fiction was a theatrical gold mine now wrote to an unidentified correspondent:

I will never allow plays to be made from my books,
and I cannot understand that anyone should propose
such a thing to authors who respect their art.

Such is the difference between the nature of the novel
and that of the play that the change of form removes
all value from a work. The novel's strength is in the
atmosphere created by the author, in the special evoca-
tion that he gives the characters for each reader, in the
style and the composition.

And you claim to replace all that with the voices of
third-rate actors and actresses, with the jargon and dis-
jointedness of the theater, which is far from giving the
effect of the writing in the book. An author who allows
his book to be turned into a play dishonors his book, and
those who have permitted it have done so only for love
of money and are not artists. . . . And scenery—just
how could it replace the thousand details of landscapes
which harmonize with the life of the book? As for me,
Monsieur, never again will I write a play—I find the
convention utterly false, odious to lovers of the real truth.

Early in his career he had maintained for a while a
not very interesting correspondence with the young Russian painter and diarist, Marie Bashkirtseff,* who had
tried to "collect" him; and now he sent to another persistent young Russian woman on the Riviera, who had
asked him for his autograph and photograph, a letter
which reveals him all too clearly in his last days:

Mademoiselle: This is the last letter that you will
receive from me. I see that we live in different worlds,
and that you do not possess the slightest conception of
what a man can be who lives entirely occupied with his
work and with modern science and absolutely disdainful
of all the nonsense of life.

The album questionnaire which you sent me was an
amazing revelation.

* Admirers of Marie Bashkirtseff can find this correspondence excellently
translated by Lewis Galantière in *The Portable Maupassant* (The Viking Press,
New York).

I keep my life so secret that no one knows what it is.
I am without illusions, a solitary, a savage. I work—that
is *all* I do—and in order to be isolated I live in so wandering a fashion that for whole months at a time only my
mother knows where I am.

No one knows anything about me. In Paris I am considered an enigma, an unknown creature acquainted
only with a few scientists (for I adore science) and with
a few artists whom I admire, the friend of a few women—
the most intelligent in the world, perhaps, but who think
as I do—that is, who have a kind of disdain for life and
for the world which causes us to look on at life with
curiosity, detached from everything we love.

I have broken with all the writers who spy on one for
their novels. I never permit a journalist to enter my
house, and I have given orders that nothing be written
about me. All the articles that have been published are
false. Only my books do I allow to be spoken of.

I have twice refused the Legion of Honor, and last
year the Academy, in order to be free of all ties and all
necessity for gratitude, and to devote myself to nothing
in the world but work.

I live almost always on my yacht, to be in communication with no one. I go to Paris only to see how others
live, and to find material.

If I sent you my photograph it is because I have been
so plagued by letters asking for it that I finally allowed
it to be sold. As for letting you see me—no. I am about
to disappear again for six months, to be rid of everyone.

You see that our characters are not at all alike.

And there was a torrent to Maître Jacob about the
New York *Star*.

"I am so ill that I fear I may be dead in a few days as
the result of a treatment I have been made to follow,"
he wrote him; and he enclosed a letter he had written
Theodore Child, offering to deposit a sum of money with
him if he could persuade Harper's—his legitimate New

York publishers—to act for him in a suit, apparently
already instituted, against the *Star* in the New York
courts.

The court claims not to know who I am [that letter
to Jacob continues], and says that I must be an unimportant, little known, poorly paid writer. Harper's are
in a position to give them correct information.

It was I who brought back the short story and the
novelette into great vogue in France. My volumes have
been translated all over the world and sell in large quanti-
ties; for newspaper publication I am paid the highest
rates ever known, receiving a franc a line for my novels
and five hundred francs for a single tale. You know this
very well. More editions of my works have been sold
than of anyone else's except Zola's. In a few days I will
send you an almost complete list, and some newspaper
articles concerning me.

Attached to that letter is a note in Maupassant's
handwriting:

M. Guy de Maupassant is the first French writer to
bring about a renascence of the national taste for the
short story and novelette. His writings, first published
in newspapers, form a collection of twenty-one volumes,
which have sold an average of thirteen thousand copies,
a figure attested by his publishers' quarterly accountings. . . . He has sold 169,000 copies of his collected
volumes of short stories, 180,000 copies of his novels,
24,000 copies of his travel books—total, 373,000 volumes.

But Jacob's New York correspondent suddenly informed him that continuation of the suit would require
Maupassant to deposit a sum considerably larger than
anyone had dreamed of, and there was agitation about
the New York lawyer's good faith, about finding the
money, and about Maupassant's stubborn insistence on
continuing. (Since the *Star* had by this time ceased pub-

lication, success of the suit would seem to have been
dubious.)

While this agitation was at its height, Maupassant
learned that Havard, in violation of contract terms, had
allowed *La Maison Tellier* to remain out of print for
three months, and through Jacob he gave him twenty-
four hours to print a new edition. Havard had to ask
him for twelve hours grace. And at this very time Edmond de Goncourt was writing in his journal:

Tuesday, December 8, 1891. Maupassant is said to
be suffering from delusions of grandeur; he thinks that
he has been made a Count, and insists on being so addressed. Popelin [a friend of Princesse Mathilde Bona-
parte] says that although he had been warned this summer that Maupassant was beginning to hesitate in his
speech, he did not notice it at St. Gratien, but was struck
by the unlikeliness and preposterousness of some of his
remarks. Maupassant spoke of a visit which he had made
to Admiral Duperré with the Mediterranean fleet, and of
a certain number of guns that had been fired in his honor
—a salute costing hundreds of thousands of francs—so
that Popelin could not help exclaiming over the hugeness
of the sum. The extraordinary thing about the story is
that Duperré told Popelin a short while afterward that
he had not seen Maupassant.

The delusions multiplied: the rest of December was
phantasmagorial. "I discovered yesterday," he wrote to
one of his doctors, "that my entire body, flesh and skin,
was impregnated with salt. I have no more saliva—the
salt has dried it up completely—only a hateful, salty
paste drips from my lips. I am in an abominable state.
I think it is the beginning of the end. . . . My head
pains are so terrible that I press my head between my
hands and it feels like a death's head." On someone's
advice, François sent his master's will to Maître Jacob

in Paris for safekeeping; out walking (for he was allowed
to walk and sail), Maupassant saw a ghost on a road near
a cemetery; he had a coughing fit, and told François
that a piece of filet of sole he had just eaten had passed
into his lung and might cause his death. Marie Kahn and
her sister visited him Christmas Eve, and seem to have
been so horrified by his condition that they fled; on the
27th Raymond told François that for the first time Maupassant had had trouble getting in and out of his boat:
"He was clearly losing control of his legs; at times he
raised them too high or lowered them too quickly." One
or another of his doctors constantly visited him; François
was warned that his master's brain was in danger, but
the doctors did not confine the patient, and laughed and
joked and exchanged stories with him when he was lucid.
But Maupassant knew that the end—some kind of an
end—was near. "I am dying," he wrote Jacob. "I think
that I will be dead in two days. Take care of my affairs
and put yourself in touch with M. Colle, my notary in
Cannes. This is a farewell that I send you." And to
Cazalis:

I AM ABSOLUTELY LOST. I AM EVEN DYING. I have a
softening of the brain, the result of washing out my nasal
passages with salt water. A saline fermentation has taken
place in my brain, and every night my brain runs out
through my nose and mouth in a sticky paste. This is
imminent death and I am MAD. My head is delirious.
FAREWELL, MY FRIEND, YOU WILL NOT SEE ME AGAIN.

New Year's day, 1892, he took the train with François to Nice, and lunched with Laure, her sister, and
Hervé's widow and little daughter. Back in Cannes that
night François sat up as usual until his master closed his
eyes, and at about quarter past two in the morning he
was awakened:

I heard a noise and ran into the little room at the top of the stairs. I found M. de Maupassant standing there, his throat cut. He immediately said: "See what I have done. I have cut my throat, it is an absolute case of madness."

I called Raymond. We placed my master on the bed in the next room and I temporarily bandaged the wound. Doctor Valcourt, notified of the emergency, quickly came to help us in the sad circumstance. Despite my emotion, I held a lamp while the doctor rapidly made the necessary stitches; he was aided by Raymond, who acquitted himself skillfully and without flinching. [Only in the unpublished portion of his memoirs does François tell that he himself fainted during the operation.] The operation succeeded perfectly.

My master was absolutely calm; he did not utter a word in the doctor's presence. When the doctor had left, he expressed his regret at having done "such a thing," of having caused us so much trouble. He took Raymond's hand and mine and begged our pardon for what he had done. He speculated as to the full extent of his misfortune, staring at us with his large eyes as though to ask us for a few words of consolation, of hope, if it were possible. . . . I did my best with what calming words I could find. I repeated them twenty times over, and they seemed to do a little something for my poor master. Finally his head fell forward, his eyes closed, and he slept.

Raymond, standing at the foot of the bed, was exhausted; he had given of himself to the utmost; he was frighteningly pale. I advised him to take a little rum, which he did, and then from his powerful chest there came sobs that made you think it would burst; his eyes remained dry. We both watched over our good master; I did not move, for one of his hands rested on my arm; I was so afraid of waking him that we no longer spoke. We had lowered the lamps, and in the darkness we thought about this irreparable disaster.

When he awoke, at eight o'clock, I was convinced that he was better. Bernard arrived and was shocked

at the sight of the patient, and indeed he had grown
terribly pale. I felt his hand, to see whether he had a
fever, but no, it was cool. At noon he was still in a state
of complete prostration, indifferent to everything. His
calm frightened me. All that day and the next he lay
prostrate.

At eight o'clock that night he roused himself and said
to me suddenly, feverishly, "François, are you ready?
We're leaving; war is declared!" I replied that we were
not to leave until the next morning. "What!" he cried,
astonished at my failure to fall in with his plans. "You're
delaying, when it's urgent that we act as quickly as
possible? You know we have always agreed that we
would go together when the time came for the revenge
against Prussia. You know we must have our revenge,
and we will have it."

He had indeed made me promise to follow him in
case of war with Germany; we were to go together to
defend the eastern frontier. During our various voyagings
he had given me his military papers to keep, lest they
be lost among the great quantity of his other papers.

As the night advanced, my poor master persisted in
his ideas and became irritated at my slowness. The
situation was becoming critical, for he could not understand why I, of all people, should put an obstacle in the
way of our departure. Happily Rose, the woman who
came by the day, appeared. She had an authority and
influence over him that were really surprising; she was
a tall woman, with pronounced features like those of a
Neapolitan, and wavy pepper-and-salt hair. Everything
she said made an impression on him; he was docile with
her and did not argue.

The next day, the attendant from Dr. Blanche's sanitarium arrived. . . .

CHAPTER 4

FAREWELL TO MAUPASSANT

Shortly before the last days in Cannes, Maupassant had written:

I keep thinking of my poor Flaubert, and I tell myself that I should like to be dead if I were sure that someone would think of me as I think of him.

Even in his manner of dying he resembled his uncle Alfred Le Poittevin, of whom Flaubert had written: "For me he died twice." Maupassant had slowly entered into one death at Cannes. The second was also to be slow. Transported in a strait-jacket to Paris to the accompaniment of considerable macabre newspaper publicity, he lingered on for more than a year in Dr. Blanche's sanitarium in Passy.

Laure at first supported the news of his incarceration with courage, but she could not take the step of visiting him, and his continued inability to write her finally brought her a degree of realization of his state that was all but unbearable. In March she suffered a series of wild hysterical attacks, during which she maltreated her daughter-in-law and tried to kill herself by taking laudanum and then by choking herself with her own hair. For a time it seemed that she, too, would have to be committed; but she gradually recovered, and resumed what had been her normal life, with an accentuation of her hypochondria. Neither she nor her husband ever visited their son. She was never fully informed of the nature of his malady, and until the very end she hoped for improvement.

So, too, at first, did Maupassant's friends:

You will be glad to know, speaking of art and artists [Paul Bourget wrote Henry James on March 24, 1892], that poor Maupassant is better—at least I am told so. The secret of the reasons which brought about his despair has remained impenetrable. But it seems that they have passed. How long it is since we spoke of him in Paris after his journey to England. . . .*

But Maupassant's disintegration continued—the European name for the last stage of his syphilis, progressive paralysis, is more descriptive than the English equivalent, paresis—and its inexorable, violent progress was freely reported by Dr. Blanche to Paris society in the salon of Princesse Mathilde Bonaparte. One of Dr. Blanche's assistants, either Dr. Meuriot or Dr. Franklin Grout (the latter was the second husband of Flaubert's beloved niece Caroline), kept a notebook of the patient's condition, and allowed it to leave his hands, and parts of it were published. On a macabre evening, March 6, 1893, Maupassant's comedy, *La Paix du Ménage*, was performed at the Comédie Française, causing a flurry of rather hushed newspaper comment. Considerably earlier than this all visits to him had been stopped (an occasional grieving or curious friend or relative had at first been admitted, and François had come every day as long as it was possible, continuing to serve). Death came to the body on July 6, 1893. No one thought to notify Monsieur de Maupassant: he read about it in his newspaper the

* See Note 14: Maupassant, Henry James, and Sigma, page 412.

next day at Sainte-Maxime. Burial was in the Mont-
parnasse cemetery in Paris on the ninth; Laure did not
come; and the closest intimates present were François,
Blanche Roosevelt, Clémence Brun, and Madame Pasca,
an elderly actress who had been a friend of Flaubert's.
During the past few days French newspapers had been
printing articles by literary men commemorating Maupassant and his work, and they were to continue printing
them for some time, but few of them equalled the eloquence of the words Zola uttered beside the grave:

What impressed us, those of us who had been watching [the young] Maupassant with interest and sympathy,
was the promptness with which he conquered the hearts
of the public. He had only to appear and tell his stories,
and instantly everyone loved him. He was a celebrity
overnight; he was not even discussed; smiling good fortune seemed simply to have taken him by the hand, eager
to lead him as high as he chose to go. I certainly know no
other example of such happy beginnings, such an instan-
taneous, unanimous success. Readers accepted everything he wrote: things that would have shocked them
had they come from others, from him made them smile.
He satisfied all intelligences, he touched all sensibilities,
and we had the extraordinary spectacle of a robust, frank
talent, making not the slightest concession, and yet immediately capturing the admiration and even the affection of the reading public, the great, average public
which ordinarily makes original artists pay so dearly for
the privilege of growing and developing independently.
All of Maupassant's genius lies in the explanation of
this phenomenon. If he was understood and loved from
the first, it was because the French soul found in him the
gifts and the qualities that have created its finest achieve-
ments. He was understood because he had clarity, simplicity, moderation and strength. He was loved because
he possessed a laughing goodness, a profound satire which
miraculously is not unkind, and a brave gaiety which

persists even through tears. He was in the great tradition
that can be traced from the first babblings of our tongue
down to our own day. He had as ancestors Rabelais,
Montaigne, Molière, La Fontaine, those who wrote
strongly and clearly, those who are the reason and the
light of our literature. His readers and admirers were not
mistaken; they made their way instinctively to the
limpid, gushing spring, to the wonderful humor of his
thought and style which satisfied their need. And they
were grateful to a writer, pessimist though he was, for
giving them, in the perfect clarity of his works, the joyful
sensation of well-being and vigor.

There must, of course, be no attempt to set limits
to art; complicated, ultra-refined and obscure artists
must be accepted along with the others; but to me it
seems that these latter provide, as it were, a momentary
debauch, or a sumptuous banquet, and that we must always return to simple and clear art as we always return
without satiety to the nourishment of our daily
bread. . . .

Apart from his glory as a writer, [Maupassant] will
always remain one of the happiest, and one of the un-
happiest, men the world has ever seen: one of those in
whom the rest of us see our own humanity aspire, and
then see it shattered; the adored, spoiled brother, dying
amid our tears. . . .

When the doctors had certified Maupassant incapable
of managing his own affairs, an administrator had been
appointed, and Laure had advised on matters concerning
writings and publishers. This she continued to do as her
son's heir, authorizing the publication of several volumes
of hitherto uncollected tales, the writing of a play based
on *Yvette*, and the appearance in magazines of the frag-
ments of *L'Ame étrangère* and *L'Angélus*.

For a time she corresponded with Hermine Lecomte
du Nouy in a series of beautifully written letters lament-

ing her fate and the disappearance of her loved ones,
telling of her doses of chloral, her nightmares, and constantly announcing her own approaching end. A hearse
stopped at her villa by mistake one morning to pick up
a body, she wrote Hermine in 1895, and she was tempted
to go along. The next year, however, she broke off relations with Hermine, on the appearance of the latter's
novel, *Amitié Amoureuse (Amorous Friendship)*. Maupassant was several times casually mentioned in the text,
but Laure, to whom the book was dedicated, believed
that the letters of which the novel is composed contained
whole passages taken from Guy's letters to Hermine, and
she was offended by what she considered disloyalty.

She lived on in her villa in Nice, visited every day by
her doctor. Curtains were kept drawn, and the occasional
writer who came sufficiently well recommended to be
granted an audience and a talk about her son found her
lying on a chaise longue in the darkness. She retained a
capacity for drama, which showed itself occasionally.
When someone asked her about the rumor (apparently
false) that three children of Guy's had been found living
in Paris, she pointed to her shelf of his books, saying,
"Children? I know only these." In 1900 a monument was
erected to Maupassant in Rouen, and Laure, invited to
the unveiling, replied to José-Maria de Heredia, president
of the committee:

Villa Monge, Nice, May 20.
Monsieur le Président,
If I were not forced to leave in the realm of vain
fancies all thought of travel, I should already have set
out for the old Norman city in which I was born, and
should not be confiding to this small sheet of paper the
mission of expressing my deep gratitude. It would be a
joy to me to shake the hands of friends, to be with the

committee which has aided you so well in the touching
care which you have never ceased to give the memory of
my dear departed.

But illness and grief, even more than years, have laid
heavy hands upon me, and I must no longer leave the
retreat in which I have taken shelter.

Heart and soul I will be with you all on Sunday, and
I cannot believe that a few words of the speeches, a few
notes of the music, will not reach me, through some
miracle well merited by a poor mother's heart.

My sight is almost extinguished, my hands are trembling, and I write with infinite difficulty. This you can
see, monsieur le Président, but I wished to send you my
reply myself.

Eleanora Duse once called on her, to pay tribute to
the mother of a great artist, and as they parted Laure
asked: "You have genius and fame: what can I wish for
you?" Duse answered "Peace," and Laure replied: "In
return, wish it for one who will find it only in the grave."

She constantly referred to herself as "scarcely belonging to the land of the living," and to one literary
man, to whom she had loaned some papers that she
wished returned, she said: "Above all, do not delay! I
am very old, very ill! And the doctor assures me that
my deliverance is close at hand!" That was in 1897. She
lived six years longer, succumbing to pneumonia on December 8, 1903, at the age of 82, having survived Guy by
more than ten years and her husband by almost five.

She had subscribed to a clipping service, but cancelled
it in 1900, when the speeches at the unveiling of the
Rouen monument dwelt too unbearably on Guy's tragedy. She never forgave fate his early extinction, and she
remained strongly agnostic to the end: "If God exists,"
she said to Hermine, "I will see him, and we will have it
out." And she well realized some, at least, of the im-

portance of her own role in her son's career: "My own genius was but latent and scattered," she told Hermine, "but it was within me that Guy acquired the gift of writing."

Laure's words are close to the truth; and it is not until we have taken leave of her that we can finally say farewell to her son—with his confusions and obsessions, his highlife mania, the simplicity and goodness that brought him devotion from François, Raymond and Bernard, his vulgarity (most apparent in the cruelty of some of his farces and in some of his descriptions of the physically maimed), his provincialism, his conflicting and shifting needs for society and for solitude, his extraordinary senses, his humor, his reserve, his intelligence, his capacity for work, the magic of some of his phrases and sentences—the description of a waltz in *Yvette*, of eating oysters in *Mon Oncle Jules*, of a collector's honeymoon with a new acquisition in *La Chevelure*—and the greater magic that makes out of a thousand trivialities, banalities, tragedies and jokes, a world of its own that illumines the real world.

It was never more true of anyone that his strength was in his weakness—even in the weakness of some of his work. "I feel a deep interest in Maupassant," Henry Adams wrote to John Hay from Paris during that January, 1892, when the patient was first removed to Dr. Blanche's. "[His] mental condition in his healthiest state worried me greatly, because he seemed totally unconscious whether he wrote excessively funny or excessively stupid things." It was Maupassant's very freedom to write "stupid" things and not worry about them as Henry Adams worried—and his lucky ability to get them

published, and to earn part of his living from them, so
that he could keep writing—that enabled him to produce
the great bulk of work that contained his masterpieces;
the masterpieces that like the rest were the fruition of his
childhood, Normandy, Flaubert, his manias, his disease
—of all those elements which from the beginning had
gone to make him, and some of which combined in the
end to destroy him.

SIXTY-FIVE FAKE
''MAUPASSANT''
STORIES

Sixty-five Fake "Maupassant" Stories

ALTHOUGH MAUPASSANT'S WORKS have been translated into most of the languages of the world, he is for a particular reason one of the least completely translatable of authors.

"It is through [the senses] alone, or almost alone, that life appeals to him," Henry James said; "it is almost alone by their help that he describes it, that he produces brilliant works." And Benedetto Croce has written of Maupassant's almost exclusively sensual materials and his transformation of them:

> Because he is a poet, Maupassant, who knows nothing save the material and the sensual, and depicts nothing save the obscure shudder of matter and spasm of senses, makes use of so much objective truth in his narrative that, thanks to grief, pity and disgust, it seems to be alive and to present ethical ideality: thanks to the comic and laughable, the superiority of well-balanced intellect: thanks to desolation and despair, the necessity for religion. . . .* He is a poet and is distinguished by emerging from such of his contemporary compatriots as Zola, Daudet and others who may be possessed of many noteworthy characteristics, but are not fundamentally and substantially poetic as he is. Truly he was born a poet and in pouring out poetry with facile creative power, he consumed his short life: he entered the world of literature and disappeared from it (as he said of himself one day when in pain and contemplating suicide) "like a meteor."

It is Maupassant's dependence on sensual materials, his "objectivity," that trick the ordinary translator. For his objective observations translate easily and well, whereas the

* See Note 15: Maupassant and Religion, page 413.

poetry he distills from them is, like most poetry, scarcely translatable at all; and the result is that a Maupassant story in translation is apt to be little more than a mere factual narrative—in Croce's words, a "shudder of matter and spasm of senses." Such, at least, has been to a considerable degree the fate of his writings in English. The extent to which they have been perverted in most existing English translations is a tragedy in after-fame.

English and American prudery delayed large-scale translation. An occasional longer work—*A Woman's Life, A Ladies' Man (Bel-Ami), Pierre and Jean*—appeared in England during his lifetime, but very few of the stories; and in the United States those of the stories that were so excellently translated by Lafcadio Hearn and Jonathan Sturges were very carefully chosen. It is clear from Henry James's essay in *Partial Portraits* that the Anglo-Saxon reading public was thought to require protection from most of Maupassant's work, and this is clear also from the preface to a small edition of five tales published in the United States in French in 1891: *

The great charmer named Guy de Maupassant is a marvellous storyteller. Like his godmothers the fairies, he makes lavish gifts of gold, pearls and flowers. But his gold is not always without alloy, his pearls are not all equally fine, and certain of his flowers give off a heady perfume. We have had to do much gleaning before finding these pretty field-flowers which we have gathered for you. Here they are, arranged in a bouquet. . . .

And Barrett Wendell's famous *English Composition*, first published in 1894 and used in two generations of American college classrooms, contains the following:

The French are finer artists than we; but according to our standards, at all events, they are apt to apply their art to very abominable subjects. More than half the time M. de Maupassant's stories deal with matters that no decent man out of France would for a moment think worthy of his pains. The impression left on you by reading these stories is unpleasantly debasing—at least, if you happen to have been born a re-

---

* *Contes et Nouvelles* par Guy de Maupassant, avec Une Etude sur l'Auteur par Adolphe Brisson. New York: William R. Jenkins, Editeur et Libraire Français, 851 & 853 Sixth Avenue. Boston: Carl Schoenhof.

spectable Yankee; but you will have to read far and wide before you can find stories in which every word and every turn of sentence is adapted to its purpose with more subtile skill. And some of the stories that are in themselves most hateful can give, and rightly, to the technical critic the keenest delight. As style, his style often seems perfect.*

Silly though those passages are,† Maupassant was nevertheless at that time regarded as a literary artist—an artist largely unsuited to Anglo-Saxon eyes and ears, but an artist nonetheless; and whatever of his work was presented to Anglo-Saxons was presented respectfully by both translator and publisher.

In 1903 all that was changed.

A smart American publisher and bookseller named M. Walter Dunne, whose specialty was large and showily produced "sets," felt that the time had come to confront the American public with all of Maupassant; and he issued, in seventeen volumes, the first large-scale collection of the stories, novels, travel-writings and verse in English.‡ As a prestige device, the total printing was divided into numerous "limited editions," differing in title page, binding, purported number of copies, price (from $50 up), and name: "Salon Edition," "Alliance Française Edition," etc. The collection was put together with ludicrously execrable taste: every detail of make-up and editing bears the mark of vulgar hands.§ Translations are anonymous, and for the most part of appalling crudity; a few, however, are recognizable as previously-issued translations by various hands. Robert Arnot, M.A., who on the supplementary frontispiece of

* Copyright by Charles Scribner's Sons.

† Let no one think, however, that the reading public of today is unprotected against Maupassant. The editor of an American reprint magazine recently estimated that of the more than two hundred tales only thirty could be offered to his readers. But then there has grown up a strange double standard of "morality" concerning what can be published in America and England in books, and what can be published there in magazines.

‡ *The Life Work of Henri René Guy de Maupassant*, Embracing Romance, Travel, Comedy and Verse, For the first time Complete in English. With a Critical Preface by Paul Bourget of the French Academy and an Introduction by Robert Arnot, M.A. Illustrated from original drawings by Eminent French and American artists. M. Walter Dunne, Publisher, New York and London.

§ The "Salon Edition," for example, contains a supplementary double-page frontispiece depicting an almost naked woman bearing in one hand a skull and in the other a glass of champagne, from which a winged cupid is sipping.

the "Salon Edition" is identified as "Managing Editor," is not
further identifiable; the preface by Bourget, crudely translated,
appears to be genuine; and no data is available as to whether
M. Walter Dunne, about whom little is known, had dealt with
Maupassant's publishers or with Laure or had merely engaged
in piracy—like the New York *Star* which had so enraged
Maupassant in 1891.

On the title page of certain of the "editions" the publisher's
name is given not as M. Walter Dunne, but as "The St. Dunston
Society, London and New York"—apparently a mere name,
perhaps a grandiose echo of his own, placed there by Dunne for
show. Dunne later failed, and the Werner Publishing Company,
of Akron, Ohio, which had done his printing and binding, took
over the remaining sets, legally organized on paper a "St.
Dunstan Society" (correcting the spelling of the name Dunstan),
printed title pages giving the publisher's name as "The St.
Dunstan Society, Akron, Ohio," and continued to market the
books until it, too, failed about 1912. Such seems, at least, to
be the correct history of this confused venture. A number of
the Maupassant sets, in "mint" condition, are at present in the
hands of a New York book-dealer.

But the most remarkable feature of the Dunne -St. Dunston-
St. Dunstan collection is its contents: for in it are included no
less than sixty-five stories which are not the work of Maupassant.

None of these sixty-five stories has ever been included in
any French edition of Maupassant's works; I have been able to
identify four as tales from the collected works of one of Maupassant's fellow-journalists, René Maizeroy; the authorship
of the remainder is unknown; but almost without exception internal evidence shows them to be non-Maupassantian. Falsity
is particularly obvious in those dealing with Central and Eastern
European life, especially Vienna and Budapest society, territory never explored by Maupassant and here described in
very non-Maupassant style. Almost all of the sixty-five give
the impression of having been trash in their original language or
languages, whatever it or they may have been.

The Dunne collection was followed, during subsequent years,
by many smaller, less elaborate Maupassant collections for

smaller purses; and although Dunne's collection was copyright it seems to have been without real protection, for in the later collections various of the fake stories first published by Dunne continued to appear and reappear. The most recent collection to contain some of them was published by Halcyon House, Garden City, New York, in 1947.* Fifty of its 223 stories are not by Maupassant; but the entire collection, Eastern European stories and all, was described by "Bookwright," a reviewer for the *New York Herald Tribune,* as being "the whole world of France seen piecemeal under a microscope." At no time before my investigations was the authenticity of any of these sixty-five grossly inferior stories questioned: an indication of the general American misconception of Maupassant.

How and why these non-Maupassant tales found their way into Dunne's collection, who the authors of most of them are, whether some are deliberate forgeries in Maupassant's manner, or whether all are like the Maizeroy stories, merely low-grade stories fraudulently presented as Maupassant's only in Dunne's collection—all these are mysteries whose solution seems unlikely, and would in any case demand research on a formidable scale, considering the immense numbers of short stories published in French newspapers of the period, the non-French character of many of the stories, and the disappearance of M. Walter Dunne and others connected with the collection.

In view of the continued reappearance of the fake stories, it would seem well to give their names. Here they are, with their English and (purported) French titles as listed in the index in Volume XVII of the Dunne collection:

1. *Babette* (*Babette*)
2. *Mamma Stirling* (*Maman Stirling*) (By René Maizeroy)
3. *Lilie Lala* (*Lilie Lala*) (By René Maizeroy)
4. *The Bandmaster's Sister* (*Lucie*)
5. *The Mountebanks* (*Les Jongleurs*)
6. *Ugly* (*Difforme*)
7. *The Debt* (*Fanny*)
8. *The Artist* (*L'Artiste*)

* The editors of Halcyon House had not known of the fraud, and on being told of it stated their intention of not republishing the stories in question.

9. *False Alarm* (*L'Epouvante*)
10. *The Venus of Braniza* (*La Vénus de Braniza*)
11. *La Morillonne* (*La Morillonne*)
12. *The Sequel to a Divorce* (*Rencontre*) (Not Maupassant's story entitled *Rencontre—The Meeting.*)
13. *The Clown* (*Le Scapin*)
14. *Mademoiselle* (*Mademoiselle*)
15. *The Man with the Dogs* (*L'Homme aux Chiens*)
16. *In Various Roles* (*Wanda*)
17. *Countess Satan* (*Comtesse Satan*)
18. *A Useful House* (*Finesse*)
19. *The Viaticum* (*Viaticum*)
20. *The Hermaphrodite* (*L'Hermaphrodite*) (By René Maizeroy)
21. *Violated* (*Violé*)
22. *Ghosts* (*Le Noyé*) (Not Maupassant's story entitled *Le Noyé—The Drowned Man.*)
23. *The New Sensation* (*Parisine*)
24. *Virtue!* (*Chasteté*)
25. *The Thief* (*Le Voleur*) (This story, about a girl's lover discovered in her house at night by her parents, was written by René Maizeroy. It is not Maupassant's *Le Voleur*, which concerns a group of painters and a thief discovered in a studio.)
26. *In Flagrante Delictu* (*In Flagrante Delictu*)
27. *On Perfumes* (*Les Parfums*)
28. *In His Sweetheart's Livery* (*Irma*)
29. *The Confession* (*Confession*) (Not one of Maupassant's several stories entitled *La Confession*)
30. *An Unfortunate Likeness* (*Similitude*)
31. *A Night in Whitechapel* (*Une Nuit*) (Not Maupassant's story entitled *La Nuit—Cauchemar—Night: A Nightmare*)
32. *Lost* (*Craque*)
33. *The Relics* (*Vieux Objets*) (Not Maupassant's story entitled *Vieux Objets—Old Objects;* nor his *La Relique—The Relic*)
34. *A Rupture* (*Lalie Spring*) (No relation to a story by René Maizeroy entitled *Lalie Spring* and included in Maizeroy's collected volume bearing the same title.)
35. *Margot's Tapers* (*Noces de Margot*)

36. *The Accent (L'Accent)*
37. *Profitable Business (Charité)*
38. *The Last Step (Une Ruse)* (Not Maupassant's story entitled *Une Ruse—A Ruse*)
39. *A Misalliance (Mésalliance)*
40. *An Honest Ideal (Désabusée)*
41. *Delila (Delila)*
42. *The Ill-Omened Groom (Zoë)*
43. *The Odalisque of Senichou (L'Odalisque de Senichou)*
44. *The Real One and the Other (Mlle. Dardenne)*
45. *The Carter's Wench (Glaizette)*
46. *The Carnival of Love (Carnival d'Amour)*
47. *The Man with the Blue Eyes (L'Homme aux Yeux Bleus)*
48. *A Good Match (Angélique)*
49. *The Old Maid (Marie des Anges)*
50. *The Marquis (Le Marquis)*
51. *A Deer Park in the Provinces (En Campagne)*
52. *An Adventure (Une Aventure)*
53. *The Jennet (Le Genêt)*
54. *Under the Yoke (Wanda Pulska)*
55. *A Fashionable Woman (Goldskind)*
56. *The Upstart (Le Parvenu)*
57. *Happiness (Le Bonheur)* (Not Maupassant's story entitled *Le Bonheur*)
58. *The White Lady (La Dame Blanche)*
59. *Wife and Mistress (Imprudence)* (Not Maupassant's story entitled *Imprudence*)
60. *Sympathy (Compassion)*
61. *Julot's Opinion (Julot)*
62. *The Lancer's Wife (La Revanche)* (Not Maupassant's story entitled *La Revanche—Revenge*)
63. *Caught (Valeska)*
64. *Jeroboam (Jeroboam)*
65. *Virtue in the Ballet (Henriette)*

Maupassant, subtly difficult to translate well, has suffered the misfortune of being translated particularly crudely and commercially, and the further misfortune of being proclaimed the author of a large body of trash written by others.

Such is his position in the United States. In England he suffered only a portion of that fate, but even there crude translation has deformed his art and distorted his reputation. In America his tales—or what purport to be his tales—have become the cheapest kind of merchandise, often given away free with other, more highly considered products. The following two advertisements are from issues of the *New York Times* during the past few years:

. . . and this thrilling, shocking 502-page SHORT STORIES OF DE MAUPASSANT. IN ADDITION TO THE STRANGE WOMAN, you will ALSO get (for only $1.39) this great 502-page volume— the greatest works of literature's most daring storyteller! Here *complete and unexpurgated*, are the frankest, most realistic stories of their kind ever written! . . . (Since this is a great classic which you will always cherish in your life-time library, you may prefer the beautiful edition bound in genuine pin seal grain *leather*. Just take your choice.)

. . . ALSO FREE—Nearly 100 of the World's Most Daring Short Stories! In addition to receiving free THE SUN IS MY UNDOING, you ALSO get—on this special offer—the 502-page SHORT STORIES OF DE MAUPASSANT: *complete, unexpurgated*. Nearly 100 stories of love, hate, intrigue, passion, madness, jealousy—the frankest, most daring stories of their kind ever written! *Ball-of-Fat, The Diamond Necklace, Love, The Piece of String, The Mad Woman, Mademoiselle Fifi, Story of a Farm Girl, Bed No. 29, The Wedding Night*, all the best works that made de Maupassant "father of the modern short story."

Readers of Maupassant in English will do well to avoid such collections as those, and to seek, rather, one of the more recent editions (there are at least two) which contain only stories which Maupassant himself wrote, and which have been translated with a certain skill and respect.

FOUR HITHERTO UNREPRINTED MAUPASSANT STORIES

Four Hitherto Unreprinted Maupassant Stories

———————————————

Here are four Maupassant stories which have never been reprinted since their original appearance in the newspaper columns of the *Gaulois* and the *Gil-Blas* in the 1880's.

Following Maupassant's death, numerous stories unreprinted during his lifetime were resurrected from newspaper files, issued in volumes, eventually translated into various languages, and included in collected editions of his work. These four, each of which is of interest in the history of Maupassant's writing, were not among them. They appear here for the first time, outside their newspapers, in any language.

AN OLD MAN*

ALL THE NEWSPAPERS had carried the advertisement: "The new watering place of Rondelis offers all desired advantages for a long stay and even for permanent residence. Its ferruginous waters, recognized as the best in the world for counteracting all impurities of the blood, seem also to possess particular qualities calculated to prolong human life. This singular circumstance is perhaps due in part to the exceptional situation of the town, which lies surrounded by mountains and in the very center of a pine forest. For several centuries it has been celebrated for numerous cases of extraordinary longevity."

And the public came in droves.

One morning the doctor in charge of the springs was asked to call on a new arrival, Monsieur Daron, who had come to Rondelis only a few days before and had rented a charming villa on the edge of the forest. He was a little old man of eighty-six, still sprightly, wiry, healthy, active, who went to infinite pains to conceal his age.

He asked the doctor to be seated, and immediately questioned him: "Doctor, if I am well, it is thanks to hygienic living. I am not very old, but have reached a cer-

* "Un Vieux," *Gil-Blas*, September 26, 1882. The first of various short stories and articles about watering-places that culminated in the writing of the novel *Mont-Oriol*.

tain age, and I keep free of all illness, all indisposition, even the slightest discomfort, by means of hygiene. I am told that the climate of this place is very favorable for the health. I am very willing to believe it, but before establishing myself here I want proof. I am therefore going to ask you to call on me once a week, to give me, very exactly, the following information:

"I wish first of all to have a complete, utterly complete, list of all the inhabitants of the town and surroundings who are more than eighty years old. I also need a few physical and psychological details concerning each. I wish to know their professions, their kinds of life, their habits. Each time one of these people dies, you will inform me, indicating the precise cause of death, as well as the circumstances."

Then he graciously added: "I hope, Doctor, that we may become good friends," and he stretched out his wrinkled little hand. The doctor took it, promising his devoted co-operation.

M. Daron had always had a strange fear of death. He had deprived himself of almost all the pleasures because they are dangerous, and whenever anyone expressed surprise that he did not drink wine—wine, that bringer of fancy and gaiety—he replied in a voice containing a note of fear: "I value my life." And he pronounced *My*, as if that life, *His* life, possessed some generally unknown value. He put into that *My* such a difference between his life and the life of others, that no answer was possible.

Indeed, he had a very particular way of accentuating the possessive pronouns designating all the parts of his person or even things belonging to him. When he said "My eyes, my legs, my arms, my hands," it was clear that no mistake must be made: those organs did not belong to everyone. But this distinction was particularly noticeable when he spoke of his physician: "My doctor." One would have said that this doctor was his, only his, destined for him alone, to take care of his illnesses and nobody else's, and that he was superior to all the doctors in the universe, all, without exception.

He had never considered other men except as kinds of puppets, created as furniture for the natural world. He divided them into two classes: those whom he greeted because some chance had put him in contact with them, and those whom he did not greet. Both categories of individuals were to him equally insignificant.

But beginning with the day when the doctor of Rondelis brought him the list of the seventeen inhabitants of the town who were over eighty, he felt awaken in his heart a new interest, an unfamiliar solicitude for these old people whom he was going to see fall by the wayside one after the other.

He had no desire to make their acquaintance, but he had a very clear idea of their persons, and with the doctor, who dined with him every Thursday, he spoke only of them. "Well, doctor, how is Joseph Poinçot today? We left him a little ill last week." And when the doctor had given him the patient's bill of health M. Daron proposed modifications in diet, experiments, methods of treatment which he might later apply to himself if they succeeded with the others. The seventeen old people were an experimental field from which much was to be learned.

One evening the doctor came in and announced: "Rosalie Tournel is dead." M. Daron shuddered and immediately demanded, "What of?" "Of an angina."

The little old man uttered an "ah" of relief. Then he declared: "She was too fat, too big; she must have eaten too much. When I get to be her age, I'll be more careful." (He was two years older than Rosalie, but never admitted to being over seventy.)

A few months later, it was the turn of Henri Brissot. M. Daron was very moved. This time it was a man— thin, within three months of his own age, and very prudent. He dared ask for no details, but waited anxiously for the doctor to tell him. "Ah, he died suddenly, just like that? He was very well last week. He must have done something unwise, Doctor." The doctor, who was enjoying himself, replied, "I believe not. His children tell me he was very careful."

Then, no longer able to contain himself, M. Daron demanded, with anguish, "But . . . but . . . What did he die of, then?"

"Of pleurisy."

That was joyful news, really joyful. The little old man clapped his dry hands. "I knew it! I told you he had done something unwise. Pleurisy doesn't come just by itself. He took a breath of fresh air after his dinner, and the cold lodged on his chest. Pleurisy! That is an accident, not an illness. Only crazy men die of pleurisy."

And he ate his dinner gaily, talking of those who remained. "There are only fifteen now, but they are all strong, aren't they? All of life is like that, the weakest fall first; people who go beyond thirty have a good chance to reach sixty, those who pass sixty often get to eighty; and those who pass eighty almost always reach the century mark, because they are the most robust, the most careful, the most hardened."

Still two others disappeared during the year, one of dysentery and the other of a choking fit. M. Daron derived a great deal of amusement from the death of the former, and concluded that he must have eaten something exciting the day before. "Dysentery is the disease of the imprudent; you should have watched over his hygiene, Doctor." As for the choking fit, it could only have come from a heart condition, hitherto unrecognized.

But one evening the doctor announced the passing of Paul Timonet, a kind of mummy, of whom it had been hoped to make a centenarian, a living advertisement for the watering place. When M. Daron asked, as usual, "What did he die of?" the doctor replied, "Really, I don't know."

"What do you mean, you don't know? One always knows. Wasn't there some organic lesion?"

The doctor shook his head. "No. None."

"Perhaps some infection of the liver or kidneys?"

"No—they were perfectly sound."

"Did you observe whether the stomach functioned regularly? A stroke is often caused by bad digestion."

"There was no stroke."

M. Daron, very perplexed, became excited. "But he certainly died of something! What is your opinion?"

The doctor raised his arms. "I absolutely do not know. He died because he died, that's all."

Then M. Daron, in a voice full of emotion, demanded: "Exactly how old was that one? I can't remember."

"Eighty-nine."

And the little old man, with an air at once incredulous and reassured, cried, "Eighty-nine! So it wasn't old age! . . ."

A SURPRISE*

MY BROTHER and I were brought up by our uncle, the abbé Loisel—the curé Loisel, as we called him. Our parents died when we were small, and he had taken us into his rectory and raised us.

For eighteen years he had had the parish of Join-le-Sault, not far from Yvetot. It was a small village, set in the very middle of the Norman plateau known as the *pays de Caux*, dotted with farms whose orchards rose up here and there amidst the fields.

The village, apart from the farm cottages scattered over the plain, consisted of a mere six houses fronting on both sides of the main road, with the church at one end and the new town hall at the other.

My brother and I passed our childhood playing in the cemetery. The place was sheltered from the wind, and there my uncle gave us our lessons, the three of us sitting side by side on the one stone tomb, that of my uncle's predecessor, whose wealthy family had seen to it that he was buried sumptuously.

To train our memories, my uncle made us learn by heart the names of the deceased that were painted on the black wooden crosses; and to train us in observation as

* "Une Surprise," *Gil-Blas*, May 15, 1883. A rewritten version of one of the first pieces Maupassant ever wrote for the *Gaulois: Une Triste Histoire (A Sad Story)*, in the 1880 series *Les Dimanches d'un Bourgeois de Paris*.

well he made us begin our odd recitation now from one
end of the graveyard, now from the other, or sometimes
from the middle. He would point abruptly to a grave,
and say, "The one in the third row, with the cross
leaning to the left: whose is that?" When a burial took
place, we made haste to learn what was to be painted
on the wooden symbol, and we often went to the carpenter's shop, to see the epitaph before it was placed on the
tomb. My uncle would ask, "Do you know the new one?"
And we would reply in unison, "Yes, uncle," and immediately begin to recite: "Here lies Joséphine Rosalie
Gertrude Malandain, widow of Theodore Magloire
Césaire, deceased at the age of seventy-two years,
mourned by her family: a faithful daughter, faithful wife
and faithful mother. Her soul is in heaven."

My uncle was a tall, big-boned priest, square-built
in his ideas as in his frame. His soul itself seemed hard
and definite, like an answer in a catechism. He often
spoke to us of God in a thundering voice, always uttering
the word as violently as though he were firing a pistol.
His God was not God the good and just, but simply God.
He seemed to think of Him as a burglar thinks of a
policeman, or a prisoner of the judge.

He brought us up harshly, teaching us to tremble
rather than to love.

When one of us was fourteen and the other fifteen, he
sent us to board, at a special reduced rate, at the seminary in Yvetot. This was a large, dreary building, full of
curés, whose pupils were almost without exception
destined for the priesthood. I can never think of the
place even now without a shudder. It smelled of prayers
the way a fish-market smells of fish. Oh! That dreary
school, with its eternal religious ceremonies, its freezing
Mass every morning, its periods of meditation, its

gospel-recitations, and the reading from pious books during meals! Oh! Those dreary days passed within those cloistering walls, where nothing was spoken of but God— the explosive God of my uncle.

We lived there in narrow, contemplative, unnatural piety—and also in a truly meritorious state of filth, for I well remember that the boys were made to wash their feet but three times a year, the night before each vacation. As for baths, they were as unknown as the name of Victor Hugo. Our masters apparently held them in the greatest contempt.

My brother and I graduated the same year, and with a few sous in our pockets we woke up one morning to find ourselves in Paris, working at eighteen hundred francs a year in a government office, thanks to the influence, exercised on our behalf, of the Archbishop of Rouen.

For a while we continued to be very good boys, my brother and I, living together in the little lodging we had rented, like two night-birds torn from their nest and cast out into the dazzling sunlight, blinded and bewildered.

But little by little the Paris air, new comrades, and the theaters took away a little of our numbness. Certain new desires, different from heavenly joys, began to awaken within us, and, on a certain evening—the same evening—after long hesitation and uneasiness and the fears of a soldier before his first battle, we allowed ourselves to—how shall I put it?—allowed ourselves to be seduced by two little neighbors, two shopgirls, who worked and lived together.

Soon an exchange took place between our two establishments, a division. My brother took the girls' flat and kept one of them to live with him. The other came to live with me. Mine was named Louise. She was

twenty-two, perhaps. A good girl, fresh, gay and round—
especially round in a certain place. She moved in with
me like a little wife taking possession of a man and of
everything connected with that man. She organized
the household, made everything neat, cooked, kept
careful account of expenses, and in addition introduced
me to many pleasant things with which I was unfamiliar.

My brother was also very happy. The four of us
always had dinner together, one day in his rooms, the
next day in mine, and there was never a cloud or a care.

For time to time I received a letter from my uncle,
who continued to think that I was living with my
brother, and who gave me news of the village, of his
maid, of recent deaths, of the crops and harvests—all
mixed in with bits of advice on the dangers of life and the
turpitudes of the world.

These letters arrived in the morning, by the eight
o'clock mail. The concierge slipped them under the door,
giving a knock with her broom handle to attract our
attention. Louise would get out of bed, pick up the blue
envelope, and sit down beside me and read me the letter
from the "curé Loisel," as she also came to call him.

For six months we were happy.

Then, one night, about one o'clock in the morning, a
violent peal of the doorbell made us jump. We hadn't
been asleep—far from it—at that particular moment.
Louise said, "What can that be?" And I answered, "I
haven't any idea. Probably a mistake." And we stopped
what we were doing and lay there pressed closely one
against the other, our ears strained to catch any sound,
very much on edge.

And then there was a second peal of the bell, and
then a third, and then a fourth long peal filled our room

with so much noise that we both sat up. This was no mistake: whoever it was, wanted *us.* I quickly pulled on my drawers and slippers and ran to the vestibule door, fearing some disaster. But before opening, I called, "Who is there? What do you want?"

A voice, a loud voice, the voice of my uncle, replied: "It's me, Jean. Open your door, I don't want to sleep on the stairs!"

I thought I would go crazy. But what was there to do? I rushed back into the bedroom and in a trembling voice said to Louise: "It's my uncle. Hide!" Then I opened the outer door and the curé Loisel almost knocked me down with his carpetbag.

"What were you up to, you scamp? Why didn't you open?"

I stammered that I had been asleep.

"Asleep at first, perhaps, but just now after you spoke to me—what were you up to then?"

I stammered that I had left my key in my trousers, and to prevent further discussion I threw my arms around his neck and kissed him violently on both cheeks.

That calmed him, and he explained his presence. "I'm here for four days, scapegrace," he announced. "I wanted to take a look at the hell-hole of Paris, to give myself an idea of what the real hell is like." He gave a laugh like a roaring storm, then continued: "Put me up any way you can. We can lay one of your mattresses on the floor. But where's your brother? Asleep? Wake him up! Wake him up!"

I felt that I was rapidly losing my wits, but managed to say, "Jacques isn't home yet. He had a lot of extra work, night work, at the office."

My uncle accepted that, rubbed his hands, and asked me how my work was going. Then he made for the door of my bedroom. I almost seized him by his collar. "No, no, this way, uncle." An idea came to me. "You must be hungry after your trip. Come and have a bite of something."

He smiled. "You're right. I am hungry. I wouldn't mind a snack." And I pushed him into the dining room.

Dinner had been at our house that night, and the cupboard was full. I took out a piece of cold beef, and the curé lit into it heartily. I kept urging him to eat, kept filling his glass and reminding him of wonderful meals we had had in Normandy, to stimulate his appetite. When he had finished he pushed away his plate and said, "That's that: I've had all I can manage." But I had other things in reserve—I knew the good man's weakness—and I brought out a chicken paté, a potato salad, a pot of cream, and some excellent wine that was left over from dinner. He almost fell over backwards in astonishment at my scale of living, pulled his plate toward him, and began all over again. It was getting late, and as he kept eating I kept trying to think of a way out, but nothing practical occurred to me.

Finally he got up from the table, and I felt my knees weaken. I tried to keep him where we were. "Here, uncle—some brandy. It's old, it's good." But he declared, "No, this time I'm really through. Let's see the rest of your quarters."

I well knew that there was no holding him back, and shivers ran up and down my spine. What would happen? What kind of a scene and scandal? What violence, perhaps?

I followed him, filled with a wild desire to open the window and throw myself into the street. I followed him stupidly, not daring to say a word to restrain him, knowing myself lost, almost fainting with anguish, yet nevertheless hoping that some chance would come to my aid.

He entered the bedroom. One last hope lifted my heart: Louise, sweet thing, had drawn the bed curtains, and not a thing in the room betrayed the presence of a woman. Her dresses, her collars and cuffs, her stockings, her shoes, her gloves, her pins and rings—everything had disappeared. I stammered: "Let's not go to bed now, uncle. The sun is almost up."

"You're a good boy to be willing to sit talking with an old man," he answered. "But I could do with an hour or two of sleep."

And he approached the bed, candle in hand. I waited, breathless, frantic. With one gesture he pulled the curtains open! It was a warm June night, and Louise and I had taken off the blankets, and on the bed was only a sheet, which Louise, in her desperation, had pulled over her head. Doubtless to make herself feel more securely hidden, she had rolled herself into a ball, and pressed tight against the sheet her—her contours were clearly visible.

I could hardly stand up.

My uncle turned to me, grinning so widely that I almost collapsed with astonishment. "So!" he cried, merrily. "Joking, were you! You didn't want to wake your brother. Well—*I'll* wake him, and you'll see how." And I saw his hand, his big peasant's hand, upraised; and as he choked with laughter it fell, with a terrific sound, on the—contours before him.

There was a terrible cry in the bed; and then a furious tempest under the sheet. It heaved, billowed and shook: the poor girl couldn't get out, so tightly had she rolled herself in.

Finally a leg appeared at one end, an arm at the other, then the head, then the bosom, naked and panting; and

Louise, furious, sat up and looked at us with eyes shining like lanterns.

My uncle, speechless, started back, his mouth open, as though he had seen the devil himself. He was breathing like an ox.

I considered the situation too serious to cope with, and rushed madly out.

I didn't return for two days. Louise had gone, leaving the key with the concierge. I never saw her again.

My uncle? He disinherited me in favor of my brother, who, warned by Louise, swore that he had refused to continue living with me because of my dissolute behavior, which he was unwilling to countenance.

I will never marry. Women are too dangerous.

THE LEGACY*

MONSIEUR and Madame Serbois were lunching, sitting opposite each other. Both looked gloomy.

She, a little blonde with rosy skin and blue eyes and a gentle manner, was eating slowly without raising her head, as though she were haunted by some sad and persistent thought. He, tall, broad, with side-whiskers and the air of a statesman or business man, seemed nervous and preoccupied. Finally he said, as though speaking to himself, "Really, it's astonishing."

"What is?" his wife asked.

"That Vaudrec shouldn't have left us anything."

Madame Serbois blushed; she blushed instantly, as though a rosy veil had suddenly been drawn over the skin of her throat and face. "Perhaps there is a will at the notary's," she said. "It is too early for us to know."

She said it with assurance, and Serbois answered reflectively: "Yes, that is possible. After all, he was the best friend of both of us, always here, staying for dinner every other day. I know he gave you many presents—that was perhaps his way of repaying our hospitality—but really, one does think of friends like us in a will. I know that if it had been I who had not felt well, I would

* "Le Legs," *Gil-Blas*, September 23, 1884. Published during the writing of *Bel-Ami*, and similar to an episode in that novel.

have made some provision for him, even though you are my natural heir."

Mme. Serbois lowered her eyes. And as her husband carved a chicken she touched her handkerchief to her nose the way one does in weeping.

He continued. "Yes, it is possible that there is a will at the notary's, and a little legacy for us. I wouldn't expect anything much, just a remembrance, nothing but a remembrance, a thought, to prove to me that he had an affection for us."

Then his wife said, in a hesitant voice: "If you like, after lunch we might call on Maître Lemaneur, and we would know where we stand."

"An excellent idea," said M. Serbois. "That is what we shall do." He had tied a napkin around his neck to keep from spotting his clothes with gravy, and he had the look of a decapitated man continuing to talk; his fine black whiskers stood out against the white of the linen, and his face was that of a very superior butler.

When they entered the notary's office there was a slight stir among the clerks, and when M. Serbois announced himself—even though he was perfectly well known—the chief clerk jumped to his feet with noticeable alacrity and his assistant smiled. Then they were shown into Lemaneur's private office.

He was a round little man, his head looked like a ball fastened to another ball, to which in turn were fastened a pair of legs so very short and round that they too almost seemed like balls. He greeted them, pointed to chairs, and said, with a slightly significant glance at Mme. Serbois: "I was just going to write you to ask you to come in. I wanted to acquaint you with M. Vaudrec's will. It concerns you."

M. Serbois could not refrain from saying "Ah! I was sure of it."

The notary said, "I will read you the document. It is very short." And taking up a paper he read:

"I, Paul-Emile-Cyprien Vaudrec, the undersigned, being of sound body and mind, do hereby express my last wishes.

"Since death can come at any moment, unexpectedly, I wish to take the precaution of writing my last will and testament, which will be deposited with my notary, Maître Lemaneur.

"Being without direct heirs, I bequeath my entire estate, consisting of securities amounting to 400,000 francs, and real property amounting to about 600,000 francs, to Mme. Clair-Hortense Serbois, unconditionally. I beg her to accept this gift from a friend who has died, as proof of his devoted, profound and respectful affection.

"Signed in Paris, June 15, 1883.

"Vaudrec."

Mme. Serbois had lowered her head and sat motionless, whereas her husband was glancing with stupefaction at her and at the notary. Maître Lemaneur continued, after a moment: "Madame cannot, of course, accept this legacy without your consent, Monsieur."

M. Serbois rose. "I must have time to think," he said.

The notary, who was smiling with a certain air of malice, agreed. "I understand the scruples that make you hesitate; society sometimes judges unkindly. Will you come back tomorrow at the same time and give me your answer?"

M. Serbois bowed. "Until tomorrow."

He took a ceremonious leave of the notary, offered

his arm to his wife, who was redder than a peony and
kept her eyes obstinately lowered, and he left the office
with so imposing an air that the clerks were positively
frightened.

Once inside their own house, behind closed doors, M.
Serbois curtly declared: "You were Vaudrec's mistress."

His wife, taking off her hat, turned toward him with a
spasmodic movement. "I?" she cried. "Oh!"

"Yes, you. No one leaves his entire estate to a woman
unless . . ."

She had gone utterly pale, and her hands trembled a
little as she tried to tie the long ribbons together to keep
them from trailing on the floor. After a moment she said,
"But . . . You're crazy, crazy . . . An hour ago
weren't you yourself hoping that he would—would leave
you something?"

"Yes—he could have left me something. Me—not
you."

She looked at him deeply, as though trying to cap-
ture that unknown something in another human being
which can scarcely be sensed even during those rare
moments when guards are down, and which are like
half-open gateways to the mysterious recesses of the
soul. Then she said, slowly, "But it seems to me that if—
that a legacy of such a size would have looked just as
strange coming from him to you, as to me."

"Why?"

"Because . . ." She turned her head in embarrassment, and did not go on.

He began to pace the room, and said: "Surely you
cannot accept?"

She answered with indifference: "Very well. But in

that case there is no need to wait until tomorrow. We
can write Maître Lemaneur now."

Serbois stopped his pacing, and for several moments
they stared at each other, trying to see, to know, to
understand, to uncover and fathom the depths of each
other's thoughts, in one of those ardent, mute question-
ings between two people who live together, who never
get to know each other, but who constantly suspect and
watch.

Then he suddenly murmured, close to her ear:
"Admit that you were Vaudrec's mistress."

She shrugged. "Don't be stupid. Vaudrec loved me, I
think, but he was never my lover."

He stamped his foot. "You lie. What you say is impossible."

She said calmly, "Nevertheless, it is true."

He resumed his pacing, then, stopping again, said,
"Then explain to me why he left you everything."

She answered nonchalantly. "It is very simple. As you
yourself said earlier, we were his only friends, he lived
as much with us as in his own home, and when the time
came to make his will he thought of us. Then, out of
gallantry, he wrote my name because my name came to
him naturally, just as it was always to me that he gave
presents—not to you. He had the habit of bringing me
flowers, of giving me a little gift on the fifth of every
month, because it was the fifth of a month that we met.
You know that. He almost never gave you anything—
he didn't think of it. Men give remembrances to the
wives of their friends—not to the husbands—so he left
his last remembrance to me rather than to you. It is as
simple as that."

She was so calm, so natural, that Serbois hesitated.
Then: "Still, it would make a very bad impression.

Everyone would believe the other thing. We cannot accept."

"Then we won't accept. It will be a million less in our pockets, that's all."

He began to talk the way one thinks aloud, without addressing his wife directly. "Yes, a million—impossible—our reputations would be ruined—too bad—he should have left half to me . . . that would have taken care of everything." And he sat down, crossed his legs and played with his whiskers—always his behavior at moments of deep meditation.

Mme. Serbois opened her work basket, took out a bit of embroidery and began to sew. "I don't in the least insist on accepting. It is up to you to think about it."

For a long time he did not answer; then, hesitantly: "Look—there would be one way, perhaps. You could sign half over to me, by deed of gift. We have no children: it would be perfectly legal. In that way nobody could talk."

She said, seriously: "I don't quite see how that would keep them from talking."

He lost his temper: "You must be stupid. We'll tell everyone that he left each of us half: and it will be true. No need to explain that the will was in your name."

Once again she gave him a piercing look. "As you like. I am willing."

Then he rose and resumed his pacing. He appeared to hesitate again, although by now his face was radiant. "No—perhaps it would be better to renounce it altogether—more dignified—still—in this way nothing could be said. . . . Even the most scrupulous could find nothing to object to. . . . Yes—that solves everything. . . ."

He stood close to his wife. "So, if you like, my darling,

I'll go back alone to Maître Lemaneur and consult him and explain. I will tell him that you prefer this arrangement, that it is more fitting, that it will stop gossip. My accepting half shows that I am on sure ground, perfectly acquainted with the whole situation, that I know everything to be honorable and clear. It is as though I said to you, 'Accept, my dear: why shouldn't you, since I do?' Otherwise it would really be undignified."

"As you wish," said Mme. Serbois, simply.

He went on, speaking fluently now: "Yes, by dividing the legacy everything is made crystal clear. We inherit from a friend who wanted to make no difference between us, who didn't want to seem to be saying, 'I prefer one of you to the other after my death, just as I did during my life.' And you may be sure that if he had reflected a little, that is what he would have done. He didn't think, he didn't foresee the consequences. As you rightly said, it was to you that he always gave presents. It was to you that he wanted to offer a last remembrance."

She stopped him, a shade impatiently. "All right, I understand. You don't have to do so much explaining. Now go to the notary."

He stammered, blushing, suddenly confused. "You're right. I'm going."

He took his hat, and approaching her he held out his lips for a kiss, murmuring, "I'll be back soon, my darling."

She held up her forehead and he gave her a big kiss, his thick whiskers tickling her cheeks.

Then he went out, beaming happily.

And Madame Serbois let her embroidery fall and began to weep.

LETTER FROM A MADMAN*

M Y DEAR DOCTOR: I am putting myself in your hands.
Do with me as you please.

I am going to tell you very frankly my strange state
of mind, and you will decide whether it might not be
better to have me cared for, during a certain time, in a
sanitarium, rather than leave me prey to the hallucinations and sufferings that harass me.

This is the story, long and exact, of the strange sickness of my soul.

I used to live like everyone else, looking at life with
man's open, blind eyes, without wonder and without
understanding. I lived as animals live, as we all live,
fulfilling all the functions of existence, looking and thinking that I saw, thinking that I knew and understood
what surrounded me; when one day I realized that all is
false.

It was a phrase of Montesquieu's that suddenly
illuminated my mind. Here it is: "One organ more or less
in our mechanism would have caused us to have a different intelligence. . . . In short, all laws established
on the basis of our mechanism being of a certain kind
would be different if our mechanism were not of this
kind."

* "Lettre d'un Fou," *Gil-Blas*, February 17, 1885. The first, crude, almost
completely undramatized version of *Le Horla*.

I reflected on that for months, for months and months, and little by little I was permeated by a strange clarity, and this clarity has brought on darkness.

Actually, our organs are the only intermediaries between the external world and ourselves. That is to say, our internal existence, what constitutes the *I*, makes contact by means of certain networks of nerves, with the external existence that constitutes the world.

Now, not to mention the fact that we fail to comprehend this external existence because of its proportions, its duration, its innumerable and impenetrable properties, its origins, its future or its ends, its distant forms and its infinite manifestations, our organs supply us, concerning that portion of it which we are able to understand at all, with information as uncertain as it is sparse.

Uncertain, because it is solely the properties of our organs which determine for us the apparent properties of matter.

Sparse, because since our senses are but five, the field of their investigations and the nature of their revelations are very restricted.

Let me explain. The eye acquaints us with dimensions, forms, and colors. It deceives us on these three points.

It can reveal to us only objects and beings of medium dimensions, in proportion to human size—thus causing us to apply the word large to certain things and the word small to certain others, solely because its weakness does not permit it to comprehend what is too vast or too minute for it. As a result, it knows and sees almost nothing; almost the entire universe remains hidden from it—the star in space and the animalcule in a drop of water.

Even if it had a hundred million times its normal

power, if it perceived in the air we breathe all the races of invisible beings, as well as the inhabitants of neighboring planets, there would still exist infinite numbers of races of yet smaller beings, and worlds so very distant that it could not reach them.

Thus all our ideas of proportion are false, since there is no possible limit of largeness or smallness.

Our estimation of dimensions and forms has no absolute value, being determined solely by the power of one organ and by constant comparison with ourselves.

Furthermore, the eye is also incapable of seeing the transparent. It is deceived by a flawless sheet of glass. It confuses it with the air, which it also does not see.

Let us go on to color.

Color exists because our eye is so constituted that it transmits to the brain, in the form of color, the various ways in which bodies absorb and decompose, according to their chemical composition, the light rays which strike them.

The varying degrees of this absorption and decomposition constitute shades and tints.

Thus this organ imposes on the mind its manner of seeing, or rather its arbitrary manner of recording dimensions and estimating the relations between light and matter.

Let us examine hearing.

Even to a greater extent than with the eye, we are the dupes and playthings of this whimsical organ.

Two colliding bodies produce a certain disturbance of the atmosphere. This movement causes to vibrate in our ear a certain small membrane which immediately changes into sound what is really only vibration.

Nature is mute. But the eardrum possesses the miraculous property of transmitting to us in the form of a sense, a sense that differs according to the number of vibrations, all the quiverings of the invisible waves in space.

This metamorphosis accomplished by the auditory nerve in the short journey from ear to brain has enabled us to create a strange art, music, the most poetic and the most precise of the arts, vague as a dream and exact as algebra.

What shall we say of taste and smell? Would we know the flavors and the quality of foods if it were not for the bizarre properties of our nose and our palate?

Humanity could, however, exist without hearing, without taste, and without smell—that is, without any notion of sound, taste, or odor.

Thus, if we had several fewer organs, we would be ignorant of things that are admirable and strange, but if we had several additional organs, we should discover about us an infinity of other things that we should never suspect due to lack of means of ascertaining them.

Thus, we are deceived when we judge what we know, and we are surrounded by unexplored things that we do not know.

Thus, everything is uncertain and capable of being estimated in different ways.

Everything is false, everything is possible, everything is doubtful.

Let us formulate that certainty by making use of the old dictum: "What is true on one side of the Pyrenees is false on the other."

And let us say: "What is true within the field of our organism is false outside it."

Two and two do not necessarily make four outside our atmosphere.

What is true on earth is false beyond, whence I

conclude that such imperfectly perceived mysteries as electricity, hypnotic sleep, thought transference, suggestion, all the magnetic phenomena, remain hidden from us only because nature has not furnished us with the organ or organs necessary for their understanding.

After having convinced myself that everything revealed to me by my senses exists, as I perceive it, only for me, and would be totally different for another being otherwise constituted, after having concluded that a humanity differently made would have, concerning the world, concerning life, concerning everything, ideas absolutely opposed to ours, because agreement of beliefs results only from the similarity of human organs, and divergences of opinion only from the slight differences in the functioning of our nervous systems, I made a superhuman effort of thought to infer the impenetrable that surrounds me.

Have I gone mad?

I told myself: I am enclosed in things unknown. I thought of a man without ears inferring sound, as we infer so many hidden mysteries, a man establishing the existence of acoustical phenomena of which he could determine neither the nature nor the source. And I became afraid of everything around me, afraid of the air, afraid of the night. From the moment we can know almost nothing, and from the moment all is limitless, what remains? The void—is it not so? What is there in that apparent void?

And that confused terror of the supernatural that has haunted mankind since the birth of the world is legitimate, since the supernatural is nothing but that which remains veiled from us!

Then I understood dread. It seemed to me that I was on the verge of discovering a secret of the universe.

I tried to sharpen my organs, to excite them, to make them momentarily perceive the invisible.

I told myself: Everything is a being. The cry that passes through the air is a being comparable to an animal, since it is born, moves, transforms itself and dies. Thus the fearful mind that believes in non-corporeal beings is not wrong. What are they?

How many men have a presentiment of them, shudder at their approach, tremble at their barely perceptible contact! We feel them near us, all about us, but we cannot distinguish them, for we haven't the eye that could see them, or rather the unknown organ that could detect them.

Then, more than anyone else, I felt them, these supernatural passers-by. Beings or mysteries? I do not know. I could not say what they were, but I could always distinguish their presence. And I have seen—*seen*—an invisible being, as much as one can see such a thing.

I passed entire nights sitting motionless at my table, my head in my hands, thinking of them. Often I believed that an intangible hand, or rather an imperceptible body, was hovering over my hair. It did not touch me, not being of fleshy essence, but of an essence that was imponderable, unknowable.

Then, one night, I heard my floor creak behind me. It creaked in a strange way. I shuddered. I turned. I saw nothing. And I thought no more of it.

But the next night, at the same hour, I heard the same sound. I was so frightened that I stood up, sure, sure, sure that I was not alone in my room. Nothing, however, was to be seen. The air was limpid, transparent everywhere. My two lamps made every corner bright.

The sound did not begin again, and I gradually

became calmer; still, I remained uneasy, and often turned
to look.

The next night I shut myself in my room early,
wondering how I might succeed in seeing the Invisible
that was visiting me.

And I saw It. I almost died of terror.

I had lit all the candles on my mantel and in my
chandelier. The room was lighted as though for a party.
My two lamps were burning on my table.

Opposite me, my bed, an old oak four-poster. To the
right, my fireplace. To the left, my door, which I had
locked. Behind me, a very large closet with mirrored
doors. I looked at myself in the mirrors for a moment.
My eyes were strange, the pupils very dilated.

Then I sat at my table as usual.

The sound had occurred, the preceding nights, at
nine twenty-two. I waited. When the exact moment
arrived, I was conscious of an indescribable sensation, as
though a fluid, an irresistible fluid, had penetrated every
part of my body, drowning my soul in a dread that was
excruciating and rapturous. And the floor creaked, just
behind me.

I jumped up, turning so fast that I almost fell. All
was as clear as daylight, and I did not see myself in the
mirror! It was empty, bright, full of light. I was not in
it, and yet I was just opposite it. I stared, terrified. I
dared not go near it, sensing full well that it was between
us, it, the Invisible, and that it was concealing me from
the glass.

Oh! How terrified I was! And then I began to see
myself, as in a fog, in the depths of the mirror, as though
through water; and it seemed to me that this water was
sliding from left to right, slowly, making my image more

precise from second to second. It was like the end of an eclipse. What was hiding me had no outlines, but a sort of opaque transparency, gradually becoming clearer.

And finally I was able to see myself perfectly, as I do every day when I look at myself.

So, I have seen it!

And I have never seen it again.

But I am waiting for it, and I feel that I am losing my mind as I wait.

I spend hours, nights, days, weeks, before my mirror, waiting! It does not come.

It knew that I had seen it. But I feel that I shall wait for it always, until death; that I shall wait without rest before that mirror, like a huntsman on the watch.

And in that mirror I am beginning to see mad images, monsters, hideous corpses, all sorts of frightful beasts, dreadful beings, all the unlikely visions that must haunt the minds of madmen.

That is my confession, Doctor. Tell me: what must I do?

LONGER NOTES

1

Note on Bibliography, etc.

FOR A MAUPASSANT BIBLIOGRAPHY the reader is referred to
Artine Artinian's *Maupassant Criticism in France, 1880–1940,
With an Inquiry into his Present Fame and a Bibliography*
(King's Crown Press, Morningside Heights, New York, 1941).
An enlarged edition of this useful work is at present in preparation. It would be superfluous to print here a list of all the books
and articles which I have consulted, since the majority are
already listed by Professor Artinian. The names of others, outside the scope of his bibliography or not included in his 1941
edition, will be found among those in my text and notes.

One recently published French work on Maupassant should
perhaps be mentioned: Paul Morand, *Vie de Guy de Maupassant*
(Paris, Flammarion, 1942). As the date indicates, this volume
was published with the German and Vichy imprimaturs, and
it presents a portrait of the author of *Boule de Suif* and the
other stories about the Franco-Prussian war denigrated and
animalized to a degree that was pleasing to the licensed "French"
press of the time. As an article in the Resistance press remarked:
"C'est une façon comme une autre de trahir."

The most complete edition of Maupassant's works is that
published by the Librairie de France in fifteen volumes (Paris,
1934–38); the student should be warned, however, against the
many inaccuracies of title, date, omission, etc., contained in
the bibliographical listings in Volume XV. Some of these errors
are corrected in the article by Sullivan and Steegmuller indicated in the footnote on page 138 of the present work. This
article is also the chief source of information concerning Maupassant's newspaper articles, most of which remain unreprinted.

Maupassant's letters, published and unpublished, are
widely scattered. The chief published collection is contained in
*Chroniques, Etudes, Correspondance de Guy de Maupassant,
Recueillies, Préfacées et Annotées par René Dumesnil avec la
collaboration de Jean Loize* (Librairie Gründ, Paris, 1938; forming Volume XV of the Librairie de France edition). Forty-
three manuscript letters from Maupassant to Zola, all but five

of them hitherto unpublished, are in the collection of Zola correspondence in the Bibliothèque Nationale. Innumerable unpublished letters remain in private hands, and through the kindness of the owners I have been privileged to see and quote from some of these. In this connection let me express thanks to Mina Curtiss, Madame Magda Sibilat, Marc Loliée, and particularly to Professor Artinian, who is himself preparing for eventual publication an enlarged edition of Maupassant's correspondence, and whose generous sharing of his Maupassant documents and knowledge has greatly aided in the preparation of the present work.

I also take this occasion to express thanks for assistance given me by the following persons, whom I name neither in alphabetical order nor in any other order save that in which I find their names listed, with much gratitude, in my records: Robert N. Linscott, Mlle. Gabrielle Leleu, Stanley Martin, Lombard Jones, Daniel Halévy, Dr. Fritz Wittels, Dr. Alvin A. Schaye, Frank MacGregor, Leon Edel, John Derby, Ralph Ellison, the late François Tassart and my friend, his nephew, also named François Tassart, Miss Margaret Hackett, Mlle. Liliane Yacoël, Professor F. O. Matthiessen, Professor Gilbert Chinard, Professor Edward D. Sullivan, André Vial, Edouard Maynial, René Dumesnil, Madame Léon Deffoux, Dr. J.-E. Zola, Jean Sarrut, Madame Julien Cain, Mlle. Thérèse d'Alverny, Madame Lydie Fischer and her mother, Madame Marthe Olivié (members of whose family were friends of Laure and Guy de Maupassant), Mrs. Percy W. Mitchell (the charming and hospitable present owner of La Guillette), Comte Cahen d'Anvers, Comte de Suzannet, Peter Quennell, Sir Osbert Sitwell, Jim Scott of the *Akron Beacon Journal*, Suzanne Crotti-Duchamp, Alfred A. Knopf, B. W. Huebsch, Maître Roger Fondevielle, Albert McVitty.

Officers and staff members of the following libraries have given valuable assistance: The Library of Columbia University, the New York Public Library, the New York Society Library, the Houghton Library of Harvard University (which kindly permitted me to see and quote from Paul Bourget's letters to Henry James), the Library of the Boston Athenaeum, the Bibliothèque Nationale, the Bibliothèque de l'Institut de

France, the Library of the French Embassy Press and Information Division, New York.

Except where noted, I am responsible for the English versions of all French documents used in the present text. Most documents have not been quoted in their entirety, and the custom of printing dots to indicate omissions has usually not been observed.

2

(Page 66)

A Henry James Letter

AMONG THE CURIOSITIES of literature must be included a letter from Henry James to Edmund Gosse, dated from Lamb House, Rye, October 17, 1912, concerning Maupassant. In an issue of the *Cornhill Magazine* of that year Gosse had written an account of Swinburne's near-drowning at Etretat in the summer of 1868, in which Maupassant was mentioned. "With your letter of last night came the Cornhill with the beautifully done little Swinburne chapter," James wrote Gosse on October 15, and he continued with the two sentences quoted on page 66. Gosse immediately wrote to ask James for further details, and on the 17th James replied as follows:

. . . it is indeed a thrill to think that I *am* perhaps the last living depositary of Maupassant's wonderful confidence or legend. I really believe myself the last survivor of those then surrounding Gustave Flaubert. I shrink a good deal at the same time, I confess, under the burden of an honour "unto which I was not born"; or, more exactly, hadn't been properly brought up to or pre-admonished and pre-inspired to. I pull myself together, I invoke fond memory, as you urge upon me, and I feel the huge responsibility of my office and privilege; but at the same time I must remind you of certain inevitable weaknesses in my position, certain essential infirmities of my relation to the precious fact (meaning by the precious fact Maupassant's having, in that night of time and that general failure of inspiring prescience, so remarkably regaled me). You will see in a moment everything that was wanting to make me the conscious recipient of a priceless treasure. You will see in fact how little I could have *any* of the right mental preparation. I didn't in

the least know that M. himself was going to be so remarkable;
I didn't in the least know that *I* was going to be; I didn't in the
least know (and this was above all most frivolous of me) that
you were going to be; I didn't even know that the monkey was
going to be, or even realize the peculiar degree and nuance of
the preserved lustre awaiting ces messieurs, the three taken
together. Guy's story (he was only known as "Guy" then)
dropped into my mind but as an unrelated thing, or rather as
one related, and indeed with much intensity, to the peculiarly
"rum," weird, macabre and unimaginable light in which the
interesting, or in other words the delirious, in English conduct
and in English character, are—or were especially then—viewed
in French circles sufficiently self-respecting to have views on
the general matter at all, or in other words among the truly
refined and enquiring. 'Here they are at it!' I remember that
as my main inward comment on Maupassant's vivid little history; which was thus thereby somehow more vivid to me about
him, than about either our friends or the monkey; as to whom,
as I say, I didn't in the least foresee this present hour of ar-
raignment!

At the same time I think I'm quite prepared to say, in fact
absolutely, that of the two versions of the tale, the two quite
distinct ones, to which you attribute a mystic and separate
currency over there, Maupassant's story to me was essentially
Version No. 1. It wasn't at all the minor, the comparatively
banal anecdote. Really what has remained with me is but the
note of two elements—that of the monkey's jealousy, and that
of the monkey's death; how brought about the latter I can't
at all at this time of day be sure, though I am haunted as with
the vague impression that the poor beast figured as having
somehow destroyed *himself*, committed suicide through the
separate injuria formae. The third person in the fantastic com-
plication was either a young man employed as servant (within
doors) or one employed as boatman, and in either case I think
English; and some thin ghost of an impression abides with me
that the "jealousy" was more on the monkey's part toward him
than on his toward the monkey; with which the circumstance
that the Death I seem most (yet so dimly) to disembroil is
simply and solely, or at least predominantly, that of the resent-
ful and impassioned beast: who hovers about me as having seen
the other fellow, the jeune anglais or whoever, installed on the
scene after he was more or less lord of it, and so invade his
province. You see how light and thin and confused are my data!

How I wish I had known or guessed enough in advance to be able to oblige you better now: not a stone then would I have left unturned, not an i would I have allowed to remain undotted; no analysis or exhibition of the national character (of *either* of the national characters) so involved would I have failed to catch in the act. Yet I do so far serve you, it strikes me, as to be clear about *this*—that, whatever turn the dénouement took, whichever life was most luridly sacrificed (of those of the two humble dependants), the drama had essentially been one of the affections, the passions, the last *cocasserie*, with each member of the quartette involved! Disentangle it as you can—I think Browning alone could really do so! Does this at any rate—the best I can do for you—throw any sufficient light? I recognize the importance, the historic bearing and value, of the most perfectly worked-out view of it. *Such* a pity, with this, that as I recover the fleeting moments from across the long years it is my then active figuration of the so tremendously *averti* young Guy's intellectual, critical, vital, experience of the subject-matter that hovers before me, rather than my comparatively detached curiosity as to the greater or less originality of ces messieurs!—even though, with this, highly original they would appear to have been. I seem moreover to mix up the occasion a little (I mean the occasion of that confidence) with another, still more dim, on which the so communicative Guy put it to me, àpropos of I scarce remember what, that though he had remained quite outside of the complexity I have been glancing at, some jeune anglais, in some other connection, had sought to draw him into some scarcely less fantastic or abnormal one, to the necessary determination on his part of some prompt and energetic action to the contrary: the details of which now escape me—it's all such a golden blur of old-time Flaubertism and Goncourtism! How many more strange flowers one *might* have gathered up and preserved! [Letters of Henry James, Selected and Edited by Percy Lubbock, New York, Charles Scribner's Sons, 1920; II, 257-260.]

Almost 25 years before that letter, James had written the *Partial Portraits* essay in which he praised Maupassant's style for its "masculine firmness" and "quiet force," and his brother William had written him: "In your Maupassant [essay] you used that author's own directness more than is your wont, and I think with great good effect. If you keep on writing like that I'll never utter another cavil as long as I live"!

3
(Page 84)
Something Very Hard to Believe

TOLSTOY HAS RECORDED * that Turgenev told him "something astonishing, something very hard to believe" about the nature of Maupassant's relations with women. What was this? It is excusable to wonder, since Turgenev considered it worth telling and Tolstoy worth referring to. Throughout the biographical literature that has grown up around Maupassant there are hints of what it may have been, but there is no statement sufficiently worthy of belief to be included in a text. Here are some of the references:

Maupassant se plaisit alors à provoquer chez lui certain état qui, même pour l'adulte le mieux constitué, ne peut se répéter à volonté et au sujet de quoi un maître du xvi siècle se plaignait de ne disposer que d'une "capacité rare et incertaine." Maupassant ne connaissait ni cette rareté, ni cette incertitude. Malheureusement il ne les connut jamais. (Léon Deffoux & Emile Zavie, *Le Groupe de Médan*, Paris, Payot, 1920, p. 67.)

. . . si Guy de Maupassant parvenait à donner de la joie aux femmes avec une réitération exceptionnelle cela tenait à une rétention peut-être volontaire, peut-être spasmodique, peut-être volontaire et spasmodique ensemble et au moins anormale, de la semence humaine. (Georges Normandy, *La Fin de Maupassant*, Paris, Albin Michel, 1927, p. 70).

"I suppose I am a little out of the common sexually," he [Maupassant] resumed, "for I can make my instrument stand whenever I please."

"Really?" I exclaimed, too astonished to think.

"Look at my trousers," he remarked, laughing, and there on the road he showed me that he was telling the truth. . . .

"Have you always had that power?" I could not help asking.

"Always," he replied. "They used to wonder at it in the Marine when I was a youth."

* In his preface to an edition of Maupassant's works in Russian, reprinted as an essay in *Zola, Dumas, Guy de Maupassant*, Traduit . . . par E. Halperine-Kalminsky. (Paris, Crès, 1896)

"But fancy keeping it right up to thirty-five or thirty-six.
You must be an ideal lover for a sensuous woman."

"That is the worst of it," he remarked quietly. "If you get a
reputation, some of them practically offer themselves." (Frank
Harris, *My Life*, Vol. 2, Chap. XX.)

The ever-present ability to induce an erection at will, as
certain rare persons can regulate their own heart-beats, might
presumably be called active priapism, as distinguished from
"normal," or involuntary, priapism; but no medical or psychological student of sexual matters has ever recorded such a
case. It has been suggested that if Maupassant did have this
power it was perhaps related to his extraordinary degree of
fantasy. But perhaps he was merely treating Harris to one of
the mystifications which he so enjoyed.

4
(Page 95)
Flaubert, Naturalism, and Critics

AS FLAUBERT INDICATES, Zola did not invent the word naturalism; and in an article entitled *Le Naturalisme*, which appeared
in the *Figaro* in 1881 and was subsequently reprinted in the
volume *Une Campagne*, he specifically denies what Flaubert
accuses him of—*thinking* that he had invented it:

Mon Dieu—I invented nothing, not even the word naturalism, which is found in Montaigne with the meaning we give it
today. It has been used in Russia for thirty years, and by twenty
critics in France, particularly by M. Taine. One day I repeat
the word—to excess, it is true—and all the jokesters of the press
find it funny and burst out laughing. *Aimables farceurs!*

There are several adjectival indications of Flaubert's feelings concerning the naturalists' novels and concerning his own
various works as compared with them in a passage from a
letter which he wrote a friend on April 2, 1877, shortly after
the publication of Edmond de Goncourt's *La Fille Elisa* and
before the appearance of his own *Trois Contes:*

Do you know *La Fille Elisa?* It is summary and anemic, and
beside it *L'Assommoir* is a masterpiece. For truly, in the long,

grubby pages of the latter book there is a real power and an undeniable temperament. Coming after these two books I shall seem to be writing for young ladies' boarding schools. I shall be reproached for being decent, and everyone will refer me to my preceding works.

But his chief reproach, often reiterated, was the naturalists' lack of interest in beauty. "Goncourt is very happy when he has picked up a word in the street that he can stick into a book; *I* am very satisfied when I have written a page without repetitions of sounds or of words," he wrote George Sand in 1876. And the naturalist novelists were not the only literary men against whom he leveled that reproach:

I am *burning* with desire to see your literary criticism [he had written Turgenev in 1869], for yours will be that of a practitioner—important consideration. What shocks me in my friends Sainte-Beuve and Taine is that they do not take into sufficient account *Art*, the work in itself, the composition, the style—in short, the elements that make Beauty. Critics were grammarians in the time of La Harpe; now they are historians— that is the only difference. With your manner of feeling—so original and so intense—your criticism will equal your creation, I am sure.

A modern critic of literary critics,* quoting a similar passage which Flaubert wrote the same day to George Sand and which ends with the question, "When will they [the critics] be artists—really artists?", comments: "It was a question not to be answered for half a century." By that he seems to mean that Flaubert would grant the title of artist to practitioners of "modern" criticism. Since the version of the passage sent to Turgenev shows that what Flaubert particularly valued was the criticism of "practitioners"—fellow-creators—it seems questionable that he would consider as "artists" the authors of most of the critical essays printed in today's little magazines.

5
(Page 150)
Maupassant and Normandy

READERS INTRIGUED by the many Norman landscapes, types, and dialect conversations in Maupassant's writings should see

---

* Stanley Edgar Hyman, *The Armed Vision* (New York, Knopf, 1948), p. 13.

the first chapter, "Le Pays," in René Dumesnil, *Guy de Maupassant* (Paris, Colin, 1933; reprinted with a few additions, Paris, Tallandier, 1947), excellent for its portrayal of the background.

There has always been something of a cult of Maupassant's stories about Norman peasants, and they are often praised at the expense of his other work. Elémir Bourges * seems to have been the first to express this preference:

How I prefer, to these two novels [*Une Vie* and *Bel-Ami*], his country tales, his Norman stories! In them M. de Maupassant shows himself an excellent painter of grotesques. He is a Teniers, a Le Nain. . . . When we are all forgotten, big and little, weak and strong, those of us who write of passion and those of us who write of neurosis, perhaps some old woman, sitting beside her fire, will tell some transformed and transfigured tale, some broad peasant tale once told by Maupassant: —and who knows whether there will remain, in the entire world, any trace of our customs and of our passions except what is contained in that story?

Henry James shared the preference to a certain extent (see pp. 238–9), and it continues to be expressed today. For example, Jean-Paul Sartre's unfavorable mentions of Maupassant in his *Qu'est-ce que la littérature? (What Is Literature?)*, in which he machine-guns most nineteenth-century French fiction, brought an indignant protest in the late magazine *Fontaine* (No. 63, November 1947, "A Propos de 'Qu'est-ce que la Littérature' de Jean-Paul Sartre—Réflexions sur une Exégèse," par Rachel Bespaloff): "What is displeasing in this work is its systematic procedure of defamation. If Sartre speaks of Maupassant, he bases himself, for purposes of belittlement, on his society stories, which are worthless, and makes no mention of the Norman tales, which are masterpieces."

Thus are preferences translated into dogma!

* The title of Bourges' article, already cited ("Un Normand," *Gaulois*, December 5, 1885), is not without significance. The word Norman is associated in France with extreme shrewdness and caution, particularly of a financial variety. Maupassant's French biographers seldom fail to mention his Norman ancestry in connection with his interest in money, his going on leave from his ministry after *Boule de Suif* instead of resigning outright, etc.)

6
(Page 152)
Maupassant and Degas

IN HIS *Souvenirs d'un Marchand de Tableaux* (*Recollections of a Picture Dealer*) Ambroise Vollard speaks of Arthur Meyer's copy of *La Maison Tellier:*

The editor-in-chief of the *Gaulois* had a very beautiful library. Each of his books was enriched by the addition of an original work by some artist, his choice always testifying to his perfect taste. Thus, for *La Maison Tellier* he had thought of Degas, and he showed me a letter from the painter himself, promising a drawing. A short time later, in Degas' home, I saw a sketch on his desk. "It is for a book in Arthur Meyer's library," he told me.
"But I thought you couldn't stand Jews."
"True, but this one has the right principles. . . ."
. . . . Degas never finished his drawing—due to excess of conscience, one might say. Since he always endeavored to improve a work by successive stages, using tracing paper and going beyond his original lines, the sketch which he destined for Monsieur Arthur Meyer ended by being more than three feet high. In other words the bibliophile had to say good-bye to his illustration. But he did not give up. He bought, to adorn *La Maison Tellier*, a Degas monotype which represented two women on a sofa, and which was far better adapted to Maupassant's story than a drawing of a dancer. At the sale of Meyer's library someone paid a high price for the book that was thus embellished and to which had been attached Degas' letter promising the drawing.

It was perhaps this whim of Meyer's that gave Vollard his idea of printing his de-luxe edition of *La Maison Tellier* in 1934. This consists of 305 numbered copies plus twenty special copies; in the text are printed seventeen engravings on wood by Degas, *hors-texte* are nineteen more. But—like so many elaborate volumes published without the author's participation, by persons whose chief interest is not in the author's words— this one is a kind of monstrosity. For although the title-page bears the words *Illustrations d'Edgar Degas*, those words are misleading; as Vollard states elsewhere in his memoirs, Degas engraved his plates not as illustrations to *La Maison Tellier* or anything else, but merely as a series of compositions which he called *Scènes de Maisons Closes* (Brothel Scenes). Most of them are in his bitterest manner, far removed from the good-humored gaiety of Maupassant's story. Vollard was doubtless proud of his idea, but both the author and the artist would almost certainly have considered it grotesque. (Note that the drawing which Degas had destined for Meyer's copy of *La Maison Tellier* was a drawing of a dancer—not any attempt to "illustrate" the story.)

Nevertheless, it is easy to think of Degas in connection with many Maupassant stories. The two men resemble each other in the graceful strength of their skills, in the combination of classic and modern elements characterizing their arts, and in many of the human materials which they use. They are said to have met in the salon of Madame Howland, a Frenchwoman married to a usually absent American: too bad that there is no record of conversation between them.

7

(Page 156)

Turgenev, Tolstoy, and *La Maison Tellier*

TOLSTOY TELLS in *Zola, Dumas, Guy de Maupassant* (see footnote to Note 3) of Turgenev's attempt to interest him in Maupassant in 1881:

During the visit he paid me in 1881, I think it was, Turgenev took from his valise a little French book called *La Maison Tellier* and handed it to me. "Read this when you have the opportunity," he said, in a seemingly detached tone. "It is by a young French writer—not bad. He knows your work and admires it very much," he added, as though he wanted to predispose me in his favor. . . .

At this time, in 1881, I was at the height of the transformation of my concept of the world, and in that transformation, the activity called artistic, to which I had previously devoted myself completely, had not only lost for me the importance that I had formerly attributed to it, but it had become for me frankly disagreeable. Thus, writings like those recommended to me by Turgenev had no attraction for me at that time. But to please him I read the book he gave me. From the first story in *La Maison Tellier*, despite the unseemliness and the vacuousness of the subject-matter, I could not deny that the author possessed what is called talent. But the little volume was unhappily lacking the chief of three conditions which, in addition to talent, are indispensable to any work of art. These are: 1, a normal relationship, that is, a moral relationship, between the author and his subject; 2, clarity of exposition or beauty of form, which are one and the same; and 3, sincerity, that is, a real feeling of love or hatred for what the artist depicts. Of these three conditions, Maupassant possessed only the last two. He was completely devoid of the first.

Tolstoy was particularly displeased by the lack of indignation in Maupassant's descriptions of seductions, and by what he considered his tendency to describe peasants "not only with indifference, but with scorn, as though they were brute beasts":

The stories *Une Partie de Campagne*, *La Femme de Paul*, and *Histoire d'une fille de Ferme* seemed so repugnant to me at that time that I did not even notice the beautiful story *Le Papa de Simon* or *Sur l'Eau*, with its remarkable description of night on the river. I said to myself, and I told Turgenev: "In these times, when so many people are eager to write, there is no lack of gifted men who do not know on what to use their talent, or who boldly use it to describe what should not be described and what it is profitless to describe." And I thought no more of Maupassant.

Tolstoy was later converted to Maupassant by *Une Vie*. For his comment on that novel see p. 170 of the present work; for his comment on *Yvette* see p. 222–3.

8
(Page 170)
"Silvius" in *La Jeune France*

HACHETTE'S REFUSAL to stock *Une Vie* in the railway station bookstalls inspired the following verses, by an author who has not been identified, in the magazine *La Jeune France* for May 1, 1883:

—*GUY DE MAUPASSANT*—

Cet effronté de Maupassant
Révolte la pudeur des gares:
Des horreurs, n'en dit-il pas cent,
Cet effronté de Maupassant!
Par son cynisme dépassant
Les Cosaques et les Bulgares,
Cet effronté de Maupassant
Révolte la pudeur des gares.

O romancier, l'ignorais-tu,
La rigueur des lignes ferrées?
Elles sont "la même vertu"!
O romancier l'ignorais-tu?
Le lis seul, de candeur vêtu,
Parcourt ces routes éthérées . . .
O romancier l'ignorais-tu,
La rigueur des lignes ferrées?

Bien que fumant comme un dragon,
La locomotive est bégueule;
Elle répugne à tout jargon,
Bien que fumant comme un dragon.
Le toit honnête du wagon
N'abrite que la vierge seule!
Bien que fumant comme un dragon,
La locomotive est bégueule.

Le danger pour les voyageurs,
Ce n'est pas que le train dévie.
Quel est, demandez-vous songeurs,
Le danger pour les voyageurs?
C'est qu'il leur monte des rougeurs
Au front, en lisant "Une Vie"!
Le danger pour les voyageurs
Ce n'est pas que le train dévie.

Amende-toi, jeune écrivain,
Pour que la vapeur te colporte;
Sans cela tout ton art est vain!
Amende-toi, jeune écrivain.
Mets de l'eau claire dans le vin
De ta prose quelque peu forte.

Amende-toi, jeune écrivain,
Pour que la vapeur te colporte.

O Guy! pille Octave Feuillet,
Où maint Ohnet déjà grapille,
Pour te faire un style douillet,
O Guy! pille Octave Feuillet!
Pour avoir droit à ce billet
De confession: l'estampille,
O Guy! pille Octave Feuillet,
Où maint Ohnet déjà grapille!

—*Silvius*

9
(Page 183)
The Memoirs of François Tassart

READERS OF THE *Revue des Deux Mondes* for March 1, 1911, found themselves presented by the editors with something unusual: an article entitled *La Mort de Guy de Maupassant,* unsigned, but with a footnote stating that it was a portion of a forthcoming book about Maupassant by his *valet de chambre,* François Tassart. A writing valet was a novelty, especially one who wrote as well as François (he referred to himself in the text by his first name only); and his article attracted considerable attention because he had been Maupassant's valet, because of the vividness of its details, and because of its worshipful tone.

Later the same year the book appeared, *Souvenirs sur Guy de Maupassant par François son valet de chambre (1883–1893).* The next year it appeared in English in London and New York, in an edition illustrated with photographs of Algerian scenes taken by Maupassant himself; and in 1915 it was translated into Russian.

It wins the reader from the first paragraphs, in which something of the characters of the two men becomes immediately apparent. François, in the shop of the tailor who has recommended him, declines to enter M. de Maupassant's service since M. de Maupassant requires that he wear livery; M. de Maupassant, after a few moments' conversation with the courteous but firm applicant, and after brief consultation with his cousin, M. Le Poittevin, tacitly withdraws the requirement. From then on, Maupassant and François are all the reader could wish: very much the master, very much the valet, but also very much, each of them, himself, with confidence in the other. The book is full of incorrect dates, naïveté, devotion, charm, liveliness and information.

François died January 22, 1949, in Roubaix, northern France, at the age of ninety-two. He was also the author of an unpublished manuscript on Maupassant, from which I have been kindly allowed to quote. Although it has been commonly conjectured that the *Souvenirs* owe something of their excellence to the skill of a ghost-writer, François' nephew and namesake declares that only his aunt, *"une femme fort instruite,"* aided his uncle in their preparation. "My uncle married my aunt after M. de Maupassant became hopelessly ill," the younger François Tassart says. "He would never have married otherwise. He was too devoted to his master."

10
(Page 195)
Mars et Vénus

THE VERSES Maupassant gave Hermine Lecomte du Nouy read as follows:

Mars et Vénus

Mars trouva Vénus à Paphos,
La belle dormait sur le dos,
Voyons, dit-il, tout ce qu'elle a,
    Alleluia!

Il alla déranger soudain
L'écharpe qui couvrait son sein;
Plus blanc que neige il le trouva,
    Alleluia!

Sa main eut la témérité
D'en tâter la rotondité,
Le sentant ferme il s'écria:
    Alleluia!

Enivré de si doux plaisirs
Il forma de nouveaux désirs,
Et de baisers se régala,
   Alleluia!

De cent façons pour l'admirer
Il se mit à la revirer . . .
Ce qui s'augmente s'augmenta,
   Alleluia!

Vénus fermant toujours les yeux
Se plaça pourtant de son mieux,
Et le guerrier en profita . . .
   Alleluia!

Bon, bon, disait Mars qui sentait
Qu'en dormant on le secondait,
Dormez toujours comme cela . . .
   Alleluia!

A peine un jeu se finissait
Qu'un autre se recommençait;
Trois jours entiers cela dura
   Alleluia!

Mais enfin Vénus s'éveillant
Dit au Dieu presqu'en rougissant:
Eh quoi, Monsieur, vous étiez là?

   Alleluia!

11
(Page 230)
Maupassant's Travel Writings

THOSE OF MAUPASSANT'S travel pieces which were reprinted
during his lifetime following their original newspaper appearance are to be found in three volumes: *Au Soleil* (*In the Sun*),
Sur l'Eau (*On the Water*, or *Afloat*), and *La Vie Errante* (*The
Wandering Life*). Other pieces were posthumously printed in
collected editions of his works, and still others are to be found

only in the columns of the *Gaulois*, the *Gil-Blas*, the *Figaro* and
the *Echo de Paris*.

Au Soleil (1884) consists chiefly of African pieces originally
published in the *Gaulois* in 1881. Just before book publication
they were reprinted in a magazine, the *Revue Bleue* for November and December 1883 and January 1884.

Sur l'Eau (1888) is in large part a cool fraud perpetrated by
Maupassant. Its foreword declares:

This diary contains no interesting story or adventures. Last
spring I made a little cruise along the shores of the Mediterranean, and I amused myself by writing, each day, what I saw
and what I thought.
What I saw was water, sun, clouds and rocks, and I can tell
of nothing else; and my thoughts were simple—the kind that
come as one is cradled and lulled and borne along by the sea.

From that, the reader naturally assumes that he is about
to read the diary of a cruise which Maupassant made in the
spring of 1887. The truth is somewhat different. Such a cruise
did take place—or rather, during the winter and spring of
1886–87 Maupassant made numerous short cruises off the
Riviera in his newly-acquired, first *Bel-Ami*—but only a portion of *Sur l'Eau* has anything to do with it. Most of the text
is made up of articles which he had published in newspapers
over the years, and which were cut and rearranged for publication in diary form. As Professor Edward D. Sullivan says in
"Sur l'Eau: A Maupassant Scrap-Book" (*Romanic Review*,
October, 1949), "If [Maupassant] did compose his book on the
Bel-Ami in 1887, the yacht's gear must have included a file
of clippings of his old articles in the *Gaulois* and the *Gil-Blas*,
as well as scissors and an ample supply of paste."

Many persons, including Laure de Maupassant herself (see
page 281), have claimed that *Sur l'Eau* reveals Maupassant's
particularly somber state of mind at the time of its composition,
that it is thus important in marking "the beginning of the end."
Considering that the book's contents were written at various
times beginning in 1881, that is scarcely the case. There are
charming bits in *Sur l'Eau*, particularly those which *do* have
to do with cruising in the Mediterranean (the opening section

and short connecting sections between disquisitions). The chief point of psychological interest concerning Maupassant's state of mind contained in *Sur l'Eau* is the fact that one of the old newspaper articles incorporated into the text is *Les Employés,* a piece about government clerks originally published in the *Gaulois* in 1882 (see pp. 149–50), and that Maupassant, by now less bitter concerning his own father, omits from it the scathing phrase about fathers which it originally included.

In *La Vie Errante* (1890) Maupassant tells of his joy in escaping to sea and gives charming glimpses of life aboard the *Bel-Ami*, of his cruise along the Ligurian coast (he falsifies to the extent of combining his two Italian trips, of 1885 and 1889), of night life in Tunis, etc. This is the best of the travel books and contains the celebrated, very Maupassantian expression of ecstasy before the headless Venus of Syracuse.

12

(Page 253)

The Credibility of Axel Munthe

IN THE EIGHTEENTH CHAPTER of *The Story of San Michele*, of which the section quoted on page 253 is a portion of the first paragraph, Munthe goes on to tell of visiting Maupassant aboard the *Bel-Ami*, where "the MS. of his 'Sur l'Eau' was lying on the table between us." On board he found an eighteen-year-old ballet dancer named Yvonne, and he recounts Yvonne's subsequent tragic end. Despite the testimony of one of Maupassant's friends that *"nul ne vit de jupe familière frou-frouter à l'ombre du maître tenant la barre ou maniant la plume,"* the rustle of "familiar skirts" was undoubtedly heard from time to time aboard the yacht. But Munthe's credibility is somewhat weakened by his statement that Maupassant spoke of his Paris home at this time as being in the rue Clauzel—from which he had moved in 1880. This slip is of a certain importance in bringing into question Munthe's further testimony on Maupassant, including his statement: "The fear that haunted his restless brain day and night was already visible in his eyes, I for one considered him already then a doomed man."

13

(Page 295)

Articles de Commerce

AFTER ORIGINALLY APPEARING in an issue of the *Mercure de France* over the signature Don Junipérien, the following verses by Laurent Tailhade were published in his collected volume of verse, *Au Pays du Mufle* (Paris, Edouard Joseph, 1920):

Articles de Commerce

Bourget, Maupassant et Loti
Se trouvent dans toutes les gares.
On les offre avec le rôti,
Bourget, Maupassant et Loti.
De ces auteurs soyez loti
En même temps que de cigares:
Bourget, Maupassant et Loti
Se trouvent dans toutes les gares.

Achetez aussi du Zola
Ça sert dans les water-closette.
Balzac est faible. Pour Rolla,
Maheu sent le gorgonzola,
Jésus-Christ fait bien la chosette,
Achetez aussi du Zola
Ça sert dans les water-closette.

Au pays où copahu
Met Jean Chouart bien à son aise,
Patara lève Rarahu.
Sous les arbres à copahu,
Mon frère Yves, que Pierre a eu,
Fait le trottoir en javanaise,
Aux pays où le copahu
Met Jean Couart bien à son aise.

Bourget, qui manque un peu de jet,
Convoite, Maupassant, ta force
Est-il plus langoureux objet:
Tant de grâce avec peu de jet!

*Cil que Mélissandre logeait
Rate parfois quand il amorce,
Bourget, qui manque un peu de jet,
Convoite, Maupassant, ta force.*

14
(Page 343)
Maupassant, Henry James, and Sigma

THERE HAS BEEN SPECULATION as to whether Maupassant and Henry James met more than twice: at Flaubert's apartment in Paris during the winter of 1875–76 and in London in 1886. The only indication that they did is given by Sigma.

Sigma is the author of an article in *The Cornhill Magazine* for August, 1925, entitled "Guy de Maupassant: A Recollection." He knew Maupassant, he says, when Guy was "a big, healthy, witty fellow, best described as full of the old Nick, merrily swimming through the warm waters flowing from thirty to forty." He had been introduced to him "as an Englishman who admired him by a man he thought very highly of—Charles Yriarte [a magazine editor and writer who frequented the salon of Princesse Mathilde Bonaparte]. He liked me a little, I think: I am certain I liked him very much. We had some curious experiences together, some of which I will narrate and some I dare not. For a time we saw not a little of each other, then we drifted apart owing to my absence for a time from Paris to look after some race horses I had. . . ."

Rather early in his article Sigma discusses Maupassant's final illness, and it is in connection with that that he makes mention of James:

. . . There was yet another factor in the acceleration of de Maupassant's physical decay—a small one in itself, no doubt; but as one knows, a mere feather may decide the incline of the already weighted beam. I do not certainly want to be deemed unkind, but I must in all honesty chronicle the fact that I always found poor de Maupassant very much worse after any visit from Henry James. . . . I feel sure that for a highly strung, very clever, very nervous man like de Maupassant—as susceptible to external influences as an aeolian harp—the presence, even if mute, of Henry James—the brow—that special massive brow only built in Boston, the lifeless eyes, the solemnity—was harmful; and if vocal—the metallic voice from which the native twang had been so successfully and mercifully [sic] hammered out as to have deprived it of all life and resonance, conveying platitudes heavily garbed to represent profound paradoxes, molluscs presented as grasshoppers, very harmful. . . . Maupassant had no possible use for James: didn't like him: knew nothing about him. Why James came to him I never could understand. It was cruel to plaster a poor quivering Paphian Parisian like Guy—a Cyprian Champs Elysees cavalier—with a thick layer of undiluted Boston, Beacon Street, and Bunker Hill. Emerson is splendid tipple; very, very, good; personally I am very fond of it—can drink tumblers of it; but it does not mix well with Boule de Suif. But to resume; it may, of course, be all imagination or mere coincidence; but I most gravely repeat and truly chronicle the fact that directly after seeing Henry James Guy de Maupassant always became much more ill.

Such is Sigma's testimony. It sounds preposterous, and its credibility is not increased when Sigma is revealed to be none other than Julian Osgood Field, the American adventurer and moneylender who mulcted, among others, Lady Ida Sitwell, and who in 1901 served an English prison term for forgery (See Osbert Sitwell, *Great Morning*, London, Macmillan, 1948, pages 161–65, 315–18).

15

(Page 353)

Maupassant and Religion

CROCE'S STATEMENT that Maupassant's narrative "seems . . . to present . . . the necessity for religion" should not be taken to mean that Maupassant himself felt any such necessity. In a letter to Flaubert written about the time of *Boule de Suif* he said, sarcastically, "Religion attracts me greatly. For, among the —— [word considered unprintable by French editors] of humanity, religion seems to me capital—the vastest, the most multiple, and the deepest." That was a bit of youthful exuberance, but his later correspondence displays his continued ag-

nosticism, and a diatribe against the creator in *L'Angélus*, his
very last, fragmentary piece of fiction, is in the tone of Laure's
agnostic remarks following his death (see p. 347).

In his ravings in the sanitarium Maupassant spoke frequently of God, and someone wrote Laure that he seemed to
wish to see a priest, and asked her advice.

I shall try to answer the delicate question you put before
me [she replied], which I assure you surprises me as much as it
perplexes me.

Without being among the clamorous and absolute enemies
of Catholicism, Guy was nevertheless far from being a believer,
and for many years had not practised religion. He was a pupil
at the seminary in Yvetot, where he was excellent in studies and
behavior—which did not prevent his being expelled, when he
was about sixteen, for an utterly unimportant peccadillo. He
finished his studies at the lycée in Rouen.

I give you these details because they may help you to
understand him. Are there, perhaps, in his sick brain, certain
memories of those far-off days, some need of support, of refuge?
Who can know?

All that I can tell you is that I have never seen any religious
inclination in my son during his mature years. Nor have I seen
any aversion or scorn for what he did not believe.

I am utterly incapable of understanding the horrible dis-
ruption that has taken place in my poor boy's brain, and I am
prepared to do anything that might bring him some relief. So do
what the circumstances require, and grant the patient's wish.
But are you not afraid of agitating him, arousing a dangerous
fanaticism? Perhaps this is but a sick man's delusion.

I confess that I, too, do not practise any religion, but I have
the greatest respect for religious convictions, and I have but
one wish: that my poor son should be cured. Whether he be
more or less of a believer, he will remain what he always has
been: generous, noble, delicate in feeling, with the best heart
that a son ever had.

I can write no longer, yet I have something more to say.
In case there should take place a kind of conversion—naturally
it could scarcely go very deep, considering the patient's condition—I particularly beg you to watch over the preservation
of the unfinished manuscripts, by which Guy set great store and
whose contents may no longer coincide with these new ideas
that have arisen in his sick brain.

According to the unpublished memoirs of François (who throughout his writings strains to indicate that Maupassant was less thoroughly agnostic than his mother), Maupassant confessed to a priest in the sanitarium; but of this there is no direct evidence, and the patient would seem, by this time, to have been far too confused to be able to confess with lucidity.

Certain commentators have written of Maupassant as violently anti-clerical, pointing to his scathing portrait of the Abbé Tolbiac in *Une Vie*. They usually omit to mention that this same novel includes another priest, the Abbé Picot, who is genially presented. Throughout Maupassant's work priests are treated as individuals, varying in character like other human beings. Unlike the works of, for example, Anatole France, Maupassant's are not listed in the Roman Catholic index of prohibited books. "Stranger though he may be to religious matters," says a Catholic writer (Michel Sinvast, in "Les Yeux Baissés de Maupassant," *La Vie Catholique*, September 12, 1925), "Maupassant is not, properly speaking, an anti-clerical. He is one of the rare writers of his period who dared make fun of the Freemasons."